Arctic Circles and Imperial Knowledge

Empire's Other Histories

Series Editor

Victoria Haskins (University of Newcastle, Australia), Emily Manktelow (Royal Holloway, University of London, UK), Jonathan Saha (University of Durham, UK) and Fae Dussart (University of Sussex, UK)

Editorial Board

Esme Cleall (University of Sheffield, UK), Swapna Banerjee (CUNY, USA), Lynette Russell (Monash, Australia), Tony Ballantyne (University of Otago, New Zealand), Samita Sen (Jadavpur University, India, and University of Cambridge, UK), Nurfadzilah Yahaya (National University of Singapore, Singapore), Onni Gust (University of Nottingham, UK), Martina Nguyen (CUNY, USA), Meleisa Ono-George (University of Oxford, UK)

Empire's Other Histories is an innovative series devoted to the shared and diverse experiences of the marginalised, dispossessed and disenfranchized in modern imperial and colonial histories. It responds to an ever-growing academic and popular interest in the histories of those erased, dismissed, or ignored in traditional historiographies of empire. It will elaborate on and analyze new questions of perspective, identity, agency, motilities, intersectionality and power relations.

Published:

Unhomely Empire: Whiteness and Belonging, c.1760-1830, Onni Gust

Extreme Violence and the 'British Way': Colonial Warfare in Perak, Sierra Leone and Sudan, Michelle Gordon

Unexpected Voices in Imperial Parliaments, edited by José María Portillo, Josep M. Fradera, Teresa Segura-Garcia

The Making and Remaking of 'Australasia': Southern Circulations, edited by Tony Ballantyne

Across Colonial Lines: Commodities, Networks and Empire Building, edited by Devyani Gupta and Purba Hossain

Imperial Gallows: Murder, Violence and the Death Penalty in British Colonial Africa, c.1915-60, Stacey Hynd

Forthcoming:

Early Capitalism in Colonial Missions: Moravian Household Economies in the Global Eighteenth Century, Christina Petterson

Vagrant Lives in Colonial Australasia: Regulating Mobility and Movement 1840-1920, Catherine Coleborne

Arctic Circles and Imperial Knowledge

The Franklin Family, Indigenous Intermediaries, and the Politics of Truth

Annaliese Jacobs Claydon

BLOOMSBURY ACADEMIC
LONDON • NEW YORK • OXFORD • NEW DELHI • SYDNEY

BLOOMSBURY ACADEMIC
Bloomsbury Publishing Plc, 50 Bedford Square, London, WC1B 3DP, UK
Bloomsbury Publishing Inc, 1385 Broadway, New York, NY 10018, USA
Bloomsbury Publishing Ireland, 29 Earlsfort Terrace, Dublin 2, D02 AY28, Ireland

BLOOMSBURY, BLOOMSBURY ACADEMIC and the Diana logo are trademarks of
Bloomsbury Publishing Plc

First published in Great Britain 2024
This paperback edition published in 2025

Copyright © Annaliese Jacobs Claydon, 2024

Annaliese Jacobs Claydon has asserted her right under the Copyright,
Designs and Patents Act, 1988, to be identified as Author of this work.

For legal purposes the Acknowledgments on pp. x–xii constitute an extension
of this copyright page.

Series design by Tjaša Krivec.
Cover image © Halo with Three Parhelia, Winter Harbour Melville Island, Charles Hamilton
Smith, 1776–1859. Photo by Sepia Times/Universal Images Group via Getty Images.

All rights reserved. No part of this publication may be: i) reproduced or transmitted in any form,
electronic or mechanical, including photocopying, recording or by means of any information storage or
retrieval system without prior permission in writing from the publishers; or ii) used or reproduced in
any way for the training, development or operation of artificial intelligence (AI) technologies, including
generative AI technologies. The rights holders expressly reserve this publication from the text and
data mining exception as per Article 4(3) of the Digital Single Market Directive (EU) 2019/790.

Bloomsbury Publishing Plc does not have any control over, or responsibility for, any third-
party websites referred to or in this book. All internet addresses given in this book were
correct at the time of going to press. The author and publisher regret any inconvenience
caused if addresses have changed or sites have ceased to exist, but can accept no
responsibility for any such changes.

A catalogue record for this book is available from the British Library.

A catalog record for this book is available from the Library of Congress.

ISBN: HB: 978-1-3502-9294-9
PB: 978-1-3502-9297-0
ePDF: 978-1-3502-9295-6
eBook: 978-1-3502-9296-3

Series: Empire's Other Histories

Typeset by Deanta Global Publishing Services, Chennai, India

For product safety related questions contact productsafety@bloomsbury.com.

To find out more about our authors and books visit www.bloomsbury.com
and sign up for our newsletters.

*For my parents and grandparents
Who loved me and told me stories.*

*And for my sweet Harriet
Who has so many yet to tell.*

Contents

List of Illustrations	viii
Acknowledgments	x
Abbreviations	xiii
Individuals	xiv
Introduction	1
1 "Which Is the Counterfeit, and Which the Real Man?": Stories of Suffering and Questions of Credibility, 1819–25	21
2 "He a Discoverer, Forsooth!": Arctic Circles and Scientific Sociability, 1818–29	57
3 "All Things Are Queer and Opposite": Arctic Circles on the Far Side of the World, 1837–43	93
4 "Have You Seen the Esquimaux Sketch of the Ships?": Disappearing Ships and Inuit Maps, 1845–9	139
5 "The Argument from Negative Evidence": The Many Lives of the Open Polar Sea, 1850–3	169
6 Full Circles: Relics, Stories, and Silences	205
Bibliography	229
Index	252

Illustrations

Maps

1. The Canadian Archipelago, Barren Grounds, and Northwest Passages — xviii
2. *lutruwita*/Tasmania — xix
3. John Thompson and James Wyld. Discoveries of Capts. Ross, Parry, and Franklin in the Arctic regions in 1818, 1819, 1820, 1821, and 1822 — xx
4. Charles W. Morse and Charles A. Colby. Chart showing the recent search for the Northwest Passage and also the coast explored in search of Sir John Franklin between the years 1848 and 1854 — xxi

Timelines

1. Polar Expeditions, 1818–27 — xxii
2. Polar Expeditions, 1829–43 — xxii
3. Polar Expeditions, the search for Franklin, 1848–59 — xxiii

Figures

1.1 Robert Hood's portrait of Akaitcho, chief of the Yellowknives Dene, and his son, 1821 — 25
1.2 Portrait of John Franklin by G. B. Lewis, 1828 — 27
1.3 Robert Hood's portrait of the Yellowknife Dene girl known as "Greenstockings," 1821 — 29
1.4 Portrait of John Richardson by E. Finden, 1828 — 36
1.5 Portrait of Eleanor Porden by her friend Mary Flaxman, 1818, around the time that Porden wrote *The Arctic Expeditions* — 38
2.1 George Francis Lyon, "Interior of an Eskimaux snow-hut, Winter Island, 1822" — 65
2.2 Iligjaq, map drawn at Winter Island, 1822 — 67
3.1 Thomas Bock's portrait of Lady Jane Franklin, 1838 — 101
3.2 Thomas Bock, *Observatory, Domain, Sir John Franklin, Captain Crozier and Captain James Ross, RN*, 1840 — 112
3.3 Thomas Bock's portrait of Mithina, c. 1841 — 114
3.4 A small doll found among Eleanor Franklin Gell's collection in the Derbyshire Record Office — 117

4.1	Usky's map drawn at Mittimatalik, Baffin Island, July 1849	148
4.2	Inuluapik, from *A Narrative of Some Passages in the History of Eenoolooapik*, by Alexander McDonald	151
4.3	Broadside Linen Poster, "Captain Austin's Expedition in Search of Sir John Franklin: *Intrepid, Resolute, Assistance, Pioneer*"	161
5.1	Elisha Kent Kane, "Beechey Island—Franklin's first winter quarters"	170
5.2	Stephen Pearce, *William Penny*, 1851	182
5.3	Portrait of Qalasirssuaq, "The Esquimaux Erasmus York." Illustration for *The Illustrated London News*, 25 October 1851	185
5.4	Qalasirssuaq's drawing of the "Anchor Ship" in a letter addressed to Eleanor Gell and signed "Kalli," St. Augustine's College (Canterbury), May 11, 1853	194
6.1	"The Franklin Relics" originally published in the *Illustrated London News*, November 4, 1854	208
6.2	Victory Point Cairn record, found by the expedition of Leopold McClintock on King William Island, May 6, 1859	218
6.3	A portrait photograph of Captain Leopold McClintock with a few of the Franklin relics	219

Acknowledgments

This book has taken fifteen years to write, and what follows is an incomplete account of my many debts. I wrote this book on Dena'ina land in Alaska; on the land of the Peoria, Kaskaskia, Peankashaw, Wea, Miami, Mascouten, Odawa, Sauk, Mesquaki, Kickapoo, Potawatomi, Ojibwe, and Chickasaw Nations in Illinois; on Dakota and Ojibwe land in Minnesota; and on the ancestral land of the muwinina people; and among today's *palawa* community in *lutruwita* Tasmania. I pay my respects to elders past, present, and emerging. I apologize for my errors, which I know are many and which I hope do no harm.

I received generous financial support for the dissertation from the Social Sciences Research Council—International Dissertation Research Fellowship, and the American Council of Learned Societies Dissertation Completion Fellowship. The University of Illinois supported me with the Graduate College Dissertation Fellowship, the Illinois Program for Research in the Humanities Dissertation Fellowship, and the Catherine B. and Bruce T. Bastian Fellowships for Global and Transnational History. My heartfelt thanks are due to those who helped me at the Scott Polar Research Institute, the National Maritime Museum, the National Archives, the British Library, the Royal Geographical Society, the Royal Naval Museum, the Derbyshire Record Office, the Whitby Museum, the Orkney Archive, the National Library of Scotland, the Hudson's Bay Company Archives, the Manitoba Archives, the Mitchell Library, the Royal Society of Tasmania, and the Tasmanian Archives. Special thanks are due to Naomi Boneham at the Scott Polar Research Institute, Sarah Strong at the RGS-IBG, and to Fiona Barnard at the Whitby Museum. Many thanks are also due to Adele Perry, who helped me to organize my trip to Winnipeg in the summer of 2010. I am also so grateful to my adopted British family of the Simuyandi-Palmers, who have loved and supported me in so many ways.

Excerpts from manuscript material appear by the kind permission of the University of Cambridge, Scott Polar Research Institute, the Derbyshire Record Office, the Hudson's Bay Company Archives, the Archives of Manitoba, the Royal Geographical Society (with IBG), the National Maritime Museum Greenwich, the Whitby Museum, and the Royal Society of Tasmania and Special and Rare Collections, University of Tasmania. My grateful thanks to the copyright holders of material in the Richardson-Voss collection and the Back Loan at the University of Cambridge, Scott Polar Research Institute, for granting permission to quote from their collections. Portions of Chapters 1 and 2 were previously published as "Arctic Circles: Circuits of Sociability, Intimacy and Imperial Knowledge in Britain and North American, 1818-1828" in Penelope Edmonds and Amanda Nettelbeck, eds., *Intimacies of Violence in the Settler Colony: Economies of Dispossession Around the Pacific Rim*, Cambridge Imperial and Postcolonial Studies Series (Cham, Switzerland: Palgrave Macmillan, 2018), 203–23.

Acknowledgments

I accumulated enormous debts in my time in the History Department at the University of Illinois, particularly to the members of my dissertation committee: Tony Ballantyne, Harry Liebersohn, Dana Rabin, John Randolph, and Adele Perry. Venetta Ivanova, Olga Svinarski, Karen Rodriguez'G, Anca Glont, Jesse Murray, Karen Phoenix, and Fedja Buric all sustained me spiritually and intellectually for many years in the American midlands. Parts of this book have been presented at different conferences in Britain, North America, and Australia, and I am indebted to all those scholars who engaged with me. These include, but are by no means limited to, Felix Driver, Penelope Edmonds, Dane Kennedy, David Lambert, Greg Lehman, Alan Lester, Jane Lydon, Marcus Rediker, Phillip Stern, Amanda Nettelbeck, Penny Russell, and Lyndall Ryan. You may not remember me, but I certainly remember your insightful comments and am grateful for them. The Illinois Program for Research in the Humanities Fellows' Seminar in 2011 pushed me to new engagements with borderlands. Michael Palin shared wisdom and encouragement during his visits to Hobart, which I am sure no one will ever forget!

I cannot express the gratitude and affection I feel for my cherished adviser, Antoinette Burton. Since 2006, she has debated with me and condoled with me in equal measure, encouraged me, written many letters for me (usually at short notice), read so very much, forgiven my many faults, and pushed me to be the best scholar I could be, even when thousands of miles away. To say that she has been generous is a great understatement, and I only hope that she knows how much I treasure her.

In Hobart, Elizabeth Leane, Kristyn Harman, and Alison Alexander have all encouraged me for years, and Alison has generously shared her own research and insights time and again. Elizabeth Claydon is a *rara avis*. Thank you to all my patient readers, especially those who read the whole manuscript: Alison Alexander, Dean Greeno, Kirstie Ross, Carmel Denholm, David Rish, Gabrielle Rish, Keith Mearnes, and my dear Vati, William Jacobs. I am very grateful to Kristyn Harman and Honey Dower for their thoughtful comments on Chapter 3. This book was written while working as an independent scholar, and I could not have done without Janine Tan, Kim Pearce, Jessica Walters, Nolan Navarre, Ian Morrison, Lydia Whitehouse, or Jaciek Pietrowski at the State Library, or Caitlin Sutton at the Allport Library. I am indebted to Dean Greeno for his kind wisdom and encouragement, and to Darrell Racine, for sharing his own research with me during our discussions of his play, "Franklin's Fate." In Hobart, Milton Andrews of Square Peg Designs created the incredible maps, and Gabrielle Rish was a fantastic editorial consultant, whose insights and sharp eye made the work so much better. At Bloomsbury, Maddie Holder has been wonderfully supportive as she has shepherded the book to press, and Megan Harris has been so helpful at every stage. I would also like to thank the anonymous reviewer for Bloomsbury, whose thoughtful suggestions sharpened and focused the work. All errors are my own.

My husband Leigh has given me unfaltering love and support for many years, and this book could not have been possible without him. Gentle, kind, and even-keeled, he is truly the best of men. We are so grateful for all the neighbors, friends, and teachers who have stepped in to help and to nurture our daughter Harriet while her mother was writing and her father was at sea—most especially Tim, Renee, Olive, Qamar, Frank, Maxwell, Charlie, Jane, Ann, Denis, Rachel, Enis, Emina, David, Carmel, Keith, Bridget,

Poppy, Angus, Nik, Clare, Oliver, Charlie, Valerie, Carol, the Fahan School community, Briony and the Frangipani crew, Uncle Rocky, Auntie Lucy, and the Gentlemen at the Cascade Hotel. Whether you have taught her in a forest or a classroom, played music with her, sewn fabulous creations, jumped on a trampoline, gone on a treasure hunt, or made an enormous mess—thank you.

I have the good fortune to have a loving father, William Jacobs, who has never faltered in his support for his children's scholarship. He has soothed a screaming baby, made timelines, read books over Skype during lockdown (and long after), and so much more. He has lived with this book as long as I have, and read every word many, many times. My loving mother, Mina Jacobs, not only painstakingly finessed bibliographies and notes, but also cheered me on and cheered me up, even if she had to travel halfway around the world to do so. This book is as much theirs as mine. And my great thanks are due to Harriet, who cheerfully embraced parental neglect by building endless cubbyhouses. She inspires me every day, and I cannot say how thankful I am.

Abbreviations

APS	Aborigines' Protection Society
BAAS	British Association for the Advancement of Science
HBC	Hudson's Bay Company
LAE	Land Arctic Expedition (First LAE 1819–22, Second LAE 1825–7)
NWC	North West Company
RAC	Russian American Company
RGS	Royal Geographical Society

Individuals

Adolphus/Timemernidic	Parperloihener or Peerapper clansman, sailor, from northwest coast of *lutruwita* Tasmania, nephew of **Tunnerminnerwait/Pevay**, spends 1839 at Government House with **Franklins**. Vanishes from records after 1847
Akaitcho (Gros Pied)	Powerful chief of the Yellowknives Dene at Great Slave Lake in 1821–3. Controlled trade with HBC and NWC, supports **John Franklin**'s first LAE (up to a point)
Anstey, Thomas	Tasmanian settler, Police Commissioner at Oatlands, Tasmania, key member of **George Arthur**'s circle and Derwent Bank circle
Arthur, George	Lt. Governor of Tasmania from 1824 to 1836
Arthur, Walter George	Son of Rolepa, senior man of the Ben Lomond Tribe in *lutruwita*/Tasmania, later claims title of Chief of Ben Lomond Tribe. Writer, activist, whaler
Austin, Capt. Horatio, RN	Arctic explorer, captain of HMS *Resolute* and commander of Arctic fleet (1850–1)
Back, Sir George, RN	Arctic explorer, companion of **Franklin** and **Richardson**, friend of **Willard Wentzel**, **Maconochies**, and **Gells**
Barrow, John (Jr.)	Keeper of the Records at the Admiralty, key supporter of **Jane Franklin**'s during searches for **John Franklin**
Barrow, Peter	Son of **Sir John Barrow (Sr.)**, younger brother of **John Barrow (Jr.)**, schoolmaster at the boy's prison at Point Puer, Tasmania in 1838
Barrow, Sir John (Sr.)	Second Secretary of the Admiralty, promoter of naval scientific expeditions around the world
Beaufort, Sir Francis, RN	Hydrographer of Navy, scientist, key member of Arctic circles
Beck, Adam	Kalaallit-Danish man employed as a translator by **John Ross** in 1850
Buxton, Sir Thomas Fowell	British humanitarian and politician, president of Aborigines Protection Society, cousin of **Anna Gurney**
Cracroft, Sophia	**John Franklin**'s niece. Fiercely devoted to **Jane Franklin** and becomes her lifelong companion
Dease, Peter Warren	Métis HBC Chief Factor and Arctic explorer, serves on **John Frankln's** Second LAE (1825-1827)
Forster, Matthew	**George Arthur**'s nephew by marriage, also Chief Police Magistrate in Tasmania under **Arthur** and **Franklin**
Forsyth, Lt. Charles, RN	Lieutenant on third voyage of HMS *Beagle*, commands *Vansittart* during survey of Bass Strait; later commands **Jane Franklin**'s *Prince Albert* in 1850 Franklin searches
Franklin, Eleanor Porden	Poet and author, first wife of **John Franklin**, mother of **Eleanor Franklin Gell**. Died from tuberculosis in 1825

Individuals

Franklin, Lady Jane Griffin	Second wife of **John Franklin**
Franklin, Sir John, RN	Arctic explorer, one-time Lt. Governor of *lutruwita*/Tasmania/Van Diemen's Land. His Northwest Passage expedition in HMS *Erebus* and *Terror* vanishes in 1845.
Fry, Elizabeth	Quaker humanitarian, activist, social reformer. Associate of **Franklins**, admired by **William Edward Parry**, cousin of **Anna Gurney** and sister-in-law of **Thomas Fowell Buxton**
Gell, Eleanor Franklin	Daughter of **John and Eleanor Franklin**, wife of curate and teacher **John Phillip Gell**
Gell, Rev. John Phillip	Curate, educator, protégé of Rugby School principal Dr. Thomas Arnold, husband of **Eleanor Franklin Gell**
Goodsir, Dr. Robert Anstruther	Scottish doctor, surgeon on whaler *Advice* in 1849
Gould, John and Elizabeth	Ornithologists and artist who stay with the **Franklins** at Government House in Tasmania, 1838-1839
Greenstockings	Niece of Yellowknives Dene leader **Akaitcho**, daughter of guide Keskarrah, possibly the mother of Lt. **Robert Hood**'s child
Gurney, Anna	Humanitarian, activist, philologist, and secret author of Select Committee on Aboriginal Tribes Report (1837), cousin of **Elizabeth Fry** and of **Thomas Fowell Buxton**. Associate of **Jane Franklin** and **Sarah Bowdich Lee** during Franklin searches
Hepburn, John	Scottish seaman, companion of **Franklin**, **Richardson**, **Back**, and **Robert Hood** on first LAE, later travels to Tasmania with **Franklins**, accompanies **William Kennedy**'s rescue expedition in 1851-2
Hood, Lt. Robert	Artist, explorer, officer on First LAE, killed 1822
Hooker, Sir William Jackson and Sir Joseph Dalton	Botanists, originally from Glasgow, keepers of Kew Gardens. Friends of **Franklins** and **Richardsons**
Iligjaq/Ilugliuk	Iglulingmiut woman, draws detailed charts for **Parry**'s expedition in 1821–3
Isbister, Alexander Kennedy	Métis (Cree-Orcadian) Arctic explorer, activist, humanitarian, educator, author, critic of HBC, nephew of **William Kennedy**, adviser to **Jane Franklin** during Franklin searches
Kay, Capt. Joseph Henry, RN	Brother of **William Porden Kay** and **Mary Anne (Kay) Kendall**, nephew of **Eleanor Porden Franklin** and **John Franklin**, son-in-law of **Louisa Ann Meredith**.
Kay, William Porden	Brother of **Joseph Henry Kay** and **Mary Anne (Kay) Kendall**, nephew of **Eleanor Porden** and **John Franklin**, colonial architect in Tasmania under **Franklin**
Kendall, Lt. Edward, RN	**John Franklin**'s lieutenant in 1825–7, husband of **Mary Anne Kay**
Kendall, Mary Anne Kay	Niece of **Eleanor Porden Franklin** and **John Franklin**, sister of **William Porden Kay** and **Joseph Henry Kay**, wife of **Edward Kendall**
Kennedy, William	Métis (Cree-Orcadian) Arctic explorer, activist, politician, humanitarian, trader, uncle of **Alexander Kennedy Isbister**. Critic of the HBC, captain of two of **Jane Franklin**'s private expeditions before returning to political life in the Red River

King, Dr. Richard	Explorer, doctor, and humanitarian. Surgeon-naturalist with **George Back** in 1832–4. Founding member of the APS and the Ethnological Society
Lee, Sarah Bowdich	African explorer, author, artist, ichthyologist, taxidermist. Widow of explorer **T. E. Bowdich**, friend of Baron Cuvier, Thomas Hodgkin, and **Anna Gurney**, adviser to **Jane Franklin** during Franklin searches
Lyon, Capt. George Francis, RN	Arctic and African explorer, artist, author, with **William Edward Parry** at Igloolik in 1821–3
Maconochie, Capt. Alexander, RN	Scottish geographer, penal reformer, humanitarian. Secretary of RGS before becoming **John Franklin**'s private secretary in Tasmania (1837–8), adviser to **Jane Franklin** during Franklin searches, close friend of **George Back**
Maconochie, Mary	Wife of **Alexander Maconochie**, naturalist and sometimes friend of the **Franklins**, close friend of **George Back**
McVicar, Robert	Commander of Fort Resolution, Great Slave Lake between 1819-1823 (1821)
Mithina/Mathinna	Indigenous Tasmanian child of Port Davey people, lives at Government House with **Franklins** between 1841 and 1843, vanishes from records after 1851
Montagu, John	Nephew of **George Arthur**, Colonial Secretary in Tasmania under **John Franklin**
Ommanney, Capt. Erasmus, RN	Captain of HMS *Assistance* in 1850–1, godfather of **Qalasirssuaq** (Erasmus York), supporter of **Jane Franklin**
Ouligbuck	Keewatin Inuk intermediary, translator, trained by **Tattannoeuck/Augustus**. Together with his son **William Ouligbuck**, travels with **John Richardson** and **John Rae** in 1848–9
Ouligbuck, William, Jr.	Keewatin Inuk intermediary, translator, son of **Ouligbuck**, works regularly with **John Rae** until 1854
Parker, Capt. John	Captain of the whaler *Truelove* in 1849
Parry, Sir William Edward (RN)	Arctic explorer, reformer, humanitarian. Close friend of **John Franklin**, linked by marriage to **Anna Gurney**
Penny, Margaret	Wife of **William Penny**, mediates between her husband and **Jane Franklin**
Penny, Capt. William	Scottish whaler and explorer, supporter of **Jane Franklin**, captains multiple Franklin search expeditions
Price, Mary (Franklin)	**John Franklin**'s niece, comes out to Tasmania with family. Married to John Price, the commandant of Norfolk Island after **Alexander Maconochie**
Qalasirssuaq, Kalli, Erasmus York	Inughuit teenager taken by **Erasmus Ommanney** from Savissivik/Cape York in 1850, brought to England. Godson of **Eleanor Gell**. Trained as a missionary, dies in 1856
Rae, John	Orkney Arctic explorer, doctor, natural historian, ethnographer, expert traveler, HBC employee. Friends with **John Richardson**, long relationship with **Ouligbuck** and **William Ouligbuck, Jr.**

Richardson, Mary Booth	Second wife of **John Richardson**, and niece of **John Franklin**. Natural historian who assists Richardson with many of his publications
Richardson, Mary Fletcher	Daughter of Edinburgh radical Eliza Fletcher. Third wife of **John Richardson**
Richardson, Mary Stiven	First wife of **John Richardson**
Richardson, Sir John	Naturalist, physician, Arctic explorer. **John Franklin**'s closest friend and nephew-in-law
Ross, Sir James Clark, RN	Arctic and Antarctic explorer, magnetic scientist, nephew of **John Ross**, shipmate of **W. E. Parry**, friend of **Franklins** and **Sabines**
Ross, Sir John, RN	Arctic explorer, uncle of **James Clark Ross**
Sabine, Sir Edward	Scientist, founding member of the BAAS, Arctic explorer. Central figure in the "Magnetic Crusade"
Scoresby, Rev. Dr. Capt. William, Jr.	Polymath, whaling captain, reverend, humanitarian, social reformer, magnetic scientist, Arctic authority. Instigator of searches for Northwest Passage in 1817, key supporter of Jane Franklin during Franklin searches.
Simpkinson (de Wesselow), Lt. Francis (RN)	Nephew of **Jane Franklin**, artist, naval officer, son of **Mary Simpkinson**
Simpkinson, Lady Mary (Griffin)	Sister of **Jane Franklin**
Simpson, Sir George	Scottish explorer, Governor-in-Chief of Rupert's Land
Swanston, Charles	Head of Derwent Bank in Tasmania
Tattannoeuck/Augustus	Keewatin Inuk, intermediary for both Dene and British in the 1820s–30s, companion of **Franklin**, **Richardson**, and **Back**, mentor to **Ouligbuck**
Trugernanner/Truganini/ Lallah Rook	Nuenonne woman of Bruny Island, *lutruwita*/Tasmania, intermediary, negotiator, resistance fighter
Tunnerminnerwait/ Pevay/Jack	Parperloihener man from Robbins Island, *lutruwita*/Tasmania, uncle of **Adolphus/Timemernidic**, intermediary, negotiator, resistance fighter
Wentzel, Willard	Norwegian fur trader with NWC, writer, musician, **Akaitcho**'s chosen intermediary on first LAE, friend of **George Back**

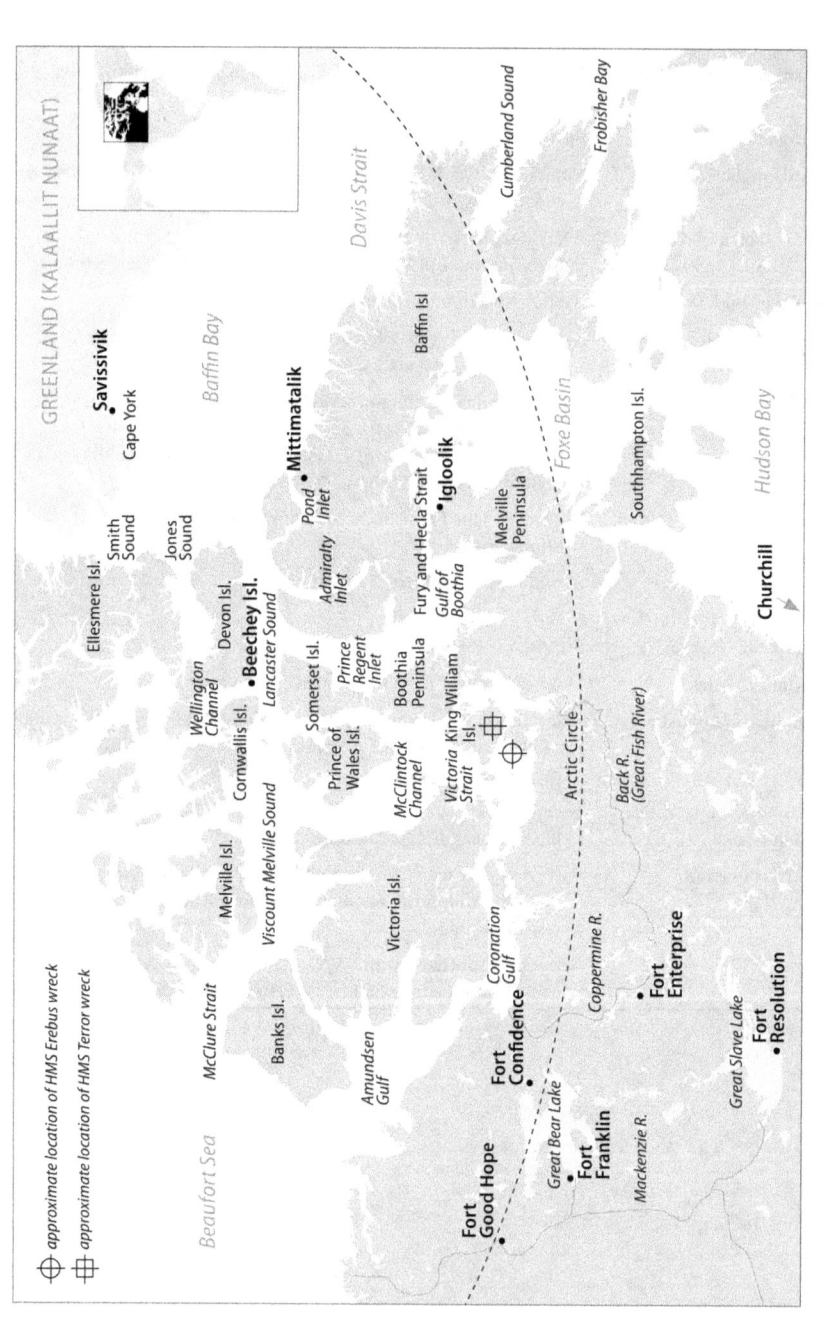

Map 1 The Canadian Archipelago, Barren Grounds, and Northwest Passages. Map by Milton Andrews, Square Peg Designs, Hobart, TAS, 2022.

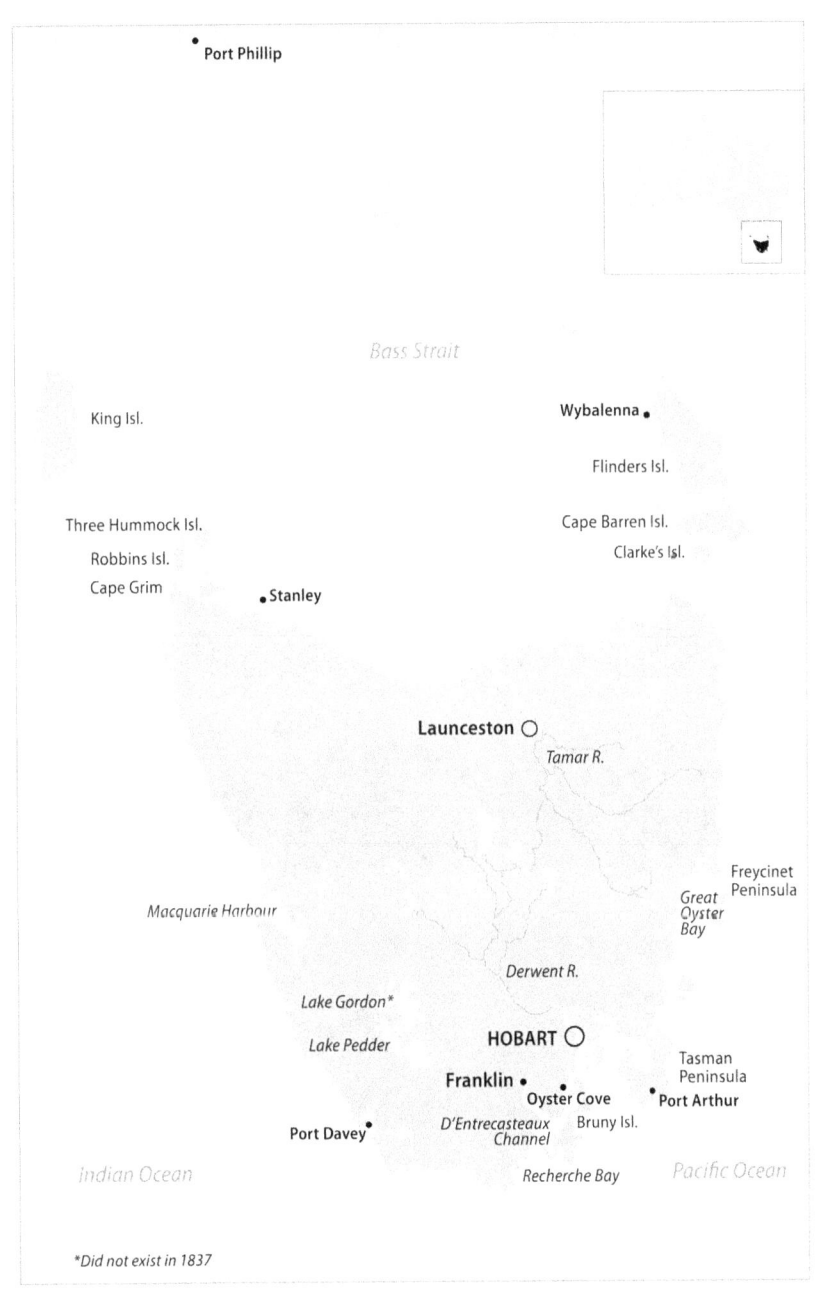

Map 2 *lutruwita*/Tasmania. Map by Milton Andrews, Square Peg Designs, Hobart, TAS, 2022.

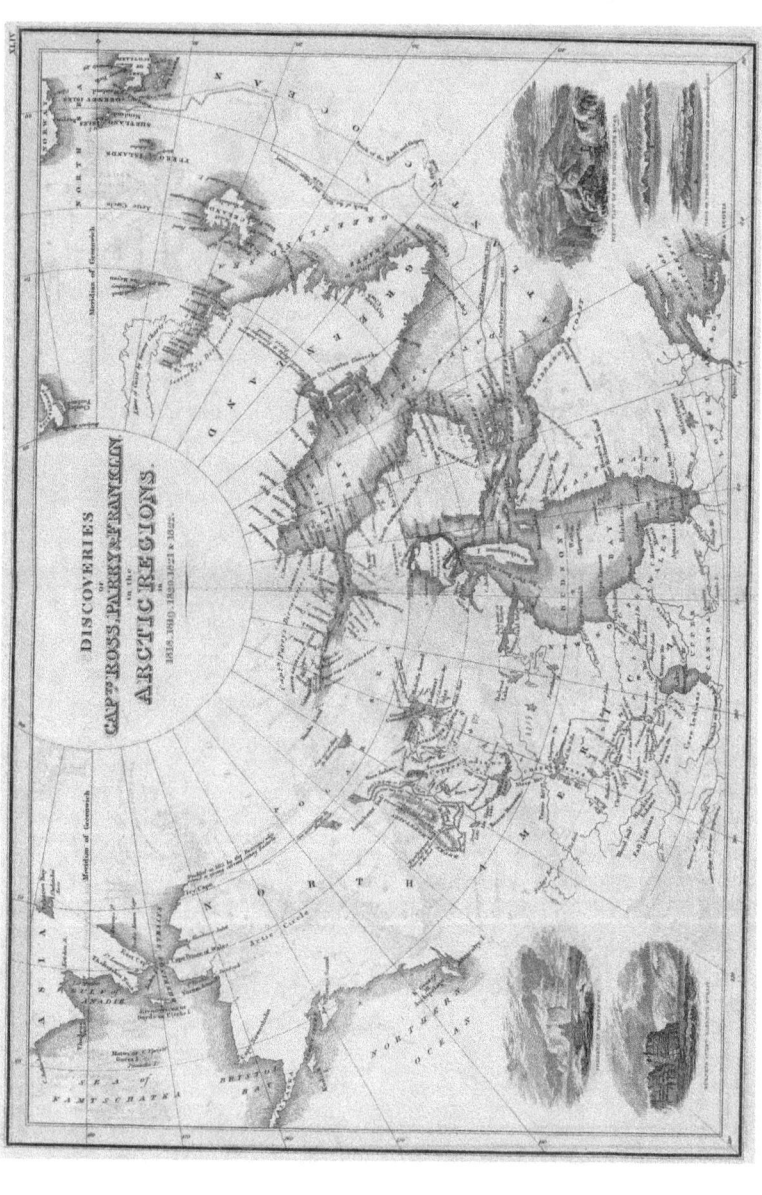

Map 3 John Thompson and James Wyld. Discoveries of Capts. Ross, Parry, and Franklin in the Arctic regions in 1818, 1819, 1820, 1821, and 1822. Edinburgh, 1824. Courtesy David Rumsey Map Collection.

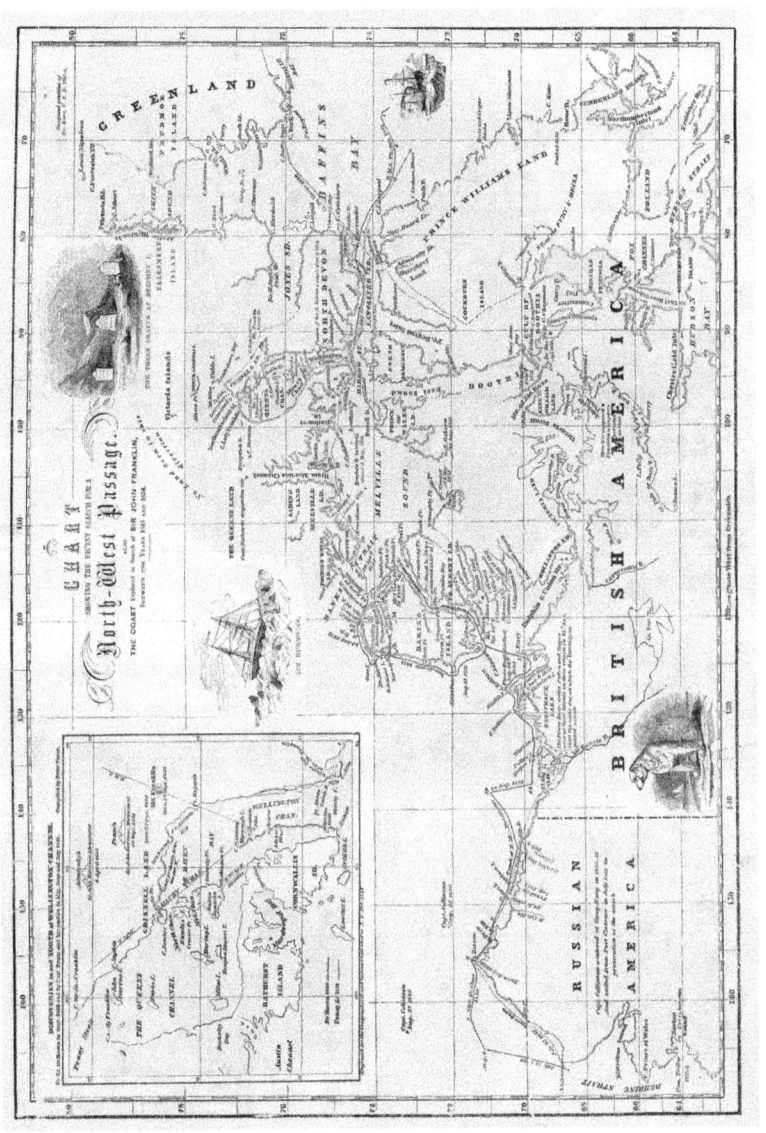

Map 4 Charles W. Morse and Charles A. Colby. Chart showing the recent search for the Northwest Passage and also the coast explored in search of Sir John Franklin between the years 1848 and 1854. Courtesy David Rumsey Map Collection.

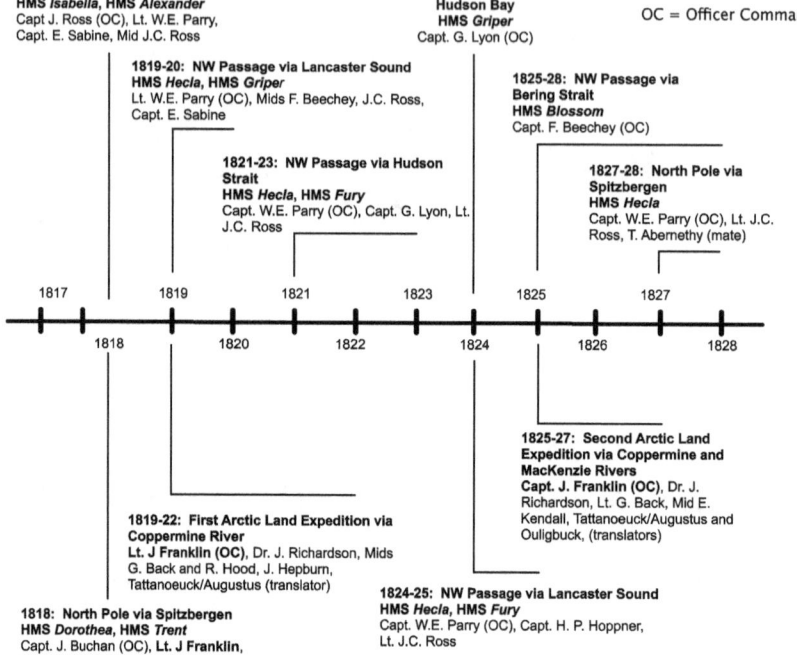

Timeline 1 Polar Expeditions, 1818–27.

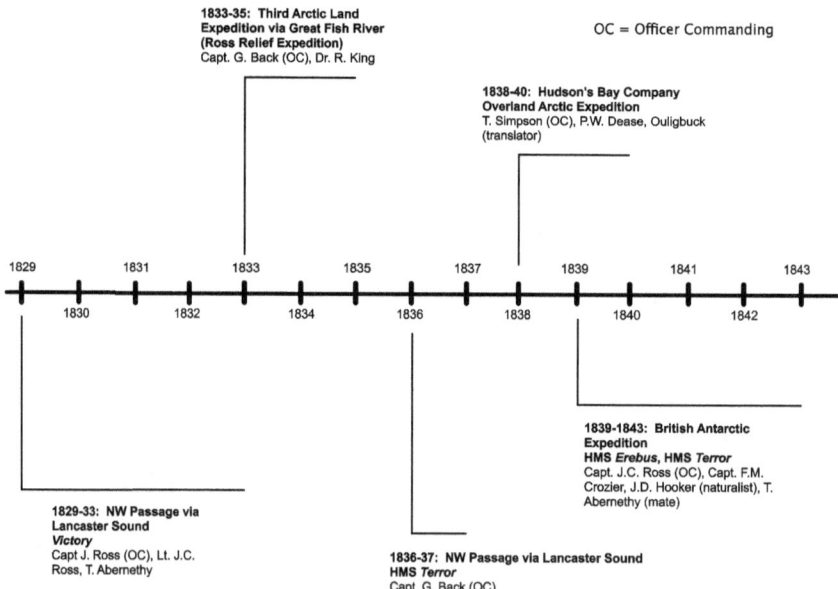

Timeline 2 Polar Expeditions, 1829–43.

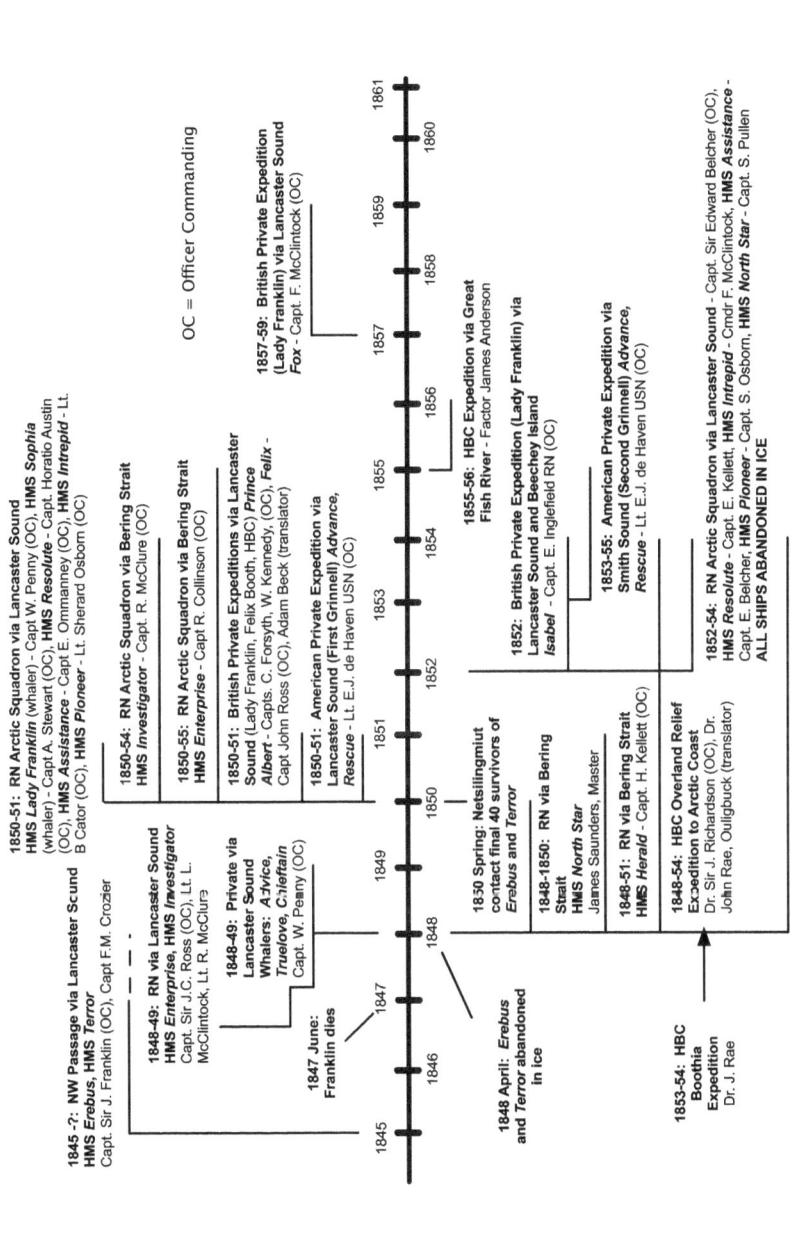

Timeline 3 Polar Expeditions, the search for Franklin, 1848–59.

Introduction

In the middle of a cold October night in 1854, a carriage drove up to a country home near Brighton. A man leapt out and pounded on the door with "violent, pealing raps." Inside were the elderly Lady Mary Simpkinson, her sister Lady Jane Franklin, and Jane's niece Sophia Cracroft. When Sophia opened her window, the man shouted that he was a special messenger from the Admiralty, and had news of her uncle Sir John Franklin's Northwest Passage expedition, which had been missing since 1845. He threw up a report from the explorer Dr. John Rae, containing information obtained from Netsilingmiut Inuit in the Gulf of Boothia. An informant had told Rae that some years before, survivors of Franklin's HMS *Erebus* and *Terror* expedition had been seen near the mouth of the Back River. The man had not seen the *qallunaat* (white men) himself, but had several items received in trade from those who had. He had also been told that there was indisputable evidence that the *qallunaat* had resorted to "the last dread alternative—cannibalism" to survive. Rae traded for several objects, including Franklin's Guelphic medal, some pieces of silverware, a knife, and a gold band from an officer's cap. "No words can describe the horror of that night," Sophia reflected.[1]

This dramatic account comes from Sophia's letter to her cousin in Australia, Mary Franklin Price, written two weeks later. Mary was no stranger to Arctic intelligence. Although she had lived for six years on Norfolk Island, a penal establishment where her husband was the commandant, she knew of Inuit maps, of rescue expeditions, of intelligence from the Bering Strait, the Hudson's Bay Company (HBC) territories, and the whaling grounds of Lancaster Sound. She knew about each of the four private expeditions that her aunt had sent out. She and her husband had subscribed to one of these through a petition organized by her cousins William and Henry Kay in *lutruwita*/Tasmania. Even on Norfolk Island, the farthest-flung jail of the British Empire, she received privileged Arctic news from nearly every point of the compass. Now Sophia told Mary that while the details about cannibalism "are everywhere rejected," nevertheless the Inuit evidence combined with the "relics" was "indisputable" and a HBC party would be dispatched in the spring to the mouth of the Back River. At the moment, she wrote, "All may speculate . . . & the speculations vary infinitely."[2]

This book is about the ways in which nineteenth-century Arctic explorers, their families, and Indigenous intermediaries traded in information. It is about how they defined what was and was not true, and who could and could not be believed. These questions of credibility and trustworthiness were central both to exploration and to the imperial knowledge it produced, but they were far from straightforward and they were not confined to the Arctic. They extended to Indigenous geopolitics, family dynamics, scientific sociability, colonial governance, and imperial humanitarianism, and from Baffin Island in the far north to Tasmania in the far south of the globe. These contests over credibility and authority were particularly apparent when rumors circulated amid the silences and pulses of information that characterized both polar exploration and long-distance communication in the nineteenth century. When explorers, their families, and the intermediaries sought to understand, control, limit, or circulate information, they did not do so alone. Rather, they were embedded in a series of interlocking "Arctic circles" formed out of shared experiences, convictions, and geographies, which cross-hatched networks of information and travel within and outside the British Empire. These contests over truth and credibility are imprinted on archives formed around a great silence—the disappearance of the Franklin expedition. For the nearly two centuries since the expedition vanished in 1845, people have scoured Arctic landscapes and archival collections for survivors, remains, and, particularly, for European documents that might attest to its fate.

In 2014 and 2016, HMS *Erebus* and *Terror* were found beneath the icy waters in the Inuit province of Nunavut. Inuit testimony helped locate the wrecks, and the publicity blitz that surrounded their discovery and the display of artifacts highlighted the vital role long played by Inuit men and women on British expeditions. Inuit were recognized as the caretakers of the wrecks, the site, and their relics by authors and curators who bemoaned the cultural blindness that had prevented Inuit testimony from being taken seriously in the first place.[3]

Arctic Circles tells a slightly different version of this story—one in which Indigenous testimony and interlocutors were always, uneasily, present within the Franklin family and the circles they inhabited. By the time John Rae's report was flung up to Sophia Cracroft on that October night, all the women in that house had been embedded in webs of information for decades. From the beginning of Franklin's career as a polar explorer in the 1820s, during his tenure as the Lieutenant Governor of Tasmania (Van Diemen's Land) in the 1830s and 1840s, and throughout the searches for his missing expedition in the 1840s and 1850s, the Franklin family had traded in information. Though they did not always realize it (and were alarmed when they did), they were often entangled within other webs of information and intimacy, including Indigenous constructions that emerged in tandem with those of British exploration and colonialism. This is the story of how these webs were woven—how, to paraphrase Tony Ballantyne, they were made, stretched, broken, and repaired over forty years.[4] It is a story that sheds light not only on the enduring obsession with the Franklin expedition but also on the "hidden histories" of science, exploration, and imperial knowledge that lie behind it. It shows how the search for Franklin was part of the fabric of the British Empire and how the one cannot be separated from the other.

Circles, Networks, and Webs of Knowledge and Intimacy

At a party in 1827, John Simpkinson pulled his sister-in-law Jane Griffin (later Franklin) aside, and "asked if I had succeeded in meeting Captain F. in arctic circles, that being the report, & whether some cape or bay was not christened in our name."[5]

Simpkinson thought he was witty. So did Jane, whom Franklin was courting at the time, and who might therefore expect to have her family name on the unfolding map of the Arctic. The "Arctic circles" to which Simpkinson referred were a feature of scientific sociability in the 1820s, comprised of Arctic officers, their friends, and relatives. They also interlocked with others—those of humanitarians, politicians, publishers, writers, artists, travelers, and families. This elite social scene was one of the realms in which explorers secured patronage, and even as scientific and geographical institutions developed in the 1830s, it would continue to be a vital sphere in which credibility was secured.[6]

Not all the members of the varied Arctic circles that made explorers famous and exploration possible would necessarily have been welcome at such parties, except perhaps as curiosities. They included mixed-race fur traders with Indigenous wives, hardened whaling captains, and Inuit guides and mapmakers, among many others. Yet they, too, were included in bounded social groups like the Arctic circles Simpkinson referred to, comprised of people who knew each other intimately; who shared experiences, sentiments, and knowledge; and whose relationships were durable over long periods and great distances. For all that, they did not necessarily trust each other. Simpkinson's comment helps us to conceptualize a dynamic that shapes this book and helped to shape practices of exploration and the circulation of knowledge.

The question of how and by whom imperial knowledge was produced, used, and circulated is one of the key questions in the historiography of the British Empire and of exploration. In one view, the state and its agents were the principal producers of colonial knowledge. Controlling territory meant conquering it conceptually; inscribing peoples, spaces, artifacts, and species on texts and in maps; trapping them in collections; and so rationalizing and categorizing them.[7] These interpretations understood explorers to be complicit actors and necessary tools of the state, extending its authority by means of their scientific instruments and rational selves.[8] Yet this view has been substantively revised over the last generation. Colonized peoples and vernacular agents are now seen as vital actors who contested, wielded, and appropriated knowledge, often producing instability on the edges of empire.[9] Practitioners of the "new imperial history" recognized that there was never a single colonial project or discourse, but rather many historically contingent agendas shaped by identities, numerous political discourses, and contested and shifting notions of difference.[10] These scholars understood the intimacies produced by colonial encounters to be crucial to the formulation of colonial knowledge and also as a source of anxiety for both colonial society and authorities.[11] Historians of exploration have shown how the business of exploration was more collective than solitary, turning their attention to people who crossed cultural boundaries, who were so crucial to expeditions, and whose work was often erased in official narratives.[12] They have shown how, in turn, official narratives were produced collectively and consumed like works of serialized fiction, and how editorial and publishing practices shaped the credibility of explorers at "home."[13] In the process, they have undermined the narratives of European exceptionalism that have long underpinned myths of the hero-explorer, in part by drawing attention to explorers' constant vulnerability, search for credibility, and reliance on intermediaries.[14] As Simon Schaeffer has put it, intermediaries "made and changed the contents and the paths of knowledge," and their relationships with explorers were often intimate, and equally as often rendered invisible.[15]

Linked to these developments was a new understanding of the British Empire's spatiality, in which the metropole–colony relationship was one strand of a web of relational networks and sites. These included networks of friendship and kinship crucial to colonial governance, intellectual and scientific networks, and transcolonial networks of humanitarians and white settlers that utilized personal connections, print culture, and strategies of mass mobilization to pressure government and to shape public opinion.[16] For settlers the ultimate goal was to secure autonomy, self-rule (including the authority to dispossess Indigenous people), and the elusive badge of respectability.[17] For humanitarians, it was to make imperialism as much a moral undertaking as a commercial, military, or political one, while securing their own moral authority as agents of civilization through practices of "humanitarian governance" that focused on the regulation of white settlement and the "protection" and assimilation of Indigenous peoples.[18] Scientific networks were embedded in practices of polite sociability and patronage, and also depended upon far-flung circuits of correspondence, on old friendships forged on voyages of discovery, and on specimen collectors in the field.[19] Women were able to carve out spaces in both humanitarian and scientific networks, whether as salon hosts, illustrators, editors, archivists, or "popularizers" of science.[20] Many of these connections and flows of knowledge were conditioned by both preexisting and developing Indigenous networks, adapting to the pressures of outsiders, working out how to maintain control of land, and leveraging multiple interests against each other. As Jane Carey and Jane Lydon have put it, imperial networks were often "shaped and even constituted through engagement with Indigenous peoples' actions, ambitions, and orientations."[21]

Tony Ballantyne has argued that we still have to assemble a full and rich understanding of the colonial information order "by identifying the place of knowledge production, the role of 'knowledgeable groups,' changing shapes of communication networks and technologies, and debates over status of particular forms of knowledge."[22] In this book, I try to address this challenge by focusing on the Arctic circles that formed around common experiences and sentiments during the British search for the Northwest Passage in the first half of the nineteenth century. These circles emerged as a result of British polar exploration, but they were never exclusively polar. Rather, they were part of the webs and networks that cross-hatched the nineteenth-century British Empire—particularly those of science, humanitarianism, commerce, and colonial governance. They also included sailors, convicts, missionaries, intellectuals, activists, travelers, settlers, and traders, among others. The parhelia on the cover of this book—the illusion of multiple suns created by particular atmospheric conditions—helps to conceptualize this phenomenon. Each apparent sun is distinct yet fuzzy, bounded and yet connected to the others, forming a whole system that only exists under certain conditions.

Within these circles, members shared experiences of curiosity, commitment, suffering, grief, love, labor, friendship, and enmity. In their search for credibility, they sometimes relied upon and sometimes undermined each other. Most were negotiating new circumstances—new environments, social structures, and technologies, changes that were often traumatic and relentless. While circles were usually formed in one place, they were also both mobile and durable, with their members maintaining connections and exchanging knowledge over great distances for many years. While they were inflected by race, class, and gender, they nevertheless included people who were male, female, Indigenous, European, the ordinary, and the elite. They were intimate, often profoundly so, but made up of relationships that are sometimes difficult to categorize. After all, what do you call the relationship between men, different in race, religion, and language, who starve together, huddling their bony bodies under a ragged caribou skin for warmth? Is that friendship? Exploitation? Companionship? John Franklin called it being "endeared by affliction", but really those relationships defied categorization in 1821 and continue to do so 200 years later.[23] Nevertheless, despite shared experiences and linked histories, the members of these circles did not entirely trust each other. Distrust and suspicion could produce and circulate knowledge just as well as (and sometimes better than) trust and confidence.[24]

Arctic Circles is concerned with how these bounded social circles of people encountered, collided, and overlapped each other as they moved through and beyond the spaces of the British Empire. It examines the kinds of knowledge produced out of these dynamics and how those collisions produced contests over authority and the truth. It is also interested in how these contests register in archives, particularly those created to tell biographies of only some of their members, subsuming the rest in silence.

Colonial Lives, Archives, and Silences

When the Franklin expedition vanished in 1845, so did all its journals, letters, and drawings. All that was left was a vast blank space on the map of North America and an endless series of possibilities. Had they starved to death? Had they gone mad? Were they poisoned by their own tinned food? Had they eaten each other? Had any of them survived by joining Inuit bands? As Heather Fisch-Davis has put it, "attempts to reconstruct what happened to the Franklin expedition break down because the material remains of the expedition produce, rather than alleviate, ambiguity."[25] These recurring ambiguities have spurred generations of explorers and researchers to try to solve the mystery of what happened to the expedition, to document the causes of the disaster, and to chart its remnants around King William Island.[26]

One of the recurring themes in the Franklin literature is how productive the absence and silence at its core is, how it begs to be filled, and how it creates a perpetual dynamic of fruitless searching.[27] This dynamic has, however, ensured that surviving archives, particularly the private papers of the Franklin family, were carefully preserved in British, Canadian, and Australian institutions. Put another way, the Franklin archive has been preserved as a counterweight to the missing expedition—to drown out, or to one day help to solve, the silence at its heart. It is not a single collection housed in one institution. Rather, it is scattered across three continents, including family bequests, odd letters, relics, and scraps of information preserved because of their association with Sir

John or Lady Jane Franklin. Created around a central absence, together they become a polyvocal archive that throws up many other connections to our sightline, concrete linkages between far distant places, people, and often-severed historiographies. As this book traces how members of heterogeneous Arctic circles made imperial knowledge, it follows not only their imperial lives but also the lives of this collective colonial archive, which produced silences of its own.

In the last fifteen years or so, histories of "imperial lives" have traced life courses across multiple imperial spaces, simultaneously illustrating the complexities and contradictions of the empire, unpicking the biographical subject and querying the project of biography itself.[28] These works attempt to wrest biography from its roots in national histories in which they have historically been entangled; explore connections between the local, imperial, and global; and bring hitherto neglected and marginalized subjects to our sightline.[29] They allow us to apprehend the mobility of imperial lives as people both traveled and remained in place, "routinely adjusting themselves—whether by choice or otherwise—to the perpetual motion" of the ground beneath their feet, as Antoinette Burton and Tony Ballantyne put it.[30] Their authors often use intimacy as a category of analysis, not one limited to conjugality but rather encompassing a broad range of relationships, tender and violent, public and private, all of which are historically, culturally, and geographically specific.[31] Doing so helps us to analyze some of the ways in which the public and private were linked through the exercise of power, and how hybridity and ambivalence were unsettling components of the everyday experience of empire. These are tall methodological and interpretive orders, but focusing on a family archive helps us to anchor these "wide, wandering, and sometimes daunting histories," as Adele Perry has put it.[32] Above all, they help us to see complexity, nuance, and contradictions within both individual lives and the worlds in which they dwelled.[33]

This scholarship is linked to a parallel interrogation of archives and archival spaces—the ways in which they are made, used, and preserved. Archives also have lives, histories, homes, intentions, and multiple contradictions. Far from being objective, passive repositories of truth, they are dynamic entities with their own biographies, genealogies, and ethnographies.[34] Like the Franklin archive, those that underpin histories of imperial lives are generally arranged around "great men" though they may have been curated for many years by women, often for the purposes of writing biographies.[35] As Antoinette Burton reminds us, the home is "both a material archive for history *and* a very real political figure in an extended moment of historical crisis."[36] Certainly that is how the Franklin archive functioned for the Franklin family. Their lives were lived in near-constant crisis across multiple imperial and extra-imperial sites, from attempts to chart the Northwest Passage, to governing a penal colony, to impossible rescues and expeditions. Like other imperial families, their homes and lives were frequently defined by absence.[37] They were governed by what Elizabeth Buettner has called "permanent impermanence," shaped by constant comings and goings, long separations, and trauma that made idealized domestic households and nuclear families almost impossible to achieve.[38] Relationships were often only sustained through correspondence, which Charlotte MacDonald has called the "intimacy of the envelope."[39] But these strained and distant relationships also offered up the opportunity to negotiate authority—and to shape archives. The Franklin women were maritime wives and partners, meaning that they could hold powers of attorney, demand support from merchant shipowners or the Admiralty, circulate information, and serve as "intermediaries between the fraternity at sea and the community on shore."[40] Their archive was formed out of what I call the "politics of truth"—their battles to define what was and was not true, to control and to suppress stories that were told of expeditions, administrations, and familial relations. For the Franklins and for other explorers, truth-telling was "far from plain and seldom unvarnished," as Innes Keighren, Charles Withers, and Bill Bell have put it.[41]

The story of the Franklin family's struggles over truth is necessarily connected with contemporary struggles over history and truth-telling in the places where they dwelled. Truth-telling is often invoked in public discourse but seldom defined. Following Antoinette Burton, I understand it as a remaking of public memory, in which conventional narratives about the past (biographies, national histories, monuments, and archives) are called into question by disenfranchised groups seeking political rights (including sovereignty) and who seek to "make visible the extent to which national identities are founded on archival elisions, distortions, and secrets."[42] It is also a question about where the histories of colonialism should properly reside—whether in archives and museums that carry their own histories of violence, or in territory, country, and memory, or in both; and if so, how can and should these stories be told?[43] Truth-telling raises questions about the ownership and definition of multiple "truths"; about the lives of the stories told, preserved, owned, and kept; about who is allowed to access and use them and under what conditions; how those that are written are to be weighed against those that are remembered; and what the consequences are for the living when we tell different stories of the dead.

In Australia, as in Canada, truth-telling focuses particularly on the often-absent histories of children, on the dignity of childhood, and on the tragedy of families severed by intervention and residential schooling.[44] This reinforces the need to understand archives and homes as mutually constituted, especially when those home are defined by the absence of children, or, as in the Franklin home, the presence of children not their own, the two Indigenous Tasmanian children they took as experiments in "improvement."

Above all, truth-telling requires blended histories of the powerful and the disenfranchised, recognizing the power of silence. Silences are comfortable for some and agonizing for others. As Maggie Walter has recently written, "full truth-telling is weighed down by 200-plus years of silence and a fondness for the comfort such silence provides."[45] Catherine Hall notes that "silencing is a practice, not something that simply happens."[46] Archival silences beckon historians the way blank places on the map once beckoned explorers—as places to be filled up with stories. Scattered, polyvocal, curated, redacted, and massive, the Franklin family archive has the capacity to shed light on a kaleidoscope of interlinked worlds, ideas, and lives across and outside the nineteenth-century British Empire. But hearing those voices requires us to reckon with silence, and the ways that the gravitational force of yearning pulls us as it pulled those whom we seek to know better.

"The Precise Line Betwixt the Possible and Impossible": Questions of Credibility and Authority

Almost immediately after HMS *Erebus* and *Terror* vanished into Lancaster Sound in 1845, rumors of their fate filtered back to Britain. Inuit maps were carried by whalers to Scotland, Inuit interpreters accompanied naval and private expeditions to Lancaster Sound, the Bering Strait, and across the Canadian Barren Grounds. Stories of lost parties of white men were passed along trade routes that crossed the top of North America, turning up in Russian trading posts on the western coast of Alaska and in British trading posts along Canadian rivers. There were stories of ships locked in open polar seas, ships frozen in icebergs, burned ships, and dead men. These were compared with physical evidence—from the remains of Franklin's 1845–6 winter camp on Beechey Island to the odd fragments of flotsam and jetsam found along shorelines. Over and over again, the same questions were asked. What constituted an authoritative source? Did it have to be a journal, a map, or a ship? Or could it be a relic, a story, a promise, or a feeling? Who was a trustworthy reporter and interpreter? How should Indigenous testimony be evaluated in a region where Inuit could travel, observe, and report in a way the British had not and could not?

Since HMS *Erebus* and *Terror* disappeared, the Franklin searches have always been framed as a quest for truth, and one that utilizes multiple methods and sources in the absence of an official archive. *Arctic Circles* examines how information, rumors, conjecture, and lies traveled amid the arrhythmic pulses of information in the early to mid-nineteenth century, and how explorers, families, and intermediaries each sought to assert their credibility and test that of others. Often these pulses were created out of a collision between Indigenous and European information orders, technology, and travel. News traveled quickly along some corridors, and slowly along others. Western technology did not guarantee either rapidity or accuracy. Indeed, steam power, postal systems, and print culture could badly distort information and give rise to destabilizing rumors. In the anxious pauses between bursts of information, spaces opened up in which knowledge and authority were contested. As the penal reformer and geographer Alexander Maconochie wrote in 1849, after using a clairvoyant to test the validity of an Inuit map, "in these days, when we make the lightning carry our messages, and the sun take our pictures, it is very difficult to draw the precise line betwixt the possible and the impossible."[47]

Nineteenth-century explorers were constantly struggling for credibility and authority. Though they were supposed to be detached and rational observers of their surroundings, it was widely understood that in practice, the physical and mental exertion of travel could easily stretch or break their reason. These included the challenges posed by environments, such as dense jungles, frozen wastes, and trackless deserts; the disordered reality of the senses caused by illness, blindness, hunger, and exhaustion; the troubled and troubling intimacies with Indigenous people and fellow travelers; the dangers that travel posed to the rational, observing self.[48] Explorers who survived were expected to return home and tell their tales. Their published narratives were key to securing their credibility with the broader public and with potential patrons, as well as opening doors to wider circuits of knowledge and sociability. These immensely popular volumes shaped both popular understanding and intellectual debates not only about the world beyond Europe's shores but also about the very nature of humanity.[49] But behind them was always the question of whether or not the men who told these stories were really trustworthy, and if so, how one could be certain.

This anxiety over credibility and authority extended to explorers' families and to intermediaries. Credibility was always shaped by identity, by shifting and slippery categories of race, class, gender, and religion, and was never straightforward. There were many subtle and contradictory ways in which people claimed truth, honor, respectability, and sovereignty, often at each other's expense. Practices of scientific sociability and imperial humanitarianism allowed the women of the Franklin family and other polar relatives to trade in information in ways that were not only allowed by but contributed to their gendered authority. When their loved ones were away in the field, relatives circulated their letters and specimens through social and intellectual circles that included female authors, scientists, travelers, and illustrators, working to secure patronage and "trust at a distance" for their absent relatives.[50] In the process, they also struggled to gain and maintain their own authority. They found models in scientific circles where they also encountered humanitarian activists, particularly women, who were central to campaigns to abolish slavery, reform prisons, ameliorate the conditions of the poor and of children, and to "protect" Indigenous people.[51] These women legitimated their activities in the public sphere as an extension of their feminine moral authority, using the "language of conscience" to argue that doing so was as an expression of duty and honor.[52] They also engaged with the contingent credibility of go-betweens by asserting their own authority as civilized, respectable, and domestic Western women. In this sense, they shared terrain and strategies with imperial feminists and colonial philanthropists who also used colonial "others" to secure their authority.[53]

Go-betweens, guides, mediators, collaborators, brokers, translators—regardless of what they were called, intermediaries were crucial to the functioning of expeditions and to early nineteenth-century imperial and scientific information systems as a whole.[54] They dwelled in a twilight of shifting, ambiguous cultural and social identifications. Sometimes they were elites, but often they were dislocated people struggling to find their place in a world that was constantly shifting beneath their feet.[55] Relationships between intermediaries and explorers could take a variety of forms, from the purely exploitative to the deeply emotional, but they were always inflected by power dynamics, both with outsiders and within their own societies. As a result, go-betweens were highly mobile, invariably indispensable, and often suspect.[56] There is an enormous methodological problem of how intermediaries' intentions, identities, and agency can be coaxed from records from which they have often been removed or never noticed in the first place.[57] This was not least because their uneasy archival presence was linked to an epistemological problem with explorers' own credibility—with how their regulated observations, aided by precise instruments, were always inadequate to the task of travel, and were almost always supplemented by necessary local and Indigenous knowledge. The end result was, Dane Kennedy has argued, a dual system of knowledge—one that operated in the field, and one that could be acknowledged at home.[58] *Arctic Circles* traces how that collision played out in the Franklin family home over forty years, and the extent to which families apprehended—and acted upon—that "epistemological rupture" between the field and home.

This struggle for credibility lies at the heart of *Arctic Circles*. It is framed by two significant developments in the first half of the nineteenth century: the making of an Indigenous Northwest Passage across the top of North America, and the emergence of Indigenous networks that interacted with colonial states and their agendas. Both of these framed the flows of information and the contests of credibility in which the Franklin family were entangled. As Kate Fullagar and Michael McDonnell have argued, "everywhere they moved Britons travelled down distinctly Indigenous pathways," and were drawn into "new and uncertain environmental, diplomatic, and commercial worlds that rested on Indigenous foundations."[59] As the British searched for a Northwest Passage after the end of the Napoleonic Wars, an Indigenous Northwest Passage developed on the northern fringes of Asia and North America. Formed haphazardly and in parts, responsive to multiple incursions of traders, whalers, hunters, and others, Indigenous networks of trade and travel expanded rapidly across sea ice, over tundra, and along river systems at the end of the Little Ice Age, roughly between the years 1800 and 1860. They developed in tandem with the movements of British, Russian, and American agents of empire, and in response to the exigencies of a changing climate and population movements. Indigenous people used visiting expeditions and wrecked ships in their territory to gain information about strangers, and where possible, to gain advantages over their neighbors. Information became a key commodity of trade along these passages, particularly as some Inuit were taken by whalers to be trained as translators, and gained experience of distant countries and peoples.[60] Explorers like Franklin found that their supplies, guides, and maps were embedded in the complicated Indigenous geopolitics around trade and travel, which they seldom fully understood but were always beholden to. When expeditions were in the field, or when they disappeared, information from these networks and informants could be simultaneously hopeful and crushing. They could also be seriously unnerving, particularly when it appeared that Indigenous intelligence extended to the heart of the empire itself, with Indigenous agents present in Britain.[61]

Other Indigenous networks were also developing within the fabric of the British Empire and far beyond it. Recent scholarship challenges the received notion of Indigenous people as autochthonous, and examines how Indigenous people and communities engaged with the institutions, ideas, individuals, industries, and networks that sought to transform, assimilate, or eliminate them.[62] This was what Tracey Banivanua Mar called an "imperial literacy" that depended partly on the written word, but also on a political literacy born of close engagement with the politics of protection, assimilation, dispossession, protest, and critique, and which developed out of an increasingly physically connected colonial world.[63] These political engagements launched far beyond the local, into developing colonial, transcolonial, and global discourses of human rights, sometimes connecting far distant communities, sometimes tapping into imperial networks of information (especially humanitarian, scientific, and missionary networks), and often operating outside of them.[64] The people at the heart of these developments were often badly traumatized as children, wrenched from their parents and communities—in Tasmania as part of the "Black War," on Baffin Island as part of whalers' desire for translators and geographers, in the fur trade countries as Scottish traders sought Scottish educations for their mixed-race sons. Some became what Zoe Laidlaw has called "conscripts of civilization" who constantly reckoned with the "tension inherent in reconciling indigenous authority and knowledge with claims to scientific authority and 'civilization.'"[65] This was never a straightforward process with clearly defined allegiances, but rather one that involved constant negotiation by people who, as Laidlaw and Lester have pointed out, often had "blended" identities.[66]

The Franklin family and their archives were shaped by these Indigenous networks, by Indigenous mobility, and by Indigenous engagement with encroaching empire. Indeed, the Franklins and their Arctic circles were sometimes the point of collision between them. Each chapter of this book is framed around one or more of these collisions, each of which was conditioned by uneven flows of information, each of which produced different crises of credibility, and each of which registered differently in the private archives of the family.

Chapter 1 examines the stories and narratives that emerged from John Franklin's disastrous First Land Arctic Expedition (LAE) to the Coppermine River (1819–22). The first half of the chapter is set at the end of the Little Ice Age, amid the unstable Indigenous and fur trade politics on the Barren Grounds and the Royal Navy's attempts to chart a Northwest Passage in the aftermath of the Napoleonic Wars. It focuses on negotiations of credibility among explorers, Indigenous leaders, intermediaries, traders, and *voyageurs* (the mobile indentured laborers of the fur trade). For these people, trust was valuable, scarce, and easily eroded. All of them attempted to control the stories and silences that emerged from the Land Expedition's dissolution into starvation, murder, and cannibalism. The second half of the chapter examines how the formal expedition narrative and circulating rumors intertwined with each other in Britain. As John Franklin and John Richardson struggled to write the narrative, their partners, Eleanor Porden Franklin and Mary Stiven Richardson, reckoned with the unsettling relationships and stories of the Barren Grounds, and their ramifications for domestic life. Out of these experiences came some of the Arctic circles that structure this book, of naval "brother officers" and their families, of Inuit interpreters and their families around Fort Churchill, and fur traders and their families in Rupert's Land.

Chapter 2 examines the crucial relationships between explorers, women, and families, both in the field and at home. On the one hand, it situates explorers and their families within the metropolitan circles of scientific sociability in which patronage was secured and reputations made in the 1820s. During their long absences, explorers' relatives circulated letters and specimens through these circles, giving patrons privileged access to restricted information while attesting to the trustworthiness (and stability) of absent men, establishing the women as gatekeepers of information, archives, and collections. Importantly, practices of sociability also brought the Arctic circles into contact with nascent humanitarian and scientific circles with whom they shared matters of conscience, religion, and reform, as well as models for women's participation in the public sphere. Metropolitan Arctic circles coexisted with Arctic circles in the field. Arctic explorers also depended upon Indigenous women and families for intimate companionship, knowledge, patronage, and logistical support. Both geographically distant circles were marketplaces of information in which credibility was negotiated in terms of intimacy, and some would shape the Franklins' imperial careers.

Chapter 3 follows the Franklin family to *lutruwita*/Tasmania, where their arrival coincided with the early years of humanitarian "protection" in the wake of the "Black War" and the exile of Indigenous Tasmanians to Flinders Island. This forced removal was one of many conflicts in Britain's settler empire that sparked the Parliamentary Select Committee on Aborigines in 1836. Members of the Arctic circles were, by the 1830s, closely linked to the humanitarian movement, and these linkages followed the Franklins to Tasmania. Anxiety over how they were perceived at "home" colored Sir John and Lady Jane Franklin's political battles in the penal colony, and particularly their promotion of colonial science as an antidote to the rumors that swirled around their family and administration. The struggle of Indigenous Tasmanians to survive intertwined with the Franklins' anxiety about their metropolitan reputations in multiple ways, but particularly through the lives of two young children they took to live in Government House in order to transform them. This chapter shows how these children fit into Jane Franklin's understanding of herself as a woman struggling for authority, both in public and in private. It also tries to apprehend the mirror image, how the Franklins may have featured in Indigenous struggles to retain their children and to define the meaning and limits of "improvement."

Chapter 4 begins with the disappearance of Sir John Franklin's expedition in HMS *Erebus* and *Terror* in 1845, not long after the family returned from Tasmania. It takes a case study from the earliest Franklin rescue expeditions to show how, in the silence that surrounded the missing expedition, authority, expertise, and truth could be debated and claimed in surprising quarters. In 1848, the first rescue missions were sent out, and in 1849, a whaler brought an Inuit map to England from Mittimatalik/Pond Inlet on Baffin Island, showing four ships stuck in the ice. This chapter follows how the map was interpreted by the Arctic circles, explorers' families, and the press. These interpretations were conditioned by a characteristic arrhythmic pulse of information, as intelligence gathered on the northern edge of the Indigenous Northwest Passage on Baffin Island made its slow way back to Britain. Rumors and conjecture accelerated wildly along expanding pathways on the telegraphs, railway, and steam press. In the midst of this disjuncture, different members of the Franklin family and Arctic circles stepped forward and claimed authority to interpret the map based on their emotional interest or professional expertise. They formulated an argument linking Arctic exploration with national identity and humanitarian rhetoric—that hope remained for the missing men who were deserving subjects of British philanthropy.

Chapter 5 examines one of the defining themes of the Franklin search—the possibility that the missing expedition was trapped in an open polar sea with plentiful animal life. It traces how the open polar sea, a relic of the Renaissance geographical imagination, came to be entangled in literate Indigenous networks of activism and imperial critique, as well as the fragmenting humanitarian movement in the aftermath of the failed Niger Expedition of 1841. In 1850-1, the open polar sea revolved around uneven, dynamic, contested intelligence, and was elaborated by a new Arctic circle centered on Jane Franklin. Members included the veteran humanitarian

Anna Gurney, the science writer Sarah Bowdich Lee, and the Indigenous activist Alexander Kennedy Isbister. Responding to a combination of new Indigenous and vernacular testimony, and the continuing absence of any records from the missing Franklin expedition, these women and men put together an "argument from negative evidence"—a campaign to both silence the testimony of one Inuk interpreter, to push the Admiralty to send more ships northward, and to assert Jane Franklin's moral authority over information. The case they made—that the British government was failing in its duty toward the deserving and vulnerable—was highly transportable, articulating with local concerns in Britain and far beyond. The chapter concludes with a brief examination of how Tasmanian settlers adopted the open polar sea as their own. Amid their crusade to end transportation and in the aftermath of an Indigenous petition to Queen Victoria, settlers used the Franklin expedition to claim that they, like Jane Franklin and the missing explorers, were vulnerable subjects devoted to the pursuit of science.

The concluding chapter returns us to the Franklin relics—items that had entered Netsilingmiut economies of reuse and exchange, and been brought back to Britain. Members of the Arctic circles selectively used these "relics" and the Indigenous testimony that accompanied them to memorialize the dead. In doing so, they not only created a narrative of the expedition's success *in* failure (by claiming that they had "forged the last link" of the Northwest Passage with their lives) but also reflected on their attachments over forty years, revisiting the precarious authority of Indigenous intermediaries and vernacular authorities. These efforts did not dispel but rather preserved the silence at the heart of the mystery, as it was understood that without written records, the story of the Franklin expedition would never be complete. The compelling nature of that silence lay behind the preservation of so many archives of the Franklin family. Assembled for the purposes of biography, the gravitational pull of their subjects tended to obscure the contests over truth and credibility that lay at their heart. That tension has not vanished. The Canadian discovery of the wrecks of *Erebus* and *Terror* in 2014 and 2016, Inuit contributions to the search, and the negotiation over the ownership of wrecks and artifacts, together with the Franklin family's increasing presence in Tasmanian truth-telling about the impact of child removal, colonial science, and the myth of extinction on Indigenous communities, are all linked to the interconnected stories of the nineteenth-century Arctic circles.

This is not an Arctic history, and it makes no claims to being an Indigenous history. There have been a number of Indigenous-centered histories and studies that would fill that role, written by a new generation of scholars who have spent much more time on country than I have, learning languages and listening to elders.[67] Rather, it is an attempt to write a history of exploration and colonialism that is attentive to both stories and to silence, because every pause contains something important. Often, our desire to fill up pauses and gaps leads us badly astray, and in our urgency to tell stories, we ignore or forget the important things that we have been told but have not properly heard. I am still learning that lesson, and I have much more to learn. This is my attempt to try to tell stories together, to show how Arctic, Indigenous, and imperial histories are entangled, through the archive made around an immense silence and about one family.

Notes

1. TA NS 1004/1/15, Sophia Cracroft to Mary Franklin Price, November 4, 1854; "The Arctic Expedition," *Times*, October 23, 1854.
2. TA NS 1004/1/15, Sophia Cracroft to Mary Franklin Price, November 4, 1854.
3. John Geiger and Alanna Mitchell, *Franklin's Lost Ship: The Historic Discovery of HMS Erebus* (Toronto: HarperCollins, Ltd., 2015); Gillian Hutchinson, *Sir John Franklin's Erebus and Terror Expedition: Lost and Found* (London, New York, and Sydney: Bloomsbury, 2017).
4. Tony Ballantyne, *Orientalism and Race: Aryanism in the British Empire* (New York: Palgrave-Macmillan, 2002), 15.
5. Quoted in Frances Woodward, *Portrait of Jane: A Life of Lady Franklin* (London: Hodder and Stoughton, 1951), 157–8.
6. Samuel J. M. M. Alberti, "Conversaziones and the Experience of Science in Victorian England," *Journal of Victorian Culture* 8, no. 2 (Autumn 2003): 208–30; James A. Secord, "How Scientific Conversation Became Shop Talk," in *Science in the Marketplace: Nineteenth-Century Sites and Experiences*, eds. Aileen Fyfe and Bernard Lightman (Chicago and London: University of Chicago Press, 2007), 23–59.
7. Bernard Cohn, *Colonialism and Its Forms of Knowledge* (Princeton: Princeton University Press, 1996); Nicholas Dirks, *Castes of Mind: Colonialism and the Making of Modern India* (Princeton: Princeton University Press, 2001); Matthew Edney, *Mapping an Empire: The Geographical Construction of British India, 1765-1843* (Chicago: University of Chicago Press, 1997).
8. Edward W. Said, *Orientalism* (London: Routledge, 1978); Morag Bell, Robin Butlin, and Michael Heffernan, eds., *Geography and Imperialism, 1820-1940* (Manchester: Manchester University Press, 1995); Mary Louise Pratt, *Imperial Eyes: Travel Writing and Transculturation* (London: Routledge, 1992).
9. John Darwin, "Imperialism and the Victorians: The Dynamics of Territorial Expansion," *The English Historical Review* 112, no. 447 (June 1997): 614–42.
10. Antoinette Burton, *Burdens of History: British Feminists, Indian Women, and Imperial Culture, 1865-1915* (Durham and London: University of North Carolina Press, 1994); Frederick Cooper and Anna Laura Stoler, eds., *Tensions of Empire: Colonial Cultures in a Bourgeois World* (Berkeley: University of California Press, 1997); Catherine Hall, *Civilising Subjects: Metropole and Colony in the English Imagination* (Chicago and London: University of Chicago Press, 2002); Kathleen Wilson, ed., *A New Imperial History: Culture, Identity and Modernity in Britain and Empire, 1660-1840* (Cambridge: Cambridge University Press, 2004).
11. Ann Laura Stoler, "Tense and Tender Ties: The Politics of Comparison in North American History and (Post) Colonial Studies," *Journal of American History* 88, no. 3 (December 2001): 829–65; Lynn Zastoupil, "Intimacy and Colonial Knowledge," *Journal of Colonialism and Colonial History* 3, no. 2 (2002). doi: 10.1353/cch.2002.0053 (Accessed April 4, 2013);Tony Ballantyne and Antoinette Burton, eds., *Bodies in Contact: Rethinking Colonial Encounters in World History* (Durham and London: Duke University Press, 2005); Tony Ballantyne and Antoinette Burton, eds., *Moving Subjects: Gender, Mobility and Intimacy in an Age of Global Empire* (Urbana and Chicago: University of Illinois Press, 2009).
12. Felix Driver and Lowri Jones, *Hidden Histories of Exploration: Researching the RGS-IBG Collections* (London: Royal Holloway, University of London and Royal

Geographical Society – Institute of British Geographers, 2009); Dane Kennedy, *The Last Blank Spaces: Exploring Africa and Australia* (Cambridge, MA and London: Harvard University Press, 2013); Shino Konishi, Maria Nugent, and Tiffany Shellam, eds., *Indigenous Intermediaries: New Perspectives on Exploration Archives* (Canberra: ANU Press, 2015).

13 Innes M. Keighren, Charles W. J. Withers, and Bill Bell, *Travels Into Print: Exploration, Writing and Publishing with John Murray, 1773-1859* (Chicago and London: Chicago University Press, 2015); Janice Cavell, *Tracing the Connected Narrative: Arctic Exploration in British Print Culture, 1818-1860* (Toronto and London: University of Toronto Press, 2008).

14 Dane Kennedy, ed., *Reinterpreting Exploration: The West in the World* (Oxford: Oxford University Press, 2014); Dorinda Outram, "On Being Perseus: New Knowledge, Dislocation, and Enlightenment Exploration," in *Geography and Enlightenment*, ed. David N. Livingstone and Charles W. J. Withers (Chicago and London: University of Chicago Press, 1999), 281–94; Johannes Fabian, *Out of Our Minds: Reason and Madness in the Exploration of Central Africa* (Berkeley and London: University of California Press, 2000); Jonathan Lamb, *Preserving the Self in the South Seas: 1680-1840* (Chicago and London: University of Chicago Press, 2001).

15 Simon Schaffer et al., eds., *The Brokered World: Go-Betweens and Global Intelligence* (Canton: Science History Publications, 2009), x; Konishi et al., *Indigenous Intermediaries*; Tiffany Shellam et al., eds., *Brokers and Boundaries: Colonial Exploration in Indigenous Territory* (Acton, ACT: ANU Press and Aboriginal History, Inc., 2016).

16 Ballantyne, *Orientalism and Race*; Zoe Laidlaw, *Colonial Connections, 1815-1845: Patronage, the Information Revolution and Colonial Government* (Manchester: Manchester University Press, 2005); Alan Lester, *Imperial Networks: Creating Identities in Nineteenth Century South Africa and Britain* (London: Routledge, 2001); David Lambert and Alan Lester, "Geographies of Colonial Philanthropy," *Progress in Human Geography* 28, no. 3 (2004): 320–41.

17 Alan Lester, "Humanitarians and White Settlers in the Nineteenth Century," in *Missions and Empire. Oxford History of the British Empire, Companion Series*, ed. Norman Etherington (Oxford: Oxford University Press, 2005), 64–85; Elizabeth Elbourne, "The Sin of the Settler: The 1835-36 Select Committee on Aborigines and Debates Over Virtue and Conquest in the Early Nineteenth-Century British White Settler Empire," *Journal of Colonialism and Colonial History* 4, no. 3 (2003). doi: 10.1353/cch.2004.0003 (accessed September 27, 2013).

18 Clare Midgley, "Female Emancipation in an Imperial Frame: English Women and the Campaign Against Sati (Widow-Burning) in India, 1813-30," *Women's History Review* 9, no. 1 (2000): 95–121; Susan Thorne, "'The Conversion of Englishmen and the Conversion of the World Inseparable': Missionary Imperialism and the Language of Class in Early Industrial Britain," in *Tensions of Empire: Colonial Cultures in a Bourgeois World*, eds. Frederick Cooper and Anna Laura Stoler (Berkeley: University of California Press, 1997), 238–62; Alan Lester and Fae Dussart, *Colonization and the Origins of Humanitarian Governance: Protecting Aborigines across the Nineteenth-Century British Empire* (Cambridge: Cambridge University Press, 2014).

19 Jim Endersby, *Imperial Nature: Joseph Hooker and the Practices of Victorian Science* (Chicago and London: Chicago University Press, 2008); Anne Secord, "Corresponding Interests: Artisans and Gentlemen in Nineteenth-Century Natural History," *British Journal for the History of Science* 27, no. 4 (December 1994): 383–408;

Harry Liebersohn, *The Travelers' World: Europe to the Pacific* (Cambridge, MA and London: Harvard University Press, 2006); Iain McCalman, *Darwin's Armada: Four Voyages and the Battle for the Theory of Evolution* (New York: W. W. Norton & Co., Inc., 2009).

20 Secord, "Scientific Conversation"; Ann B. Shteir, *Cultivating Women, Cultivating Science: Flora's Daughters and Botany in England 1760-1860* (Baltimore: The Johns Hopkins University Press, 1996); Carl Thompson, "Earthquakes and Petticoats: Maria Graham, Geology, and Early Nineteenth Century 'Polite' Science," *Journal of Victorian Culture* 17, no. 3 (September 2012): 329–46.

21 Jane Carey and Jane Lyon, eds., *Indigenous Networks: Mobility, Connections and Exchange* (New York and London: Routledge, 2014), 2.

22 Tony Ballantyne, *Webs of Empire: Locating New Zealand's Colonial Past* (Wellington: Bridget Williams Books, 2012), 187.

23 SPRI MS 395/70/5; BL, John Franklin to George Back, October 15, 1821.

24 See, for example, Joshua Piker, "Lying Together: The Imperial Implications of Cross-Cultural Untruths," *The American Historical Review* 116, no. 4 (October 2011): 964–86.

25 Heather Fisch-Davis, *Loss and Cultural Remains in Performance: The Ghosts of the Franklin Expedition* (New York: Palgrave Macmillan, 2012), 5.

26 See Russell A. Potter, *Finding Franklin: The Untold Story of a 165-Year Search* (Montreal and Kingston: McGill-Queen's University Press, 2016).

27 Adriana Craciun, "The Franklin Relics in the Arctic Archive," *Victorian Literature and Culture* 42, no. 1 (March 2014): 3.

28 David Lambert and Alan Lester, eds., *Colonial Lives Across the British Empire: Imperial Careering in the Long Nineteenth Century* (Cambridge: Cambridge University Press, 2006); Desley Deacon, Penny Russell, and Angela Woollacott, eds., *Transnational Lives: Biographies of Global Modernity, 1700-Present* (New York: Palgrave-MacMillan, 2010); Catherine Hall, *Macauley and Son: Architects of Imperial Britain* (New Haven and London: Yale University Press, 2012); Adele Perry, *Colonial Relations: The Douglas-Connolly Family and the Nineteenth-Century Imperial World* (Cambridge and New York: Cambridge University Press, 2015); Zoe Laidlaw, *Protecting the Empire's Humanity: Thomas Hodgkin and British Colonial Activism, 1830-1870* (Cambridge: Cambridge University Press, 2021).

29 Lydon and Carey, *Indigenous Networks*, 10–11; Emma Rothschild, *The Inner Life of Empires: An Eighteenth-Century History* (Princeton and Oxford: Princeton University Press, 2011).

30 Ballantyne and Burton, *Moving Subjects*, 3.

31 Ibid., 4–5.

32 Perry, *Colonial Relations*, 5.

33 Laidaw, *Protecting the Empire's Humanity*, 1–27; Lydon and Carey, *Indigenous Networks*, 10–11.

34 Antoinette Burton, *Dwelling in the Archive: Women Writing House, Home and History in Late Colonial India* (Oxford: Oxford University Press, 2003); Antoinette Burton, ed., *Archive Stories: Facts, Fictions, and the Writing of History* (Durham and London: Duke University Press, 2006); Ann Laura Stoler, *Along the Archival Grain: Epistemic Anxieties and Colonial Common Sense* (Princeton: Princeton University Press, 2009).

35 Burton, *Dwelling in the Archive*; Perry, *Colonial Relations*; Laidlaw, *Protecting the Empire's Humanity*.

36 Burton, *Dwelling in the Archive*, 5.

37 Lambert and Lester, *Colonial Lives*, 26.

38 Elizabeth Buettner, *Empire Families: Britons and Late Imperial India* (Oxford: Oxford University Press, 2004), 1, 14.
39 Charlotte MacDonald, "Intimacy of the Envelope: Fiction, Commerce, and Empire in the Correspondence of Friends Mary Taylor and Charlotte Bronte, c. 1845-1855," in Ballantyne and Burton, *Moving Subjects: Gender, Mobility and Intimacy in an Age of Global Empire*, eds. Tony Ballantyne and Antoinette Burton (Urbana and Chicago: University of Illinois Press, 2009), 89–108.
40 Margaret Hunt, "Women and the Fiscal Imperial State," in *New Imperial History: Culture, Identity and Modernity in Britain and Empire, 1660-1840*, ed. Kathleen Wilson (Cambridge: Cambridge University Press, 2004), 29–47; Lisa Norling, *Captain Ahab Had a Wife: New England Women and the Whalefishery, 1720-1870* (Chapel Hill and London: University of North Carolina Press, 2000), 142–50; Lisa Norling, "Ahab's Wife: Women and the American Whaling Industry, 1820-1870," in *Iron Men, Wooden Women: Gender and Seafaring in the Atlantic World, 1700-1920*, ed. Margaret S. Creighton and Lisa Norling (Baltimore: Johns Hopkins University Press, 1996), 85; Margarette Lincoln, *Naval Wives & Mistresses* (London: The National Maritime Museum, 2011), 50–7; Margot Finn, "Women, Consumption, and Coverture in England, c. 1700-1860," *The Historical Journal* 39, no. 3 (1996): 703–22.
41 Keighren et al., *Travels Into Print*, 2.
42 Burton, *Archive Stories*, 2.
43 Julie Gough et al., *Tense Past* (Hobart: Tebrikunna Press, 2021).
44 Henry Reynolds, *Truth-Telling: History, Sovereignty, and the Uluru Statement* (Sydney: NewSouth Publishing, 2021), 3.
45 Maggie Walter, "Tasmania Needs to do its own Truth-Telling," *Mercury*, January 21, 2023.
46 Hall, *Macauley and Son*, xvii.
47 [Alexander Maconochie] "The Bolton Clairvoyante," *Morning Chronicle*, October 4, 1849, 3. I discuss this further in Chapter 4.
48 The literature here is vast, but see especially Outram, "On Being Perseus," 281–94; Fabian, *Out of Our Minds*; Lamb, *Preserving the Self*; D. Graham Burnett, *Masters of All They Surveyed: Exploration, Geography, and a British El Dorado* (Chicago and London: University of Chicago Press, 2001); Anne Salmond, *The Trial of the Cannibal Dog: The Remarkable Story of Captain Cook's Encounters in the South Seas* (New Haven and London: Yale University Press, 2003); Vanessa Smith, "Banks, Tupaia and Mai: Cross-Cultural Exchanges and Friendship in the Pacific," *Parergon* 26, no. 2 (2009): 139–60; Michael T. Bravo, "Ethnographic Navigation and the Geographical Gift," in *Geography and Enlightenment*, eds. David N. Livingston and Charles W. J. Withers (Chicago and London: University of Chicago Press, 1999), 199–235.
49 Liebersohn, *The Travelers' World*, 15–76.
50 The concept of "trust at a distance" and how explorers secured it through their correspondence are discussed in Keighren et al., *Travels Into Print*. For women and scientific sociability, see James A. Secord, "Scientific Conversation"; Alberti, "Conversaziones"; Thompson, "Earthquakes and Petticoats."
51 See, for example, Zoe Laidlaw, "'Aunt Anna's Report': The Buxton Women and the Aborigine's Select Committee," *Journal of Imperial and Commonwealth History* 32, no. 2 (May 2004): 1–28; Clare Midgely, *Women Against Slavery: The British Campaigns, 1780-1870* (London and New York: Routledge, 1995), 1–6; F. K. Prochaska, "Women and English Philanthropy, 1790-1830," *International Review of Social History* 19, no. 3 (1974): 426–45.

52 Midgely, *Women Against Slavery*, 3; Prochaska, "Women in English Philanthropy," 431–2; Leonore Davidoff and Catherine Hall, *Family Fortunes: Men and Women of the English Middle Class, 1780-1850*, rev. ed. (London and New York: Routledge, 2002), 429–36.
53 Burton, *Burdens of History*; Catherine Hall, "Rule of Difference," in *Gendered Nations: Nationalisms and Gender Order in the Long Nineteenth Century*, eds. Ida Blom, Karen Hagemann, and Catherine Hall (London and New York: Bloomsbury, 2000), especially 108–9; Midgley, "Female Emancipation," 95–121.
54 Schaffer et al., *Brokered World*, x–xi.
55 Kennedy, *Last Blank Spaces*, 162–94; Liebersohn, *The Travelers' World*, 139–85; Smith, "Banks, Tupaia, Mai," 139–60.
56 Schaffer et al., *Brokered* World, xvi.
57 Konishi et al., *Indigenous Intermediaries*, 4–6.
58 Kennedy, *Last Blank Spaces*, 193–4.
59 Kate Fullagar and Michael MacDonnell, eds., *Facing Empire: Indigenous Experiences in a Revolutionary Age, 1760-1840* (Baltimore: Johns Hopkins University Press, 2018), 13.
60 I discuss this at greater length in Chapter 1. See Claudio Aporta, "The Trail as Home: Inuit and their Pan-Arctic Network of Routes," *Human Ecology* 37 (2009): 131–46; John Bockstoce, *Furs and Frontiers in the Far North: The Contest Among Native and Foreign Nations for the Bering Strait Fur Trade* (New Haven and London: Harvard University Press, 2009); Ilya Vinkovetsky, *Russian America: An Overseas Colony of a Continental Empires, 1804-1867* (Oxford and New York: Oxford University Press, 2011); Renee Fossett, *In Order to Live Untroubled: Inuit of the Central Arctic, 1550 to 1940* (Winnipeg: The University of Manitoba Press, 2001), 115–66; Dorothy Harley Eber, *Encounters on the Passage: Inuit Meet the Explorers* (Toronto and London: University of Toronto Press, 2008).
61 T. J. Tallie, "Indigeneity, Movement, and Disrupting the Global Nineteenth Century," in *World Histories from Below: Disruption and Dissent, 1750 to the Present*, 2nd ed., eds. Antoinette Burton and Tony Ballantyne (London and New York: Bloomsbury Academic, 2022), 188–225.
62 This literature is considerable, but see, for example, Tracey Banivanua Mar, *Decolonisation and the Pacific: Indigenous Globalisation and the Ends of Empire* (Cambridge and New York: Cambridge University Press, 2016); Alan Lester and Zoe Laidlaw, *Indigenous Communities and Settler Colonialism: Landholding, Loss and Survival in an Interconnected World* (Basingstoke: Palgrave MacMillan, 2015); Fullagar and MacDonnell, *Facing Empire*; Ballantyne, *Webs of Empire*; Carey and Lydon, *Indigenous Networks*.
63 Tracey Banivanua Mar, "Imperial Literacy and Indigenous Rights: Tracing Transoceanic Circuits of a Modern Discourse," *Aboriginal History* 37 (2013): 1–28.
64 Elizabeth Elbourne, "Indigenous Peoples and Imperial Networks in the Early Nineteenth Century: The Politics of Knowledge," in *Rediscovering the British World*, eds. Phillip Buckner and R. Douglas Francis (Calgary: University of Calgary Press, 2006), 59–85; Laidlaw, *Protecting the Empire's Humanity*, especially 95, 243–54, 269–76; Carey and Lydon, *Indigenous Networks*; Mar, *Decolonization and the Pacific*.
65 Laidlaw, *Protecting the Empire's Humanity*, 278.
66 Laidlaw and Lester, *Indigenous Communities and Settler Colonialism*.
67 These include, but are by no means limited to: Keavy Martin, *Stories in a New Skin: Approaches to Inuit Literature* (Winnipeg: University of Manitoba Press, 2012);

Emilie Cameron, *Far Off Metal River: Inuit Lands, Settler Stories, and the Making of the Contemporary Arctic* (Vancouver and Toronto: University of British Columbia Press, 2015); Karen Routledge, *Do You See Ice? Inuit and Americans at Home and Away* (Chicago and London: University of Chicago Press, 2018); Bathsheba Demuth, *Floating Coast: An Environmental History of Bering Strait* (New York: W.W. Norton & Company, 2019).

1

"Which Is the Counterfeit, and Which the Real Man?"

Stories of Suffering and Questions of Credibility, 1819–25

In the winter of 1820, on the northern fringe of the boreal forest, Dr. John Richardson wrote a letter to his wife. He imagined Mary Richardson walking through Edinburgh streets, with flowers peeking from stone walls as she passed. In contrast, Richardson wrote of the intense stillness, frost, and cold at Cumberland House (modern Saskatchewan), where "the screams of a famished raven or the crash of a lofty pine rending through the intenseness of the frost are the only sounds that invade the silence. . . . I have often admired the pictures our eminent poets have drawn of absolute solitude, but never felt their full force till now."[1] Richardson was the surgeon-naturalist on the First Land Arctic Expedition (LAE), led by Lieutenant John Franklin as part of the British attempt on the fabled Northwest Passage. Before long, the two men would become the closest of friends, "endeared by affliction," as Franklin would put it. Between 1819 and 1821, during a time of regional violence and starvation, they and a party of British naval officers, Canadian *voyageurs*, Dene families, and Inuit interpreters would travel from Great Slave Lake, down the Coppermine River to the Arctic coast. They would cross a vast borderland between Dene and Inuit territory, a no-man's-land beyond the reach of the rival Hudson's Bay Company (HBC) and North West Company (NWC), a contested zone where people only ventured to hunt caribou, and then quickly departed.

Richardson wrote several more letters to Mary during the journey, teasing her about how he had become "as Dark as any Indian in the country" and "rude from want of society."[2] Over the next two years, he described their winter quarters, their future plans, and their slow progress. His letter of April 1822, however, was much different. Written from a Yellowknife Dene fort on Great Slave Lake, Richardson described the expedition's disastrous journey across the Barren Grounds in the autumn of 1821. Almost all the tough, experienced *voyageurs* had died, at least two of them murdered, and, before the Yellowknives rescued them, the survivors had subsisted on lichen, rotten caribou hides, and each other's bodies. Richardson could only tell Mary some of this. At one point, he stopped writing, refreshed his pen, and wrote, with several crossings-out, "I shall not attempt to describe the miseries we endured in this journey for no description can convey an adequate idea of them. And the bare detail would be too ~~harmful~~ harrowing to ~~the~~ your feelings ~~of humanity~~."[3] Mary found it all out anyway. Reports of starvation, murder, and cannibalism, circulated by the traders, hunters, and travelers that the expedition had left unpaid, appeared in British newspapers, just before Richardson, and his letter, arrived at Mary's doorstep in Edinburgh in October 1822.[4] Within weeks, the couple would join Franklin in London. There, Richardson and Franklin would write the heroic narrative of the expedition that would secure their enduring fame, and Mary Richardson and John Franklin's fiancée Eleanor Porden would try to work out the ramifications for their own lives.

This vignette was part of the collision between the LAE's official narrative and a multiplicity of stories and silences about what had happened on the Barren Grounds in 1819–21. It was part of a larger struggle over credibility and authority that stretched from Great Slave Lake to Britain, forming and entangling multiple circles of intermediaries, explorers, and families. As historians of science and exploration have shown, the struggle for credibility underlay the making of geographical knowledge. As travelers sought to prove themselves as trustworthy observers, armchair geographers tried to verify information supplied at second (or third, or fourth) hands.[5] An examination of the LAE shows how that contest extended far beyond the writing and publication of the narrative and reached deep into the linked worlds of traders, Indigenous leaders, and British families. For each of these groups, the politics of truth—what they knew and what they didn't, what was withheld and what was volunteered—worked differently, as each judged the other's trustworthiness, according to their own matrix of credibility, authority, knowledge, and intimacy. As they anticipated the published narrative, they engaged with what James Secord has identified as the key measures of credibility, "how knowledge travels, to whom it is available and how agreement is achieved."[6]

In looking at how expedition narratives and stories impacted each other, it is important to distinguish between them. Both were fluid rather than fixed, both were central to colonial knowledge, and both were prone to misunderstanding. Just as expeditions are now understood to have been made by a coalition of interests (European, vernacular, and Indigenous), explorers' narratives are increasingly seen not as the work of a single author, but rather as contested and multivocal, shaped by the field, publishers, and the public.[7] In the nineteenth century, exploration narratives shaped popular understanding and intellectual debates about the world and the nature of humanity.[8] Their maps, drawings, and accounts attempted to fix distant peoples and places in print, and became a key part of what Felix Driver has called the "cultures of exploration" of the nineteenth century.[9]

Stories worked differently, though they also circulated across multiple geographical, cultural, political, and linguistic contexts. They have their own subsets—legends, poems, fables, tales, rumors, lies, and skits, among many others. They can be recorded in letters, landscapes, and in stars, danced, sung, whispered, embroidered, remembered, and forgotten. They are both enduring and impermanent, and their authority changes depending on who tells them, hears them, and records them. In periods of crisis, stories—true, untrue, and contested—take on new power as political authority fragments and hierarchies of credibility collapse.[10] As Ann Stoler has pointed out, stories that swirl around dramatic, violent events "indicate a fractured social reality, one derived from fragmented knowledge as well as from competing hierarchies of credibility through which violence was read."[11] How far they traveled, who told and believed them, and how they gained credibility (to rephrase Secord) are even more difficult to trace than the readership and reception of a book, but it can be glimpsed when, occasionally, narratives and stories collide.

This chapter is set across the Barren Grounds and London, during the exceptionally cold winters between 1818 and 1825. This was the end of the Little Ice Age, when Mary Shelley published *Frankenstein*, when the Thames froze solid, and when epidemics of violence and disease raged across what is now northern Canada. These were the circumstances in which Britain turned its attention to the far north, John Franklin found his enduring fame, and the Franklin family archive and the Arctic circles began to take shape. It gave rise to important and enduring relationships and stories of suffering, and to persistent questions about what such experiences did to men and women, and how they could be trusted afterward.

Trade, Survival, and Exploration on the Barren Grounds, 1819–22

It is best, perhaps, to begin with the caribou, for this story depends upon these animals, as did all human beings on the Barren Grounds in the early nineteenth century. Like the LAE, the barren ground caribou (*Rangifer tarandus groenlandicus*) crossed three ecological and cultural zones in their annual journeys: the boreal forest (Chipewyan, Cree, Dene, and Ojibwe territory), the tundra (Dene and Inuit territory), and the Arctic coast (Inuit territory) (see Maps 1 and 3). People of the circumpolar north depended on caribou for survival. The caribou's hollow, thick fur provided the best insulation from the bitter winter cold, while their skins were used for clothing, tents, and dog harnesses. The sinews from their legs could be used as fine thread for warm boots or the seams of a skin boat. Their flesh was good food, and their bones and antlers made good tools. Yet the vast herds that ranged across Canada and Alaska were extremely fragile. As Bathsheba Demuth puts it, "there is no one historical moment when the herds are not either recovering or preparing to falter."[12] Their cyclical crashes—sometimes, though not always, linked to human behavior—could cause widespread misery, starvation, and death.[13]

Caribou are highly sensitive to climatic change, and the early nineteenth century was a volatile time. This was the end of the Little Ice Age, a period of climate instability that, in this part of the Arctic, was marked by severe cold. The years between 1810 and 1821 were especially hard, exacerbated by the catastrophic eruption of Mount Tambora in Indonesia 1815 and "the year without a summer" in 1816.[14] In these years, winter started earlier, the caribou herds declined, and their migrations became erratic. The changing climate and animal behavior also structured new encounters among both Indigenous and European peoples, as they met on old and new territory, created new relationships and enmities, and exchanged and circulated knowledge about each other and the natural world.[15] Around the Barren Grounds, coastal Inuit moved inland in the summer to hunt caribou and to fish in rivers and lakes, returning to the coast as ice formed in the autumn. Dene left the boreal forest and pushed northward, trying to catch the caribou earlier on their southward migration. Dene and Inuit might meet along the rivers or on the tundra, but they took pains to avoid doing so.[16]

The other newcomers were the competing fur traders of two British companies, the HBC and the NWC. They had only recently expanded into this region and found themselves dependent on both caribou and Indigenous people. The networks of lakes and rivers that cross-hatched the landscape formed highways for birchbark canoes, paddled and portaged by *voyageurs*—indentured laborers with their own subculture built upon shared mobility.[17] Some were French-Canadian peasants, others were Scottish islanders displaced by clearances, and others came from métis communities born of the fur trade.[18] The rivalry between the companies spilled out into open violence as both sought trade with Indigenous people, and also to keep those hunters perpetually in debt, forced to supply traders with furs and provisions—especially fish and dried caribou meat and fat, pounded into pemmican. Such trading relationships blended into kinship and marriage with Indigenous women, whose labor, connections, and knowledge were essential for men who hoped to succeed, and indeed survive, in the country.[19]

In this mixture of climate change, subsistence collapse, and commercial demands, introduced disease and warfare seriously impacted Indigenous communities.[20] The combination produced what anthropologists have called a "shatter zone" of destruction, adaptation, and regeneration.[21] Amid profound instability, new middlemen who sought to control trade developed both European connections and new kinds of leadership and power. At the same time, an Indigenous (principally Inuit) trading network began to develop at the northern fringes of the British and Russian empires in North America and Asia. It connected distant communities through a series of seasonal "trading fairs" of varying sizes, at which hostilities were temporarily suspended. From its origins in the late eighteenth century, this network developed over the first half of the nineteenth century into what was effectively an Indigenous Northwest Passage, possibly linking Siberia to the Mackenzie Delta and beyond as people, goods, and information traveled great distances to trade with outsiders of many kinds. Some of these passages and networks developed on the seasonal sea ice, while others followed rivers and overland tracks. Still others were only imaginary in 1820. One of those desired trade routes followed the Coppermine River from Yellowknives Dene territory at Great Slave Lake to Inuit country (Inuinnait) on the coast.[22]

Desirable though it was, the route along the Coppermine River was seen by many as a no-man's-land. In 1771, Yellowknife hunters had guided the HBC trader Samuel Hearne down the river. Where the river narrows at a place Inuinnait called Kugluktuk and Hearne called Bloody Falls, Hearne's party encountered and killed an Inuinnait group. Though the details were contested, stories of the massacre were very much alive fifty years later. For British readers of Hearne's published narrative, the account seemed to warn of the scale of Dene–Inuit violence in the region, and also to invite a British return, both to correct Hearne's maps and observations and to bring peace through commerce.²³ Franklin's official instructions from Lord Bathurst urged him to acquire an Inuit interpreter at all costs, in order to prevent "those disgraceful scenes described by Hearne to have occurred on the Coppermine River."²⁴ There was also a widespread understanding among the Dene that they would be killed if Inuinnait discovered them on their territory. As a result, their knowledge of parts of the Barren Grounds was vague and patchy.²⁵

These were some of the contexts that shaped the lives of the intermediaries who attached themselves to the LAE, and who shaped it in turn. The first was the powerful chief of the Yellowknives Dene, Akaitcho, whose elder brother had been with Hearne's expedition (Figure 1.1). Between 1812 and 1820, Akaitcho consolidated his power around Great Slave Lake, driving the Dog Ribs out of their homelands and controlling furs and supplies. He was an unusual and new kind of leader who demanded respect from outsiders, yet whose power still depended on the consent of his warriors. He was long remembered by his enemies as the embodiment of terror.²⁶ His name is still invoked in the dialects, politics, administration, and geography of the region around Great Slave Lake.²⁷ Akaitcho supported the LAE in order to establish relations with Inuinnait, and so gain access to trade at the mouth of the Coppermine River. The second was the Keewatin Inuit interpreter Tattannoeuck (The Belly), or Augustus, one of the first Inuit men to have a sustained, personal relationship with *qallunaat* at Fort Churchill on Hudson's Bay.²⁸ From 1812, the then-teenage boy Tattannoeuck worked at the fort alongside Orkneymen and Cree boys, sleeping in the kitchen with the cook and steward.²⁹ He learned English and Cree, as well as how to read and write.³⁰

Figure 1.1 Robert Hood's portrait of Akaitcho, chief of the Yellowknives Dene, and his son, 1821. The Picture Art Collection/Alamy Stock Photo, Image ID: MMP1KE.

By the time he joined Franklin's expedition in the winter of 1821 (together with his kinsman Hoeootoerock, or Junius), Tattannoeuck had a reputation of being "devoted to the English and good natured."[31] He would become a key broker between Inuit, Yellowknives Dene, and the British, even as each sought to use him as a human passport and a peace broker. The third was the NWC trader Willard Wentzel, a Norwegian who had built up an extensive network of relationships (good and bad) among traders and Indigenous people since about 1795. His journals and correspondence reveal a man who was simultaneously practical and brutal, widely read, and single-minded. He and his fur-trade family had experienced starvation several times, including an especially severe winter, 1810–11, which killed one of his children.[32]

At the same time as Indigenous passages of trade, travel, and information exchange were developing across the North American Arctic, British naval and scientific interests began to focus on the region. The related ideas of a northern sea route to Asia and an open polar sea had fired the imaginations of adventurers and geographers alike for more than three hundred years.[33] In the aftermath of Waterloo, the second Secretary of the Admiralty, Sir John Barrow, began to promote the discovery of a navigable Northwest Passage as a suitable use for a bloated navy with thousands of officers on half-pay.[34] This new era of exploration was also sparked by a young Whitby whaling captain, William Scoresby, who reported in 1817 that Davis Straits was largely clear of ice. Scoresby's offer to lead an expedition was supported by Sir Joseph Banks but refused by Barrow. Over the following decades, Scoresby painstakingly established himself as an authority on Arctic, scientific, and humanitarian matters (see Chapter 4).[35] Drawing on Scoresby's information, in 1818, two British naval polar expeditions undertook summer Arctic journeys: the North Polar Expedition in HMS *Dorothea* and *Trent* (Captain David Buchan and Lt. John Franklin) and the Northwest Passage Expedition in HMS *Isabella* and *Alexander* (Captain John Ross and Lt. William Edward Parry). These were followed by Franklin's LAE in 1819–21 and Parry's attempt on the Passage in HMS *Hecla* and *Griper* in 1819–20. Many more followed, which are discussed in Chapter 2 (see also Timeline 1).

The LAE's British component was made up of Franklin, Richardson, midshipmen George Back and Robert Hood, and the seaman John Hepburn. Franklin had joined the Navy in 1800 at the age of fourteen, and in 1802 joined his uncle Matthew Flinders in HMS *Investigator* to survey the Australian coast (Figure 1.2). Left onshore after Waterloo, Franklin sought out Robert Brown, his companion from the *Investigator* who was now Banks' librarian. Franklin's navigational skills, interest in terrestrial magnetism, and Brown's patronage helped Franklin get appointed first to the North Polar expedition in the *Trent* in 1818, and then to the LAE in 1819.[36] Richardson was a 31-year-old Scottish naval surgeon and naturalist, who struggled to pay the bills in peacetime Edinburgh, but was nevertheless well connected through his patron, the Edinburgh naturalist Robert Jameson.[37] Midshipman George Back, twenty-two, had been captured by the French at age twelve. After spending his adolescence in captivity, including being packed over the Alps in a saddle bag, he had previously been north with Franklin on the *Trent*.[38] Midshipman Robert Hood was also twenty-two, had been at sea since he was eleven, and was, like Back, a gifted artist.[39] Hepburn was a 24-year-old cowherd from East Lothian who

Figure 1.2 Portrait of John Franklin by G. B. Lewis, 1828. Getty Images, Boyer/Contributor, 15384-1.

had been pressed into the Navy as a teenager in 1810, and served with Franklin and Back on the *Trent*.[40] In the summer of 1819, they traveled together from Britain to York Factory on Hudson's Bay, and then made their way separately to Cumberland House and Fort Chipewyan, with *voyageurs* and volunteers joining and leaving along the way (see Map 3).

The rest of the expedition was comprised of Canadian *voyageurs* after the Orkney Islanders, whom Franklin had hired, decided against the perilous journey.[41] Most of these *voyageurs* were "Athabasca men," tough, experienced, and elite men who had spent several winters in the region, starved more than once, and were, Carolyn Podruchny has argued, driven by ambition quite as much as any explorer.[42] Some had Dene kin, but others were outsiders. This latter group included Michel Teroahaute, a Kahnawake Mohawk (Iroquois) man, one of many who sought employment in the fur trade as part of an initiation to manhood. These young Mohawk men had a reputation for being tough and ruthless canoers, trappers, and fighters. While they were sought after by the fur companies, they were often viewed as rapacious outsiders by the Indigenous groups whose lands they crossed, and Wentzel thought they would "ruin the country."[43]

These, then, were some of the Arctic circles that developed on the Barren Grounds between 1819 and 1822. Knowledge about the Inuit and the coast at the mouth of the Coppermine River was desirable to Yellowknives Dene and British alike, all of whom were keen to promote trade, build relationships, and acquire better maps of Inuit territory. All of them were ambitious men, accustomed to danger and violence from their youth, but they did not necessarily know what to expect, either from the environment or from each other. All of them were, ultimately, dependent upon both the caribou and each other's goodwill, and neither were in great supply. Those who survived would be transformed by their encounters and experiences, and many would never be the same.

The Sinews of War: Provisions, Information, and Credibility

In 1823, the fur trader Simon McGillivray wrote to Franklin: "Provisions constitute the sinews of war in the Indian country. The moment these fail, disorganization ensues—men change their nature and become unmanageable—of this you have had a terrible example."[44] McGillivray was reflecting on the perfect storm of starvation, disease, and violence that had descended on the region in 1819–21. Epidemics of measles and whooping cough swept through the country, partly spread by Franklin who coughed his way from York Factory to Cumberland House in 1819.[45] Many Dene and Cree men were so sick that they could not hunt at all, while others destroyed their weapons in mourning. The winters grew bitter, the caribou were fickle, fisheries failed, the hare population crashed, fur-bearing animals vanished, and hunger was widespread.[46] Hostilities between the NWC and HBC escalated into open warfare until, as the LAE was starving in 1821, the companies made peace and united. Robert McVicar's post journal for the HBC Fort Resolution on Great Slave Lake is full of anguish throughout the summer of 1820. His supplies of goods, ammunition, and food were constantly interrupted, and he struggled to get either furs or provisions from the Yellowknives Dene who visited the post. He wrote, "my situation at this place ... is miserable beyond measure."[47]

Understanding how the politics of provisions intertwined with those of information and intimacy is crucial to understanding both the LAE and its legacies. It has long been argued that the expedition failed because of John Franklin's Eurocentrism, and in particular his unwillingness to use Indigenous technology or to accept Indigenous advice.[48] Unwilling he certainly was, yet he and his officers were nevertheless forced into a dependence on Yellowknives Dene, *voyageurs*, and traders as they struggled to maintain their supply chain and fell deeply into debt. Accordingly, the control and consumption of food came to be intertwined with the control of information and the political dynamics within the expedition.[49] Yellowknives Dene and traders alike found the expedition's demands for supplies intolerable, yet they were all keen to acquire valuable intelligence about the others and their territories. As the explorers' debts increased, they were forced to bargain for supplies and support with their best—and often only—valuable asset. Information was exchanged for provisions and support, and the trade became entangled in the expedition's intimacies and enmities. As relationships blossomed and soured around Great Slave Lake, men and women struggled to convince each other of a good faith that had long since eroded, and Indigenous and vernacular intermediaries came to exert subtle control over the expedition, its officers, and its intelligence.

In July 1820, the British officers of the LAE met Akaitcho and Wentzel for the first time on the western shore of Great Slave Lake. This was where people hunted, fished, and gathered berries in the summer, and it suited Akaitcho much more than Franklin.[50] The officers chafed at Wentzel's insistence that they should court Akaitcho's patronage, yet they knew that their survival depended upon supplicating him. They reluctantly donned what Hood called the "remnants of our European apparel" and bestowed gifts of tobacco, ammunition, vermillion, medals, and maps on Akaitcho and his warriors. Laying out the charts of the Coppermine River drawn by the *voyageur* Beaulieu at Cumberland House, Franklin told Akaitcho that if the Northwest Passage were found, the Coppermine would become a conduit for British goods, flowing up the river into Dene territory from ships that would visit Inuit territory at the river mouth.[51] Akaitcho agreed to supply Franklin with meat, hunters, and their families for the following year, but had demands of his own. He required access to the expedition's Inuit interpreter, and an intermediary of his own choosing—a European translator with deep, long-standing Yellowknives Dene connections. Wentzel was suggested and accepted.[52]

Akaitcho had other informants within the expedition, including his own family. He asked his brother, Keskarrah, and his wife and daughter, to join the nearly forty Yellowknives who lived at Fort Enterprise on Winter Lake in the autumn of 1820. In addition to depending on Keskarrah's skill as a hunter and guide, Franklin and his officers needed Dene women to snare ptarmigan, trap hares, sew clothing, and mend snowshoes. They also needed them for information. Franklin and Richardson understood that Yellowknife women were knowledge bearers, holding what Franklin called "traditional accounts" of the tribe, which he and the other officers desired for their ethnographic collections.[53] Yet Franklin begrudged every morsel they ate, and throughout the winter sent families away to save on provisions. Ultimately, the only Yellowknives left were Akaitcho's mother, Keskarrah, and his family. Keskarrah's daughter, the teenager known as "Greenstockings," has long been seen as the source of the sexual rivalries and tensions within the expedition (Figure 1.3).[54] The two

Figure 1.3 Robert Hood's portrait of the Yellowknife Dene girl known as "Greenstockings," 1821. Getty Images, Universal Images Group Editorial.

midshipmen, Back and Hood, both pursued her, and in November 1820, Franklin wrote to Back (then away on a supply mission), "Perhaps you were prepared to expect the pleasure of a Female Companion in your room. Hood says he shall inform you of the circumstance. I need not therefore enlarge upon the subject."[55] Twenty-five years later, Hepburn said that the men had arranged to fight a duel over her, and also that the teenage girl later gave birth to Hood's daughter.[56] It may be that Greenstockings' alliances were understood by some (British, Yellowknife, or both) as one of many fur trade intimacies of the 1820s, in which Indigenous women and girls (often very young) became key intermediaries, providing labor to their husbands while sharing intelligence with their relatives. In Adele Perry's view, these kinds of partnerships were "a mechanism through which men, including newcomers, were knitted into families, communities and economies."[57] It is impossible to prove this, but it is certainly the case that Akaitcho was well informed about circumstances at Fort Enterprise. It is far from impossible that the relatives he left there—including his mother, brother, and niece—were among his informants.

As the winter dragged on, Franklin's anxiety over provisions increased, as he struggled to not only pay the Yellowknives but also negotiate the hostilities between the HBC and NWC. In October 1820, he sent Back and Wentzel on a thousand-mile overland journey to secure goods from both companies, and in the meantime, paid Yellowknife hunters with notes drawn on the NWC at Fort Providence on Great Slave Lake. He knew those notes would not be honored, for the fort had nearly run out of provisions.[58] Those bad debts opened a door for Akaitcho to require payment in information, revealing his own understanding of the expedition's goals and documentation. In December, he demanded that Franklin clarify the rumors "that we should probably deceive the Indians, by turning them off unrewarded, when we found that we could no longer be useful." Akaitcho also noted that he expected that an expedition that had not only secured an Inuit interpreter but also received so many documents and journals must not be short of cash.[59] A few months later, Akaitcho required Franklin and the officers to spread out their charts and drawings, including ethnographic material, for his approval before they sent them to England. It was only after he had inspected the material that Akaitcho chose to ignore the "idle rumours which had been floating about the barren grounds," that the expedition was broke, and asked for the Inuit interpreter Tattannoeuck/Augustus to return to his fort with him.[60] By May, when the expedition was preparing to depart for the coast and supplies were perilously low, Akaitcho refused to supply them with meat until he was assured that he would be paid, arguing that the British King "must see from the drawings and descriptions of ourselves and our Country, which you have Sent, that we are in a pitiable Condition."[61] In these ways, Akaitcho deployed his understanding of the expedition's documentary practices in order to maintain a degree of control over its officers, provisions, and information.

Tattannoeuck and Back were also entangled in these politics of provisions, information, and intimacy, which both negotiated in their own ways. From the time that he arrived at Fort Enterprise with Wentzel in February 1821, Tattannoeuck carefully observed the developing tensions within the expedition. He was keenly aware of being an outsider in many respects, but particularly as an Inuk among both *qallunaat* and Yellowknives Dene, who was expected to trespass on the territory of other Inuit, strangers with whom he did not share kin. This was an extremely perilous situation for the young man. Tattannoeuck went out of his way not only to be agreeable but to be a reputable source of information. He offered maps and ethnographic information to Franklin, Richardson, Wentzel, and Akaitcho alike, with lengthy descriptions of the changing travel routes, subsistence, beliefs, alliances, and habits of Inuit around Hudson Bay and far to the north and west. He seized opportunities to spend time with both the British and Dene, whether writing and reading in the fort in the winter evenings, or journeying to Akaitcho's camp, apparently conversing in Cree (though Franklin asked him not to).[62] Back, meanwhile, found himself increasingly at odds with the other officers on the expedition. Franklin and Richardson were drawing closer and closer together over the winter of 1820–1, and both their journals and correspondence reveal that their mutual respect was developing into a fond regard. But while both men seemed friendly enough with Back in their surviving correspondence, there was both physical and emotional distance between them. On his arduous overland journey in search of supplies in 1820–1, Back set up his own network of alliances with traders, nurturing a reputation that stood separately from the others.[63] In his journal, Back also recorded that when the *voyageurs* threatened to stop work in August 1820, Franklin lost his temper and said he would make an example of any supposed mutineer by "blowing out his brains."[64]

The politics of provisions, intimacy, and information all intertwined around the frozen shores of Great Slave Lake in 1820–1. As the vulnerabilities and divisions of the expedition and its officers became apparent, so did their acts of bad faith. These fraught dynamics underpinned negotiations of power and exchanges of knowledge in the months leading up to the LAE's departure for the polar sea. In particular, they opened spaces for Indigenous people to exert autonomy and authority over the expedition and its documentation, and for others (including its own men) to subvert it through the circulation of rumors.

"Endeared by Affliction": Stories of Starvation, 1821–2

In the summer of 1821, the LAE set out from Fort Enterprise for the Arctic coast. It was now comprised of five Britons, Wentzel, eleven *voyageurs*, two Inuit, five Yellowknife hunters (including Akaitcho), and eleven Yellowknife and Dog Rib women and children (Greenstockings was counted as a child).[65] The *voyageurs* managed the canoes, while the women dragged heavy sledges. The party shared three anxieties: to secure provisions, to avoid confrontations with Inuit, and to return alive. The last was understood differently by each person. For the naval officers, return was inconceivable until it was no longer possible to advance. For the others, return was required if the risks were too great. When combined with existing tensions within the expedition, it made a toxic mixture of fear, ignorance, and distrust.

An encounter with Inuit at Kugluktuk in June exposed serious rifts in the party. As they approached Inuit territory, the Yellowknives Dene stopped lighting fires, one hunter escorted Greenstockings back to her relatives, and there were disagreements about how to proceed. When they met Inuit at Kugluktuk, Tattannoeuck and Hoeootoerock conducted negotiations between British, Inuit, and Dene, with each exchanging gifts, information, and promises of trade. Nevertheless, from this point the Dene hunters would go no further. They were not only concerned about Inuit reprisals but also deeply concerned about the caribou migration, fearing that winter would set in early, and they would miss the herds.[66] They promised to leave depots along the river banks and to wait for Wentzel, who was to return when the expedition reached the coast. When the LAE reached the mouth of the Coppermine in July, it splintered again, as the *voyageurs* tried to convince Franklin to turn back. They pointed out the dangers of the sea voyage in birchbark canoes, their scarce provisions, and the lateness of the season. Several (including the two remaining métis interpreters, Adam and St. Germain) insisted on returning with Wentzel. Carolyn Podruchny has argued that this sort of resistance was common among *voyageurs* when rations were poor and decisions were bad, but it was anathema to naval discipline, which expected unquestioning obedience.[67] Franklin refused to turn back, and Wentzel left alone. He carried letters and dispatches with him which gave no hints of the dangerous tensions within the expedition, including one from Richardson to Mary, and one from Hood to his father. Both assured their loved ones that the Yellowknives and Wentzel would lay in depots of food all along the return route.[68]

The LAE then took two heavily laden birchbark canoes and navigated more than 500 miles east to Point Turnagain. All the while, Richardson recorded, the remaining *voyageurs* grumbled. By the middle of August, Richardson recorded that Adam and St. Germain were trying to compel Franklin to stop by refusing to hunt caribou, and that they planned to "privately . . . procure ducks and geese and . . . avoid the necessity of sharing them with the officers."[69] Finally, Franklin agreed to return, but by a new and untested route—overland via the Barren Grounds, bearing by compass for Fort Enterprise. But as they had been warned, they had missed the caribou migration. The party struggled to live off the land, sometimes making only a few miles every day.[70] On September 10, the hunters killed a caribou and the whole party fell upon it, devouring its guts while they were still warm. Within days, they were scavenging caribou carcasses left behind by wolves and eating their own shoes. Discipline broke down, and Richardson wrote that the *voyageurs* "considered the want of food as dissolving all ties between us" and that they began to steal from the officers.[71] They could only rely on *tripe de roche*, a barely edible lichen which *voyageurs* used to stave off starvation.[72] Several of the men, including Hood, could not digest it and suffered terribly.[73]

On October 4, 1821, Back took the *voyageurs* St. Germain, Solomon Belanger, and Beauparlant to seek help. The next day, the *voyageurs* in Franklin's party began to collapse and were left behind to freeze to death. Hoeootoerock went hunting and never returned. On October 7, the party divided again. Hood (who could barely move), Richardson and Hepburn volunteered to camp with the equipment, while Franklin and the rest slogged on to Fort Enterprise, to return with provisions when they could. Within two days, the Mohawk guide Michel Teroahaute and the *voyageurs* Jean Baptiste Belanger and Ignace Perrault left Franklin to return to Richardson's camp. When Franklin reached Fort Enterprise a few days later, he found it deserted. Wentzel had taken their books and papers, but they could not find any note from him to say where he or the Yellowknives Dene had gone. Unable to send help back to their companions, they settled down to wait for relief, in the meantime cooking pounded bones and singed caribou hides with *tripe de roche* in a nasty broth. When a messenger from Back arrived asking for further instructions, Franklin wrote a despairing letter that excoriated the "miserable wretched treachery of the Indians" and the "indifference" of Wentzel as he mourned those "endeared to me by affliction."[74] His surviving journal catalogs his descent into despair: how their legs, joints, and groins swelled so they could not walk; how caribou came near but could not be killed; and how hope fled from him.[75]

Meanwhile, according to Richardson, Teroahaute arrived at their camp alone.[76] The next day he took a hatchet and went into the woods, returning with what he claimed was wolf meat. Richardson and Hepburn later came to believe, from "indisputable evidence," that it was part of Belanger's body. Richardson claimed that Teroahaute became increasingly argumentative and aggressive, treating the British as if they were "completely in his power," and "[giving] vent to several expressions of hatred towards the white people," claiming that traders had killed and eaten his uncle and two relations.[77] Within days, Michel killed Hood; Richardson killed Michel; and then the last survivors, Hepburn and Richardson, headed to Fort Enterprise. There they found Franklin and the others barely alive.[78] Hepburn would later recall that, "inarticulate sounds, issuing from the nose like grunts, were their only means of conversation."[79] They remained at Fort Enterprise for another eight days, during which two more men died, leaving only Franklin, Richardson, Hepburn, and the Yellowknife Dene interpreter Jean Baptiste Adam barely alive. They pinned their hopes for survival on Back and Tattannoeuck, both of whom were now looking for Akaitcho to the south.

Over these eight days, some of the men formed a fellowship of suffering that endured for decades, built on their shared religious understanding and conversion experience. Jonathan Lamb has argued that scurvy on Pacific voyages caused "despair and joy [to be] blended in a moment of suspense in which privation and pleasure were dilated to fantastic extremes," and that seems to have been replicated at Fort Enterprise.[80] Their minds wandered, and at one point, Hepburn said, "Dear me, if we are spared to return to England, I wonder if we shall recover our understandings?"[81] They structured their days around scavenging food and reading religious tracts, and these exerted a profound influence on them.[82] Later, Franklin wrote, "I can truly say I never experienced such positive happiness from the comforts of religion as in the moments of greatest distress, when there scarcely appeared any reason to hope that my existence could be prolonged beyond a few days."[83] Richardson wrote to Mary that his religious reflections "produced a calmness of mind and resignation to His will under the prospect of approaching death that I could not have previously hoped to attain."[84]

On November 7, three Yellowknife hunters arrived at Fort Enterprise. Akaitcho had dispatched them after Tattannoeuck and Back had arrived to beg for help. Franklin and Richardson saw the Yellowknives Dene as superhuman; Franklin wrote, "contrasted with our emaciated figures and extreme debility, their frames appeared to us gigantic, and their strength supernatural," while Richardson wrote to Mary, "these savages, as they have been termed, wept upon beholding the deplorable condition to which we were reduced."[85] Richardson and Hepburn struggled to remove the corpses from the house, and to hide the singed caribou hides to avoid offending the hunters, "for these simple people imagine that burning deer-skin renders them unsuccessful in hunting."[86] After feeding, bathing, shaving, and nursing the emaciated men, the Yellowknives took the survivors to Akaitcho's lodge. They used to be able to cover the 8 miles or so in a day, but this was now an arduous journey for starving men with swollen legs.[87]

It soon became clear Franklin would not be able to pay his rescuers. The union of the rival fur companies in 1821 meant that the expedition's credit with the NWC had evaporated, and there were no goods to pay the Yellowknives.[88] Earlier, Akaitcho had told Franklin, "I know you write down occurrences in your journals but probably you only take notice of the bad things we Say or do and are Silent as to the good," and now he requested a favorable portrayal in the narrative in partial payment of Franklin's debts.[89] Richardson claimed that he said this "in a tone of good humor" and added "it is the first time that the White people have been indebted to the Red Knife Indians."[90] The degree to which Franklin followed through on this promise is debatable. Cavell has observed that Franklin was bound by a sense of obligation to Akaitcho and removed many of the accusations of the Leader's "fickleness" and "vanity" that peppered his journal, though Davis points out in his edited and annotated version of Franklin's journal that it was more nuanced and fine-grained in its representation of Akaitcho and the Yellowknives Dene, though not more favorable.[91]

In January, Franklin, Richardson, and Hepburn left Akaitcho's lodge and traveled to the HBC Fort Resolution. Here, Franklin rewrote his lost journal, basing it on Richardson's surviving account, Wentzel having taken the rest of their records. Neither wrote to their families, nor to Hood's father, for months. In the end, it didn't matter. All of their letters from March 1821 until October 1822 arrived at the same time, only a few days before they returned home themselves. Rumors and stories traveled ahead of them. Even in those hungry years, the loss of so many experienced men was shocking, and the news traveled far and fast. Pierre St. Germain, the *voyageur* who had often challenged Franklin's authority and who traveled with Back's party in the autumn of 1821, arrived at Fort Chipewyan in January 1822.[92] It was from him that the new HBC governor George Simpson learned the news, which was "truly melancholy and distressing to the feelings of humanity," that "while crossing the Barren Lands Mr Hood and 10 of the common men fell sacrificed to starvation."[93] Simpson's phrasing echoes one of the standard euphemisms for cannibalism, of men being "sacrificed to sustain life," though whether that was his intention, or St. Germain's, is impossible to determine. The news traveled to Montreal, and then to London. Just as the HBC ship *Prince of Wales* docked in Stromness with Franklin, Richardson, and Hepburn on board, it was reported in the *Times* that they had been "driven to the necessity of prolonging a miserable existence by feeding upon the tattered remnants of their shoes, and, we fear, upon a more forbidding and unpalatable fare."[94]

Information had been currency on the fraught and unpredictable Barren Grounds during the LAE. Geographical and ethnographical information was desirable to Akaitcho and Franklin, and structured both their tense relationship and the precarious positions of intermediaries like Tattannoeuck/Augustus. The flow of information had been entangled with the control of provisions, the threat of starvation, and the trustworthiness of men engaged in business many thought both reckless and lucrative.

The tragedy of the LAE and its loss of life was, in the end, only part of a greater story of suffering in 1819–22 around Great Slave Lake. As the survivors returned to Britain and crafted their suffering into a published narrative, that process was conditioned by another set of relationships, with other questions of trustworthiness. These were patrons, publishers, wives, and families, none of whom fully comprehended the debts the expedition left behind. Amid a proliferation of both stories and silences, these other Arctic circles struggled to understand what the legacy of suffering meant for the rest of their lives.

"There Is No Nourishment in Pepper": Narratives and Marriages, 1822–3

As the *Prince of Wales* approached the Scottish shore in October 1822, John Franklin wrote to his family that he would tell them "every particular of which they may desire to be informed" in person. He was, he reminded them, under an "injunction of silence" from the Admiralty, and he feared his letters would be published before he arrived.[95] Meanwhile, the young poet Eleanor Ann Porden wrote to him that the newspaper reports were "enough to frighten all of your friends."[96] Hood's father had learned of his son's death from the press and wrote to Richardson, begging for information.[97] Mary Richardson also received a parcel of letters from her husband, written over the previous two years. In his last, he wrote "you must be prepared to behold traces of age upon my face that have been impressed since we parted—I feel at least ten years older than I did two years ago."[98] He arrived two days later (Figure 1.4).

From the ship, Franklin wrote to Eleanor how he dreaded the "disagreeable task" of writing the book.[99] Like most narratives, *Journey to the Polar Sea* would be a collective enterprise, produced by a constellation of interests that included patrons, collaborators, fellow travelers, editors, publishers, and engravers.[100] These books were an important source of colonial knowledge, selling out multiple editions, and being excerpted and summarized in periodicals.[101] But all this depended, of course, on the trustworthiness, credibility, and character of the explorer-author, for these were key to the claims that he made about the places, peoples, and things he had observed. As Dorinda Outram has put it, "the dazzle and the glitter of the world really did pose a threat to a unitary personality capable of moral discipline, capable of being trusted."[102] A man's trustworthiness was central not only to his reputation as an explorer but also to his identity as a husband and was one of the essential foundations of the early nineteenth-century home and family.[103] Women like Mary Richardson and Eleanor Porden now needed to chart the dimensions of the changes wrought on the Barren Grounds and map the ramifications for their own lives. This was especially tricky because of the enduring relationship between Franklin and Richardson, which entwined with the production of the narrative.

Franklin and Richardson may have decided to write the narrative together at Fort Resolution in early 1822, as they rewrote their journals.[104] Certainly, the decision had been finalized well before they returned to Britain or before Richardson spoke to Mary,

Figure 1.4 Portrait of John Richardson by E. Finden, 1828. Getty Images, Hulton Archive/Stringer, HF9367.

with Franklin heading on to London and securing lodgings for the men at Frith Street in Soho. The expectation was that Richardson would come straight from Dumfries to 60 Frith Street, a small seventeenth-century house in the middle of a bustling commercial district.[105] Franklin discouraged Richardson from bringing Mary, writing, "I still fear she will be greatly disappointed in London, it certainly won't do after a residence in Edinburgh."[106] But after three years of separation, the Richardsons would not be parted, and so she came.

Mary Richardson was described as an intelligent and well-read woman with a fine sense of humor.[107] Her Edinburgh neighbor, the wife of a celebrated American botanist, described her as "a most gentle, amiable, but very delicate lady."[108] In John Richardson's words, she was "an admirer of the works of God in the beauties of Nature," placing her in company with natural theologians.[109] Franklin came to admire Mary's "amiable simplicity of character, purity of mind, [and] tender regard for others' feelings and steadfast faith in Christ." Her piety and sympathy, he later wrote, "endeared her to me as a sister."[110] Yet she may also have been worldly, in her way. Her mother was an author, and both women circulated in Edinburgh's and St. Andrew's medical, scientific, and literary circles, and kept Richardson well informed while he was in the field. Certainly, she had shared his field correspondence within those circles of natural historians, for they had made their way into the Scottish newspapers during his absence, to his great dismay (see Chapter 2).[111]

It is only possible to speculate on Mary Richardson's role at Frith Street, but it is probable that she brought Richardson's correspondence with her from Edinburgh.

After all, it was an on-the-spot account of the explorers' understandings, expectations, and promises. It provided color, put flesh on the bones, so to speak, of Richardson's journal. As I argue in Chapter 2, these kinds of letters could be seen as early drafts of a narrative which needed to appeal to a broad audience, including well-read women. It is reasonable to suggest that Mary saw and commented on the drafts. Based on Franklin's recollection of her piety, it is also tempting to think that through prayer and discussion, Mary may have tried to reconcile the religious sentiments developed on the Barren Grounds with those of her home.

Franklin and Richardson had always been religious, but their experiences on the Barren Grounds had confirmed for them that suffering and salvation were linked. As Cavell has shown, these feelings were shaped by the Evangelical tracts donated to the expedition by the Anglo-Irish aristocrat, Lady Lucy Barry, which, according to Richardson, Hood had been reading when he was killed.[112] At Frith Street, Franklin and Richardson wove these sentiments through the narrative, and it became one of its most wildly popular features, setting the moral tone for a generation of Arctic narratives.[113] Both men also saw their new relationship with God as central to their domestic lives and identities. In his letter to Mary from Great Slave Lake, Richardson wrote, "Through the protection of God I have escaped from still greater dangers.... I feel that I can never by the utmost devotion of my future life sufficiently express my gratitude."[114] Franklin would later write to Eleanor Porden that his faith "has been my support in the most trying occasions and I fervently pray it may continue to sustain me and you until our eyes are closed on this world."[115] As Franklin began to court Eleanor in the winter of 1822, he may have hoped that she would emulate Mary Richardson's apparent acceptance of a doctrine of pious suffering and resignation, and of his and Richardson's companionship. If so, he was badly mistaken.

Eleanor Porden was a 27-year-old Romantic poet, an independently wealthy woman who published with John Murray under her own name (Figure 1.5). She had been a member of the French Academy of Sciences for ten years, and frequently attended the meetings of the Royal Society. In 1816, her scientific epic "The Veils" had received wide acclaim, as had her poem *The Arctic Expeditions* in 1818. Franklin had read both when he returned from his voyage in the *Trent*, and begged for an introduction to the author. Apparently smitten, he may not have fully understood the poem's message. While *The Arctic Expeditions* was clearly a patriotic tribute to scientific exploration, at the same time, Porden (like her contemporary Mary Shelley) warned polar explorers against hubris, conjuring a nightmarish vision of, "Your prows drawn downward and your sterns in air,/ To waste with cold, and grief, and famine, there."[116] In 1822, Porden had only a little over two years to live, though she did not know it. She suffered from tuberculosis, and it would kill her in February 1825. Well acquainted with suffering from both her illness and her long nursing of her parents (both of whom had died in Franklin's absence), Porden nevertheless firmly rejected Franklin's intertwining of piety with pain. Her remarkable correspondence narrates how she came to grips with her prospective husband's trustworthiness, with the consequences of his actions, and with how conjugal and fraternal relationships might have to coexist.

Figure 1.5 Portrait of Eleanor Porden by her friend Mary Flaxman, 1818, around the time that Porden wrote *The Arctic Expeditions*. The History Collection/Alamy Stock Photo, Image ID: J3BT0G.

Franklin described the writing of his book to Porden as "a sad plague," "irksome," and "a wearying task."[117] She, in turn, teased him in verse about how the hero of the Arctic could not bring himself to write:

> A field of snow's but one blank page
> > Bears, Icebergs, Buffaloes together
> I'd rather all their might engage
> > Than touch that one poor Goose's feather.[118]

Her milieu was the world of scientific and literary sociability, in which she ran her own salon, held soirees, and attended lectures.[119] As I discuss in Chapter 2, it was a world in which Franklin and Richardson, like other writers and travelers, were in high demand as "lions." They both dreaded the role. Porden invited Franklin to her parties, but he seldom attended, and seemed constrained and out of sorts when he did. He thought the gatherings were frivolous, and the company flippant. As for being a "lion," he felt that "such attention may prompt me to assume individual merit for results which are entirely to be ascribed to the superintending blessing of a Divine Providence."[120] Nevertheless, Porden accepted his offer of marriage, but it came at a social and professional cost to her. She wrote to him later, "I could not with propriety receive any company of which you did not form a part," but because "you were then too much occupied with your book and withal too anxious not to be seen," there were friends she missed for nearly a year.[121]

As the year turned, the weather grew colder, the Thames froze, and Franklin and Richardson started writing about the Barren Grounds. They retreated into Frith Street and saw only each other and Mary. Franklin would later write to his aunt, Ann Flinders, "the recollection of scenes which had been soothed by time and reflection, so distressed me that I felt quite unequal to correspondence with any of my friends."[122] This was when Porden began to interrogate Franklin's trustworthiness. On an unusually cold day in January, she teased that the "Most Faithless Saxon" must have forsaken her. "Think not that I expect to melt you," she wrote, "for had you not been already hardened by three polar winters, you must be now like my tears, and like everything else in this great town, completely frozen."[123] On Valentine's Day, she sent Franklin and Richardson duplicate poems to their shared address. Written in disguised handwriting, the poems, entitled "The Esquimaux Girl's Lament," were signed "Miss Greenstockings" and dated February 14, Coppermine River.[124] As she addressed her "faithless admirer" in the character of the girl, she enticed him to return, promising to care for him in the Arctic winter, to smooth his way and "blow the icebergs from thy path," and to keep him in perfect comfort. However, she warned him against an ill-conceived marriage to an Englishwoman:

Nor think in thy Green Isle some Fair one to wed,
For in tempest and snow shall my vengeance pursue,
My bidding at noonday shall darken the air,
And the rage of my climate shall Follow thee there.[125]

She ended the poem proclaiming her/Greenstockings' constancy, with the lines "By the Lake, by the Mountain, the Forest & River / In the Wilds of the North I am Thine & Forever."[126]

Francis Spufford suggested that Eleanor Porden cast Greenstockings as a "purely notional rival" for Franklin's attention, and translated it into "harmless female frippery," while Jen Hill has argued that it was part of a pattern in Eleanor's poetry, in which women were mistresses of an Arctic that punished male hubris.[127] But it seems likely that the "Miss Greenstockings" poem, addressed to both Franklin and Richardson, was intended as both a commentary on the relationships inside Frith Street, and on the legacy of obligation from the Barren Grounds. The form echoes the "ventriloquized laments" of Samuel Taylor Coleridge and William Wordsworth, both of which were inspired by Hearne's account of the Bloody Falls massacre. In the years that followed, John O'Leary has argued, poets in white settler colonies would use "Indigenous ventriloquists" to call attention to settler violence, idealize a precontact past, and create an emotional middle ground where settlers could find sympathy with displaced peoples.[128] In this case, Porden used Greenstockings' imagined voice to remind the men of how they had been fed and clothed, their snowshoes mended, and their fires kindled—in short, to remind them of their many debts. Neither man ever referred to the poem directly while Porden was alive, but Franklin memorized it. More than twenty years later, he wrote it down from memory (flipping some stanzas and phrases) and enclosed it with his final letter to his second wife, Jane Franklin, just before he disappeared into the ice of Lancaster Sound.[129]

A few weeks after Porden wrote the Greenstockings poem, Franklin remarked to her sister Sarah Kay that he had "an objection almost amounting to horror to anything like publication in any one connected with [him]." He was referring to the narrative, which was bound for the printers, but the implication was that he expected Porden to abandon her writing after their marriage. Porden immediately confronted Franklin about his trustworthiness, both in the field and at home, and about the return to the Barren Grounds she knew he was already planning (see below). He had always led her to believe, she wrote, that "my studies would not only be encouraged but shared," and reminded him, "When you return from the Pole you will have another book to write, and you will expect my assistance.... [S]urely you would not selfishly take advantage of my facility in composition for our ease, and restrain me in its exercise for my own relaxation?" She added:

> One word too on the subject of your Expedition. Whatever your objections may be, and I pretend not to guess them, you must feel that nothing which I might publish could possibly give you one tenth part of the uneasiness which that Expedition must necessarily cost me, but I know that you ought to undertake it, and therefore you should find me the last person in the world that would endeavour to detain you.[130]

Spufford argued that in this letter, Porden effectively refused the role of a "conventional polar wife," which he understood to consist of patient waiting and resignation.[131] But her letter can best be understood as defining, rather than rejecting, that role—after all, she had no role model apart from Mary Richardson. She expected she would help produce narratives for the sake of her husband's career—as did other wives of naturalists, botanists, astronomers, geologists, and practitioners of gentlemanly science. She also expected, like other maritime wives, to be repeatedly abandoned, perhaps for years.[132] In that context, she argued, she had a right to knowledge—particularly about Franklin's relationships, traumas, and how those were likely to impact their shared life. She thought Richardson was the root cause of the trouble, writing to Franklin that "your prejudices are of recent origin" and that "they may have been suggested to you by those with whom you conversed." He had entertained no such feeling about her writing when he left in 1819, she pointed out, which made her wonder, "which is the counterfeit, and which the true man?"[133]

When *Journey to the Polar Sea* was published in April 1823, it was rapturously received by the reading public. As Cavell and others have shown, the Evangelical sentiments woven throughout the text gave meaning and structure to British Arctic suffering. Hepburn was cast as a Christian hero of the lower deck, while French-Canadian voyageurs were painted as feckless and irreligious men who thought only of their bellies, and were ultimately unable to bear the physical strain of starvation without the moral strength of Protestant faith.[134] Richardson's narrative of accidental cannibalism and Hood's and Michel's deaths was published within the text as its own chapter, embedded within the march to Fort Enterprise and the sufferings they endured at the fort. Throughout the text, Franklin and Richardson claimed that the NWC and HBC traders' unwillingness to provide provisions, men, and goods was one of the main causes of the expedition's high mortality. Franklin's struggles with Akaitcho were toned down, but the overall portrait of the Yellowknives Dene emphasized their "fickleness" and "vanity." They and Wentzel bore the brunt of the blame for the starvation at Fort Enterprise because, Franklin wrote, they had given the expedition up for dead. Above all, the narrative gave moral value to failure, and this was its most enduring legacy, both for polar narratives and British imperial literature.[135]

After the narrative was published, the household at Frith Street broke up and the Richardsons returned to Edinburgh. Franklin accompanied them as far as his home in Lincolnshire. Both men described how the treeless landscape reminded them of the Barren Grounds, adding that they wished "that the line of our march had been as level as this and that we could have enjoyed the hospitality of a human friend and comfortable house as we are now doing."[136] But their parting loomed, and Franklin wrote to Porden, "the day of separation from such a friend with whom I have lived for four years will be a sore one for me."[137] When the Richardsons left Lincolnshire, Franklin wrote to Richardson that he was "much distressed with the idea of our separation . . . and felt very uneasy," and to Porden that the Richardsons were eager for them to spend all the next summer and autumn together in Edinburgh.[138]

When Richardson left, Porden tried to take her place as Franklin's emotional and spiritual confidante. One of Franklin's close relatives died just as Richardson departed, and Porden wrote, "your sorrows it is my peculiar privilege to share, and I feel almost defrauded of my right if you are in scenes of affliction without me."[139] Franklin evidently thought otherwise. In the same evening, he wrote letters to Richardson and Porden that were nearly exact duplicates, expressing his longing to enjoy the "meditation and reflection" of Fort Enterprise. To Richardson, he lamented that "I can scarcely hope for a return of such pleasurable sensations."[140] To both, he wrote of his regret that in London, "the parties and cares of mixed society and an active life tend to dissipate such emotions."[141] In the following days, Franklin became more insistent that Porden share his and Richardson's religious sentiments. She responded that they were an "aberration of religious zeal," adding, "Did you pick it up in North America?"[142] He sent her copies of Lady Lucy Barry's pamphlets which he and Richardson had pored over at Fort Enterprise. She was shocked by their emphasis on suffering as a route to salvation, and threatened to break off the engagement if Franklin was "really tainted with that species of fanaticism." She wrote,

> Do not. . . . I beseech you turn the Mercies of Heaven into a curse, by letting the present state of your mind induce you to adopt that dark and unsocial view of human nature . . . to which I feel you are <u>somewhat</u> inclined. You <u>must</u> have had such strong emotions that all now appears tame; but remember that there is no nourishment in pepper.[143]

Franklin maintained that his faith was as relevant to their marriage as to his survival on the Barren Grounds, writing that it "has been my support in the most trying occasions" and that he expected it "to sustain me and you until our eyes are closed on this world." Finishing his letter well past midnight, he added, "the emotions I have had were indeed strong, they afforded me the greatest consolation at the time, and thanks be to God continue to do so."[144]

In her reply, Porden described how, in struggling to understand Franklin's trauma, she had reflected on the deaths of her parents. "I could not hear you complaining that you had no longer an interest in what surrounded you—in anything you saw or heard, and even in the society of your own friends, without recalling a similar period in my own feelings," she wrote, and assured him that he, too, would eventually come to terms with his own absorbing grief. "I therefore say to you," she added, "do not regret that your present life offers to you no sensation equally absorbing with those that are past. They were like the excitement of opium and must be followed by a corresponding state of exhaustion."[145] Later, Porden wrote that she had "the strongest reliance on the worth of [Franklin's] character, and his regard for me. I have at least proved that the latter only derived strength from time, distance and suffering."[146]

When John Franklin and Eleanor Porden were married on August 9, 1823, Eleanor had her wedding dress embroidered with flowers illustrated in *Journey to the Polar Sea*: the *Eutoca franklinii*, *Heuchera richardsonii*, and *Phlox hoodii*. The flowers formed an intricate pattern intertwined all over the dress, with the eutoca named after Franklin at the center of each cluster.[147] Robed in the flora of the Barren Grounds, Porden paid tribute to the dead, to surviving friendships, and to lasting scientific achievements. But she also may have acknowledged that her married life would be defined by places she would never see, experiences she could not understand, and relationships she could not access. Her wedding dress telegraphed that she understood her marriage to be relative to her husband's other companionships. The subtlety was lost on Franklin. He later wrote to Richardson, "I did not discover the compliment paid to us on the first day, nor indeed until it was pointed out to me, though I could sufficiently appreciate it when my attention was directed towards it."[148]

"Stones Sometimes Speak": Rumors and Narratives, 1823–5

As Porden's wedding dress was being embroidered, Franklin wrote to Richardson to tell him "that a few persons are of opinion that you have not made out sufficiently clear that Michel actually murdered poor Hood—and the fact that you have not expressed yourself sufficiently on the dreadful necessity to which you were reduced taking away the life of Michel." Barrow feared that "these men . . . may chatter on these points with other persons who will receive it on their authority without even reading the account in the Narrative."[149]

Franklin was so worried that he visited a lawyer, who, he later wrote to Richardson, "knows more of the circumstances than any other man except for you, Hepburn and myself, [and] is decidedly of the opinion that your having failed in courage to take the step would have proved fatal to the all party (sic)." Franklin encouraged his friend to continue to "enjoy the peace of mind and happiness, which religion alone can afford."[150]

What were these rumors, where were they circulating, and who was responsible? While it is impossible to be certain, it is likely they originated at Fort Chipewyan in June 1822, with George Back and Willard Wentzel. Though their exact content is unclear, the echoes of these stories help us glimpse how vernacular intermediaries and junior officers engaged with the politics of truth, using rumor and innuendo to cast doubt on the reliability of official narratives and their authors. Stories of "things which must not be known" swirled around and collided with both Franklin and Richardson's narrative and their domestic lives for years to come, from Canada to Tasmania, and their destabilizing potential was never far away.

Men like Wentzel were both indispensable and awkward on expeditions. Their linguistic skills, experience, judgment, and local connections were invaluable to explorers, and, as Franklin and Richardson knew well, failure followed when these were withdrawn. Their polar narrative had rationalized that failure by giving it moral purpose, securing their reputations in the process. But they had done so at the personal expense of Wentzel and his NWC patrons, despite promising to forward their interests in Britain. Wentzel, like other colonial agents, collectors, and savants, was on an unequal, precarious footing with explorers.[151] With the right patrons, these men could engage with literary, scientific, and philosophical circles, their observations and experiences might be noted and quoted, but equality was elusive, if not impossible (see Chapter 2). Their reputations were as important—and as vulnerable—as that of any naval explorer. For Wentzel, there was no romance in failure, nor redemption in suffering. Both were cold and hard and cruelly ordinary for a man who, a decade earlier, had watched his child starve to death. His loyalty, moreover, was to a company that no longer existed, that had been absorbed into its rival, and whose agents were also subject to public critique by Franklin and Richardson.

Wentzel was keenly aware of the power of an expedition's narrative. In 1807, when Roderick McKenzie (cousin of the explorer Alexander Mackenzie) was contemplating a history of the NWC, he asked Wentzel to draw up a narrative about the peoples and the country around the Mackenzie River district.[152] The Norwegian was known as an avid reader, prolific writer, and lover of music, and he compiled a brief but detailed geography, natural history, ethnography, and vocabulary for McKenzie's use, but then cautioned him against publication because "swarms of adventurers will, I fear, inundate the North."[153] When the LAE arrived twelve years later, Wentzel was highly suspicious of what he saw as its secrecy. In May 1820, as he was conducting early negotiations with Akaitcho, Wentzel wrote to McKenzie, noting that the expedition was causing a great deal of "noise . . . amongst all classes of people" in the country, although, as he added, "the intent and purpose must conceal some mystery which may be developed hereafter." He promised to convey any intelligence that he could.

Akaitcho saw Wentzel as a guarantor of Yellowknife interests, but Wentzel saw himself as a loyal agent of the NWC and his patron McKenzie.[154] Wentzel's later reports about the dissensions among the officers may have grown out of his conversations with Back, as the two became friends.[155] After the pair returned to Fort Enterprise in 1821 with Tattannoeuck and Hoeootoerock, Wentzel complained to McKenzie that he had "become a party concerned in [the expedition's] pursuits and subjected to an order of secrecy, or rather silence, in my correspondence to my friends," adding, "it seems, by the Commander's discourse, to be his determined plan not to allow any intelligence to transpire that embraces *particular points*, until it has previously been approved and ordered for publication by the Right Honorable Earl Bathurst, secretary of State for the War and Colonial Department." While the officers kept journals, he said, "I keep none, since I cannot be allowed to retain it."[156]

While Wentzel chafed at the "order of secrecy", he drew up his own narrative, apparently for Franklin and Richardson's use. It was a survey of the ethnography and natural resources of the Mackenzie River and Great Slave Lake regions, as well as a history of the NWC in the area since 1795. He composed it soon after his arrival, while Franklin observed the aurora, Hood and Richardson dissected and sketched a white wolf caught by Keskarrah, and the ink froze in the inkwell.[157] Written from memory, the account and the accompanying map were detailed and comprehensive, sketching the tense and changing Indigenous geopolitics and trading routes of the region alongside his observations of climate change, and strong recommendations that any future trade be carried on by men well known to local Indigenous people (such as himself).

Wentzel enclosed his account with his irritated letter to McKenzie. It reached Scotland well before any of Richardson's letters to his wife. In November 1821, while Franklin and Richardson were starving at Fort Enterprise, it was read at the Wernerian Society in Edinburgh, a scientific body superintended by Richardson's patron, Dr. Robert Jameson, and known as a wellspring of geological and evolutionary theory.[158] As the members of the Wernerian awaited news of their colleague Richardson, Wentzel's narrative was one of the only "authentic" accounts of the region in circulation. The others were personal letters, which, as I discuss in Chapter 2, bore the stamp of intimate authenticity and were sought after by journalists. Mary Richardson had already published at least one.[159] Wentzel's narrative nestled at the Wernerian alongside other accounts from vernacular authorities on Arctic matters, including the whaler William Scoresby, another of Jameson's protégés. Over the following years, Wentzel's account, and the map that he drew at Fort Enterprise, continued to circulate, both before and after the official narrative was published (see Map 3).[160]

In April 1823, as the first edition of Franklin's narrative came out, Wentzel was back at the Mackenzie River, in ill health and ill temper, and writing again to McKenzie. A new HBC-sponsored expedition was being contemplated that would trace the coast west from Churchill to the Coppermine, through Inuit territory—a route that had been suggested to Franklin in 1819, and which both HBC and NWC officials had rejected as too perilous.[161] Wentzel wrote:

> I hope and wish they may not be exposed to the same difficulties and hardships which proved so fatal to the Land Arctic Expedition, whose return was clouded by the loss of eleven lives, whilst the surviving officers have left in the country impressions not altogether very creditable to themselves amongst both the trading class of people and the native inhabitants. But it is doubtful whether, from the distant scene of their transactions, an authentic account of their operations will ever meet the public eye in England. It is to be presumed, as they themselves will be the publishers of the journals which will appear, that they will be cautious in not exposing their own errors and want of conduct. In fact one of the officers was candid enough to confess to me that there were circumstances which *must* not be known: however it is said that "stones sometimes speak."[162]

Wentzel added that he had kept a "sort of journal which . . . contains matter that it is not proper should appear at present, unless I had a desire to injure some which it is my interest to conceal at least for a time." He added that one of the officers knew he had it, and "requested me . . . to remain a year or two more in this country, I presume with a view to let the storm in some measure subside, or, what is as likely, to take advantage of my not being in the way for examination."[163]

It was George Back who begged Wentzel to hold on to his journal. The two companions had met again at Fort Chipewyan in June 1822, as the survivors of the LAE made their way back to York Factory. At the time, Wentzel explained to Franklin in writing that he had not abandoned the expedition at Fort Enterprise, but had fulfilled his mission as he understood it.[164] Wentzel and Back then spent five days together, their only opportunity to exchange information. It was one of many unrecorded moments when stories were exchanged and elaborated as men traveled from post to post. Those unnamed rumors survived for many years, buoyed, perhaps, by the popularity of Franklin's narrative. Some were translated into a skit that poked fun at the incompetence and quarrelsomeness of the British officers, and which concluded with the explorers agreeing that "all difference of opinion should be buried in oblivion and that the public were only to know us by the perfect unanimity that marked our proceedings."[165] Years later, ghosts of these rumors would recirculate in Tasmania, as Franklin's political foes received letters from correspondents in Rupert's Land that "pronounced the old man, many years ago, to be a fool.—Sir George Back, at a later period declared the same aged person to be that, and something more."[166]

When the Franklins embarked on their honeymoon in 1823, Franklin and Richardson were already planning a return to Canada. As I discuss in Chapter 2, they argued that a new expedition was necessary to forestall Russian expansion in the region, and particularly to prevent Russian infiltration of Indigenous trading networks. In doing so, they drew heavily on Wentzel's narrative and its description of geopolitics of the Mackenzie River region. Using the Russian threat as leverage, Franklin, Richardson, and Parry convinced the Admiralty to dispatch a new set of expeditions, despite "the humane repugnance of the British Government" to expose officers to the Arctic's dangers.[167] Parry would command HMS *Fury* and *Hecla* and head for the eastern entrance to the Passage, following an Inuit map obtained on his previous voyage (see Chapter 2). William Frederick Beechey would take HMS *Blossom* into the Bering Strait and then through Iñupiat territory to meet Franklin on the northern coast of Alaska. Franklin and Richardson would ascend the Mackenzie River and Franklin would head west to meet Beechey, while Richardson turned east to chart the coast between the Mackenzie and Coppermine drainages (see Timeline 1). Both Franklin and Richardson tried to keep Back at a distance. Franklin used his influence to get Back on HMS *Superb* in the West Indies, ostensibly to gain sea time, but in effect keeping him away from both the expedition and from Eleanor's niece Mary Anne Kay, whom he was courting.[168] But Back returned early from the Caribbean, and even as Richardson insisted that he would not serve under him, and as Hepburn raised concerns about his management of stores, at the Admiralty, Barrow pushed for his appointment.[169] Franklin wrote to Richardson that if he explained why they were so reluctant to take Back, "it might be retorted on me, Why did you permit these to be dormant so long? An explanation on this point would only lead further to the mire."[170]

Eleanor Porden Franklin, meanwhile, had become fond of the Richardsons and they of her. Throughout 1823 and 1824, they corresponded on subjects ranging from architecture to natural history, and they all expected that she would help to write the narrative of the second expedition. Franklin wrote to Richardson that he was about to be supplanted, for "I may calculate on some assistance from a near and dear friend of whom you know is not a little experienced in both composition and the detail of publishing."[171] Richardson, in turn, sought Eleanor's advice for one of his female relatives who was an aspiring author.[172] When the Richardsons moved to Chatham in the spring of 1824, the Franklins stayed with them after their daughter (also named Eleanor) was born in June.[173] Eleanor's tuberculosis grew worse during her difficult pregnancy, and she was housebound for much of 1824, but nevertheless helped to correct the third edition of Franklin and Richardson's narrative.[174] She also read Franklin's correspondence, inspected his supply lists, and learned what she could about the hostilities between the Yellowknives Dene and the Dog Ribs, which had driven Akaitcho's band from their territories. She reassured their relatives that all the preparations were models of prudence, forethought, and caution, and that the Yellowknives were prepared to support the expedition again (though in this, she was mistaken).[175] In January 1825, her condition worsened. Franklin wrote, "my occupations necessarily keep me from her the whole day—and by the Evening she is fatigued and agitated by having to be left to reflect on my going."[176] Nevertheless, he and Richardson left in February, and she died three days later. In a ceremony that recalled the imagery of her wedding dress, Franklin's brother Arctic officers, Captains Buchan, Beaufort, Lyon, and Beechey, served as her pallbearers.[177] The Franklins' nine-month-old daughter was left in the care of Franklin's sister, Isabella Cracroft, with whom she would spend most of her young life.

Meanwhile, Franklin's bad credit was coming back to haunt him. The Yellowknives had refused to "accompany the Expedition under the Command of Captain Franklin to Bear Lake either in the capacity of Hunters or otherwise."[178] Moreover, the HBC was having difficulty recruiting guides and *voyageurs*, forcing them to pay exorbitant wages.[179] In March 1825, the recruiters wrote with relief that they had finally assembled a crew, including "Charles the Iroquois" who knew the whole route and was "an expert Guide and excellent voyageur."[180] He was Charles Teroahaute, Michel Teroahaute's brother, and he was well acquainted with the rumors in the country. In April, Franklin learned of Eleanor's death, as he was in the midst of writing to her.[181] The expedition paused for a few days, and during this time Charles Teroahaute walked into the tent that Franklin and Richardson shared, sat on the floor, and demanded to know the circumstances of his brother's death.[182] Back wrote that Charles "wished also to know what had become of [Michel's] wages, and requested that he might receive them." Franklin and Richardson promised to pay, but Back recorded that Charles went away dissatisfied and that "we determined . . . to keep a keen Eye on his and his Countrymen's Actions."[183] Franklin wrote furious letters to the HBC officials, demanding to know why Charles and the rest of the Iroquois men had been engaged, and swearing that he would leave them all at Fort William.[184]

When Eleanor Porden demanded that John Franklin compare his past and present behavior and tell her "which is the counterfeit, and which the real man," she pointed at the heart of a big problem. She was one of many (including Charles Teroahaute), from Edinburgh to London to York Factory to Great Slave Lake, who questioned

Franklin's trustworthiness during the First LAE and in the months leading up to and following the publication of *Journey to the Polar Sea*. The narrative he wrote with John Richardson was shaped by the many crises on the Barren Grounds in 1819–22 and was just one of many tales of suffering caused by the shifting rhythms of caribou herds and the demands of the fur trade.

Teasing apart these stories and silences helps us glimpse some of the myriad ways in which Indigenous intermediaries, vernacular authorities, and explorers' families engaged with the politics of truth. It demonstrates how Indigenous leaders like Akaitcho not only used expeditions to gather useful intelligence in a time of crisis but also tried to control how they were portrayed on a global stage. It shows how vernacular intermediaries like Wentzel and junior officers like Back engaged with the narrative both before and after its publication, through both their own narratives and journals and through the circulation of rumors. It helps us glimpse how wives and prospective wives like Eleanor Porden and Mary Richardson tried to come to terms with the intimacies and traumas that lay behind the book's celebration of heroic and pious suffering in the face of failure. Each of them nursed their own secrets and suspicions, and each questioned, in their own way, the trustworthiness of others.

Notes

1 SPRI MS 1503/2/5, John to Mary Richardson, March 6, 1820.
2 SPRI MS 1503/2/8, John to Mary Richardson, July 29, 1820, Great Slave Lake. See also SPRI MS 1503/2, John Richardson Correspondence 1819-1820, MS 1503/3, John Richardson Correspondence 1820-21, and SPRI MS 1503/3, John Richardson Correspondence, 1821-22.
3 The corrections are marked features of this letter, as Richardson's handwriting changes to accommodate the freshly recut nib and its flow of ink. SPRI MS 1503/4/3, John to Mary Richardson, April, 1822.
4 Mary received Richardson's April letter on October 16. Four days earlier, reports of cannibalism on the expedition appeared in the British press. Three days after Mary received her letter, a correction appeared that claimed to be from an "authentic source," giving Richardson's version of events. "The Arctic Expedition," *Northampton Mercury*, October 12, 1822; "The North West Land Expedition," *The Times*, October 18, 1822,2; "North West Expedition," *Morning Post*, October 19, 1822.
5 Nigel Leask, *Curiosity and the Aesthetics of Travel Writing, 1770-1840* (Oxford: Oxford University Press, 2002), 54; Keighren et al., *Travels Into Print*, 68–99.
6 James A. Secord, "Knowledge in Transit," *ISIS* 95 (2004): 660.
7 Keighren et al., *Travels Into Print*; Cavell, *Tracing the Connected Narrative*; Adriana Craciun, *Writing Arctic Disaster: Authorship and Exploration*, Cambridge Studies in Nineteenth-Century Literature and Culture (Cambridge and New York: Cambridge University Press, 2016).
8 Liebersohn, *The Travelers' World*; Kennedy, ed., *Reinterpreting Exploration*.
9 Felix Driver, *Geography Militant: Cultures of Exploration and Empire* (Oxford and Malden: Blackwell Publishers, 2001).

10 C. A. Bayly, *Empire and Information: Intelligence Gathering and Social Communication in India, 1780-1870*. Cambridge Studies in Indian History & Society (Cambridge and New York: Cambridge University Press, 1996); Piker, "Lying Together," 964-86.
11 Ann Laura Stoler, "'In Cold Blood': Hierarchies of Credibility and the Politics of Colonial Narratives," *Representations* 37, Winter (1992): 153.
12 Demuth, *Floating Coast*, 171.
13 Ibid., 137-68; Richard K. Nelson, *Make Prayers to the Raven: A Koyukon View of the Northern Forest* (Chicago and London: University of Chicago Press, 1986); Farley Mowat, *People of the Deer* (New York: Carroll & Graf Publishers, 1975), 66-84.
14 Julie Cruikshank, *Do Glaciers Listen? Local Knowledge: Colonial Encounters, and Social Imagination*. (Vancouver and Toronto: University of British Columbia Press, 2005), 23-49; Fossett, *In Order to Live Untroubled*, 115-37; Lloyd Keith, ed., *North of Athabasca: Slave Lake and Mackenzie River Documents of the North West Company, 1800-1821*. Rupert's Land Record Society Series (Montreal and Kingston: McGill-Queen's University Press, 2001), 67.
15 Here I am paraphrasing one of Cruikshank's central arguments in *Do Glaciers Listen?*
16 Beryl C. Gillespie, "Changes in the Territory and Technology of the Chipewyan," *Arctic Anthropology* 13, no. 1 (1976): 6-11; James G. E. Smith, "Chipewyan, Cree and Inuit Relations West of Hudson Bay, 1714-1955," *Ethnohistory* 28, no. 2 (Spring 1981): 133-56.
17 Carolyn Podruchny, *Making the Voyageur World: Travelers and Traders in the North American Fur Trade* (Lincoln and London: University of Nebraska Press, 2006).
18 The use of métis/Métis is complex, but following Heather Devine, I use the lower-case métis to refer to people of mixed ancestry in the fur trade countries, and Métis to refer to the specific ethnic group centered on the Red River Colony from the mid-nineteenth century. Heather Devine, *The People Who Own Themselves: Aboriginal Ethnogenesis in a Canadian Family, 1660-1900* (Calgary: University of Calgary Press, 2013), xviii.
19 Sylvia Van Kirk, *Many Tender Ties: Women in Fur-Trade Society, 1670-1870* (Winnipeg: Watson & Dwyer Publishing, Ltd., 1980); Jennifer S. H. Brown, *Strangers in Blood: Fur Trade Company Families in Indian Country* (Norman: University of Oklahoma Press, 1980); Susan Sleeper-Smith, ed., *Rethinking the Fur Trade: Cultures of Exchange in an Atlantic World* (Lincoln and London: University of Nebraska Press, 2009).
20 See James Daschuk, *Clearing the Plains: Disease, Politics of Starvation, and the Loss of Indigenous Life*, 2nd ed. (Regina: University of Regina Press, 2019), 41-57.
21 For a survey and critique of the concept of the "shatter zone," see Denise Ileana Bossy, "Shattering Together, Merging Apart: Colonialism, Violence and the Remaking of the Native South," *William and Mary Quarterly*, 3rd ser. 71, no. 2 (October 2014): 611-31. For conditions around Great Slave Lake, see Shepherd Krech III, "Disease, Starvation and Northern Athapaskan Social Organization," *American Ethnologist* 5, no. 4 (November 1978): 710-32 and also Daschuk, *Clearing*, 55-7.
22 SPRI MS802/1-2;D Willard Wentzel, account of the MacKenzie Region, February 26, 1821; Aporta, "The Trail as Home," 131-46; Bockstoce, *Furs and Frontiers*; Vinkovetsky, *Russian America*.
23 Strother Roberts, "Trans-Indian Identity and the Inuit 'Other': Relations between the Chipewyan and Neighboring Aboriginal Communities in the Eighteenth Century," *Ethnohistory* 57, no. 4 (Fall 2010): 597-624; Cameron, *Far Off Metal River*. The

actual scale, distribution, and magnitude of conflict between Inuit and Dene people across northern North America is debated, as is the significance of the Kugluktuk massacre. See Katherine L. Reedy-Maschner and Herbert D. G. Maschner, "Marauding Middlemen: Western Expansion and Violent Conflict in the Subarctic," *Ethnohistory* 46, no. 4 (Fall 1999): 704–43; Ernest S. Burch, Jr., *Alliance and Conflict: The World System of the Iñupiaq Eskimos* (Lincoln and London: University of Nebraska Press, 2005), 64, 107–25; Smith, "Chipewyan, Cree and Inuit," 133–56.

24 TNA CO6/15, Sketch of Official Instructions from Lord Bathurst, April 29, 1819.
25 See John Richardson, *Arctic Ordeal: The Journal of John Richardson, Surgeon-Naturalist with Franklin, 1820-1822*, ed. C. Stuart Houston (Kingston and Montreal: McGill-Queen's University Press, 1984), 26, 44–5. Robert Hood, *To the Arctic by Canoe, 1819-1821: The Journal and Paintings of Robert Hood, Midshipman with Franklin*, ed. C. Stuart Houston (Montreal and London: McGill-Queen's University Press, 1974), 133; George Back, *Arctic Artist: The Journal and Paintings of George Back, Midshipman with Franklin, 1819-1822*, ed. C. Stuart Houston (Kingston and Montreal: McGill-Queen's University Press, 1994), 49, 54, 61, 73. See the correspondence between Alexander McKenzie and the officers of the NWC and the HBC with the officers of the expedition in SPRI MS 248/276 and TNA CO6/15, some of which are reproduced in John Franklin, *Sir John Franklin's Journals and Correspondence: The First Arctic Land Expedition, 1819-1822*, ed. Richard C. Davis (Toronto: The Champlain Society, 1995), 289–90 and 303–18.
26 June Helm and Beryl C. Gillespie, "Dogrib Oral Tradition as History: War and Peace in the 1820s," *Journal of Anthropological Research* 37, no. 1 (Spring 1981): 8–27.
27 "Dene Nation," https://denenation.com/ (accessed April 1, 2023); "Yellowknives Dene First Nation," https://ykdene.com/ (accessed April 1, 2023).
28 HBCA B.42/a/140, Churchill Factory Post Journal 1813-14; HBCA B.42/a/141, Churchill Factory Post Journal 1814-15, 3 May 1815. Fossett identifies him as a Keewatin Inuit man, *In Order to Live Untroubled*, 123–5.
29 HBCA B.42/a/140, 12 July, 1814; HBCA B.42/a/141, June 22–24, 1815.
30 John Franklin, *Narrative of a Journey to the Shores of the Polar Sea, in the Years 1819-20-21-22*, 3rd ed. (London: John Murray, 1824), 41; George Back, *Arctic Artist*, 119.
31 TNA CO 6/15, "Queries answered by Mr Snodie, Chief of Churchill Fort."
32 Keith, *North of Athabasca*, 54–69.
33 Ann Savours, *The Search for the North West Passage* (New York: St. Martin's Press, 1999), 1–18; Christopher Carter, "'The Sea Fryseth Not': Science and the Open Polar Sea in the Nineteenth Century," *Earth Sciences History* 32, no. 2 (2013): 235–51. I discuss the open polar sea theory in more depth in Chapter 5.
34 Savours, *Search for the North West Passage*, 39–55; I. S. MacLaren, "John Barrow's Darling Project (1816-1846)," in *Arctic Exploration in the Nineteenth Century: Discovering the Northwest Passage*, ed. Frederic Regard (London: Pickering and Chatto, 2013), 19–36.
35 Michael Bravo, "Geographies of Exploration and Improvement: William Scoresby and Arctic Whaling, 1782-1922," *Journal of Historical Geography* 32 (2006): 512–38.
36 Andrew Lambert, *The Gates of Hell: Sir John Franklin's Tragic Quest for the North West Passage* (New Haven and London: Yale University Press, 2009), 22–9.
37 John McIlraith, *Life of Sir John Richardson* (London: Longman, Green and Co, 1868), 58–61.
38 Peter Steele, *The Man Who Mapped the Arctic: The Intrepid Life of George Back, Franklin's Lieutenant*. (Vancouver: Raincoast Books, 2003), 3–54.

39 Hood, *To the Arctic*.
40 *Haddingtonshire Courier*, "An East Lothian Polar Explorer," August 22, 1913; Joseph Rene Bellot, *Memoirs of Lieutenant Joseph Rene Bellot* (London: Hurst and Blackett, 1855), 130.
41 Hood, *To the Arctic*, 125; Franklin, *Narrative of a Journey*, 6.
42 Podruchny, *Making*, 64–71.
43 Nicole St-Onge, "'He was Neither a Solder Nor a Slave: He was Under the Control of No Man': Kahnawake Mohawks in the Northwest Fur Trade, 1790-1850," *Canadian Journal of History* 51, no. 1 (2016): 1–32; Louis-Rodrigue Masson, ed., *Les Bourgeois de la Compagnie du Nord-Ouest: Récits de Voyages, Lettres et Rapports Inédits Relatifs au Nord-Ouest Canadien* (New York: Antiquarian Press, 1960), 109.
44 SPRI MS 248/281/1 BJ, Simon McGillivray to John Franklin, nd.
45 Hood, *To the Arctic*, 33.
46 James Daschuk, *Clearing the Plains*, 55–7; Hood, *To the Arctic*, 49; Keith, *North of Athabasca*, 69; HBCA B.1818/a/3, Robert MacVicar, Journal Fort Resolution and Great Slave Lake.
47 HBCA B.1818/a/3, Robert McVicar, Journal Fort Resolution and Great Slave Lake, June 29, 1820, 5.
48 See Richard C. Davis, introduction to *Sir John Franklin's Journals and Correspondence: The First Arctic Land Expedition, 1819-1822*, ed. Richard C. Davis (Toronto: The Champlain Society, 1995), xi–cix, especially lxxviii–cvii.
49 For the role of food in the exercise of power in fur trade county, see Leslie Ritchie, "'Expectations of Grease & Provisions': The Circulation and Regulation of Fur Trade Foodstuffs," *Eighteenth-Century Life* 23, no. 2 (1999): 124–42.
50 It is now the site of a giant mine. See map at Yellowknives Dene First Nation, https://ykdene.com/, accessed April 1, 2023.
51 Hood, *To the Arctic*, 132–5.
52 See TNA CO 6/15, William Wentzel to Edward Smith, May 22, 1820.
53 SPRI MS 1503/2/9, John to Mary Richardson, 18 October 1820; Franklin, *Journals and Correspondence: 1819-1822?*, 119. See also Van Kirk, *Many Tender Ties*.
54 In the narrative, Franklin described her as a lascivious "great beauty" who "although under sixteen years of age has belonged successively to two husbands, and would probably have been the wife of many more, if her mother had not required her services as a nurse." Franklin, *Narrative of a Journey*, 229. See also Richard Davis, "Fact and Fancy in History and Biography: The Case of Greenstockings," *Polar Record* 37, no. 200 (2001): 5–12.
55 SPRI MS 395/70/2 BL, John Franklin to George Back, Fort Enterprise, November 21, 1820.
56 Bellot, *Memoirs*, 252.
57 Perry, *Colonial Relations*, 43.
58 Richardson, *Arctic Ordeal*, 29; Franklin, *Journal*, 110–11. See also HBCA B.1818/a/3, Robert McVicar, Journal Fort Resolution and Great Slave Lake.
59 Franklin, *Journal*, 80.
60 Franklin, *Journal*, 113.
61 Franklin, *Journal*, 136–7.
62 Franklin, *Journal*, 95, 114, 129–30, 142; Richardson, *Arctic Ordeal*, 26–9; Back, *Arctic Artist*, 118–19; Franklin, *Narrative of a Journey*, 42–6, 215, 223, 234.
63 Back's absence has long been linked to the expedition's sexual tensions, while his biographers have also suggested that it reflected his ambition and physical

toughness. See Leslie Neatby, *The Search for Franklin* (Toronto and Edmonton: M. G. Hurtig, 1970), 47; Davis, "Fact and Fancy," 9; Houston, introduction to *Arctic Artist*, xx–xxv.
64 Back, *Arctic Artist*, 81.
65 Franklin's census of the expedition included the names of all the women, except for Greenstockings, who was counted among the children. Franklin later referred to her as "Keskarrah's fascinating daughter." See Franklin, *Journal*, 158–9, and Franklin, *Narrative of a Journey*, 154.
66 For Inuit tactics, see Burch, *Alliance and Conflict*, 55–7.
67 Podruchny, *Making*, 151.
68 SPRI MS1503/4/2, John to Mary Richardson, July 18, 1822. The letter from Hood is referenced in SPRI MS1503/4/4, Dr Richard Hood to John Richardson, October 1822.
69 Richardson, *Arctic Ordeal*, 110, 83–4.
70 Richardson, *Arctic Ordeal*, 62–3. Franklin later attributed "our Want of provision . . . to the duplicity and fickleness of our Indian Companions." Franklin, *Journal*, 167.
71 Richardson, *Arctic Ordeal*, 129, 140.
72 Podruchny, *Making*, 119.
73 Richardson, *Arctic Ordeal*, 144–5.
74 SPRI MS 395/70/5 BL, John Franklin to George Back, October 15, 1821.
75 NLS, John Murray Archive, MS.42237.
76 Hepburn later confirmed portions of Richardson's account. It has been suggested that Richardson's account was also part of an elaborate cover-up, but Cavell has argued that hard evidence is lacking. Bellot, *Memoirs*, 140, 263; M. A. MacLeod and R. Glover, "Franklin's First Expedition As Seen By the Fur Traders," *Polar Record* 15, no. 98 (1971): 669–82; Janice Cavell, "The Hidden Crime of Dr. Richardson," *Polar Record* 43, no. 2 (April 2007): 155–64.
77 John Richardson, "Dr. Richardson's Narrative," in John Franklin, *Narrative of a Journey to the Shores of the Polar Sea, in the Years 1819-20-21-22*, 3rd ed. (London: John Murray, 1824), 341–2.
78 Richardson in Franklin, *Narrative of a Journey*, 343.
79 Bellot, *Memoirs*, 263.
80 Lamb, *Preserving the Self*, 126.
81 Franklin, *Narrative of a Journey*, 355.
82 Janice Cavell, "Lady Lucy Barry and Evangelical Reading on the First Franklin Expedition," *Arctic* 63, no. 2 (June 2010): 1–10.
83 SPRI MS 248/305 John Franklin to Willingham Franklin, Jr., April 8, 1822.
84 SPRI MS 1503/4/3, John to Mary Richardson, April 1822.
85 Franklin, *Narrative of a Journey*, 359; SPRI MS 1503/4/3, John to Mary Richardson, April, 1822.
86 Richardson, *Arctic Ordeal*, 167.
87 Franklin, *Journal*, 289; Back, *Arctic Artist*, 190–1.
88 Franklin, *Journal*, 229.
89 Franklin, *Journal*, 231.
90 Richardson, *Arctic Ordeal*, 178.
91 Janice Cavell, "Representing Akaitcho: European Vision and Revision in the Writing of John Franklin's *Narrative of a Journey to the Shores of the Polar Sea* . . . ." *Polar Record* 44, no. 228 (2008): 32; Franklin, *Journal*, 231, fn 511.
92 In C. Stuart Houston's view, St. Germain was responsible for the survival of the Britons on the expedition. See Houston, "Commentary," *Arctic Ordeal*, 215.

93 Back, *Arctic Artist*, 352.
94 "The North West Land Expedition," *The Times*, October 18, 1822, 2.
95 John Franklin to Eleanor Porden, October 2, 1822, in Edith Mary Gell, *John Franklin's Bride: Eleanor Anne Porden* (London: John Murray, 1930), 66–71; Richard C. Davis, "'... Which an Affectionate Heart Would Say': John Franklin's Personal Correspondence, 1819-1824," *Polar Record* 33, no. 186 (1997): 202–4.
96 Porden to Franklin, October 19, 1822, in Gell, *John Franklin's Bride*, 71–2.
97 SPRI MS1503/4/4, Richard Hood to John Richardson, October 1822.
98 SPRI MS1503/4/3, John to Mary Richardson, April 1822 (received October 16, 1822).
99 Franklin to Porden, October 2, 1822, in Gell, *John Franklin's Bride*, 66–71.
100 Liebersohn, *The Travelers' World*, 8.
101 Cavell, *Tracing the Connected Narrative*, 7–12.
102 Outram, "On Being Perseus," 285.
103 John Tosh, *A Man's Place: Masculinity and the Middle-Class Home in Victorian England* (New Haven and London: Yale University Press, 1999); Davidoff and Hall, *Family Fortunes*.
104 Franklin had lost his journal covering the period from June to October 1821 when his canoe overturned in the Hood River. Richardson's journal for August–October 1821 contain a number of passages that refer to later conversations with Yellowknives and traders alike, as well as evidence of this early collaboration. See Franklin, *Journal*, 160, fn 344, 179, fn 398, 181, fn 402, 196, fn 446; Richardson, *Arctic Ordeal*, 135, 140, 143. They could not have drawn on Hood's or Back's journals, as Franklin had already dispatched them to Britain.
105 Frith and Bateman Street: Portland Estate: Frith Street, Survey of London: volumes 33 and 34: St Anne Soho, F. H. W. Sheppard (General Editor), in British History Online, http://www.british-history.ac.uk/report.aspx?compid=41075 (accessed April 14, 2014).
106 DRO D8760/F/FJR/1/1/3, Franklin to Richardson, October 24, 1822.
107 McIlraith, *Life of Sir John Richardson*, 73; DRO D3311/53/32, John and Eleanor Franklin to John and Mary Richardson, August 24, 1824.
108 McIlraith, *Life of Sir John Richardson*, 122.
109 SPRI MS 1503/2/5, John to Mary Richardson, March 6, 1820, Cumberland House; see also Sujit Sivasundarum, *Nature and the Godly Empire: Science and Evangelical Mission in the Pacific, 1795-1850* (Cambridge: Cambridge University Press, 2005).
110 DRO D8760/F/FJR/1/1/62, Franklin to Richardson, February 24, 1832.
111 Richardson alludes to these in his correspondence with Mary, see especially SPRI 1503/4/1.
112 Cavell, "Lady Lucy Barry," 5.
113 Cavell, *Tracing the Connected Narrative*, 92–116.
114 SPRI MS 1503/4/3, John to Mary Richardson, April 1822.
115 Franklin to Porden, July 11, 1823, in Gell, *John Franklin's Bride*, 216–17.
116 Eleanor Anne Porden, *The Arctic Expeditions. A Poem* (London: John Murray, 1818), 14. For a comparison of Porden and Shelley's work, see Jen Hill, *White Horizon: The Arctic in the Nineteenth-Century British Imagination* (Albany: State University of New York Press, 2008), 53–88.
117 Franklin to Porden, December 5 and 16, 1822, in Gell, *John Franklin's Bride*, 77, 82.
118 DRO D8760/F/FEP/3/6/1, "Lines written to John Franklin on hearing that he has been persuaded to write his Travels."

119 See Gillian Russell and Clara Tuite, eds., *Romantic Sociability: Social Networks and Literary Culture in Britain, 1770-1840* (Cambridge and New York: Cambridge University Press, 2002).
120 Franklin to Porden, December 16, 1822, in Gell, *John Franklin's Bride*, 82.
121 Porden to Franklin, May 28, 1823, in Gell, *John Franklin's Bride*, 145.
122 Quoted in Cavell, *Tracing the Connected Narrative*, 10.
123 Porden to Franklin, London, January 1823, in Gell, *John Franklin's Bride*, 95–6.
124 DRO D8760/F/FEP/3/7/2 addressed to Captn Franklin R. N. 60 Frith Street Soho, February 14, 1823; SPRI MS 1503/5/3, addressed to Dr. Richardson, 60 Frith Street Soho, February 14, 1823.
125 "The Esquimaux Girl's Lament," in Gell, *John Franklin's Bride*, 97–8.
126 Ibid.
127 Francis Spufford, *I May Be Some Time: Ice and the English Imagination* (London: Faber and Faber, 1996), 111; Hill, *White Horizon*, 76–7.
128 See John O'Leary, "Speaking the Suffering Indigene: 'Native' Songs and Laments, 1820–1850," *Kunapipi* 31, no. 1 (2009): 47–59.
129 RGS-IBG SJF/7/5, "Miss Greenstockings to her Faithless Admirer," in John Franklin's handwriting. It is identified in RGS-IBG catalog as having been sent by John Franklin to Jane Franklin from the *Erebus* in 1845.
130 Porden to Franklin, March 29, 1823, in Gell, *John Franklin's Bride*, 109.
131 Spufford, *I May Be Some Time*, 111.
132 Lisa Norling, "'How Frought with Sorrow and Heartpangs': Mariners' Wives and the Ideology of Domesticity in New England, 1790-1880," *The New England Quarterly* 65, no. 3 (September 1992): 422–46.
133 Porden to Franklin, March 29, 1823, in Gell, *John Franklin's Bride*, 107–9.
134 Cavell, *Tracing the Connected Narrative*, especially 100–15.
135 Max Jones, *The Last Great Quest: Captain Scott's Antarctic Sacrifice* (Oxford and New York: Oxford University Press, 2003), 26; Stephanie Barczewski, *Heroic Failure and the British* (New Haven and London: Yale University Press, 2016).
136 Franklin to Porden, May 17, 1823, in Gell, *John Franklin's Bride*, 132–4.
137 Franklin to Porden, May 26, 1823, in Gell, *John Franklin's Bride*, 138–41.
138 DRO D8760/F/FJR/1/1/5, Franklin to Richardson, 13 June 1823; Franklin to Porden, June 7, 1823, in Gell, *John Franklin's Bride*, 166–7.
139 Porden to Franklin, June 17, 1823, in Gell, *John Franklin's Bride*, 187–92.
140 DRO D8760/F/FJR/1/1/6, Franklin to Richardson, June 19, 1823.
141 Franklin to Porden, June 19, 1823, in Gell, *John Franklin's Bride*, 192–5.
142 Porden to Franklin, June 28, 1823 (dated May, but June by context), in Gell, *John Franklin's Bride*, 149.
143 Porden to Franklin, July 9, 1823, in Gell, *John Franklin's Bride*, 205–6. For a deeper discussion of this conflict and the content of the pamphlets, see Cavell, "Lady Lucy Barry."
144 Franklin to Porden, in Gell, *John Franklin's Bride*, July 11, 1823, 216–17.
145 Porden to Franklin, July 12, 1823, in Gell, *John Franklin's Bride*, 226–7.
146 Porden to Mr. Elliott, July 21, 1823, in Gell, *John Franklin's Bride*, 228.
147 Franklin, *Narrative of a Journey*, 733, 767, and plate 27.
148 SPRI MS 1503/5/5, Franklin to Richardson, September 19, 1823.
149 DRO D8760/F/FJR/1/1/8, Franklin to Richardson, August 1, 1823.
150 SPRI MS 1503/5/4, Franklin to Richardson, August 11, 1823.

151 For vernacular intermediaries, explorers, and scientific practitioners, see A. Secord, "Corresponding Interests," 383–408; Ballantyne, *Webs of Empire*, 124–36; Kennedy, *The Last Blank Spaces*, 166–7; Bravo, "Geographies of Exploration and Improvement."
152 The spelling of McKenzie, Mackenzie, and M'Kenzie was used interchangeably by this family. See Keith, *North of Athabasca*, introduction and 54–71.
153 Masson, *Les Bourgeois*, 105.
154 Wentzel to McKenzie, May 23, 1820, in Masson, *Les Bourgeois*, 130. For Wentzel's relationship with the McKenzie family, see Keith, *North of Athabasca*, introduction and 54–71.
155 Back, *Arctic Artist*, 91.
156 Wentzel to McKenzie, March 26, 1821, in Masson, *Les Bourgeois*, 138.
157 Keith, *North of Athabasca*, 71.
158 Ibid., 72; James A. Secord, "Edinburgh Lamarkians: Robert Jameson and Robert E. Grant," *Journal of the History of Biology* 24, no. 1 (Spring 1991): 1–18; Bill Jenkins, "Neptunism and Transformism: Robert Jameson and Other Evolutionary Theorists in Early Nineteenth-Century Scotland," *Journal of the History of Biology* 49 no. 3 (Fall 2016): 527–57.
159 SPRI MS 1503/2/10, John to Mary Richardson, December 1, 1820.
160 See, for example, "Attempts to Reach the Sea by the Mackenzie River," *Hereford Journal*, March 26, 1823, 1; "Captain Franklin's Journey," *Caledonian Mercury*, May 15, 1823, 4.
161 See TNA CO 6/15, "Queries answered" file.
162 Willard Wentzel to Roderick Mackenzie, April 23, 1823, in Masson, *Les Bourgeois*, 145–6.
163 Ibid.
164 Franklin, *Narrative of a Journey*, 492–3; Back, *Arctic Artist*, 225–6.
165 MacLeod and Glover, "Franklin's 1st Expedition," 675.
166 TA NS6102, Thomas Anstey to George Swanston, November 14, 1841.
167 In Chapter 2, I discuss in more detail how Franklin used this argument to regain the favor and patronage of HBC officials. See CO 6/16, John Franklin to John Barrow, November 26, 1823; HBCA B. 200/e/3 A. R. MacLeod, MacKenzie River District Report, 1823–4.
168 DRO D8760/F/FJR/1/1/34, Franklin to Richardson, November 4, [1823]; DRO D8760/F/FJR/1/1/15, Franklin to Richardson, December 30, 1823; NMM FRN1/2, John Franklin to Mary Anne Kay, November 22, 1823.
169 DRO D8760/F/FJR/1/1/13, Franklin to Richardson, December 15, 1823.
170 DRO D8760/F/FJR/1/1/29, Franklin to Richardson, August 24, 1824.
171 DRO D8760/F/FJR/1/1/16, Franklin to Richardson, January 14, 1824.
172 DRO D8760/F/FSJ/1/9/7, Richardson to Franklin, March 10, 1824.
173 DRO D8760/F/FSJ/1/9/9, Richardson to Franklin, June 29, 1824; Eleanor Franklin to Sarah Kay, August 14, 1824, in Gell, *John Franklin's Bride*, 280–2.
174 SPRI MS248/388/2 Eleanor Franklin to Isabella Cracroft, March 17, 1824; Eleanor Franklin to Sarah Kay, October 28, 1824, in Gell, *John Franklin's Bride*, 284–5; John to Eleanor Franklin, December 16, 1824, in in Gell, *John Franklin's Bride*, 293.
175 Eleanor Franklin to Sarah Kay, August 14, 1824, in Gell, *John Franklin's Bride*, 280–4; SPRI MS 248/389/2, Eleanor Franklin to Elizabeth Franklin, September 10, 1824.
176 DRO D8760/F/FKA/1/1/1, John Franklin to Sarah Kay, January 26, 1825.
177 Martyn Beardsley, *Deadly Winter: The Life of Sir John Franklin*. (London: Chatham Publishing, 2002), 124.

178 HBCA B.39/b/2, Fort Chipewyan Correspondence Book, Edward Smith & A R MacLeod to Charles Dease & John Hutchinson, March 7, 1824.
179 SPRI MS 248/281/1 BJ, Messrs McGilivray, Thane & Co to Franklin, March 23, 1825.
180 SPRI MS 248/281/1 BJ, Messrs McGillivrays & Co to Franklin, March 26, 1825 and March 30, 1825.
181 DRO D8760/F/FEP/1/1/26, John to Eleanor Franklin, April 22, 1825; Richardson wrote to Mary that he was "unhinged" by the news. SPRI MS 1503/6/1, John to Mary Richardson, April 22, 1825.
182 SPRI MS 248/281/1 BJ, Franklin to Messrs McGillivray, Thain & Co, May 2, 1825.
183 SPRI MS 395/6 BL, George Back, Journal of the Second Expedition, 1824-1826, 33–4.
184 SPRI MS 248/281/1 BJ, John Franklin to Messrs McGillivray, Thain & Co, May 2, 1825.

2

"He a Discoverer, Forsooth!"
Arctic Circles and Scientific Sociability, 1818–29

In 1827, Jane Griffin's brother-in-law Sir John Simpkinson pulled her aside at a party and "asked if I had succeeded in meeting Captain F. in arctic circles, that being the report, & whether some cape or bay was not christened in our name."[1] Franklin and Richardson had recently returned from their Second Land Arctic Expedition (LAE), and it was an open secret that the widower was looking for a new wife and mother for little Eleanor, now three years old. He had, indeed, christened a "Point Griffin" in Jane's honor and also stopped by her house "begging acceptance of reindeer tongues and 3 prs shoes made by native Ind. [Indian] women."[2] He also brought home an Iroquois corn husk doll for Eleanor, who had no memory of her father. He sent a raccoon skin as a wedding present to Edward and Isabella Parry. They used it as a hearth rug in a home filled with "curiosities" from Parry's Arctic voyages, including maps and sketches drawn by Iglulingmiut at Winter Island in 1821–3, artifacts of a (temporarily) shared world.[3]

As these gifts and conversations suggest, the geographical circle at 66° 33' N was echoed in several very different metropolitan social circles in which explorers and their families claimed credibility and sought patronage. In the heyday of British Arctic exploration in the 1820s, circles of scientific sociability in London and Edinburgh were marketplaces of information. They linked explorers and their families to the people who would develop both scientific institutions and humanitarian networks over the next thirty years. In circles of polite science, the female relatives of explorers encountered other knowledgeable, educated women who negotiated the public sphere as authors, reformers, artists, and philanthropists. This was a vital and perilous sphere that required endless self-fashioning, particularly as explorers' wives and families became intermediaries and gatekeepers of information from the field.[4] Men and women needed to be simultaneously charming and reticent, original and conventional, and above all trustworthy and credible. In the process, the women of the Franklin family became keepers of archives and information, of correspondence, specimens, curiosities, and ephemera. These collections expressed their own taste, refinement, and accomplishments in a gendered counterpart of their partners' profession. But they also helped to establish explorers' credibility, particularly as they returned from the field to become "curiosities" themselves, as men who had starved, lived among unknown peoples, been immured in ice, and returned. It fell to relatives to reassure their intimate friends that explorers were unchanged in essentials, were reliable reporters about the strange lands and peoples they trespassed upon, and above all, were still conventionally attached and domestic.

Lions and Bluestockings: The Perils of Fame in Arctic Circles

In the 1820s, Arctic expeditions departed relentlessly, one on the heels of another, all of them inconclusive and incomplete (see Timeline 1). As the sea ice in the Canadian archipelago, Beaufort Sea, and the Bering Strait advanced and retreated at the end of the Little Ice Age, eleven expeditions set out between 1818 and 1829, all but one of them sponsored by the Admiralty or Colonial Office. These were the voyages and journeys through which Franklin, Richardson, John Ross, William Edward Parry, George Francis Lyon, Frederick William Beechey, and many others made their fame. Junior officers like James Clark Ross, George Back, Francis Moira Crozier, and Edward Kendall gained experience of ice navigation, long polar winters, and tough Arctic travel. Along the way, they made Indigenous and vernacular connections, glimpsing but never fully comprehending the scale of Indigenous trade and travel across the passage that the British sought to find before the Russians.[5]

The social world of polite science in London thrived on such accounts. Fifty years earlier, Joseph Banks and the Tahitian nobleman Mai circulated through salons and soirees of the eighteenth-century "conversable world."[6] It was as true in the 1820s as it was in the 1770s that it was only by "circulating, talking about, and looking at" curiosities that expeditionary information could be, as Gillian Russell has put it, "properly assimilated and activated."[7] Travelers were curiosities to be displayed, paraded, and interrogated by fellow guests, along with other "lions"—the writers, musicians, and travelers of the Romantic period.[8] This elite world of scientific sociability was the genesis of the institutions, networks, and infrastructures of "professional" science that emerged later in the century.[9] It was a scene in which, according to James Secord, "people differing in gender, rank and depth of experience not only talked about science but in doing so contributed directly to its making."[10] Yet navigating it was also a struggle, one as marked for explorers and their families as it was for others who sought entry on the basis of merit.

Circles of polite science acquired a distinctive Arctic flavor during the 1820s. Visiting the Arctic ships became one of the highlights of the London Season. In 1818, Franklin wrote to his sister Isabella Cracroft that "Deptford has been covered with carriages and the ships with visitors every day since they were in a state to be seen," and they had to move the *Dorothea* and *Trent* further down river to finish equipping them in peace.[11] Jane Griffin also visited the ships, going down into the fo'c'sle to examine the crew's sleeping quarters on the *Isabella*. A young woman named Charlotte Grimstone described how she managed to get on board the *Isabella* by flirting with Parry and was rewarded by watching the Inuit interpreter, Jack Saccheuse, paddling his *qayaq* in the Thames.[12] In 1824, Parry threw a ball aboard the departing HMS *Hecla*, made famous by her two years immured in the ice in Iglulingmiut territory. The Franklins and Richardsons attended, together with 320 others, and more than 6,000 people signed the *Hecla*'s visitor book.[13] The rigging was hung with lanterns and flags, and small parties were taken down to the cramped confines of the captain's cabin to take cake and wine.[14] In the same Season, Jane Griffin and her sisters "joyfully accepted" Franklin's offer to test the new boats for the Second LAE—known as the "Walnut Shells." These were based upon the design of an Inuit *umiaq*, but "Mr. Mackintosh's Prepared Canvas" replaced the seal skin that normally stretched tight over a wooden frame. Franklin later wrote, "So secure was this little vessel that several ladies ... fearlessly embarked in it, and were paddled across the Thames in a fresh breeze."[15] Three years later, in 1827, the newlywed Parrys spent a week on board the *Hecla* at Deptford before she departed for the North Pole, and the Thames obligingly froze around the ship so that Isabella could hear the ice grating along the sides.[16] Arctic delicacies like bison tongue, musk ox steak, reindeer haunch, and pemmican were consumed at dinner parties, introducing young women like Franklin's niece, Mary Anne Kay, to the taste of pemmican. She found it revolting.[17] Her younger sister later remembered, "We used ... to treasure up the remnants of pemmican which reached our house on the return of the Expedition, and I have often tasted it, but always thought it very unpalatable."[18] One imagines that the variety would have appealed to William Buckland, who was famous both for his geological research and for his determination to eat every known animal.[19]

At one of the Season's many gatherings, one might converse with travelers, have the bumps on one's skull "read" by a phrenologist, examine tiny creatures under a microscope, or view the heavens through a telescope.[20] Like her friend Eleanor Porden, Jane Griffin regularly attended Royal Institution lectures, including Michael Faraday's lecture on electricity and magnetism and Peter Mark Roget's on optics. Fascinated by phrenology, Jane had her cranium "read" after she spoke to the mathematician Charles Babbage about it, and once took flight in a hot air balloon. When she was introduced to Captain John Ross at a dinner in 1819, she leapt at his joking suggestion that she accompany him on a voyage to the Bering Strait. Ross replied that "I came 6th upon his list, for that he meant to take 12 young ladies with him."[21] In Edinburgh's winter Season, the scene was somewhat different. Eliza Fletcher (who would later become Richardson's third mother-in-law) reflected that from around 1815, dinner parties gave way to conversational evenings, hosted by either (or both) ladies and professors. Beginning around 9 p.m. and running until at least midnight, a few light refreshments were served along the way, but, she insisted, "people did not in these parties meet to eat, but to talk and listen."[22] Franklin and Richardson loathed such experiences when they returned from the First LAE in 1823, but Parry loved them, writing to his parents in Bath daily about the parties he attended and the acquaintances he made.[23] In London, one might meet Captain Francis Beaufort, who later became the Hydrographer of the Admiralty; the polymath William Whewell; the geologists William and Mary Buckland, Roderick and Charlotte Murchison, Adam Sedgwick, and Charles Lyell; the astronomers John Herschel and Caroline Herschel; the scientists Mary and William Somerville; the mathematicians Henry and Mary Frances Kater; the author Maria Edgeworth; and the traveler, author, and geologist Maria Graham.[24] In Edinburgh, the mixture might include the natural historian Robert Jameson, the botanist William Jackson Hooker, the physicist John Leslie, the anatomist Robert Knox, and several others. These men would shepherd official expeditions and set the agenda for scientific and mathematical research for the first half of the nineteenth century.[25]

This was an environment in which women could enjoy a degree of scientific or literary distinction—so long as they positioned themselves strategically, obtained the sponsorship of a male mentor, and constantly, as Mary Orr has put it, "dressed [their] learning in the modesty of potential female error."[26] Among the inner circles of the Franklins' acquaintances were Sarah Fitton, the sister of the geologist Dr. William Fitton, who wrote anonymous works on botany for women, children, and working-class men.[27] William Herschel's sister Caroline was a very highly respected astronomer, who later in life received a £50 per annum royal pension on account of her work. Mary Frances Kater shared her husband's mathematical pursuits and also published *A History of England* in her own name.[28] Maria Graham was a seasoned traveler and a published author, who both contributed to geological debates (in print but anonymously) and edited narratives of exploration.[29] Charlotte Murchison was a geologist who accompanied her husband Roderick on several of his expeditions (and was better known in some circles as a conchologist than Roderick was as a geologist), while Buckland's wife Mary was also an accomplished geologist. They met in a carriage when they both were reading Baron Georges Cuvier's most recent volume. Mary's was a present from the naturalist himself.[30] Sarah Bowdich Lee, the young widow of the explorer T. E. Bowdich, was also one of Cuvier's close friends and protégées. She would associate with the Franklins for decades (see Chapters 3–5). The Bowdiches had partly funded their own expeditions to the west coast of Africa by Sarah's influential work on taxidermy, designed to help amateurs prepare specimens.[31] She began traveling to Africa in 1816, accompanied by her young children, to join her husband on diplomatic missions to the Asante kingdom until his death in 1824, after which she and her children lived with the Cuviers in Paris. She was in London in the last half of the 1820s, when she began the mammoth project, *The Freshwater Fishes of Great Britain*, a series of books illustrated with her own original paintings (the paints mixed from ground fish scales to preserve their iridescence) which ornamented the libraries of naturalists and dukes.[32]

Within these circles of polite science, both explorers and educated women were constantly negotiating their own credibility, trustworthiness, and authority. Their positioning and self-fashioning were not the same, but they echoed each other. When explorers turned authors, they needed to appear to do so unwillingly, compelled by duty rather than ambition or love of fame.[33] When women engaged in science or geography, they had to profess modesty, ignorance, or inexperience, and then proceed to demonstrate the breadth of their scholarship, whether in conversation or in print.[34] As Carl Thompson has put it, for women in circles of polite science, "pretence of . . . ignorance was a deft rhetorical manoeuvre."[35] It was one of many strategies required to navigate the gendered perils of the public sphere. Mary Somerville, for example, only discussed scientific matters with those whom she thought might have an interest in the subject, and "feared being seen as a bizarre specimen, a bluestocking."[36] Jane Griffin was horrified when, after one of John Millington's lectures on mechanics, his wife came up to her and her sister Fanny to say that they were "very learned—people were frightened at us—we had quite the character of bluestockings." A shocked Jane assured Mrs. Millington that she "had no accomplishments" to speak of.[37]

These fears were not, however, universal. Eleanor Porden, for example, once dressed down a man at the Royal Society who suggested that young women would be better to stay home and make puddings than to attend scientific lectures. She replied, "oh, we did that before we came out."[38] In 1834, Maria Graham was singled out by the president of the Geological Society, George Greenough, as an unreliable eyewitness to a Chilean earthquake (part of his broader attack on Charles Lyell's *Principles of Geology*). She responded to his attacks (which she deplored as being made "through my petticoats") both in print and via intermediaries at the Geological Society, and became part of a long-running argument in circles of polite science. It continued until 1836, when Charles Darwin finally resolved the issue at question (whether or not earthquakes can cause dramatic elevations of land masses) when he observed a similar phenomenon while on board HMS *Beagle*.[39] The women of the Franklin family would learn, forget, and then painfully relearn these lessons over decades.

Society could be equally perilous for explorers, who were expected to seek patronage, curry favor, and put up with being put on display like other tastes, crazes, and fads.[40] William Edward Parry became a nineteenth-century pinup, as engravings of his portrait were collected by young women like Franklin's niece Mary Anne Kay and pasted into scrapbooks.[41] But as flattering as this attention might be, navigating it could be like pirouetting on a seesaw, easy to put a foot wrong, to be made an object of barbed wit rather than admiring conversation. Explorers seeking to establish their credibility were particularly vulnerable, first because they were naval officers (many of whom came from humble backgrounds—Franklin was the son of a linen draper), second because they had no formal education beyond what they had gleaned at the midshipmen's berth, and third because the whole source of their fame lay in their experiences beyond the pale. Author Mary Russell Mitford mocked John Ross in a letter to one of her friends after his failed 1818 expedition, writing, "He a discoverer, forsooth! All that he did was to go about christening rocks, capes, bays, and mountains after all the great men, dead and living, whom he thought to gain by, and then to come home and write a huge quarto about nothing."[42] John Richardson's brother Peter visited him in London in 1828 and kept a journal about the Season's activities, including the observation that "Capt Franklin has named two mountains, one after Professor Buckland a stout short man & the other after Copplestone a tall thin man—Copplestone on being told this said they ought to have been called Copplestone Crag & Bucklands Bluff."[43] William Scoresby was still employed as a whaling captain when he began circulating in Edinburgh's scientific scene under Robert Jameson's patronage. He was nearly paralyzed with anxiety when he attended a scientific soiree, reflecting that "my introduction into a party consisting of scientific men of eminence, with accomplished and intelligent women [was] at first inconceivably painful." But presently, he found the society much more welcoming to someone with his peculiar set of experiences, for "the free and encouraging manner of the professor and his friends, however, and the frankness of the ladies, soon dissipated every painful feeling, and enabled me at length to enjoy the uncommon treat that such a party presented."[44]

Arctic officers had spent their adolescence aboard ships in wartime—experiences that had taught them seamanship, navigation, instrumentation, and observation, but not how to write. As Parry wrote to his parents in 1820, after he returned from his furthest trip west to Melville Island, "though I can write a tolerable Manuscript Journal, I begin to feel that a life spent at sea since 12 years of age does not qualify one altogether to write such an account as the public expect in print."[45] Women helped compose and correct their narratives. Franklin and Richardson drew on Eleanor Franklin's assistance when revising the third edition of *Journey to the Polar Sea* and expected her help with the next (see Chapter 1). After Eleanor's death in 1825, Mary Anne Kay helped Franklin prepare the narrative of the second expedition, making clean copies of pages, correcting appendices, and managing his (evidently chaotic) library, all packed away in trunks that she supervised.[46] Explorers also sought an education from their polite and learned acquaintances. Before his second expedition in 1819, for example, Parry attended a course of lectures on mineralogy given by Rebecca Lowry, the wife of a famous engraver. He wrote to his parents that his Arctic companion, the astronomer Edward Sabine, was also attending, and later asked his parents to send Mrs. Lowry some of his mineral specimens, as "I am deriving very great advantage from her lectures which I attend regularly three times a week."[47]

Some Arctic explorers also sought connections of conscience among the Evangelical and humanitarian movements. The development of scientific and humanitarian networks went hand in hand and was part of a broader set of complex relationships between science, medicine, religion, and reform in Britain and its empire in the early nineteenth century.[48] There were several trajectories that brought explorers and humanitarians together. The first and simplest was geography—they moved in the same circles and they lived alongside each other. Thomas Fowell Buxton, for example, was William Wilberforce's designated successor to the antislavery cause. He was also Franklin's neighbor in 1828.[49] The second stemmed from conviction. The experiences of profound isolation, intense cold, otherworldly landscapes, extremes of light and dark, and physical suffering all worked on men's minds and shifted their understandings of the relationships between themselves, the environment, the divine, and their fellow men. Their reflections in their narratives, together with expedition artwork, gave rise to a popular phenomenon later dubbed the Arctic Sublime. Visitors flocked to exhibitions, panoramas, and theatrical productions that sought to recreate the sense of human frailty against pitiless, beautiful Nature.[50] Like Franklin and Richardson, Parry and Scoresby also had profound religious experiences on their Arctic voyages. Scoresby gave up the sea and became a minister, publishing the sermons he wrote for his whaling crews, which were used by Arctic navigators for years to come.[51] They all saw Arctic expeditions as spaces for personal and social reform, particularly because they feared what might happen when seamen were "secluded for an uncertain and indefinite period form the rest of the world; having little or no employment ... and subject to a degree of tedious monotony."[52] Convinced that both scurvy and "vice" (specifically homosexuality) flourished alongside depression and inactivity, Parry established a program of "rational and useful occupation" on board the *Fury* and *Hecla* in 1821–3, including schools run by literate seamen, plays performed by officers, lectures on improving subjects (illustrated with glass lantern slides donated by "a lady"), regular exercise in the open air, and excursions to nearby Inuit settlements.[53] Parry would boast for years that every man who went to sea with him could read his Bible when he came home.[54]

Programs of Arctic spiritual and moral reform echoed those of humanitarians directed toward convicts, slaves, Indigenous people, and the poor. Sparked first by the antislavery and emancipation movements, Evangelicals and humanitarians sought to ameliorate, convert, civilize, domesticate, and improve "heathen peoples" from industrial Lancashire to the West Indies to Van Diemen's Land. Many were nonconformists or Dissenters who believed not only that they could make themselves anew in their relationship to Christ but that they also bore a responsibility to civilize their fellow men and women.[55] The Buxton, Fry, and Gurney families were at the center of these circles, maintaining elaborate and far-flung correspondence networks throughout the empire.[56] They were deeply involved in antislavery and philanthropic networks, and Buxton's sister Sarah Maria, daughter Priscilla, and cousin Anna Gurney were very active in the 1820s and 1830s (see Chapter 3).[57] In 1817, Elizabeth Fry set up a school for the female prisoners' children in Newgate Prison, sparking a larger and longer project of moral reform of convict women through religious readings and industrious labor.[58] Humanitarianism as a political movement did not only allow but also depended upon women's participation in the public sphere as petitioners, subscribers, audiences, writers, and patrons, justified as a matter of womanly and maternal conscience.[59] These humanitarian men and women also found a home in circles of scientific sociability, in which religious Dissenters and nonconformists could engage in the public sphere prior to the abolition of the Test and Corporation Acts in 1828.[60]

In time, humanitarians and Evangelicals would occupy key positions in the Colonial Office and so directly influence the careers of Arctic men in the colonies (see Chapter 3). But in the 1820s, these men and women were just beginning to develop social, emotional, and religious attachments to each other. For some, it began with their reading in the field. Franklin had been so impressed with the writing of Wilberforce that he read during the First LAE that he named Wilberforce Falls after him. For others, it happened in London, often at Newgate Prison. Visiting the prison became one of many outings for respectable women during the Season. Some found it elevating, like the Edinburgh radical Eliza Fletcher and her daughter Mary. They visited Fry at the women's prison in 1820, accompanied by the socialist Robert Owen, and were struck by how "her sympathy and kindness did them good."[61] Jane Griffin was less impressed. When she visited Newgate in 1822, she thought that "the few words [Mrs. Fry] uttered could not ... have produced any kind of impression on them & I was convinced that she must have used at other times much more effectual methods ... in order to have made them as decent & well-behaved as we saw them."[62]

Parry, on the other hand, was smitten with Fry and felt her work with convicts echoed his own with sailors. After he returned from Igloolik in 1823, and amid the controversy over his romantic attachments at Igloolik (see below), Parry went to Norfolk and renewed his connections both with the Gurneys and Cresswells. He thought Fry and her daughters were "the most delightful women I almost ever met with," and they compared notes on programs of "improvement" during isolation and incarceration.[63] But Parry's fondness for Fry nearly wrecked the prospect of his marriage to Isabella

Stanley, the daughter of the formidable Lady Maria Stanley. In 1827, Parry wrote to his sister that Lady Maria "has been trying to scold me out of my religious sentiment, and informing me of her utter abhorrence of 'Mrs Fry and all saints.'" He reassured his sister that the reason was most likely that Lady Maria was "a very worldly woman," who was, it later transpired, also ill at ease about Parry's treatment of both British and Inuit women.[64] The marriage did come off, and Parry maintained his relationships with the Frys, Gurneys, and Cresswells. When he and Isabella set off for New South Wales in 1828 to work for the Australian Agricultural Company, they continued to correspond with the Frys and Gurneys about their attempts to "improve" both convicts and Indigenous people.[65]

Women and men, intellectuals and explorers, travelers and authors, wits and reformers were all fixtures of polite science in metropolitan Britain in the 1820s. It was a vital sphere for making useful and enduring connections, but it was also a perilous one. Quests for authority and attempts at self-fashioning for both men and women happened in tandem, and in the Franklin family would do so for years to come. Women not only facilitated connections by hosting parties; they also gave lectures, published books, collected specimens, experimented, observed, traveled, drew, wrote, and argued, filling gaps in explorers' educations and perhaps shaping and refining their understandings.

"Miss Ilugliuk's Hydrographical Tact," or, Intermediaries at the Dinner Table

In April 1824, John and Eleanor Franklin held a dinner party for William Edward Parry and George Francis Lyon, who had just returned from two years immured in the ice around Melville Peninsula and Repulse Bay. Jane Griffin and her sister Fanny attended, and when they sat down to dinner, Parry asked Lyon to reach under the table and show Fanny his arm, which had been tattooed by Iglulingmiut women the previous year.[66] It was a charged moment. Tattoos were maps on sailors' bodies, physical marks of their journeys to strange places, conjuring the moment of closeness, curiosity, and intimacy in which they were made (Figure 2.1).[67] This was certainly the case with Lyon's tattoo, for it had been inscribed at Igloolik as Parry's expedition drew heavily on Inuit resources, including the geographical knowledge and sexual companionship of Inuit women. As Lyon pulled up his sleeve and showed the unmarried Fanny his naked arm under the table, she and Jane were thinking about those intimacies, which had been one of the favorite topics of conversation the previous year. Jane observed that Parry "seems far from light-hearted and exhibits traces of heartfelt and recent suffering." Fanny made oblique references to how excited he and his men must be when they came within range of shore, and began thinking about those waiting for them.[68] It echoed one of the final scenes of *Persuasion*, when Anne Elliott and Captain Harville argue about whose constancy is greater, the man at sea or the woman on shore. Perhaps it was meant to; after all, both *Persuasion* and Porden's *The Arctic Expeditions* had been published by John Murray in 1818. The observation also referred to Parry's broken

Figure 2.1 George Francis Lyon, "Interior of an Eskimaux snow-hut, Winter Island, 1822," Lyon sketched a number of intimate scenes during the time that HMS *Hecla* and *Fury* spent alongside Iglulingmiut settlements between 1821 and 1823. His own tattoos would have been made in the same way as the traditional tattoos on this woman's face. In W. F. Parry, *Journal of a Second Voyage for the Discovery of a North-West Passage* . . . (London: John Murray, 1824), sourced from Wikimedia Commons.

engagement with Miss Browne (Captain Edward Sabine's niece), a breach of promise entangled with his use of Inuit geographical knowledge provided by the Iglulingmiut woman, Iligjaq. Both at home and as they circulated in society, explorers' wives, families, and friends were constantly negotiating with the presence, real and imagined, of Indigenous intermediaries. Eleanor Porden had not been alone in her attempts to reconcile explorers' companionships, constancy, credibility, and lingering obligations and attachments (see Chapter 1). The intimacies of the field were also the subject of wider inquiry, interest, and intrigue, particularly as both narratives and stories about expeditions and encounters were consumed.

Sabine and Parry had become close friends on John Ross's first expedition, united in their frustration with Ross and particularly his decision to turn his ships around in Lancaster Sound when he saw a mirage that he named the "Croker Mountains." They had shipped out again together in 1819 in HMS *Hecla* under Parry's command, making it as far as Melville Island. Just before they left, Parry began courting Sabine's niece Miss Browne, inviting her on board HMS *Hecla* for the ship's ball and later taking her and her parents on a rowboat and a picnic at Greenwich where he persuaded her to inflate his life-vest.[69] They became engaged before he departed for his second expedition in 1821. Within months, *Hecla* and *Fury* were frozen up in what is now called Hecla and Fury Strait—a narrow channel between the Melville Peninsula and Baffin Island. They felt themselves to be at the ends of the earth, and perhaps on the threshold of the Northwest Passage. They were wrong in one respect and right in another, for they had frozen up between the Inuit settlements of Igloolik and Aivilik, held to be the "cultural epicentre for the Inuit people."[70]

If Parry had had access to Franklin's journal, he would have read Tattannoeuck/Augustus's account of the far-flung trading networks, maintained through a series of regional fairs at specific locations, that linked his home territory near Churchill with these eastern Inuit.[71] Goods and information were exchanged at these fairs.[72] This included information about Dene and Cree people to the south, and *qallunaat* traders and whalers who were pushing deeper into Cumberland and Lancaster Sounds from Davis Strait. Gathering places on Baffin Island, such as Mittimatalik/Pond Inlet and Admiralty Inlet, were becoming places for trade with whalers. By the end of the nineteenth century, Inuit would be enmeshed in a trade economy they could no longer control.[73] But that was still a long way off, and at this time, Inuit trading practices would structure the lives of the crews of the *Fury* and *Hecla*. The ships became a new trading site, as Parry and Lyon took a role that Franklin had refused at Fort Enterprise—acting as hosts and supplying provisions to women and children. Starvation occurred in other parts of the territory during the dreadful years of 1820–2, but around the *Fury* and *Hecla*, it was kept at bay.[74] There were friendly exchanges of music, dance, and information on all sides, which allowed Inuit to gather information about both *qallunaat* and strange Inuit beyond their territories. A teenage boy named Toolooak sketched the officers, Inuit, and animals, while others taught James Clark Ross, Francis Crozier, Parry, Lyon, and William Hooper how to drive dogs, build snow houses, and hunt seal.

Over these winters, Parry formed a relationship with Toolooak's sister, Iligjaq. Years later, as he reflected on the controversy that followed, he wrote to his brother that no matter where he went in the world, he always "felt a desire to be <u>attached somewhere</u>," and "contrived to fancy myself in love with some virtuous woman."[75] In his narrative, he described Iligjaq as a woman with a "superiority of understanding," a love of music, and a fine voice.[76] He seems to have understood the relationship as consensual (so did his officers) and it is possible that Iligjaq and her husband understood it as a spousal exchange, an important cultural practice that cemented trading partnerships and established enduring links of trust and reciprocity.[77] Iligjaq's geographical knowledge became one of the expedition's signature features. In March 1822, Parry asked Iligjaq to draw the coastline to the north and west of where the *Fury* and *Hecla* were stuck.

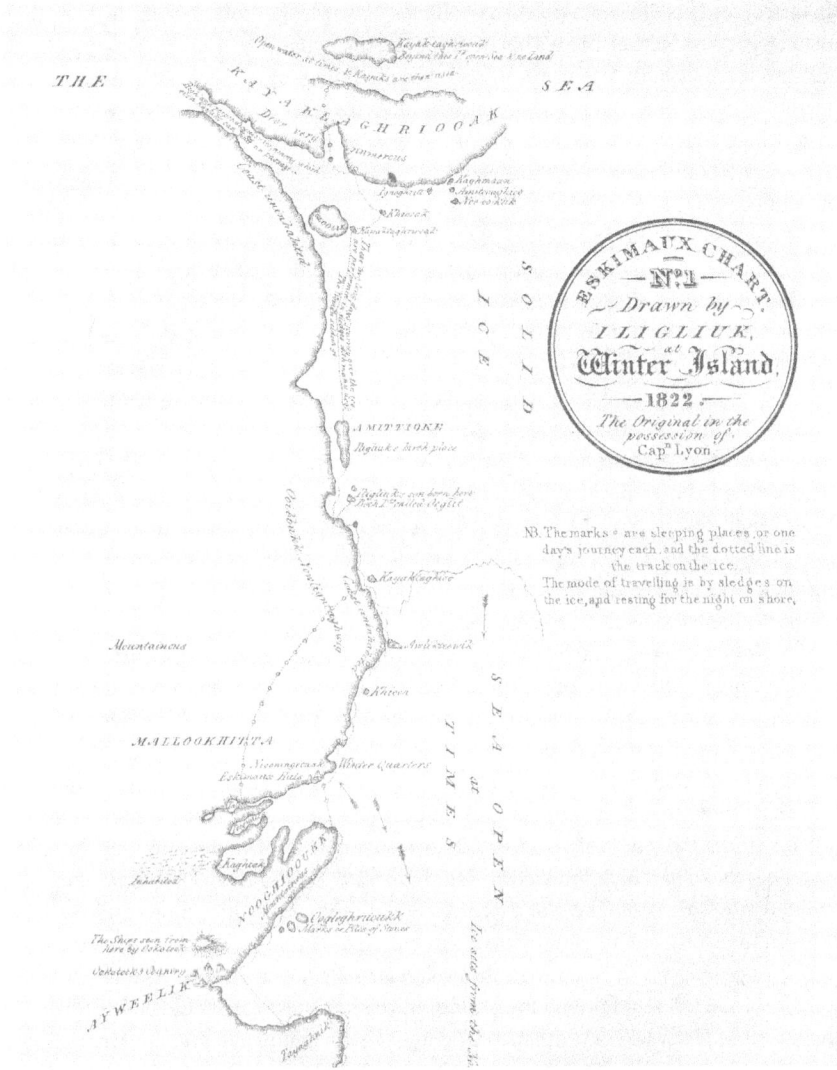

Figure 2.2 Iligjaq, map drawn at Winter Island, 1822. From W. E. Parry, *Journal of a Second Voyage for the Discovery of a North-West Passage* . . . (London: John Murray, 1824) image courtesy Wikimedia Commons.

She drew a detailed map over several sheets of paper, noting where the coast was inhabited, where game could be procured, where she and her son were born (Figure 2.2). It was a paper record of her gendered geographical knowledge, a country that she knew intimately, yet differently from men who were hunters. Iligjaq took a memorized and animate landscape, both human and more-than-human, and translated it into a cartographic projection.[78] Her listeners, who only partially understood her, annotated the map, and inscribed it with an Inuktitut compass rose.[79] Michael Bravo has argued that Parry and his officers tried to make Iligjaq's knowledge "commensurate" with their own, as they edited her map. They focused on the usual extent of the new winter ice and the ice that held fast to the shore, the directions of currents, the strength and heights of tides, and, most important for them, a great expanse of open water to the west, which they took to be the opening of the Northwest Passage.[80] Parry published Iligjaq's charts in his narrative and would insist for decades on the unfailing accuracy of Inuit geographical knowledge (see Chapter 4).

At the end of the winter of 1823, relationships at Winter Island soured. The expedition's demands had become importunate, and neither the region nor the Iglulingmiut could sustain them any longer. Iglulingmiut only expected a particular site to sustain a small band for three winters, and never anticipated the demands of hundreds of mouths on two discovery ships.[81] Parry, Lyon, and Lt. W. H. Hooper wrote that the Iglulingmiut became irritable, sullen, and prone to thieving as the winter of 1822–3 progressed, culminating in the theft of a shovel from the *Hecla*. Thefts of this kind were often understood by Inuit as a way to assert authority, but Parry responded by asserting his own naval authority and flogging the man.[82] While Parry interpreted the shocked reaction of the assembled Inuit as a sign of subordination, it may have been a sign of *ilira*, the vulnerability and fear felt in the presence of abusive and unpredictable people, the feeling that it is better to yield than to engage in conflict. As Karen Routledge puts it, "The emotional state of *ilirasuktuq* is part of the reason that Inuit so often obeyed intolerable requests from colonial authority figures."[83] It may also have been *isuma*, the counterpart of *ilira*, an expression of emotional detachment and restraint that creates a space for rational thought.[84] It may have been neither, and a response that it is not possible for an historian and an outsider to understand. But it appears that both these responses were common features of Inuit-*qallunaat* meetings, though seldom understood by outsiders as anything but compliance, and not as a studied way to avoid conflict. There were many local stories about the incident, including those in which the victim was an *angekok* (shaman) and the *qallunaat* were trying to steal his wife. The *qallunaat* tried to kill him, tying him down and trying to chop off his limbs, but no blow could harm him. In retribution, the shaman sent a spirit to chew up or crush the ship, and the *qallunaat* sailed away in fear. As a result, ships were forbidden to visit Igloolik for a hundred years.[85] These stories linked the arrival of the *Fury* and *Hecla* with a fundamental change in the region as *qallunaat* arrived more often on its fringes. They did not, however, return to Igloolik for nearly a century.[86]

When Parry returned to Britain in 1823, he discovered that Miss Browne had broken off their engagement. While Parry was celebrated as a polar hero, both he and Miss Browne were also exposed to ridicule.[87] A humiliating rhyme made the rounds in Bath and London, which ran, "Parry, why that distracted air? Why for a jilt so cast down? None but the *Brave* deserve the *Fair*, but *Any One* may have *the Brown*."[88] The play on Miss Browne's name also referred to Inuit complexions, of course. Miss Browne's mother retaliated by saying that Parry was the jilt, and rumors of his faithlessness circulated amid accounts of his relationship with Iligjaq and the evidence of her maps.[89] Thomas Hood published an "Ode to Captain Parry" entreating him not to forsake English beauties for a "Polar Mrs. Parry," and conjured developing stereotypes of Inuit as a filthy and thieving people:

To dote on hair, an oily fleece!
As tho' it hung from Helen o' Greece—
  They say that love prevails
  Ev'n in the veriest polar land—
And surely she may steal thy hand
  That used to steal thy nails![90]

William Henry Glascock mocked Parry's reliance on "Miss Ilugliuk's hydrographical tact" in a book, *The Naval Sketchbook*, which offered a broader condemnation of explorers' use of Indigenous geographical knowledge, particularly in the Arctic.[91] George Lyon's wife, Lucy, privately described the book as libelous, but nevertheless "cannot but say how excellent it is."[92] Meanwhile, Sabine and Parry's friendship faltered and would not be mended for more than a decade.[93]

Stories of the invented love triangle between Iligjaq, Parry, and Miss Browne continued to circulate in society for years. As Jane Griffin recorded, it was very much a topic of conversation at Arctic soirees in 1824, with Miss Browne's name still juxtaposed with the tattoos inscribed at Igloolik. In 1826, Parry's prospective mother-in-law, Lady Maria Stanley, counted his relationships with Iligjaq, Miss Browne, and Elizabeth Fry among her many objections to her daughter's marriage.[94] Around the same time, an anonymous woman published a little book for children entitled *A Peep at the Esquimaux*, in which Inuit children set moral examples for spoiled English children, as they cheerfully embraced a modest life in the ice.[95] The polar historian Ann Savours suspected that the anonymous author was Lucy Lyon, though it might have been one of her contemporaries.[96] The book distilled ethnographic information from the expedition into several pages of verse, illustrated by her husband's drawings. It was followed by a "Polar Pastoral," which was attributed to a "Friend of the Authoress" who claimed to have overheard an argument between an Inuk man and woman, caused by the arrival of discovery ships, their trade goods, and their sailors. Sprinkled throughout with words and phrases of Inuktitut, it concluded with a message of thanks to those Inuit who sheltered wet and shivering explorers.[97]

It is tempting to rank *A Peep at the Esquimaux* alongside Eleanor Porden's ventriloquist "Miss Greenstockings" poem, though they were aimed at very different audiences. Both may have represented women's attempts to wrestle with the consequences of men's attachments in the field, the obligations they had undertaken, the ways in which they had allowed themselves to become beholden, and the degrees to which they could be trusted in future. Both conjured the presence of Indigenous women within the British home and family, and both questioned explorers' trustworthiness as men, while they asserted their own authority as women to interpret and comment on those relationships, in the context of their own ethnographic and intimate assessments.

When explorers returned to Britain, the relationships formed in the field could follow them and demand entry to their social circles. Traders could expect a degree of patronage from men like Franklin and Richardson, for introductions to society were understood as a small return for the support given in the field. Not everyone, however, shared the same understanding. While explorers needed social capital and patronage both in Britain and in the fur trade countries, they were not necessarily always willing to reciprocate. It is worthwhile examining how Franklin and Richardson dealt with two fur traders, Robert McVicar and Peter Warren Dease, in the London social scene, how their interests aligned to broader Arctic geopolitical tensions, and how both patronage and politics dovetailed with family life in Britain and in the fur trade countries.

Robert McVicar had left Islay for York Factory when he was thirteen, and by his mid-twenties had become Chief Factor at Fort Resolution on Great Slave Lake.[98] He had looked after Franklin, Richardson, Hepburn, and Back while they recuperated in 1822 after the ordeal of the First LAE. In 1824, he was on leave in London. Franklin and Richardson both met with him, introduced him to their wives, and offered to show him "the lions of London." Richardson also begged him for the Cree and Northern Indian names for a number of animals he was describing for Parry's narrative.[99] It was only a few short months after the rumors from Great Slave Lake had caused Franklin and Richardson to reconsider their account of Michel Teroahaute's death for the second edition of *Narrative of a Journey to the Polar Sea* (see Chapter 1). Now Franklin was planning a second expedition and was keenly aware of how desperately he needed McVicar's patronage—both in the newly united Hudson's Bay Company (HBC) and in the increasingly unstable area around Great Slave Lake, where conflict between the Yellowknives and Dog Ribs had reached a crisis. McVicar's presence in London and Edinburgh may have turned the tide for the second expedition, not only reordering how it was planned and conducted but also reestablishing the officers' trustworthiness among Arctic circles in North America.

In 1823, the Dog Ribs annihilated the band of Yellowknives led by Long Legs, a severe blow that led both to the decline of Yellowknife power around Great Slave Lake and later to a significant peace treaty between Akaitcho and the Dog Rib leader Edzo that united the two tribes.[100] At the same time, Inuvialuit at the mouth of the Mackenzie River had been indicating their willingness to engage in trade with *qallunaat* to the south. These constituted major shifts in an already destabilized region. Meanwhile, the British were very anxious about Russian exploration and expansion. After the HBC had merged with the North West Company (NWC) in 1821, the Russian American Company (RAC) was also reorganized, and turned its attention to the Alaskan interior, which placed it in direct competition with the HBC in some locations.[101] Then in November 1823, the Russian admiral and Arctic explorer Ivan von Krusenstern told John Barrow about a new Russian attempt on the Northwest Passage. In response, Franklin, Richardson, and Parry began agitating for a new series of British overland and maritime expeditions to chart the passage from the west, the east, and overland. Franklin argued that supporting these expeditions was in the HBC's interest, particularly as they would be able to assess Russian infiltration of Indigenous trading networks.[102] Together with Richardson, Hepburn, and McVicar, they developed a plan for the Second LAE. Mary Richardson was "very averse" to it, but Richardson hoped that "she will be brought to consider the business more calmly in a short time."[103]

If Eleanor Franklin was as troubled as Mary Richardson by the idea of her husband departing again for the Barren Grounds, she did not show it. While recuperating from pregnancy, nursing a newborn, and coughing up blood, Eleanor managed an important traffic in information as both the Franklin and Richardson homes became staging grounds for the expedition. In August 1824, the Franklins visited the Richardsons at

Chatham with their two-month-old baby. Eleanor wrote to her sister Sarah Kay that when they were making meridian observations, they "had to dislodge Miss Baby from her sky-parlour at rather a crucial juncture, because the sun would not wait for them."[104] Back at home, Eleanor sewed a silken flag to be unfurled on the polar sea and oversaw ladies' donations of books for the traveling library. Some, she declared, were "a mass of Calvinistic verbiage which I should be sorry to prostitute my reason or taste in the perusal of." Others she described to be "fitter to be under a glass case in a drawing room with pet china and essences, than to toss about among the Esquimaux."[105] When several officers came to the house to try to get a place on the expedition, she wrote to Franklin, "I wish you would come home and do your own business, for I feel it very ridiculous to have all these gentlemen coming to me to try the effect of petticoat influence."[106]

Eleanor's correspondence indicates that she knew about the details of supplies, engagements of men, and the disposition of the HBC.[107] She inspected the boats designed by John Hepburn at Woolwich, which she described to Franklin's sister Elizabeth as "varnished and adorned with blue and gold, and painted with all sorts of mythological devices," which she speculated would "make the Indians wonder at the strange beasts we have in our country."[108] She wrote to Franklin's sister Isabella Cracroft in February 1824 to assure her, "there is no danger of his again encountering the sufferings of his last journey." She explained how the HBC trader Peter Warren Dease had been sent ahead to build the forts and establish supplies, and how others in the HBC "have their interest now so much involved in the success of the Expedition that there can be no doubt of their . . . complete support."[109] Eight months later, she wrote to her sister Sarah Kay and gave her a digest of the information contained in Franklin's northern correspondence, and optimistically concluded, "As far as human prudence can foresee or provide, all seems most auspicious."[110]

Peter Warren Dease's support was crucial in reassuring both the Franklin family and the fur traders that the Second LAE was better planned than the first. He had spent twenty years with the NWC in the Athabasca and Mackenzie River districts, becoming a chief trader during the merger of the companies. He had trading and kinship connections across multiple Indigenous groups, including the Yellowknives Dene (Akaitcho had proposed him as an alternative intermediary to Wentzel on Franklin's first expedition). In early 1824, probably at McVicar's suggestion, Franklin hired Dease to build the expedition's forward base, Fort Franklin, on Great Bear Lake, where he established a winter fishery, built up supplies, engaged and actually paid Dene hunters and an interpreter.[111] When McVicar returned to Canada in 1824, he personally took the expedition's canoes to Fort Chipewyan, along with a bundle of letters from Franklin addressed to HBC officials. These cast the expedition as a commercial, rather than geographical, venture, pointing out that "it is expected the encroachment of the Russian Fur Traders towards your posts will be prevented."[112] When McVicar delivered the letters, he was able to explain how he and Dease had advised Franklin from the earliest stages. According to Franklin, Dease and McVicar helped broker the truce between Akaitcho and Edzo, though Dog Rib oral tradition recognizes several other Indigenous intermediaries who were involved.[113]

The effort paid off, as HBC officials wrote to Franklin to congratulate him on his prudence. Two years before, they had been in the midst of swirling rumors about the secrets of his expedition, but Dease's involvement laid their lingering concerns to rest. In August 1824, the governor of the new Northern Department, George Simpson, wrote to Franklin from York Factory "There is but one feeling towards yourself . . . in this Country, that of the highest respect, regard, and esteem," and that the expedition was considered "so important both in a political and Commercial point of view . . . that we are all anxious to meet your views, and to render you our most cordial assistance and support."[114] He also entreated Franklin, "do not part with Mr. Dease under any circumstances," not only because he could help the expedition "in trying or distressing circumstances" but also because "his presence would . . . give a confidence to the people which that of strangers to the country cannot inspire."[115] Chief Factor Edward Smith wrote to Franklin that Dease was "well acquainted with the nature of the Country and its natives," while Chief Factor George McTavish wrote from York Factory, "I cannot help congratulating you upon the judicious choice you made . . . his experience, local knowledge . . . the equanimity of his temper, added to gentell [sic] unassuming manners, point him out as by far the most suitable character for your purposes."[116]

Dease's wife Elizabeth was also crucial to the expedition's comfort, survival, and collections. She and the other Indigenous women not only made the expedition's shoes and clothing but also gathered and prepared faunal specimens for Richardson long before he even arrived in the country. (Franklin noted in one letter that "the women know how to stuff them too well to need description from me.")[117] They also made the birch boxes to transport the specimens and were paid in red cloth, a highly valued commodity.[118] Franklin ensured that Dease and other expedition members brought their families to Fort Franklin so that the women could make the shoes and clothing for the expedition.[119] In some cases, they arranged this before they left. In the Orkney Islands, there was a growing population of mixed-race families whose fathers decided to send their sons "home" to be educated, especially after the merger of the companies in 1821.[120] In 1824, Lyon requested the Admiralty to arrange for "24 pairs of snow shoes to be made at the Orkneys by Indian Women who are there."[121]

But when it came to Dease's reward, things were rather different. When the expedition returned in 1827, it was a qualified success. Although it did not find the passage, it had charted a great deal of the northern coast of North America, and only a few men had died. The traders apparently expected that Franklin would reciprocate Dease's patronage, and there was a widespread feeling that Franklin ought to take him to Britain at the end of the expedition at his own expense and there, as Franklin wrote to Back, "to have introduced him most particularly to the Committee and generally to the public—Then they thought his promotion would be ensured!"[122] Though this was exactly what he had done with McVicar three years earlier, Franklin declined to do so for Dease. He explained that he, too, was seeking patronage and could scarcely be Dease's patron, though he did promise to speak well of him in his official report and in his meetings with Governor Simpson and the HBC Council. Dease was effectively left to look after his own interests.

Franklin's snub of Dease may have rested partly on his status as a métis man, and partly on his marriage. Ambitious company men like Simpson and McVicar were beginning to see "country wives" as professional impediments and began to abandon their Indigenous partners in favor of British kinship and friendship ties.[123] However, this too had its problems. European brides were prestigious but were also viewed as impractical, unskilled encumbrances.[124] This was certainly the case with McVicar, who met the teenage Chrissy MacBeath at Norway House as he was en route with the LAE's canoes. They exchanged vows and he took her with him to Great Slave Lake; Franklin married them legally in 1827 at Fort Chipewyan.[125] Privately, Richardson and Franklin were dubious about whether she was a help or a hindrance. Richardson wrote to Franklin, "I am afraid that the additional load of a wife of no light weight will not increase his speed" with their canoes.[126]

Dease did still make his appearance in the social scenes of London—but only as a joke. One Sunday evening not long after his return, Richardson mentioned that Dease had been praising Englishwomen in front of his wife Elizabeth, "not aware she understood him she attacked him furiously and gave him a good cuffing for giving them the preference."[127] The incident appears in the journal of John Richardson's brother Peter, who was staying with his brother in London. It was not recorded as a private conversation, but as an amusing anecdote at a Sunday evening soiree at the Fittons' home, to which Buckland, Sabine, Brown, Lyell, Murchison, and John Griffin were invited along with Franklin, the Richardson brothers, and, of course, their wives, daughters, and relatives. Peter Richardson also recorded how, two weeks earlier, Mary Anne Kay played *voyageur* songs, recently transcribed by George Back, on the piano while the inebriated Franklin, Richardson, and Back seized poker and tongs from the fireplace and paddled an imaginary canoe around the room, to the delight of the company.[128] For Peter Richardson, the Dease story was just one of many amusing tales from his sojourn in London. But it was also an opportunity for the women of the party to publicly think about, talk about, and process all those experiences, obligations, and debts, both known and imagined. When explorers were present, those discussions might be sparked—or laid to rest—by tattoos, songs, and stories. But when explorers were absent, the focus shifted to those left behind, to their intimates and the information they possessed. Women became intermediaries themselves, acting as gatekeepers of information, and asserting their relatives' credibility at the same time as their own.

Souvenirs, Specimens, and Correspondence: Families as Intermediaries

Iroquois dolls, raccoon hearthrugs, and Dene moccasins were only three examples of the collections that filled explorers' homes and circulated in society. The Parrys' home was crammed with Inuit legacies, including objects and art now in the collections of the British Museum and the Scott Polar Research Institute, alongside material gathered during their time in New South Wales.[129] From the Second LAE, Edward Kendall sent his mother an Inuit parka, later asking her to "write to Uncle Buller and say that I shall feel much obliged to him if he will pack up the Esquimaux fur woman's jacket and send it to Dr Tract" at the Liverpool Institution, for "he is one of the Astronomical Society to which I hope to belong on my return and it may get me a vote."[130] Despite her poverty, the widowed Sarah Bowdich Lee held onto the golden Asante ritual objects that she and her first husband had collected in West Africa in 1817. They were only donated to the British Museum a year before her death in 1856.[131] The Franklins' homes in Tasmania and London were always remarked upon for their strange, confronting arrays of ethnographic objects, portraits of explorers, maps, libraries, and casts of human heads (see Chapter 3). While their collections were sold and split up at least twice, as late as the 1860s, visitors remarked upon the portraits and collections crammed into the elderly Jane Franklin's tiny dining room. They were later bequeathed to the National Portrait Gallery.[132]

The specimens, objects, and artwork were displayed in explorers' homes by their families, but their archives were the real gold mines. For explorers and their families, correspondence sustained fragile relationships over immense distances and uncertain times—what Elizabeth Vibert has called the "cold space of empire."[133] Letters from the other side of the world created a private, intimate space that juxtaposed the familiar and strange, safe and dangerous, comfortable and strenuous. Circles of polite science craved these letters, both for their ring of authenticity and for information that would not be public until the narrative was published. Under these circumstances, families became important gatekeepers of information, nodes in a broader web of scientific and imperial knowledge, and agents in establishing explorers' trustworthiness and credibility. They were, in effect, intermediaries between the field and influential "friends" at home. Presents, souvenirs, and mementos sent home for amusement and diversion were distributed through social circles and networks, like Uncle Buller sending the Inuit parka to Dr. Tract in Liverpool. The traffic went both ways, as relatives sent news, gossip, books, mittens, and marmalade to men in the field. These practices ultimately produced key archives of exploration, as families later donated letters and artifacts to institutions. But they also did the work of downplaying the importance of other intermediaries upon whom explorers depended in the field. In this way, explorers' correspondence with their families might be seen as an attempt to reconcile what Dane Kennedy has called the "epistemological rupture" between the chaotic experiences of the explorer in the field and the armchair geographer's rational study, or "cabinet," in Britain—a crucial step, in other words, in the making of imperial knowledge.[134]

The families of an island nation and a maritime empire had been "gatekeepers" of information long before the Arctic expeditions began. For at least two hundred years, women had acted as intermediaries between the ship and shore, whether in the merchant fleet, deep sea and whaling fisheries, or the Royal Navy.[135] During men's prolonged absences, many women—wives, mistresses, girlfriends, even publicans—were given powers of attorney, which they were not always keen to relinquish.[136] A traffic in information accompanied control over financial and legal matters. On both sides of the Atlantic, naval wives and whalers' wives received information from long-absent men, including their planned routes, the movements of the fleet, disagreements among the crew, and other matters, which they might (or might not) share with the ship's owners, other officers, or the Admiralty.[137] In the 1820s, this feature of the early modern maritime world articulated with the circles of polite science and the broader capillary system of the nineteenth-century information order—the correspondence networks that spread knowledge and sustained relationships. Recent work has illuminated the vital role that women played in maintaining these networks, both in their own rights as reformers, naturalists, writers, and artists and as amanuenses, editors, collectors, and illustrators for the men in their lives. The abolitionist and humanitarian work of the Buxton and Gurney women has received particular attention, as has the work of Darwin's female correspondents.[138] In both cases, women's authority over information both rested on and was limited by their gender, and their trade in knowledge and specimens always needed to remain within the bounds of propriety.

Most of the letters sent to explorers by their families do not survive, and their contents have to be inferred from explorers' notes and replies. Extracts of some of Mary Anne Kay's letters, however, give a tantalizing glimpse into how the seventeen-year-old acted as her Uncle Franklin's intermediary in the naval hub of Greenwich. Scientists and naval officers visited her at home, and asked her to include excerpts of book reviews and accounts of experiments in her letters, which she combined with summaries of her own reading and notes on lectures that she attended.[139] She scrupulously reported on the latest news of the Herschels, the Astronomical Society, the Royal Observatory, the court-martial of a fellow Arctic explorer, Parry's debut as the Hydrographer of the Navy, and her own recent expedition prospecting for fossils at Folkestone.[140] At Greenwich, she inspected departing discovery ships bound for Australia and passed judgment on them. She also passed on gossip, describing Parry's proposed expedition to the North Pole as "a six months trip founded in all essential points on a plan of yours laid down I believe in 1819," and noting that the general opinion in Greenwich was that success was doubtful, for "he is grown enormously fat (of which he had no need) and has suffered a good deal with his head."[141] As she built a reputation as a young woman of taste, accomplishments, and connections, she gathered and circulated information on her uncle's behalf.

Correspondence from home, via canoe, snowshoe, or whaleship, kept explorers informed about matters crucial to their interests. Like Mary Anne, relatives often summarized the news in their letters, intertwining it with the latest domestic gossip and supplementing it with packets of newspapers and magazines. Franklin received a packet from Sarah Kay in February 1826 that included the *Literary Gazette*, *Quarterly Review*, the *Mechanics Magazine*, and the *Edinburgh Review*, which put them "in possession of every intelligence domestic and general which was stirring among you in May last."[142] This information was not only entertaining but could be highly valuable. Sarah Kay also told Franklin what she had learned from Lady Beechey about her son's progress in the *Blossom* toward the Bering Strait, while her daughter Mary Anne wrote, "I hear Capt Beechey is ordered to remain 2 years off Icy Cape, for chance of falling in with you"—crucial information, if Franklin received it early enough, for his summers' travels.[143]

As families funneled information to the field, they also circulated news of the expedition at home. Private letters gave families privileged information that only the Colonial Office or Admiralty might possess—and therefore valuable social capital in circles that thrived on the curious and unique. As Gillian Beer has put it, "the personal moment, the record of what is smelt, touched, tasted, seen and heard . . . provides convincing written evidence of the authenticity of what is told."[144] This was both useful and dangerous. Confidentiality had to be balanced with circulation, because there was always the danger that a letter might fall into the wrong hands. The press actively sought explorers' private letters because they were thought to contain the most honest and truthful account of the events of the expedition.[145] Officers and their families might also publish their private journals once they were returned by the Admiralty. Lyon published his own *Private Journal* after Parry's official account of the Igloolik expedition. He wrote in the preface that "it was written solely for the amusement of my own fire-side; and without the most distant idea that it would ever see the light in any other shape."[146]

Having a letter published could be fatal to one's professional interests because, technically, the Admiralty prohibited private correspondence. Nevertheless, officers still wrote compulsively to their families by every available channel and cautiously encouraged circulation to a trusted few. In a letter marked with his latitude and longitude, Parry wrote to his parents in 1820, "I beg and intreat you that this letter may only be shewn to your own circle of friends—but by no means published in any shape."[147] At Igloolik in 1822–3, he constructed a letter so that certain pages could be removed and shared with a select circle (whom he named). Parry was contemplating sending Lyon home with his journals, letters, and dispatches while he continued to press the Passage, using Iligjaq's maps as a guide. The letter became a valuable insurance policy, a way to ensure that an authorized version of the expedition would make it home if he did not. He wrote to his parents that if his dispatches were published, they would recognize many passages from this letter, "for it is not easy to tell the same story half a dozen different ways," and he hoped that his "friends" would not judge him harshly.[148] On the Second LAE, Franklin ordered his officers to "use the greatest caution in mentioning . . . proceedings in their correspondence, and strictly prohibit their friends from publishing their accounts."[149] Nevertheless, Richardson asked Mary to pass along extracts to all of their family, Franklin's family, and his friends and patrons (especially Robert Jameson, William Hooker, and Mrs. Hooker).[150] He also wrote directly to his patrons, who unabashedly published these letters.[151] Edward Kendall cautioned his mother "against letting anything I may tell you relative to the expedition find its way into the public prints—it would be immediately known that some of the officers . . . had been too communicative of which our lords and masters are particularly jealous."[152] Still, he habitually asked her and his sisters to share his letters, in particular with anyone who might be instrumental in getting him promoted.[153] One letter usually had to suffice for many, especially since, as Kendall reminded his mother, "Paper is too precious in this part of the world to be wasted."[154]

Explorers occupied center stage in these letters, as the people upon whom they depended faded into the background, along with hardships and privation. Kendall hardly mentioned the *voyageurs* at all in his letters to his mother and sisters as he described their progress up the Canadian river system in the spring of 1825. He described their passage as comfortable, pleasant, and strengthening, adding "this hard marching agrees extremely well with me I assure you."[155] Richardson wrote Mary a vivid description of their daily routine: rising at 2:30 a.m., paddling, napping, smoking, eating, and sleeping. He painted a picture of contented *voyageurs* who were happy with small luxuries like a morning dram, a two-minute smoke break every half hour, singing "cheerful songs," and sleeping on "the softest turf they can find" in the evening.[156] It is impossible to tell how this resonated with Mary, who was so reluctant to part with her husband again, who knew the story of the first expedition so intimately, and the way that blame had been laid at the feet of the *voyageurs*. Indeed, Richardson and Franklin praised the support of the HBC and the Yellowknives in their correspondence, never failing to point out their ample provisions, domestic comforts, and good relationships, as well as the thoroughness of their own preparations.[157] Richardson wrote to Mary that they had been met "with the utmost civility and attention," and that "compared with our last journey this promises to be a party of pleasure."[158]

When intermediaries and their families appeared in explorers' correspondence, it was often as either a parable or a parody—and usually explicitly in contrast with the contexts in which correspondence would be read and shared. Over the winter of 1825-6, Franklin, Richardson, and Back invited their families to compare themselves with the conversation, sociability, and domesticity of the far North. Rituals, celebrations, feasts, and rendezvous were a key aspect of *voyageur* culture, blending some Indigenous customs with an annual cycle of French-Canadian carnival.[159] But occasions like the Christmas celebrations offered an opportunity to compare women on both sides of the world, which Richardson did with delight. He told Mary that "all the rank and fashion of Bear Lake" had attended the Christmas ball at Fort Franklin in 1825, "their raven hair dripping with unguents prepared from the marrow of the rein-deer, and their expanded countenances ornamented with twin rows of ivory teeth gracefully contrasting with their lovely bronze features wheron streaks of lamp black and rudge [sic] were harmoniously blended."[160] In contrast, he and Franklin both described their orderly, separate chambers at Fort Franklin as an isolated, domestic, and rational space, quite apart from the rest of the fort, where "conversation" was frequently interrupted by the "squalling of an unruly child—or the growling and fighting of some ungovernable dogs."[161] In their private chambers, they arranged specimens, redrafted journals, read books and old newspapers—artifacts that Back described as "manna in the wilderness" when they were "at a weary distance from Society and civilization."[162] Their chambers, they told their families, were where they ate homemade pickles and marmalade, wore their home-knitted mittens, drank cherry brandy, swaddled themselves in woolen blankets, and played chess—all, Franklin wrote to Mary Anne, "so that we have daily mementos of you."[163] This also had the effect of contrasting the industriousness of children in Britain and the fur trade countries. Many of the hats, scarves, and "ditty bags" that Franklin referred to had been made by his nieces and nephews; one niece recalled that they knitted as many as "their juvenile skill could manufacture."[164] The children of the fort, on the other hand, were depicted as "unruly," though many performed the work of adults long before they were fully grown.

In letters like these, explorers appeared as rational men who were fundamentally unchanged by their experiences, as capable Arctic travelers engaged in detached observation, and as domestic men who were amused, rather than tainted, by the mixed-race culture of the frontier. All the while, they gestured to the presence of the Arctic in their own homes in Britain, especially as they invited their correspondents to find them on a map or to compare their progress with Hearne's or MacKenzie's narratives on the bookshelves.[165] In doing so, they and their correspondents were both continuing the essential work of shoring up their credibility. The reason that formed the basis of the explorer's authority was often disordered by disease, hunger, distance, isolation, and dislocation.[166] Yet this was paradoxical, for the explorer's authority—and popularity—also partly derived from the fact that they placed themselves in peril for the sake of science.[167] Circulating explorers' correspondence helped them walk this line before they returned home. Letters could function as testimonials to their safety, competence, and detachment from the world they observed, while it served as valuable evidence of their authentic experiences.[168] Amid both the mixed-race society of the forts and the homosocial society of their own chambers, explorers insisted that their compasses pointed resolutely "home."

Explorers were keenly aware, however, that their letters were not the only accounts of their voyage that their families received. They also saw snippets of intelligence from vernacular and Indigenous sources that traveled along the same channels. News circulated through the HBC's posts, was discussed and elaborated over long winters, and was eventually passed to the London office and the press.[169] Explorers often cautioned their families that such information was inherently unreliable. Parry warned his parents in 1818 that the whalers carrying his letter "may like to tell wonderful stories about us," and to be aware that "in an expedition which excited so lively & general an interest, every seaman's account of us will be greedily devoured and quickly circulated."[170] In 1825, Kendall cautioned his mother not to believe anything except information from him, the Colonial Office, or the Admiralty "for this is the very country of exaggeration, every little incident that may occur is magnified into a circumstance of vital importance and the most absurd falsehoods are circulated and credited, losing in their passage from fort to fort about as much as a snowball does in running downhill."[171]

Despite their cautions to their families, the men's own reliance on Indigenous and vernacular intelligence occasionally crept into their letters. In January 1826, a party of Yellowknives arrived at Great Slave Lake after traveling up the Great Fish River to the coast, where they reported having seen "some certain indicators of White People"—footsteps, a cache of deer, and a sawpit. Eager to leave Inuit territory, they returned to Great Slave Lake with a map of their route, which they gave to Robert McVicar.[172] The news arrived at Fort Franklin in March, and the officers interpreted it to mean that Parry was wintering on the coast and that Richardson might meet him the following summer.[173] Franklin sent off a special dispatch to ask McVicar to investigate, and Richardson and Kendall both used it to send excited letters home.[174] Richardson told Mary that the Indians had been "not far . . . from Bathurst's Inlet," and lamented that they had not been able to interview them personally.[175] Six months later, they learned that the Yellowknives had actually seen an Inuit camp, and that "the story had been wonderfully exaggerated in its passage to Fort Franklin." In his journal, Franklin wrote that both the officers and traders had read too much into "circumstantial evidence."[176] Richardson wrote to McVicar that the story "came to us . . . tricked out with many adventitious (sic) circumstances, which we scarcely could suppose the Indians possessed ingenuity enough to invent."[177] By this time, however, all the expedition families already knew not only that the report had been debunked but also that Parry had returned to England. Kendall's mother had sent him the excerpt of an HBC report on the intelligence that appeared in the London papers that the story was, as Kendall later put it, "one of those fabrications in . . . which the Indians are too apt to place implicit confidence, and then to circulate until like the story of the three black crows, the whole is discovered to have its foundation in error."[178]

Episodes like this were a ubiquitous feature not only of Arctic exploration but also of colonial intelligence orders plagued by "information panics," which reminded officials of their inability to fully tap into local information orders.[179] In Arctic circles, the circulation of poorly understood Indigenous intelligence was amplified by the long and anxious silences that characterized travel and correspondence, followed by the rapid, almost breathless circulation of letters in Britain. As I explore in Chapter 4, this was a signature feature of the searches for Franklin in the 1840s and 1850s—an arrhythmic pulse of information which was, by then, central to the rhythm of life in polar families. Yet British intermediaries, especially women, were told very little about their counterparts in the field, for it often lay in that vast category of information that was deemed not appropriate for their age or station. The result was that shadowy and uncertain world of the Indigenous go-between barely registered in explorers' narratives—and in their correspondence, almost not at all. Yet developing in the background, and alongside the development of the Indigenous Northwest Passage, were a group of Churchill-based Inuit intermediaries whose work would shape Arctic expeditions for thirty years, and would ultimately—though not intentionally—shape the global memory of the Franklin family. They were led by a young man who saved Franklin's and Richardson's lives more than once before he lost his own in Arctic service, the interpreter Tattannoeuck/Augustus.

Franklin's first LAE had seriously damaged Tattannoeuck's painstakingly maintained relationships, both with his kin and with traders at Churchill.[180] The missionary Benjamin West reported to Franklin in 1823 that he had been ostracized by his band, who considered him to be at least partly responsible for his comrade Hoeootoerock/Junius's disappearance in 1822 (see Chapter 1). This meant he was forced to live at Churchill, where, as Franklin wrote to Richardson, he was made to "work at drudgery . . . [sent] out daily to fish which seems to go much against the Grain and for which indeed he is not much fitted."[181] Tattannoeuck had little to lose by joining up again. As Routledge points out, it is often impossible to know how much the work of Inuit intermediaries was truly voluntary, for many went to extraordinary lengths to avoid conflict.[182] Franklin did make quite a few efforts to entice Tattannoeuck, encouraging him to bring a companion, Ouligbuck (Ullebuck or Ouglibuck) who had never worked for Europeans before.[183] The Second LAE was Ouligbuck's apprenticeship, on which Tattannoeuck trained him to be an intermediary. After the expedition, the two men would continue to work together at Churchill and York Factory until Tattannoueck's death in 1832, and Ouligbuck (and his son William) would both be centrally involved in the Franklin searches of the 1850s (see Chapter 6).[184]

The second LAE encountered many more Inuit than the first, and in much more dangerous situations, and Tattannoeuck and Ouligbuck were the only people who had any idea how to manage those interactions so that they did not boil over into conflict. In the short summer of 1826, they would follow the Mackenzie River north toward the delta, the heart of Inuvialuit territory, where Franklin, Back, and Tattannoueck would turn west and head toward Kotzebue Sound, into the Alaskan Iñupiat territory claimed by Russia. Richardson, Kendall, and Ouligbuck would turn east and chart the coast to the mouth of the Coppermine, meeting up with their tracks from the last expedition. In the space of five years, the region had become flooded with trade goods, fed by trading fairs at Ostrovnoe in Siberia and Sheshalik in western Alaska and then redistributed through at least fifty different trade routes and over more than 2,000 miles. Though these exchanges normally took place in the spring, the system was evolving and extending, and in the summer of 1826 new locations were being established, for example, at the place Franklin named Barter Island. It was all extremely tentative, however, for territorial boundaries were fiercely guarded. Trade fairs were the only opportunities for strangers to meet peacefully, and outside of these agreed times and places, a small armed party could expect to be treated as hostile.[185]

Primed both by Hearne's narrative and by Franklin's and Richardson's tales of the first expedition, explorers' relatives fully expected to hear about Inuit–Dene hostilities in letters from the field. When Tattannoeuck appeared in correspondence, it was generally as a reassuring presence, but in no way did this encompass either his real value to the expedition, or indeed, the officers' appreciation of him. Kendall wrote to his mother and sisters in September 1825 that he had encountered a group of Gwich'in on the Mackenzie River who, "endeavoured to dissuade us from proceeding any further representing the Esquimaux as a very treacherous . . . people who would certainly kill us." But Tattannoeuck's presence had ensured his safety, for, "when [the Gwich'in] understood that we had an Esquimaux interpreter . . . they were rejoiced and changed their opinion immediately."[186] Franklin wrote to Mary Anne and her siblings in February 1826 and described Tattannoeuck as

> very lively and active [but] considers himself a person of some consequence, and you would be amused with his vanity—when he goes from room to room to shew his specimen of copying writing—which by the way he does well—would you not like to have his Autograph? He is now looking over the Doctor & myself—watching our motions—I have just told him I had written his name, he smiles and says thank you and desires me to say to you "We very well!" and "Me very glad England me see."[187]

One can glimpse Tattannoeuck's concern about his position. He was determined to be set apart from the rest of the men, and insisted on serving Franklin and Richardson in their own apartment at Fort Franklin.[188] He was proud of his literacy and anxious to know how he was being portrayed in Franklin's letter. Franklin's description for Mary Anne was meant to set her mind at ease and to give her a humorous picture of frontier life. But in the process, he provided a snapshot of Tattannoeuck's efforts to shore up his own credibility, to make himself both indispensable and irreproachable, to bolster and to secure his vulnerable position.

That vulnerability was especially apparent when it came to encounters with Inuit, which the expedition only survived because of Tattannoeuck's intervention. When, for example, Franklin's and Back's boats ran aground at Barter Island on July 7, 1826, and were attacked by 300 Inuvialuit men, Tattannoeuck helped them to escape.[189] Back wrote that as he was being pinned down and the buttons cut off his jacket, he saw out of the corner of his eye, "that brave little Man rushed in the midst of a ferocious mob and commanded them to leave off."[190] When the boats grounded again, Tattannoeuck leapt onto the beach to negotiate.[191] He gave a long speech to the Inuvialuit, pointing to his naval uniform as evidence of the advantages of peaceful trade, and threatening revenge if the British were killed.[192] Franklin later wrote in his journal, "A greater instance of courage has not been I think recorded."[193] That evening, Tattannoeuck returned to the Inuvialuit camp, where he performed songs and dances that were normally performed during trade with strangers, and were intended to cement lasting relationships, and managed to persuade the Inuvialuit not to pursue and destroy the expedition.[194]

Franklin and Back were keenly aware that they owed their lives to Tattannoeuck. Richardson also understood that his safe eastward passage had depended upon Ouligbuck's interventions. (On one occasion, he carried Richardson on his back as they fled from a hostile crowd.)[195] Later, Franklin and Richardson demonstrated their gratitude, praising Tattannoeuck and Ouligbuck in the narrative and compensating them at Churchill.[196] Richardson gave his spare uniform to Tattannoeuck, not knowing that when he wore it later at Churchill, it made him an object of mockery, evidence of the "nonsencical [sic] pride taught him by the late Expedition Gentry."[197] But Franklin mentioned neither Inuk man's interventions to his correspondents, and Richardson never alluded to these lifesaving actions to Mary. He only hinted at the danger in a letter to his mother when he wrote that, "the numerous hordes and turbulent disposition of the Esquimaux . . . rendered the voyage so hazardous" that they were all filled with "gratitude to the Supreme Disposer of events."[198] Back, meanwhile, wrote to his brother John, "We have been attacked by a large number of Natives—which cannot fail to cause a six Week Wonder to the World on our arrival."[199]

These examples could be viewed as simply as cases of strategic representation and occlusion on the part of explorers; of men crafting the tales of their adventures to suit their audiences, molding them to fit what was suitable depending upon the recipient; and of representing themselves as the undisputed heroes of their journeys.[200] But these recipients were not some faceless public, but family members who were embedded in metropolitan cultures of exploration. They were widely read and were aware of the expedition's preparations for meeting, negotiating, and living with Indigenous peoples.[201] Mary Anne had asked Franklin to give "Miss Greenstockings" a kiss for her, and evidently asked for a report on how the "mythological figures" painted on the bows of the *Lion* and *Reliance* were being received.[202] Both despite and because of the limited portrait of Arctic life painted by their explorer-relatives, the women and families of Britain's Arctic circles could reasonably consider themselves to be a knowledgeable group. By the time Arctic explorers returned home, their relatives were as experienced as women in their position could ever expect to be in terms of gathering, evaluating, and processing information from the far north, without having been there themselves.

During the heyday of official Arctic expeditions, several metropolitan Arctic circles were formed. Circles of polite science connected naval officers, naturalists, humanitarians, and patrons in every sense. In them, men and women could both claim credibility, authority, and knowledge, all of which were gendered, circumscribed, and crucial for explorers' careers. Both explorers and their families were constantly struggling to maintain and shore up that credibility. Information became social currency; specimens were circulated and fondled; letters were read, excerpted, and commented upon; tattoos caused a frisson of excitement. This was how voyages were absorbed and how intermediaries vanished, or were shifted into a more comfortable place.

This could be considered to be the case for both Indigenous intermediaries in the field, and for women who acted as intermediaries between explorers in the field and their constellation of friends at home. Indigenous intermediaries were glimpsed in letters, imagined in gossip, and viewed as spectacles. More often, it was the products of Indigenous women's labor—from birchbark specimen boxes to corn husk dolls to raccoon skin rugs to tattoos—that made their way back to explorers' homes. They became, so to speak, part of the furniture. They also constituted social capital—stories and specimens to be exchanged, which would bolster the credibility of absent explorers. Yet they did not vanish altogether, for the descriptions of intermediaries in explorers' letters home may have been fleshed out on their return. Harassed by the pressures of publication and social circulation, not to mention reacquainting himself with his daughter, Franklin handed over quite a bit of copying work to his late wife's niece, Mary Anne Kay, including appendices, measurements, and tables. It is tempting to think that he may also have asked her to copy his original letterbook, for the copy in the Scott Polar Research Institute is not in his or Jane Franklin's hand, and it bears some resemblance to Mary Anne's.

There would always be an echo of this period of scientific sociability in subsequent years and subsequent homes. The next chapter examines how the Franklins would try to recreate them in an Antipodean context in Tasmania, trying to rebuild not only the feel of the soirees, the thrill of polar sociability aboard discovery ships, but also the content of scientific conversation as they continued to try to claim credibility and build authority, both within the same metropolitan Arctic circles, but also in the very different Antipodean circles, in which humanitarian projects, scientific endeavor, individual reform, and Indigenous intermediaries meant very different things.

Notes

1 Quoted in Woodward, *Portrait of Jane*, 157-8.
2 Ibid., 158.
3 Ann Parry, *Parry of the Arctic: The Life Story of Admiral Sir Edward Parry, 1790-1855* (London: Chatto & Windus, 1963), 128; Spufford, *I May Be Some Time*, 96-7; the sketches, attributed to Toolooak and annotated by George Lyon, are at the Scott Polar Research Institute Museum, accession numbers Y: 76/7/1-9—they may also have been located at Lyon's house, rather than Parry's.
4 Gillian Russell, "An 'Entertainment of Oddities': Fashionable Sociability and the Pacific in the 1770s," in *A New Imperial History: Culture, Identity and Modernity in Britain and the Empire, 1660-1840*, ed. Kathleen Wilson (Cambridge: Cambridge University Press, 2004), 48-70; Secord, "Scientific Conversation," 23-59.
5 For more thorough synopses of all of these expeditions, see Savours, *Search for the North West Passage*, 39-123; M. J. Ross, *Polar Pioneers: John Ross and James Clark*

Ross (Montreal and London: McGill-Queen's University Press, 1994), 23–108. For a detailed analysis of the expeditions and the print culture they generated, see Cavell, *Tracing the Connected Narrative*, 53–156.

6 Smith, "Banks, Tupaia and Mai," 139–60; Russell, "Entertainment of Oddities"; J. Secord, "Scientific Conversation," 23–5; Anne Secord, "Botany on a Plate: Pleasure and the Power of Pictures in Promoting Early Nineteenth-Century Scientific Knowledge," *Isis* 93, no. 1 (March 2002): 28–57.
7 Russell, "Entertainment of Oddities," 57.
8 James Secord, *Victorian Sensation: The Extraordinary Publication, Reception, and Secret Authorship of Vestiges of the Natural History of Creation* (Chicago and London: University of Chicago Press, 2000), 178–80.
9 Thompson, "Earthquakes and Petticoats," 329–46; Endersby, *Imperial Nature*, 1–30, 249–75.
10 Secord, "Scientific Conversation," 132.
11 H. Traill, *Life of Sir John Franklin, R. N.* (London: John Murray, 1896), 56.
12 SPRI MS 1145, Charlotte Grimston to Harriott Estcourt, March 26, 1818.
13 DRO D8760/F/FJR/1/1/22, John Franklin to John Richardson, April 24, 1824.
14 Parry, *Parry of the Arctic*, 89.
15 These boats were designed by Hepburn and Richardson in Edinburgh in early 1824, drawing on ethnographic information gathered by Parry and Lyon at Igloolik. DRO D8760/F/FJR/1/1/13, John Franklin to John Richardson, December 15, 1823; SPRI MS 1503/5/2, John Richardson to John Franklin, January 10, [1824]; John Franklin, *Narrative of a Second Expedition to the Shores of the Polar Sea, in the Years 1825, 1826 and 1827* (London: John Murray, 1828), xiii; Woodward, *Portrait of Jane*, 155–6.
16 Parry, *Parry of the Arctic*, 105.
17 SPRI MS 438/26/53, W. E. Parry to his parents, December 2, 1820; Willingham Franklin Rawnsley, *The Life, Diaries, and Correspondence of Jane, Lady Franklin, 1792-1875* (London: E. Macdonald, Ltd., 1923), 62. For tinned meats, see Carl Thompson, "The Heroic Age of the Tin Can: Technology and Ideology in British Arctic Exploration, 1818-1835," in *Maritime Empires: British Imperial Maritime Trade in the Nineteenth Century*, ed. David Killingray, Margarette Lincoln, and Nigel Rigby (Suffolk: Boydell Press, 2004), 84–99; Franklin teased Mary Anne about pemmican in DRO D8760/F/FKA/1/1/4, John Franklin to Sarah Kay, Lake Winnipeg, June 3, 1825.
18 Anonymous, *A Brave Man and His Belongings* (privately published), 31. Often attributed to Sophia Cracroft, this was clearly written by one of the Kay sisters, as the author identifies Eleanor Porden as her mother's sister. Likely to have been Emily Kay, as she recalls being small enough to sit on Franklin's knee and play with the epaulettes on his shoulders in 1823.
19 Richard Girling, *The Man Who Ate The Zoo: Frank Buckland, Forgotten Hero of Natural History* (London: Vintage, 2017), 14–19.
20 Russell, "Entertainment of Oddities," 48–70; Secord, "Scientific Conversation," 23–59.
21 Woodward, *Portrait of Jane*, 134–6, quote 98.
22 Eliza Dawson Fletcher, *Autobiography of Mrs. Fletcher of Edinburgh: With Letters and Other Family Memorials*, ed. Lady Mary Fletcher Richardson (Edinburgh: Edmonston and Douglas, 1875), 102–3; Tom Stamp and Cordelia Stamp, *William Scoresby: Arctic Scientist* (Whitby: Caedmon of Whitby Press, 1976), 36.
23 SPRI MS 438/26/54, William Edward Parry to Caleb and Sarah Parry, December 6, 1820.
24 Woodward, *Portrait of Jane*, 91–102, 141–9.

25 McIlraith, *Life of Sir John Richardson*, 23-33.
26 Mary Orr, "Pursuing Proper Protocol: Sarah Bowdich's Purview of the Sciences of Exploration," *Victorian Studies* 49, no. 2 (Winter 2007): 277-85.
27 H. S. Torrens and Janet Browne, "Fitton, William Henry (1780-1861)," in *Oxford Dictionary of National Biography* (Oxford University Press, 2004), accessed May 1, 2013. doi:10.1093/ref:odnb/9525.
28 Julian Holland, "Kater, Henry (1777-1835)," in *Oxford Dictionary of National Biography* (Oxford University Press, 2004), accessed May 1, 2013. doi:10.1093/ref:odnb/15186.
29 Thompson, "Earthquakes and Petticoats"; Keighren et al., *Travels Into Print*, 68-72.
30 J. Secord, "Scientific Conversation," 30; Caroline Fox, *Memories of Old Friends: Being Extracts from the Journals and Letters of Caroline Fox, from 1835-1871*, ed. Horatio Noble Pym and John Stuart Mill (London: Smith, Elder & Co., 1883), 54-5.
31 [Sarah Bowdich], *Taxidermy: Or, the Art of Collecting, Preparing and Mounting Objects of Natural History for the Use of Museums and Travellers* (London: Longman, Hurst, Rees, Orme and Brown, 1820).
32 Orr, "Pursuing Proper Protocol," 277-85; Donald deB. Beaver, "Lee, Sarah (1791-1856)," in *Oxford Dictionary of National Biography* (Oxford University Press, 2004), accessed May 1, 2013. doi:10.1093/ref:odnb/16310; Mary Orr, "Fish with a Different Angle: *The Freshwater Fishes of Great Britain* by Mrs Sarah Bowdich (1791-1856)," *Annals of Science* 71, no. 2 (2014): 206-40.
33 Keighren et al., *Travels into Print*, 100-32.
34 Orr, "Pursuing Proper Protocol," 283; Thompson, "Earthquakes and Petticoats," 339; Secord, "Scientific Conversation," 23-59.
35 Thompson, "Earthquakes and Petticoats," 345.
36 Secord, "Scientific Conversation," 37.
37 Woodward, *Portrait of Jane*, 134.
38 Quoted in Alison Alexander, *The Ambitions of Jane Franklin, Victorian Lady Adventurer* (Sydney: Allen & Unwin, 2013), 18.
39 Thompson, "Earthquakes and Petticoats," 335-8.
40 David Allen, "Tastes and Crazes," in *Cultures of Natural History*, eds. N. Jardine, J. A. Secord, and E. C. Spary (Cambridge: Cambridge University Press, 1996), 394-407.
41 NMM FRN1. For the significance of scrapbooks in a young woman's demonstration of her taste, refinement, and scientific enquiry, see James A. Secord, "Scrapbook Science: Composite Caricatures in Late Georgian England," in *Figuring It Out: Science, Gender and Visual Culture*, eds. Ann B. Shteir and Bernard Lightman (Hanover: Dartmouth College Press, 2006), 164-91.
42 Mary Russell Mitford to Barbara Hofland, April 17, 1819, quoted in Mary Russell Mitford, *The Life of Mary Russell Mitford, as Related in a Selection from Her Letters to Her Friends*, ed. Alfred Guy L'Estrange (London: Richard Bentley, 1870), Vol. 2, 68.
43 SPRI MS 1503/8/2, Peter Richardson Journal, January 11, 1828.
44 Stamp and Stamp, *William Scoresby*, 36.
45 SPRI MS 438/26/53, William Edward Parry to Caleb and Sarah Parry, December 2, 1820.
46 NMM FRN/1/17, Franklin to Mary Anne Kay, November 1827; FRN/1/19, Franklin to Mary Anne Kay, nd.
47 SPRI MS 438/26/30, William Edward Parry to his parents, February 15, 1819; SPRI MS 438/26/38, William Edward Parry to his parents, London, February 23, 1819.
48 Laidlaw, *Protecting the Empire's Humanity*, 63-98; Sivasundarum, *Nature*, 1-13.

49 SPRI MS 1503/8/2, Peter Richardson Journal.
50 Chauncey Loomis, "The Arctic Sublime," in *Nature and the Victorian Imagination*, ed. U.C. Knoepflmacher and G. B. Tennyson (Berkeley: University of California Press, 1977), 95–112; Spufford, *I May Be Some Time*, 16–40; Robert G. David, *The Arctic in the British Imagination, 1818-1914* (Manchester and New York: Manchester University Press, 2000); Russell A. Potter, *Arctic Spectacles: The Frozen North in Visual Culture, 1818-1875* (Seattle and London: University of Washington Press, 2007).
51 William Scoresby, *Memorials of the Sea: Sabbaths in the Arctic Regions, or, Testimonies of Nature and Providence to the Divine Institution and Perpetuity of the Sabbath*, 2nd ed. (London: Longman, Brown, Green, and Longmans, 1850). First published in 1830.
52 William Edward Parry, *Journal of a Second Voyage for the Discovery of a North-West Passage from the Atlantic to the Pacific: Performed in the Years 1821-22-23, in His Majesty's Ships Fury and Hecla, under the orders of Captain William Edward Parry* (London: John Murray, 1824), 123–4; John Ross, *On Intemperance in the Royal Navy* (London: Tweedie, 1852).
53 Parry, *Journal of a Second Voyage*, 123–4. Some of the slides still exist at the Mitchell Library in Sydney—ML, Slides made and used by Sir W. E. Parry to educate his crew on his second polar exploring expedition, SLIDES 8.
54 Parry, *Parry of the Arctic*, 76.
55 Hall, *Civilising Subjects*; Thorne, "'The Conversion of Englishmen and the Conversion of the World Inseparable,'" 238–62; Lester and Dussart, *Colonization*, especially 1–36.
56 Lester, *Imperial Networks*, 23–44, 105–37; Laidlaw, *Colonial Connections*, 27–31; Lambert and Lester, "Geographies of Colonial Philanthropy," 323–30.
57 Laidlaw, "Aunt Anna's Report," 1–28.
58 Elizabeth Gurney Fry, *Memoir of the Life of Elizabeth Fry, with Extracts from her Journal and Letters*, eds. Katherine Fry and Rachel Elizabeth Fry Cresswell (London: C. GIlpin, J. Hatchard & Co., 1848), vol. 1, 253–8.
59 Midgley, *Women Against Slavery*; Prochaska, "Women in English Philanthropy"; Davidoff and Hall, *Family Fortunes*, 429–36.
60 Ann Janowitz, "Amiable and Radical Sociability: Anna Barbauld's 'Free Familiar Conversation,'" in *Romantic Sociability: Social Networks and Literary Culture in Britain, 1770-1840*, eds. Gillian Russell and Clara Tuite (Cambridge and New York: Cambridge University Press, 2002), 62–81, Laidlaw, *Protecting the Empire's Humanity*, 63–8.
61 Fletcher, *Autobiography*, 135–7.
62 Woodward, *Portrait of Jane*, 144.
63 Parry, *Parry of the Arctic* 88, 95–7.
64 SPRI MS 438/26/325, W. E. Parry to Gertrude Parry, [June 1826]; Parry, *Parry of the Arctic*, 104.
65 ML A630–A632, Sir William Edward Parry Papers, 1829-1834; Parry, *Parry of the Arctic*, 154.
66 Parry, *Parry of the Arctic*, 88; Qikigtani Truth Commission, "Community Histories 1950-1975: Igloolik" (Iqaluit, Nunavut: Inhabit Media, 2013), 11.
67 Greg Dening, *Mr Bligh's Bad Language: Passion, Power and Theatre on the Bounty* (Cambridge: Cambridge University Press, 1992), 34–6; Lamb, *Preserving the Self*, 106–9.
68 Woodward, *Portrait of Jane*, 154–5.
69 SPRI MS 438/26/39, W. E. Parry to his parents. London, April 20, 1819.
70 Qikigtani Truth Commission, "Community Histories," 13.

71 Franklin, *Narrative of a Journey*, vol. 2, 40–7.
72 Fossett, *In Order to Live Untroubled*, 125–31.
73 Ibid., 129; Shelagh D. Grant, *Arctic Justice: On Trial for Murder, Pond Inlet, 1923* (Montreal and London: McGill-Queen's University Press, 2002), 14–15; Eber, *Encounters on the Passage*, 12–36.
74 Fossett, *In Order to Live Untroubled*, 128.
75 Parry, *Parry of the Arctic*, 84–5.
76 Parry, *Journal of a Second Voyage*, 165–7.
77 Qikiqtani Truth Commission, "Community Histories," 22; Kaj Birket-Smith, *The Caribou Eskimos: Material and Social Life and Their Cultural Position. Descriptive Part*. Report of the Fifth Thule Expedition, 1921–4, trans. W. E. Calvert (Copenhagen: Gyldendalske Boghandel, 1929), vol. 5, pt. 1:86–7.
78 For gendered Inuit geographical knowledge, see Beatrice Collignon, *Knowing Places: The Inuinnait, Landscapes, and the Environment*, trans. Linna Weber (Canadian Circumpolar Institute Press, 2006). See also Claudio Aporta, "The Sea, the Land, the Coast, and the Winds: Understanding Inuit Sea Ice Use in Context," in *SIKU: Knowing Our Ice: Documenting Inuit Sea Ice Knowledge and Use*, Igor Krupnik et al. (Dordrecht: Springer Netherlands, 2010), 163–80.
79 RGS-IBG SSC/73/3-4, W. H. Hooper Journals, 1821-1822.
80 Michael Bravo, *The Accuracy of Ethnoscience: A Study of Inuit Cartography and Cross-Cultural Commensurability. Manchester Papers in Social Anthropology, No. 2* (Manchester: Manchester University Press, 1996), 10–11. See also Bravo, "Ethnographic Navigation," 199–235.
81 Qikiqtani Truth Commission, "Community Histories," 17.
82 For theft as a way to assert authority, see Bockstoce, *Furs and Frontiers*, 134.
83 Routledge, *Do You See Ice?* 61.
84 Coll Thrush, "The Iceberg and the Cathedral: Encounter, Entanglement, and Isuma in Inuit London," *Journal of British Studies* 53 (January 2014): 59–79; Routledge, *Do You See Ice?*, 90–4.
85 Eber, *Encounters on the Passage*, 35.
86 Ibid., 12–36. These oral histories are supported by W. H. Hooper's journal of the expedition, RGS-IBG SSC/73/3-4.
87 This breach of promise was reported in the society sections of newspapers and ladies' magazines across England, see, for example, "The Mirror of Fashion," *Morning Chronicle*, October 24, 1823, 3; *The Mirror of Literature, Amusement and Instruction*, November 1, 1823, 384; "The North-Western Expedition," *Leeds Mercury* October 25, 1823, 3.
88 *The Mirror of Literature, Amusement and Instruction*, November 1, 1823, 384.
89 Parry, *Parry of the Arctic*, 84–5.
90 Thomas Hood, "Ode to Capt Parry" (1825) in Thomas Hood, *The Poetical Works of Thomas Hood: With a Memoir of the Author* (New York: James Miller, 1873), 508–10. I am grateful to Janice Cavell for this reference.
91 William Glascock, *The Naval Sketchbook, or, the Service Afloat and Ashore with Characteristic Reminiscences and Opinions*, 2nd ed. (London: Henry Colburn, 1831), vol. 2, 193–5.
92 SPRI MS 248/432/1, William Porden Kay to John Franklin, February 22, 1826 (Franklin's notes).
93 Parry, *Parry of the Arctic*, 85; DRO D8760/F/FJR/1/1/34, John Franklin to John Richardson, Nottingham, November 4, [1824 penciled in, but should be 1823 by

context]; SPRI MS 1503/5/6-10, correspondence between John Richardson and William Edward Parry, 1823–4.
94 Parry, *Parry of the Arctic*, 104.
95 A Lady, *A Peep at the Esquimaux; Or, Scenes on the Ice, To Which is Annexed, A Polar Pastoral* (London: H. R. Thomas, 1825), vii.
96 Savours, *Search for the North West Passage*, 123; for other possible authors, see Megan Norcia, *X Marks the Spot: Women Writers Map the Empire for British Children, 1790-1895* (Athens: Ohio University Press, 2010), 31–65.
97 Lady, *A Peep at the Esquimaux*, 57.
98 Description of 'McVicar, Robert, Robert McVicar collection, 1815-1844. Scott Polar Research Institute Archives, University of Cambridge. GB 15 ROBERT MCVICAR' on the Archives Hub website, https://archiveshub.jisc.ac.uk/data/gb15-robertmcvicar, accessed: April 20, 2023.
99 SPRI MS 961 MJ, John Richardson to Robert McVicar, January 2, 1824; Alice Lea, "Some Unpublished Letters of Sir John Franklin, Sir John Richardson, and Others, Written During the Expeditions to North-west Canada for the Purpose of Explorations, 1819-22; and 1825-27," *Transactions of the Women's Canadian Historical Society of Toronto* 17 (1915): 17; SPRI MS 1503/6/6, John Richardson to Mary Richardson, September 6, 1825.
100 Helm and Gillespie, "Dogrib Oral Tradition," 17–23.
101 See Irby C. Nichols and Richard A. Ward, "Anglo-American Relations and the Russian Ukase: A Reassessment," *Pacific Historical Review* 41, no. 4 (November 1972): 444–59; James R. Gibson, *Otter Skins, Boston Ships and China Goods: The Maritime Fur Trade of the Northwest Coast, 1785-1841* (Montreal: McGill-Queen's University Press, 2001).
102 TNA CO 6/16, John Franklin to John Barrow, November 26, 1823; HBCA B. 200/e/3 A. R. MacLeod, MacKenzie River District Report, 1823–4.
103 SPRI MS 1503/5/2, draft letter from John Richardson to John Franklin, January 10, [1824].
104 Eleanor Franklin to Sarah Kay, August 14, 1824, in Gell, *John Franklin's Bride*, 280–2.
105 Eleanor Franklin to John Franklin, December 20, 1824, in Gell, *John Franklin's Bride*, 301.
106 Eleanor Franklin to John Franklin, December 18, 1824, in Gell, *John Franklin's Bride*, 298–99.
107 Eleanor Franklin to John Franklin, April 10, 1824, in Gell, *John Franklin's Bride*, 256–7.
108 SPRI MS 248/389/1, Eleanor Franklin to Elizabeth Franklin, May 11, 1824.
109 SPRI MS 248/388/1, Eleanor Anne Franklin to Isabella Cracroft, February 5, 1824.
110 Eleanor Franklin to Sarah Kay, October 28, 1824, in Gell, *John Franklin's Bride*, 284–5.
111 SPRI MS 248/281/1 BJ, John Franklin Letter Book, John Franklin to Peter Warren Dease, March 4, 1824.
112 SPRI MS 248/281/1 BJ, John Franklin to James Keith, March 9, 1824; John Franklin to Edward Smith, March 7, 1824; John Franklin to John Halden, March 9, 1824.
113 Franklin, *Narrative of a Second Expedition*, 10; Helm and Gillespie, "Dogrib Oral Tradition," 19–23.
114 SPRI MS 248/281/1 BJ, George Simpson to John Franklin, August 8, 1824.
115 Quoted in William Barr, *From Barrow to Boothia: The Arctic Journal of Chief Factor Peter Warren Dease, 1836-1839* (Montreal and London: McGill-Queen's University Press, 2002), 10.

116 SPRI MS 248/281/1 BJ, John Franklin letter book.
117 SPRI MS 248/281/1 BJ, John Franklin to Peter Warren Dease, March 4, 1824. SPRI MS 248/281/1 BJ, John Franklin Letter Book, John Franklin to George Simpson, February 27, 1824; John Franklin to Peter Warren Dease, March 4, 1824; John Franklin to James Keith, March 9, 1824.
118 HBCA E.15/1/70, Franklin Supplies, 1824-27.
119 SPRI MS 248/281/1 BJ, John Franklin letter book.
120 Brown, *Strangers*, 27–8, 156–9, 179–85; Van Kirk, *Many Tender Ties*, 96, 140–1. According to local lore in Orkney, some of these children attended Tomison's Academy, an institution set up by Governor William Tomison. See OA D1/73/3, Short Biography of Governor William Tomison, 1739-1829. See also OA D 31/21/3/3, Ernest Marwick Collection.
121 TNA CO 6/16, George Lyon to R. Wilmot Horton, February 17, 1824.
122 SPRI MS 395/74/15 BL, John Franklin to George Back, March 9, 1827.
123 Brown, *Strangers*, 123–6.
124 Brown, *Strangers*, 128, Van Kirk, *Many Tender Ties*, 5, 290, 182.
125 Van Kirk, *Many Tender Ties*, 179–80; SPRI MS 395/41/4 BL, John Franklin to George Back, March 4, 1834.
126 SPRI MS 1503/6/6, John Richardson to Mary Richardson, September 6, 1825; SPRI MS 1503/6/12, John Richardson to Mary Richardson, September 20, 1826; NMM FRN1/9, John Franklin to Mary Anne Kay, Fort Franklin, November 8, 1825; DRO D8760/F/FSJ/1/9/12, John Richardson to John Franklin, October 29, 1824.
127 SPRI MS 1503/8/2, Peter Richardson Journal, January 20, 1828.
128 SPRI MS 1503/8/2, Peter Richardson Journal, January 4, 1828.
129 The British Museum, "Sir (William) Edward Parry," https://www.britishmuseum.org/collection/term/BIOG158477, accessed April 20, 2023; Scott Polar Research Institute Museum, accession numbers Y: 76/7/1-9.
130 RGS-IBG SCC/88/2, Edward Kendall to Mrs. M. C. Kendall, June 18, 1825.
131 The British Museum, "Mrs Sarah Bowdich", https://www.britishmuseum.org/collection/term/BIOG202972, accessed April 20, 2023. These included exquisite beads in the shapes of a drum, a bell, and a harp, as well as two "soul discs."
132 DRO D8760/F/GPL/2/1, Recollections of Lady Franklin by Phillip Lyttleton Gell.
133 Elizabeth Vibert, "Writing 'Home': Sibling Intimacy and Mobility in a Scottish Colonial Memoir," in *Moving Subjects: Gender, Mobility and Intimacy in an Age of Global Empire*, eds. Tony Ballantyne and Antoinette Burton (Urbana and Chicago: University of Illinois Press, 2009), 67; Kate Teltscher, "The Sentimental Ambassador: The Letters of George Bogle from Bengal, Bhutan, and Tibet, 1770-1801," in *Epistolary Selves: Letters and Letter-Writers, 1600-1945*, ed. Rebecca Earle (Aldershot: Ashgate, 1999), 81.
134 Kennedy, *Last Blank Spaces*, 194.
135 Norling, *Captain Ahab Had a Wife*, 140–64.
136 Hunt, "Women and the Fiscal Imperial State," 29–47; Lincoln, *Naval Wives*, 50–7; Finn, "Women, Consumption, and Coverture in England, c. 1700-1860," 703–22.
137 Norling, "Ahab's Wife: Women and the American Whaling Industry, 1820-1870," 85; Lincoln, *Naval Wives*, 50–7.
138 Amanda Vickery, ed., *Women, Privilege and Power: British Politics, 1750 to the Present* (Stanford: Stanford University Press, 2001); Kathryn Gleadle and Sarah Richardson, eds., *Women in British Politics, 1760-1860: The Power of the Petticoat* (London: Palgrave Macmillan, 2000); Midgley, *Women Against Slavery*; Jane Rendall, "Women

and the Public Sphere," *Gender and History* 11, no. 3 (November 1999): 475–88; Janet Browne, *Charles Darwin: The Power of Place* (Princeton: Princeton University Press, 2002), 2, 346–50; Joy Harvey, "Darwin's 'Angels': The Women Correspondents of Charles Darwin," *Intellectual History Review* 19, no. 2 (2009): 197–210; Paul White, "Darwin Wept: Science and the Sentimental Subject," *Journal of Victorian Culture* 16, no. 2 (August 2011): 195–213; Laidlaw, "Aunt Anna's Report."
139   See, for example, SPRI MS 248/432/2 "Extracts from Miss Kay afterwards the wife of Lieut. Kendall – to Captain Franklin" May 25, 1826.
140   DRO D8760/F/FSJ/1/10/3, Partial letter from Mary Anne Kay to John Franklin, [February 17, 1826]; SPRI MS 248/432/2 "Extracts . . ." May 25, 1826.
141   SPRI MS 248/432/2, May 25, 1826; SPRI MS 248/432/1, Mary Anne Kay to John Franklin, February 17, 1826; DRO D8760/F/FSJ/1/10/3, Partial letter from Mary Anne Kay to John Franklin, [February 17, 1826].
142   DRO D8760/F/FKA/1/1/9, Franklin to Mrs. (Sarah) Kay, February 6, 1826.
143   SPRI MS 248/432/1, Sarah Kay to John Franklin, February 7, 1826 (Franklin's notes); DRO D8760/F/FSJ/1/10/3, Partial letter from Mary Anne Kay to John Franklin, [February 17, 1826].
144   Gillian Beer, "Travelling the Other Way," in *Cultures of Natural History*, eds. N. Jardine, J. A. Secord and E. C. Spary (Cambridge: Cambridge University Press, 1996), 323.
145   Cavell, *Tracing the Connected Narrative*, 33.
146   George Francis Lyon, *The Private Journal of Captain G. F. Lyon, of H.M.S. Hecla, During the Recent Voyage of Discovery Under Captain Parry* (London: John Murray 1824), xiii.
147   SPRI MS 438/26/49, William Edward Parry to his parents, HM Ship Hecla, West Coast of Davis' Strait, Lat 70° 41′N Long 69° 17′E, September 5, 1820.
148   SPRI MS 438/26/63, W. E. Parry to his parents, November 10, 1822–July 3, 1823.
149   SPRI MS 248/281/1 BJ, John Franklin's instructions to his Officers, March 4, 1825.
150   SPRI MS 1503/6/3, John Richardson to Mary Richardson, May 29, 1825.
151   "Extract of a Letter from Dr Richardson on the Progress of the Overland Arctic Expedition, to Professor Jameson," *The Edinburgh Philosophical Journal* 13 (1825): 173.
152   RGS-IBG SSC/88/2/6, E. N. Kendall to Mrs. M. C. Kendall, June 18, 1825.
153   RGS-IBG SSC/88/2, E. N. Kendall to Mrs. Kendall, March 15, 1825; E. N. Kendall to Mrs. M. C. Kendall, June 18, 1825; E. N. Kendall to Mrs. Kendall, January 18, 1827.
154   RGS-IBG SSC/88/2, E. N. Kendall to Mrs. Kendall, January 18, 1827; John Richardson to Mrs. Richardson, September 6, 1825, in McIlraith, *Life of Sir John Richardson*, 144.
155   RGS-IBG SSC/88/2, Edward Kendall to Mrs. Kendall, July 25, 1825.
156   SPRI MS 1503/6/3, John Richardson to Mary Richardson, May 29, 1825.
157   SPRI MS 1503/6/2, John Richardson to Mary Richardson, May 12, 1825; DRO D3311/50/14, John Franklin to Sarah Kay, July 23, 1825.
158   SPRI MS 1503/6/2, John Richardson to Mary Richardson, May 12, 1825; MS 1503/6/4, John Richardson to Mary Richardson, July 20, 1825.
159   Podruchny, *Making*, 165–200.
160   SPRI MS 1503/6/8, John to Mary Richardson, February 6, 1826.
161   DRO D8760/F/FKA/1/1/10, John Franklin to Sarah Kay, June 12, 1826.
162   RGS-IBG SGB/1/4, George Back to John Back, February 19, 1827.
163   NMM FRN/1/9, John Franklin to Mary Anne Kay, November 8, 1825.
164   Anonymous, *A Brave Man and His Belongings*, 39.

165 See, for example, DRO D8760/F/FKA/1/1/4, John Franklin to Sarah Kay, June 3, 1825; John Richardson to unnamed correspondent, in McIlraith, *Life of Sir John Richardson*, 133.
166 Fabian, *Out of Our Minds*, 180–208; Lamb, *Preserving the Self*, 114–31; Salmond, *Trial of the Cannibal Dog*, ixx–xxi.
167 Outram, "On Being Perseus," 281–94.
168 Beer, "Travelling," 323.
169 See HBCA B.38/1/2-4, Fort Chipewyan Correspondence Books, 1822-6; B181/a/3-4. Robert MacVicar, Journals, Great Slave Lake, 1820-21 and 1822-23; B.181/a/6-7, Post Journal, Great Slave Lake, 1825–7.
170 SPRI MS 438/26/22, W. E. Parry to his parents, July 25, 1818.
171 RGS-IBG SSC/88/2, Edward Kendall to Mrs. Kendall, July 25, 1825.
172 SPRI MS 248/280/2 BJ, John Franklin Journal, March 22, 1826. See also John Franklin, *Narrative of a Second Expedition*, 75–6.
173 HBCA B.39/b/4, Fort Chipewyan Correspondence Book, James Keith to Robert McVicar, January 31, 1826; Franklin, *Narrative of a Second Expedition*, 76.
174 Franklin, *Narrative of a Second Expedition*, 75; SPRI MS 248/280/2 BJ, John Franklin Journal, March 22, 1826; Lea, "Some Unpublished Letters," John Franklin to Robert McVicar, March 23, 1826. Kendall's letter has not been preserved, but he referred to it in RGS-IBG SSC/88/2, Edward Kendall to Mrs. Kendall, Fort Franklin, Great Bear Lake, January 18, 1826.
175 SPRI MS 1503/6/9, John to Mary Richardson, Fort Franklin, March 23, 1826.
176 SPRI 248/280/2 BJ, June 28, 1826.
177 SPRI MS 961; MJ. John Richardson to Robert McVicar, Fort Norman, June 27, 1826.
178 RGS-IBG SSC/88/2, Edward Kendall to Mrs. Kendall, Fort Franklin, January 18, 1827.
179 Bayly, *Empire and Information*.
180 Kennedy, *Last Blank Spaces*, 164, 193.
181 DRO D8760/F/FJR/1/1/13, John Franklin to John Richardson, December 15, 1823.
182 Routledge, *Do You See Ice?* 61.
183 For Franklin's offer, see SPRI MS 248/281/1 BJ. John Franklin to George Simpson, February 27, 1824. For Ouligbuck's background, see HBCA B.42/a/151 Churchill Journal 1823/24, Ff 38, July 7, 1824.
184 B. 239/b/104b, York Factory Correspondence Book, 1852-56.
185 Bockstoce, *Furs and Frontiers*, 130–46; Burch, *Alliance and Conflict*, 61–3.
186 RGS-IBG SSC/88/2, Edward N. Kendall to Mrs Kendall, September 6, 1825.
187 NMM FRN 1/10, John Franklin to Mary Anne Kay, William Porden Kay, and Emily Kay, February 6, 1826.
188 In an earlier letter, Franklin had mentioned to Mary Anne that Tattaneouck had become his and Richardson's personal servant and that he "is never happier than when he is officiating about the apartment." NMM FRN 1/8, John Franklin to Mary Anne Kay, Fort Franklin, Great Bear Lake, November 8, 1825.
189 Franklin, *Narrative of a Second Expedition*, 107–12.
190 SPRI MS 395/6; BL, George Back Journal, 1824-1826, July 7, 1826.
191 John Franklin, *Sir John Franklin's Journals and Correspondence: The Second Arctic Land Expedition, 1825–1827*, ed. Richard C. Davis (Toronto: The Champlain Society, 1998), 205.
192 Franklin *Narrative of a Second Expedition*, 108.
193 Franklin, *Journals and Correspondence: The Second Arctic Land Expedition*, 205.

194 Franklin, *Narrative of a Second Expedition*, 110–12; Burch, *Alliance and Conflict*, 69; Kaj Birket-Smith, *The Caribou Eskimos*, 86–7.
195 Franklin, *Narrative of a Second Expedition*, 194.
196 HBCA E.15/1, List of supplies provided by the HBC to the Second Land Arctic Expedition, especially Fos 90–135.
197 SPRI MS 1503/8/2, Peter Richardson Journal, February 11, 1828; HBCA B.42/e/6, Report of Churchill Old Factory District, 1828-29, "Servants: Augustus, Esquimaux."
198 John Richardson to Mrs. Richardson, November, 1826, in McIlraith, *Life of Sir John Richardson*, 159–60.
199 RGS-IBG SGB/1/445, George Back to John Back, Fort Franklin, February 19, 1827.
200 Teltscher, "Sentimental Ambassador," 82.
201 See, for example, DRO D8760/F/FKA/1/1/4, John Franklin to Sarah Kay, June 3, 1825; John Richardson to unnamed correspondent, possibly his sister Margaret Carruthers, in McIlraith, *Life of Sir John Richardson*, 133.
202 DRO D8760/F/FKA/1/1/6, Franklin to Mrs. Kay, July 23, 1825; NMM FRN 1/10, John Franklin to Mary Anne Kay, William Porden Kay, and Emily Kay, February 6, 1826.

3

"All Things Are Queer and Opposite"
Arctic Circles on the Far Side of the World, 1837–43

In June 1841, the residents of Hobart in the penal colony of Van Diemen's Land (*lutruwita*/Tasmania) were treated to a grand spectacle.[1] The Antarctic discovery ships HMS *Erebus* and *Terror* had just returned from their summer's voyage under Captain James Ross and Captain Francis Moira Crozier, and they held a winter's ball to celebrate. The discovery ships were housed over, as though for a winter in the ice, but inside they were brightly lit and festooned with decorations. A tunnel of trees lit with lanterns led the way to the ships, where the upper deck of the *Erebus* became a ballroom, and the *Terror* was transformed into a giant dining room. The spectacle was remembered for years.[2] As Hobart prepared for the ball, the governor's daughter, sixteen-year-old Eleanor Franklin, wrote to her cousin Catherine, "I must draw my letter to a conclusion, as my little pupil Methinna (a native girl) is waiting for her lesson, and every few minutes interrupting me to shew me her work."[3] Mithina was a six-year-old Indigenous girl. Eleanor's first pupil, a fourteen-year-old boy named Timemernidic (or Adolphus, as he preferred outsiders to call him), was a ship's boy on the government cutter *Vansittart*. He might have seen the spectacle of *Erebus* and *Terror* too, but from the docks rather than from the windows of Government House.[4] Before long, he would also depart on a scientific voyage under the officers of HMS *Beagle*, surveying his own sea country in the company of strangers. Both children had been taken from their own families to join the Franklins at Government House.

Mithina and Adolphus's childhoods intertwined with the Franklin family's struggle for credibility and authority during John Franklin's governorship of Tasmania from 1837 to 1843. Both have been seen as tragic experiments in civilization and improvement, overseen by Lady Jane Franklin (John Franklin's second wife).[5] That is part of their story, but far from all of it. This chapter looks at one small section of their lives, specifically, how their time at Government House was intertwined with three struggles: the struggle of Tasmania's Indigenous people to protect and hold onto their children, the struggle of colonially educated Indigenous youth to navigate and claim authority within multiple communities, and the struggles of the Franklin family to secure their authority. Each of these circles was engaged in battles with the truth, that is, with the things that were said of them, with the legacies of broken promises, with the trustworthiness of others. Each was responding to the complex politics of settler colonialism, humanitarianism, and imperial science, all of which had profound implications for their own lives. Each turned on the perils and possibilities of education and "improvement." Yet the stakes could not have been more different, for while one fought to preserve a hard-won reputation, the others fought for survival.

Braiding these stories together helps us glimpse how, as the Franklin family took and tried to shape the lives of young children, they participated in a global project that would shape their own lives in turn. In the nineteenth century, unknown numbers of Indigenous children from the Arctic to the Antipodes were separated from their families. Some were sent to institutions like missions, orphanages, and schools, while others went to trading posts, farms, whaling stations, ships, and homes. The reasons for their removal were diverse, but the idea was always to change them, to fundamentally alter the courses of their lives. Many never saw their families again. Many also became intermediaries with complex allegiances and obligations. Some became politically active young people with blended identities and allegiances. New scholarship is showing how imperial exploration, science, humanitarianism, and governance were shaped by the practice of taking Indigenous children, and by the intermediaries whose childhoods were so disrupted.[6] Adolphus and Mithina were two of these children, along with many other Indigenous intermediaries in this book, including Tattannoueck, William Kennedy, Alexander Kennedy Isbister, Adam Beck, and Qalasirssuaq. These people shaped the Franklin family and their legacies as the Franklins tried to shape them. Yet most appear in the Franklin story as adolescents or adults and always around the edges. Placing Adolphus and Mithina's stories at the center of the Franklins' story helps to both unsettle and rebalance well-established Tasmanian narratives and reconnect them to Arctic histories.

Telling the Franklins' story alongside Adolphus's and Mithina's also helps us to understand the complex range of the Franklin women's claims to authority. When Adolphus and Mithina came to Government House, they were meant to be subject to the authority of Jane and Eleanor Franklin. This in turn was linked to Jane Franklin's own battles to understand and define her position as a governor's wife and an explorer's wife. In Tasmania, she learned that the authority of the former was considerably different than the latter. In Arctic circles, she had watched other women work as intermediaries and brokers of information. But this did not translate to a public role as the governor's wife in a penal colony with a boisterous press and entrenched settler interests. Controlling correspondence, suppressing rumors, and responding to crises became part of her everyday reality in Tasmania, as she was regularly accused of exceeding her authority and subjecting her husband and settlers to "petticoat government." In Tasmania, Jane Franklin began, very slowly, to understand how scientific and humanitarian language and credentials could both support and undermine her, and how those credentials were weighed differently in the colonial public sphere and in metropolitan Arctic circles. Adolphus and Mithina were, for her, small but significant parts of this struggle. She did not seem to realize that she might be a small but significant part of their own.

"An Absolute Moral Wilderness"—Tasmania and the Arctic Circles in the 1820s–1830s

Lutruwita/Tasmania is located south of mainland Australia, in the heart of the Roaring Forties (see Map 2). When whalers, sealers, and British and French navigators touched here in the eighteenth century, the islands' seven thousand people were divided into nine nations, speaking multiple languages, with complex political and economic relationships, long-distance trading networks, and stewardship of land and sea. It was a system developed over millennia, as people and ecosystems shaped one another.[7] These were severely disrupted when the British claimed the island they knew as Van Diemen's Land in 1803 as a new penal colony. The first decades of the settlement were a complex mixture of violence, accommodation, adaptation, and trade. In Bass Strait, women taken by sealers became known as the *tyereelore*, or island wives, and are the ancestral matriarchs of many of Tasmania's Indigenous communities today.[8] Violence increased dramatically from the mid-1820s, amid a massive influx of settlers, dispossession from traditional hunting grounds, and the widespread abduction of Indigenous children. In what came to be known as the Black War, warriors raided settler farms while some settler newspapers openly advocated extermination, and "roving parties" hunted families in the bush.[9] The full scale of the violence may never be known, but even the most conservative estimates of casualties are catastrophic. In some areas, over 60 percent of the Indigenous population were killed.[10]

Tasmania also became a battleground between settler and humanitarian interests. Lieutenant Governor George Arthur walked a fine line between accommodating the demands of colonists and the expectations of his fellow Evangelicals in the Colonial Office.[11] As settlers argued they had been abandoned by a government that valued humanitarian optics over their safety, Arthur simultaneously pursued policies of both aggression and amelioration to remove all Tasmania's Indigenous peoples. He restricted the press, declared martial law, and tried to form a human chain (known as the Black Line) across south eastern Tasmania in a failed attempt to drive all Indigenous people toward the Tasman Peninsula.[12] At the same time, Arthur chose George Augustus Robinson, a self-educated evangelical bricklayer, to "conciliate" Tasmania's first peoples.[13]

Indigenous intermediaries played crucial roles in what came to be known as Robinson's Friendly Mission. Between 1830 and 1834, a young Nuenonne woman named Trugernanner/Truganini from Bruny Island and more than a dozen other intermediaries (many of whom had been abducted as children) accompanied Robinson across the island. They acted as negotiators and translators as they tried to persuade both kin and strangers to leave their ancestral lands.[14] More than a hundred people ultimately made the journey to Flinders Island in Bass Strait, believing that they were not giving up either their sovereignty or their freedom.[15] Adolphus and Mithina's families, from the Parperloihener and Port Davey people, respectively, were among them.[16] The Wybalenna settlement on Flinders Island was intended to "civilize" them through labor, worship, and agriculture.[17] It was also deadly, riven by epidemics that killed Mithina's father and Adolphus's mother, among many others. On the island, both adults and children resisted Robinson's program of acculturation in their own ways. Many refused to speak English, using either their own languages or the vernacular introduced by the *tyereelore*. While they attended church and wrote sermons, they also conducted rituals and initiated the young. However, many children over the age of five were sent to the Orphan School in Hobart. These included Adolphus; Walter George Arthur; and Thomas, David, and Peter Brune, all of whom were sons of chiefs.[18] When these boys returned to the island in 1835, they were all fluent in English and literate. It was at this time that Robinson renamed Timemernidic "Adolphus," a name which he preferred to use with outsiders in later life. Robinson sent them to live with the catechist, Robert Clarke, and tried to enlist them as young supporters of his reforms. Yet these boys had more complex understandings of their roles, which Robinson never glimpsed.[19]

In London in 1836, the Parliamentary Select Committee on Aboriginal Tribes endorsed the narrative that the removal of Tasmania's Indigenous people was an unavoidable humanitarian measure.[20] Fuelled by information from Arthur and Robinson, the committee concluded that convicts and bushrangers (rather than the government or "respectable" settlers) were responsible for the worst of the violence. Still, the committee's 1837 report (largely written by T. F. Buxton's relative Anna Gurney) argued that the future of white settlement must go hand in hand with the "protection" of Indigenous people to prevent similar violence.[21] In the following years, protectorates would be established at Port Phillip, Aotearoa New Zealand, South Australia, and elsewhere. Arthur, meanwhile, became the governor of Lower Canada. He left a firmly entrenched circle of his advisers and relatives behind in Tasmania (including the Colonial Secretary John Montagu and the Chief Police Magistrate Matthew Forster).

Meanwhile, the Arctic circles based in Britain shifted, connecting explorers' families in new and important ways. These changing circles also began to link the Arctic to the Antipodes through explorers' colonial careers, imperial science, and humanitarianism. Amid the increasing austerity of the 1830s and the Age of Reform, there was little appetite for expensive polar exploration, so Arctic veterans turned their attention elsewhere. In 1828, the Australian Agricultural Company approached Franklin, Richardson, and Parry (all of whom had just been knighted) to superintend their sheep farming operations at Port Stephens, New South Wales.[22] Encouraged by the board of directors which was packed with fellow Evangelicals, Parry accepted. He and his family lived in New South Wales from 1829 to 1833 but left embittered by what Parry called the "absolute moral wilderness" of the colony.[23]

John Franklin and Jane Griffin married in 1828. Soon afterward, Franklin took command of HMS *Rainbow* in the Mediterranean while Jane toured the sea separately from her husband. Six-year-old Eleanor was left behind with her Cracroft relatives.[24] Meanwhile, Richardson took an appointment at Haslar Hospital. As Daniel Simpson has recently argued, Haslar was global nexus of scientific information, and Richardson received specimens and correspondence from naval expeditions around the world.[25] His wife Mary died in 1831, and after a brief period of mourning, he married one of Franklin's nieces, Mary Booth. Both Franklin and Richardson were delighted to be related to each other, and also, they thought, to shake off their old companion George

Back. He had been courting Franklin's niece Mary Anne Kay for years, but in 1832, she married their old Arctic companion Edward Kendall. Franklin wrote to Richardson from the *Rainbow*, "when I think of her escape from the heartlessness of the first proposer I thank God for his goodness in preventing their Union."[26]

As the contours of the Arctic circles changed, so did those of British science. The Royal Society disintegrated while the Franklins were in the Mediterranean, and its dissolution created space for specialist societies to emerge. These included the Geological Society, the Astronomical Society, the Zoological Society, the Royal Geographical Society (RGS), and the British Association for the Advancement of Science (BAAS). Their meetings developed alongside practices of scientific sociability. The RGS, for example, emerged from the Raleigh Dining Club, where explorers had shared reindeer haunches and leftovers from their travels.[27] In these new incarnations, societies continued to allow gentlemanly amateurs and government officials to exchange information, but they now formally excluded women. However, as the rest of this book will show, women still exerted some influence over their discussions. Arctic veterans and their friends spanned them all. Beaufort became the Hydrographer of the Admiralty and was a crucial link between the Admiralty and the RGS.[28] Sabine was a founding member of the BAAS, Richardson of the Zoological, and Murchison of the Geological, and they all were crucial to the development of the RGS. These institutions would come to complement (and in some cases, supplant) government-funded scientific expeditions.[29]

In these overlapping institutional and familial contexts, two privately financed expeditions came to link Arctic, Antipodean, and Antarctic circles of science and humanitarianism (see Timeline 2). They also began to lay the groundwork for John Franklin's troubles, first in Tasmania and then on his final, fatal expedition. In 1829, John Ross and his nephew James Clark Ross set out for the Northwest Passage in the steamboat *Victory*, backed by the gin magnate Felix Booth. They promptly disappeared. In 1832, the RGS set up a private committee to rescue them. Richardson planned a route along the river he knew as the Thew–ee-cho-dezeth (The Great Fish River/Back River), cutting through both Dene and Inuit territories.[30] After he married Mary Booth, he gave his plans to Back, though Franklin lamented, "I wish the duty had fallen into abler and more faithful hands than our Companion."[31] Captain Alexander Maconochie, the Secretary of the RGS, organized the rescue efforts. He, Richardson, Franklin, and Back had all known each other for years, but now Maconochie and Back became close friends. Maconochie circulated Back's letters, promoted his interests, secured his instruments, and made Back his son's godfather.[32]

In 1833, Back set out for Great Slave Lake with the surgeon-naturalist Dr. Richard King. When they arrived at Fort Reliance, they found Yellowknife Dene power severely diminished by years of war, disease, and famine. They also discovered that Tattannoueck/Augustus (whose help they had counted on) had died on his way from Churchill. Starvation set in over the winter, and King was horrified by what he saw as the Hudson's Bay Company (HBC)'s indifference to Dene suffering. Secretly, he collected information for his friend Thomas Hodgkin about the HBC's trading practices in firearms and alcohol.[33]

At the end of the winter, Back and King received word that the Rosses had already been rescued by whalers. They had wrecked the *Victory* in Prince Regent Inlet. They had all survived, and with Netsilingmiut Inuit support, James Ross had located the North Magnetic Pole. With their rescue expedition turned into a purely geographical one, Back and King crossed the Barren Grounds and descended the Back River, emerging in the Gulf of Boothia. When members of their party killed three Inuit, they had to leave the river mouth quickly, leaving behind them bitter memories and deep suspicion of outsiders.[34]

The Ross and Back expeditions had far-reaching consequences, both from what they left behind and what they carried away. The wreck of the *Victory* became known as Kablunaaqhiuvik ("the place for meeting white people"). It transformed the economy of the Boothia Peninsula, its wood and metal enabling the Netsilingmiut to survive the harsh conditions that would destroy the final Franklin expedition.[35] Thomas Hodgkin sent the evidence King gathered around Great Slave Lake to the Select Committee on Aboriginal Tribes. There, it nestled alongside accounts of Tasmania's "Black War," and helped fuel support for humanitarian governance.[36] When the Rosses returned to Britain, they fell out with each other, which the Arctic circles attributed to John Ross's jealousy of his nephew's discovery of the North Magnetic Pole.[37] In that awkward position, James Ross turned to Franklin, Richardson, Beaufort, and Sabine for patronage. After several years of magnetic work around the British Isles, Sabine and Beaufort sent James Ross to locate the South Magnetic Pole, as part of an effort to map the world's magnetic field.[38] The British Antarctic Expedition in HMS *Erebus* and *Terror* (1839–43) established observatories around the southern hemisphere, which the Franklins would utilize to secure their own credibility among overlapping scientific and humanitarian circles in Britain.

All these dynamics recombined at Government House in Tasmania. When Franklin accepted the appointment as Lieutenant Governor in 1836, he and his wife saw it as an opportunity to practice "benevolent government" without much of any experience.[39] Franklin invited Maconochie to accompany him as his private secretary, and he left his post at the RGS to take his large family to Hobart. From the penal colony, both Alexander and Mary Maconochie carried on a constant correspondence with their close friend Back. On the surface, it seemed a little enough thing. Yet the Maconochies' correspondence was one of many links between Arctic circles and Antipodean politics, connecting old resentments and new crises.

"The Mischief-Making Visionary": Crises of Credibility, 1837–9

On a summer's evening in January 1838, the schooner *Eliza* docked at Flinders Island. Three Indigenous chiefs stood on the beach at sunset, wearing European clothes that were complemented by Sir John Franklin's full naval dress, stretched tight over what Robinson privately described as his "elderly and corpulent" body.[40] John, Jane, and Eleanor Franklin, Alexander Maconochie, and the botanist Ronald Campbell Gunn spent the night in Robinson's house. The next day, they visited the school, where ten-year-old Adolphus was a monitor and Walter George Arthur and Thomas Bruny taught their elders English. Since their return from the Orphan School, Adolphus and the other boys had lived with the catechist rather than their parents, but also spent time in the bush together.[41] At church, they listened to Tunnerminnerwait and respected elders preach sermons in their own languages and in the Wybalenna vernacular.[42] Adolphus was scarred by both the catechist's floggings and a musket ball lodged in his body from his early childhood. The details of the shooting were unrecorded, like so much of the violence against children in colonial Tasmania.[43] The Franklin party left a few days later, and Franklin promised Robinson that he would be allowed to take people from Wybalenna with him to Port Phillip to establish a new Protectorate. Gunn was unimpressed, and later wrote to Sir William Hooker, "Unless Sir John at an early day adopts some remedial measures . . . the race in another season or two will become extinct!"[44]

As they prepared to embark, Jane and Maconochie both asked Robinson for some skulls for their collections, which he provided from his own stock.[45] He had been collecting body parts for some time, both from autopsies and from grieving mothers who kept the bones of their children with them. Later, he would send Jane Franklin the skull of Adolphus's aunt.[46]

When the Franklins and Maconochies arrived in Tasmania in 1837, they were rapturously received. Twelve-year-old Eleanor, who had only spent five years with her father, was accompanied by her cousins Sophia Cracroft and Mary Franklin. John Franklin had brought his old companion John Hepburn with him, one of many lingering obligations from the Barren Grounds (see Chapter 1). There were parties, parades, and dinners as they toured the island. Maconochie later wrote to Back that Franklin "became really half wild upon . . . the gross adulation, the 'booings,' the presentations, the 'excellencies' lauded on him by the Gov officers, who read him in a moment."[47] Alexander and Mary Maconochie, both keen naturalists, and their children also lived with the Franklins at Government House. The Maconochies, ambivalent about their hosts, kept up a regular correspondence with Back, narrating how Franklin was seduced by the flattery of the "Arthur faction," and complaining that he had "no power of Intellect" to regulate it.[48] This was one of the recurring themes in the criticism of Franklin's government, that he was well intentioned but easily influenced, and incapable of making his own decisions. They echoed Back's own views of his old commander (see Chapter 1).

Maconochie was particularly concerned about the influence of Arthur's nephews by marriage, Colonial Secretary John Montagu and Chief Police Magistrate Matthew Forster. Their offices sat at the core of the Tasmanian administration, and it is difficult to underestimate the extent of their power. They supervised all official correspondence, penal settlements, and police, as well as the armed colonial cutters *Eliza* and *Vansittart*.[49] Their loyalties lay with Arthur, entrenched settler interests, and the Derwent Bank, the colony's principal financial power.[50] Together, they constituted the center of the "Arthur circle," which also had deep ties to the Tasmanian press. Franklin, uncertain and anxious about his new role as Lieutenant Governor, leaned on these men and on his wife for support and advice, a decision which he would come to regret.

As the Maconochies attended soirees and caught insects for the children of Government House, they became increasingly distressed. Alexander Maconochie had been asked by the Society for the Improvement of Prison Discipline to write a report on convict management. Together with his Tasmanian Quaker friends, John Backhouse and George Washington Walker, he believed that the system of assigning convicts to settlers was tantamount to slavery.[51] He would later write to Back, "I was a Solitary Abolitionist, amid a host of Slave Owners and Drivers."[52] After a visit to New South Wales in early 1837, he developed two suggestions to reform management of both convicts and Indigenous peoples. On the one hand, he proposed replacing assignment with parole, in which, after an initial period of imprisonment, labor, and religious instruction, convicts were free to seek employment for wages.[53] On the other, he suggested developing an Indigenous police force similar to one at the Cape Colony.[54]

When Maconochie showed Franklin the early draft of his convict plan in 1837, Franklin wrote to Richardson that it "is full of Theories which in my opinion cannot with safety be introduced into a Community constituted as this is."[55] Jane Franklin, however, wrote to her sister Mary Simpkinson that she was interested in Maconochie's proposal, but she feared that "great use has been made of my name abroad as their known friend and supporter," and that Montagu and Forster were depicting her as "double-faced, vacillating, or even treacherous."[56] Her suspicions were well founded, for Montagu wrote to Arthur in 1837 that it was "Petticoat influence which Rules" and that Franklin was "the tool of every rogue who will flatter his wife for she in fact governs . . . he is the weakest minded man I ever had to do business with."[57] However, the Arthur circle reserved their greatest hatred for the Maconochies. They had been dubbed "Metternich" and "Madame Metternich," after the Austrian statesman, by settler Thomas Anstey and Charles Swanston, the director of the Derwent Bank.[58] Anstey wrote to Swanston in 1837, "[Maconochie] and his supercilious blue stocking Dame had better pack up and be off.—We don't want intriguing theorists here."[59]

Meanwhile, the Franklins and Maconochies sent collections of plants, animals, and insects to friends in Britain in a stream of complaining correspondence. Franklin wrote to Richardson that the Maconochies were "actively engaged in catching the subjects of [natural] History, for their own purposes—without offering any . . . either to me or Jane, though they must know we both have many friends who would be glad to receive such presents."[60] Both Maconochies kept up a regular flow of letters with scientific friends in Edinburgh and in London, further developing the narrative that Franklin was dominated by his wife.[61] "To enumerate the one half of the falsehoods got up to injure Alexander would indeed be a miserable vexation," Mary Maconochie wrote to Back, adding, "the system here is unhesitating falsehood, constant & secret, undermining."[62] Back circulated these rumors at the Raleigh Club and RGS.[63] Richardson heard them and wrote to his wife that "your Uncle is too mild for Van Diemen's Land," that "Lady F has plunged her husband into difficulty that he would otherwise have avoided," and that before Franklin "undertook the management of a colony he should have asserted his right of governing his own family."[64] Jane Franklin seemed unaware of either the Maconochies' discontent or of the damaging rumors. When she commissioned her portrait from the convict artist Thomas Bock, Mary Maconochie suggested making it a phrenological study, "to bring to light very conspicuously . . . my two great bumps of causality" (Figure 3.1).[65] At the same time, Jane purchased Bock's portraits of Indigenous Tasmanian intermediaries, including one of Adolphus's uncle

Figure 3.1 Thomas Bock's portrait of Lady Jane Franklin, 1838. Mary Maconochie asked that Bock pay particular attention to the "two great bumps of causality" on Jane Franklin's skull. Original in the Queen Victoria Museum and Art Gallery, Launceston, Tasmania. The History Collection/Alamy Stock Photo, Image ID: J4WTTN.

Tunnerminnerwait/Pevay. While her own phrenological study remained private, she often showed what she called "the Aborigines in my possession" to visitors, alongside her growing collection of artifacts, plaster busts, and mortal remains.[66]

In May 1838, Maconochie placed his report on convict discipline into Franklin's sealed diplomatic bag.[67] The ramifications were serious, for the report was given to Sir William Molesworth's Committee on Transportation.[68] It painted a picture of a colony riddled with moral decay and sexual disorder. Arthur's earlier testimony to the Select Committee on Aborigines in 1836 had laid the blame for genocidal violence at the feet of bushrangers, sealers, and ex-convicts, not respectable settlers. Maconochie now argued that the system was rotten to the core, and that the whole colony was addicted to violence and vice. It became integral to Molesworth's argument that transportation corrupted the empire and threatened the future of infant colonies.[69] The report led to the end of transportation to New South Wales in 1840 and the introduction of convict parole in Tasmania. When the report began to circulate in the Tasmanian press in September, Franklin was forced to dismiss Maconochie. This was a small consolation to settlers enraged by their depiction as immoral and irredeemable brutes. As Anstey wrote to Swanston, "The dismissal of this mischief making Visionary has given great pleasure to the sensible portion of the Settlers throughout the interior."[70]

The Franklins began to heavily promote colonial science after Maconochie's dismissal. The botanist Ronald Campbell Gunn replaced Maconochie as Franklin's private secretary and helped Jane Franklin to reorganize their fortnightly dinner parties into an informal scientific association. The Franklins wrote to friends and relatives within the Arctic circles, begging them to ignore the sensational press and to send scientific correspondence. Franklin wrote to Sabine that scientific matters are of "moral advantage" and unlikely to "excite the inflammatory propensities of our oddly constituted community."[71] He also wrote to Sir John Herschel at the Cape, suggesting that his correspondence might "stamp a character on our meetings which would go far to render them respectable in the eyes of the Community."[72] Meanwhile, the ornithologists and artists John and Elizabeth Gould arrived in Hobart and took the Maconochies' place in Government House, writing to friends at the RGS and in London about the Franklins' hospitality and genuine scientific interests.[73]

At the end of 1838, the Franklins found themselves feeling betrayed, anxious, misunderstood, and maligned. Deeply worried about how the colony was portrayed in the London press, they were also concerned about the rumors spread by the Maconochies through the Arctic circles. It was in this context that Jane Franklin sought to make Government House the center of Antipodean science, rational improvement, and Indigenous transformation. In December 1838, she asked Robinson to send her "a black boy also snakes different species."[74] He selected Adolphus.

Natural Curiosity: "Prince Adolphus" and Circles of Science and Patronage, 1839

At a dinner party at Government House in January 1839, George Augustus Robinson became upset. John Franklin was, yet again, comparing Robinson's Friendly Mission to Franklin's own journey across the Barren Grounds.[75] Robinson was already nervous about his impending departure for Port Phillip, angry about what he saw as his paltry remuneration for his services, and anxious about the repercussions of a recent execution on the mainland. Three weeks earlier, seven men were hanged for the slaughter of Indigenous families at Myall Creek, after a trial prompted by a humanitarian outcry. White settlers were now protesting against what they saw as their victimization in the British press.[76] In these circumstances, Robinson was under intense pressure to persuade the Wurundjeri people at Port Phillip to accept "protection," and to convince settlers that his methods could produce "civilized savages."[77] When Franklin compared Robinson's mission to his own naval service, Robinson snapped. "I could not endure this," Robinson wrote in his journal. "It was all humbug in Sir John. He had never been exposed to but little danger from natives."[78]

Soon afterward, John Gould and Robinson went together to Flinders Island to collect specimens, expecting to return with two children for Jane Franklin. Robinson was harboring influenza, which he would spread through the settlement with devastating impact. Gould, meanwhile, spent a week collecting birds and eggs, guided and aided by twelve people. Adolphus was one of them, and a few days later, Gould brought him and two other boys back to Hobart. He wrote to his wife Elizabeth from Launceston, "Tell Lady Franklin I have her little page with me, he is a most interesting little fellow, throws the spear waddie with the utmost dexterity and extremely useful to me in the bush, an eye like a hawk, discovers birds nests & eggs in a most astonishing manner."[79] Robinson, on the other hand, described him as "somewhat volatile in disposition" as he sent Jane another skull for her collection. The Franklins sent one boy to the Orphan School; the fate of the other is unknown.[80] Soon after, Adolphus's uncle Tunnerminnerwait/Pevay left for Port Phillip together with Robinson, Truganini, Thomas Brune, Walter, and Mary Anne Arthur and ten others.[81]

For four years, Adolphus had watched as these young people carved out a place for themselves at Wybalenna. They all occupied an unstable middle ground, in which adults and adolescents vied for authority across multiple cultural, political, and linguistic divides.[82] Now he was living with a convict groom from Yorkshire in the stables at Government House.[83] He had been a monitor at the Wybalenna school, and now he trudged up to the nursery for infrequent lessons from Eleanor Franklin, a girl only a few years older than him. For nearly a year, his life intertwined with the Franklins' political crises and struggles for credibility, shaped by rumors, patronage, and obligation. But even as Jane Franklin sought to participate in a global conversation about acculturation and improvement, Adolphus may have been, like his kin and old companions in Port Phillip, adapting circumstances to his own purposes.

Adolphus's time at Government House began with two departures. The first was that of John Montagu, the Colonial Secretary. The second was that of Sir John Barrow's younger son, Peter Barrow. Montagu's journey was ostensibly to act as Franklin's envoy at the Colonial Office; in fact, he used the time to seek a new position and to spread rumors that Jane Franklin was governing the colony by proxy.[84] Both the Maconochies and Jane Franklin sensed danger from Montagu. Mary Maconochie wrote to Back, "You will probably meet our deadly enemy Capt Montagu that snake in the grass, sleek, smooth & slippery, a specimen of our Genus homo well worthy of the attention of the naturalist." She also described Franklin as a "false friend" with "<u>certain passions</u>" and "no moral courage," though she did not describe what those passions were, assuming, perhaps, that Back understood.[85] Jane wrote to her sister Mary and described how she drafted dispatches, proposed ideas, commented upon and suggested policies, often in front of Montagu and Forster. Yet she was afraid that Mary might let something slip that might confirm the rumors about her interference. She begged Mary not to give away that "I am so much in their councils."[86]

The Franklins, however, worried far more about the dangers posed by Peter Barrow. Sir John Barrow's younger son had come to Tasmania from Sierra Leone, where he had been a schoolmaster, and was placed in charge of the convict boys at Point Puer, where he worked alongside John Hepburn. In 1838, Franklin promised Barrow a position in the new Board of Education, but the arrangement fell through.[87] Barrow complained bitterly to his father, blaming Franklin, Montagu, and Forster for undermining him, but omitting his public brawl with one of Franklin's officials in a busy Hobart street.[88] Mary Maconochie wrote to Back, "They endeavour to make him out to be mad . . . though he behaved very violently & improperly latterly, he was shamefully treated."[89] Jane blamed Maconochie for Barrow's behavior, writing to her sister Mary, "I know very well the influence he had over young Barrow's mind," that

Barrow had "beat the boys savagely," and that he "wanted to try Capt M's experiments on them." She went on:

> I see a powerful conspiracy at work against [Franklin]—Barrow, Gregory, Maconochie all against him—I pray to God I may preserve sufficient health & strength to help to avert evil from Sir John & I am sure you will do the same, while you avoid all appearance of any uneasiness & alarm . . . you may always converse freely with Captn Beaufort.[90]

She sent Mary colonial newspapers to illustrate their persecution, many of which focused on the Franklins' marital relations. Most attacks originated from the Arthur circle, and as Alison Alexander has argued, did not necessarily reflect wider views of the Franklins.[91] Montagu, Forster, Anstey, and Swanston were well connected in the boisterous colonial press, and they were constitutionally allergic to anything that smelled of metropolitan agendas, humanitarianism, or reform. In some articles, Franklin was described as "imbecilic" and impotent (in all senses).[92] After her campaign to rid the island of snakes, Jane received a revolting Valentine—a dead snake pinned to a card, with a bit of doggerel commenting on its flaccid tail.[93]

In Britain, Mary Simpkinson worked tirelessly as her sister's envoy.[94] Like Jane, she had been a fixture in circles of scientific sociability for more than twenty years, and now her son Francis was surveying the Pacific as a lieutenant in HMS *Sulphur*. Mary, therefore, had a direct line to some of the most influential naval, scientific, and humanitarian figures in British society. In 1839 and 1840, her social world was filled with farewell parties for expeditions departing to Africa and the Antarctic (see below).[95] At one of these, Mary showed Jane's letters to Parry, who was "grieved and touched" by Franklin's troubles.[96] Mary; her husband, Parry; and Montagu discussed Peter Barrow's troubles with his older brother, John Barrow Jr., over several dinners. They portrayed Peter as a misguided youth who had fallen under Maconochie's influence.[97] Yet Maconochie was in favor with the humanitarians at the Colonial Office and had now been appointed the Commandant of Norfolk Island. Indeed, Sir John Barrow invoked Peter's admiration for Maconochie as his son sought a position with the new Protectorate at Swan River on Australia's west coast.[98]

Jane was about to set out on her own expedition to the Australian mainland. For five months, she would travel, observe, and report as she journeyed from Robinson's new Protectorate at Port Phillip to Sydney. Together with Sophia Cracroft, the naturalist Dr. Edward Hobson, Captain William Moriarty (the port officer at Launceston), and Henry Elliot, the son of Lord Minto, she would travel overland from Port Philip to Sydney along the track established a few years earlier by Thomas Mitchell. As she left, Jane wrote to Eleanor, "If you see Timeo, tell him I hope he is a good boy and that I shall find him improved—tell him that I do not forget him."[99] She called him "Timmy" or "Timeo" (a diminutive of Timemernidic) rather than the name Robinson had given him. Robinson was on her mind as she headed for Port Phillip. John Franklin had just ordered an enquiry into Wybalenna that uncovered sexual "indiscretions" and misappropriation of stores. The whole staff, except for the chaplain Thomas Dove, was removed and Captain Malcolm Smith placed in command.[100] Jane read her husband's letters about the inquiry alongside her own observations of the new Protectorate. She thought the Protectors as "vulgar, illiterate men of mean appearance and figure," and recorded that "everyone laughs at them and thinks it humbug."[101] She met with some of the Tasmanians, including Truganini, who were supposed to persuade Wurundjeri people to accept protection. Mar has argued that these exchanges had the opposite effect, and sparked Wurundjeri assertions of sovereignty.[102] Though she was unaware of it, Jane may have documented some of these negotiations, both at a huge meeting between the Tasmanians and the "stranger tribes," and in her account of a feast where, "somebody is said to have told the blacks the Protectors were going to poison them . . . a few afraid to eat."[103]

Over the next five months, Jane gathered vast amounts of information as she followed Mitchell's track. Her correspondence with her sister and husband was, like Franklin's own Arctic correspondence, both intimate and strategic, and meant to be consumed and shared (see Chapter 2). She described the Indigenous intermediaries who guided the party and whom she encountered on the way, and recorded stories from stockmen and soldiers of "supposed outrages by the blacks." She also collected tales of very young Indigenous children living with settler families, particularly reports of their intelligence, appearance, literacy, and affection.[104] At church one wintry day in Sydney, she found a six-year-old Muthi Muthi girl by her side. Her name was Ballandella, and she was the daughter of Mitchell's female guide, Turandurey.[105] Mitchell, who had already left for England, had claimed that he wanted "to take back . . . an Aboriginal child, with the intention of ascertaining, what might be the effect of education upon one of that race," and that Turandurey had offered Ballandella to him, though there were rumors that he had kidnapped her.[106] Jane did not comment on how the girl had come to Sydney, or where her mother was. She only wrote, "capacity superior to what cd be expected—some of her questions surprising—is learning to read."[107]

When she met Ballandella, Jane was being hailed by the Sydney newspapers for her "spirited & enterprising tour" in Mitchell's footsteps. An editorial in the *Australian* hoped she would write a narrative on the "practical application" of colonial botany and mineralogy and wrote approvingly of her "deep interest in the aboriginal natives."[108] She met Count Paul Strzelecki, an exiled Polish nobleman and humanitarian on a geological expedition, who would soon travel to Tasmania. Meanwhile, John Franklin's letters reported how Beaufort, Sabine, and Mary Simpkinson were working to repair the Franklins' damaged relationship with Sir John Barrow at the Admiralty. It is impossible to know how this conjunction of events aligned in Jane Franklin's mind. What is clear is that when she returned to Hobart, it was with a desire to further promote colonial science and to evaluate Adolphus's capacity for "improvement." When she returned, the Tasmanian Society was formally established with John Franklin as its patron, with six official members: Franklin's secretary Gunn, Jane's traveling companion Dr. Hobson, Dr. Edward Bedford, Dr. Adam Turnbull, Rev. Thomas Ewing, and Rev. John Lillie. Its object was, as the *Australian* had suggested, to promote the "practical application" of colonial science, though it became in part a publicity machine for the Franklins (see below).

There were few accounts of Adolphus during his time at Government House. Eleanor mentioned him the most, for she recorded her days in detail—her reading about Indigenous peoples around the Pacific and Arctic, her walks in the garden with her father, her lessons in Latin and French, her developing interest in natural history, and her conversations with Gunn and the Goulds. Neither she nor her parents ever mentioned what she taught Adolphus.[109] His lessons were erratic, occurring sometimes three times a week, sometimes fortnightly, and he occasionally crossed paths with John Gould.[110] Eleanor wrote in October that "he is anxious to be able to read and write well. He waits at table and does other little things. But unfortunately he is very idle and obstinate, so that it is difficult to keep him to his duty, unless he is constantly watched."[111]

Adolphus's desire to read and write well did not necessarily reflect a desire to please Eleanor. He had a deeper relationship with literacy, linked to the complex power dynamics of Wybalenna. As Penny Van Toorn and Tony Ballantyne have argued, Indigenous writing could accommodate, rather than destroy, cultural shifts in a time of radical change, and both Indigenous elders and youth saw writing as a powerful tool to assert authority both within their community and vis-à-vis the colonial state.[112] Eleanor did not know that Adolphus had been present when his friends Walter George Arthur and Thomas Brune composed the first Indigenous newspaper in Australia, the *Flinders Island Chronicle*. In it, the boys adopted the language of "improvement," which Walter Arthur would continue to deploy in his own attempts to claim authority for many years. Written in the boys' shared quarters, each issue was designed, as Brune wrote, to "promote Christianity civilization and Learning" as well as to "excite a desire for useful knowledge and promote Learning generally."[113] They exhorted elders to adopt agriculture, praised them for taking books into the bush, and reprimanded other boys for laughing and playing in class. Some scholars have seen these articles as evidence of Robinson's coercion, but others have seen them as a reflection of developing power struggles between colonially educated sons of chiefs, their elders, and Robinson.[114] It is not possible to know where or how Adolphus fits into these complex struggles, but it is likely that the memories of them lingered during his lessons in Eleanor's schoolroom.

After Jane Franklin returned from Sydney, she found Adolphus more difficult than she expected. He frequently escaped and associated "with the most depraved and corrupt, and preferring the most miserable and most crowded quarters of the town." He was also calling himself "Jack," a name also adopted by his uncle Tunnerminnerwait/Pevay.[115] The other Indigenous boys in the Orphan School ("Duke" and Thomas Thompson) were also running away, which might have been both an act of resistance and a way to display daring, strength, and courage.[116] Earlier in the year, the *Colonial Times* had reported on the Orphan School's program to transform convict, destitute, orphan, and Indigenous children through early risings, cold baths, industrial training, and short rations. They wrote, "We have seen many assemblages of children in our time, both at home and abroad, but never did we see two hundred human beings, that exhibited so squalid an appearance, as did the majority of the Queens Orphans."[117] Now Jane asked the headmaster, Rev. Ewing, to take Adolphus, saying that though he was "idle and disobedient," she thought he "might improve under better discipline," but Ewing declined.[118] She decided instead to return Adolphus to Flinders Island.

In early December 1839, a French Antarctic expedition under Dumont D'Urville arrived in Hobart. This was D'Urville's second Pacific voyage. In 1832, he had developed an influential racial scheme that divided the people of Oceania into several ranked races, with Indigenous Tasmanians at the bottom.[119] Jane had read his work and was interested in his theories of biological racial difference. When the French officers called on Jane, they had a long conversation on phrenology and natural history, and she sent for Adolphus. The boy joined the officers in a drawing room that the phrenologist Pierre Marie Dumontier later described as filled with both life-sized and miniature paintings of Indigenous Tasmanians. This included Bock's portrait of Adolphus's uncle, as well as plaster casts of several heads made by local teachers, Mr. and Mrs. Benjamin Law.[120] Dumontier would take copies of these, and possibly also a cast of Adolphus's head, back to Paris, where they were displayed in his Museum of Phrenology and later in the Musée d'Homme, both developing hubs of new ideas of biological racial difference.[121] So far as Jane was concerned, Adolphus was now principally useful only as a specimen, and within days she sent him back to Flinders Island. She wrote to her sister, "you have heard of my unsuccessful experiment to civilize a native boy.... If my servants had helped me better in the matter, I might perhaps have been more lucky."[122]

Adolphus has usually been understood as an enigmatic precursor to Mithina's time at Government House. However, his year there has never been seen in tandem with either developing networks of Indigenous literacy and resistance, the Franklins' political crises, or the emerging Protectorates on the mainland. All these factors, however, shaped how the boy fit into the Franklins' struggles, and vice versa. As the Franklins tried to stem rumors and maintain their connections, especially within Arctic circles, they began to promote their programs of colonial "improvement" and contrast them with others, including Robinson's Protectorate. As a result of her travels on the Australian mainland, Jane Franklin came to believe that it was essential to promote Tasmanian science to Antipodean, metropolitan, and global audiences. The way she thought about Adolphus reflected this transition, as he changed in her eyes from a project in acculturation to a racial type specimen. However, it may also be that Government House played into Adolphus's own negotiation of a shifting middle ground. His time there was one of many journeys that took him back and forth from Flinders Island to Hobart, and intersected with the lives of other boys and men who tried to negotiate their own tenuous authority in both Indigenous and colonial worlds. Though Adolphus only appears briefly in the correspondence of the Franklins and their associates, those fleeting appearances suggest that the eleven-year-old engaged with multiple networks, patrons, and comrades. Whether it was making himself indispensable to Gould, escaping to Hobart's unsavory districts, listening to his peers on Flinders Island, or the lessons of Eleanor Franklin in the schoolroom, perhaps all the while Adolphus was hedging his bets and acquiring connections, skills, and credibility.

"Her Ladyship's Exploring Maggot": Rumor, Reputation, and Civilizing Missions, 1841–3

In January of 1840, the settler Thomas Anstey wrote to the banker Charles Swanston, "there will be no end to the lively wriggling of her Ladyship's exploring Maggot. The contempt, which has long been generally felt, is now changing to a feeling of aversion."[123] Anstey and Swanston's correspondence is preserved in the records of the

Derwent Bank, whose shareholders were embedded in networks of patronage derived from Army service, the East India Company, and the Black War.[124] Their letters traveled alongside carefully chosen Tasmanian periodicals that heaped scorn on the Franklins.[125] These newspapers, as Alexander has argued, represented a vocal minority in the settler community. But the rumors and accusations they contained gained traction in the colony and in Britain, particularly those about Franklin's weakness and credulity, and Jane Franklin's "unnatural" activities including her journeys, scientific interests, and intrigues.[126] It was impossible for the Franklins to stem these rumors. In 1842, prompted by a pile of English newspapers that arrived on a convict ship bearing "whole columns of abuse" that had originally been printed in the *Van Diemen's Land Chronicle* in 1841, Jane wrote to her sister Mary, "I can bear well enough to be slandered in Van Diemen's Land where the secret history of everything is pretty well-known, and where men are cowards and dastards ... but in England too—is there no refuge?"[127]

Anxiety about the press, about rumors, and about hidden enemies came to shape the Franklins' world. Their promotion of colonial science, among other schemes of improvement, was explicitly intended to drown out settler rumors in British Arctic circles. Space does not permit a full examination of their activities, such as their art museum and botanical garden at "Ancanthe," their attempts at educational reforms, their colony in the Huon Valley that still bears their name, or the college that John Phillip Gell, a protégé of Rugby School principal Dr. Thomas Arnold and Eleanor Franklin's future husband, founded in 1840.[128] Instead, I focus on their Tasmanian Society, its publication *The Tasmanian Journal of Natural Science, Agriculture, Statistics, &c.*, and their support for the British Antarctic Expedition under James Clark Ross. Each of these promoted science as a marker of colonial civility and the Franklins as civilizers of colonial society. As the Franklins used the Tasmanian Society to serve the interests of their Arctic friends, they also developed the idea of Tasmania as a remnant of the deep past, where developing ideas of evolution and extinction could be witnessed in real time. These efforts also represented Jane Franklin's early attempts to engage with periodical print culture, which she would develop further during the searches for her husband (see Chapters 4–6).

When Franklin arrived in Tasmania in 1837, scientific pursuits were seen as disinterested, gentlemanly, and virtuous, displaying civility, superiority, and strength of character, easily harnessed to settlers' claims to "improvement."[129] Yet few colonists practiced science. It was mostly the province of doctors, anatomists, and surgeon-naturalists, who were knit loosely together in a circuit of colonial correspondence. These kinds of relationships, Jim Endersby has argued, underpinned the practices of Victorian science. Colonial collectors like Ronald Campbell Gunn were crucial for metropolitan practitioners like William Jackson Hooker, who plied them with promises of precious books and paraphernalia in return for specimens. These collaborations were always tense and hierarchical, between those who were meant to collect and report and those who were supposed to interpret and publish.[130] Some women engaged in natural history—including Louisa Ann Meredith, the wife of a settler and whaleship owner, whose travel narratives and popular works of natural history would later be published to wide acclaim.[131] Mechanics' Institutes in Hobart and in Launceston were supposed to cultivate self-improvement through rational amusement, lectures, and lending libraries but were neglected. Most of their members were well-to-do settlers, rather than actual mechanics or artisans.[132]

Franklin was expected to patronize these home-grown scientific societies, and he did so, but only to a limited extent. In the winter of 1837, Jane Franklin began holding *converzationes* at Government House in an attempt to introduce scientific sociability to the colony, but her exclusive guest lists (which spurned ex-convicts and others) laid her open to criticism.[133] Louisa Meredith later recalled women declaring that they "had no idea of being asked to an evening party, and then stuck up in rooms full of pictures and books, and shells and stones, and other rubbish, with nothing to do but to hear people talk lectures, or else sit as mute as mice listening to what was called good music."[134] By October 1838, these converzationes had turned into fortnightly dinner parties, and a year later, into the Tasmanian Society. Its motto was, in Latin, "All Things Are Queer and Opposite" and its mascot was the platypus.[135] Jane called it "my Platipus society" in her letters to Mary and others. This was a marketing ploy, for the species was a source of hot debate among naturalists, particularly whether or not it laid eggs or gave birth to live young. It represented the fascinating possibilities of Australia's fauna, which threatened to upend classificatory systems established in the northern hemisphere.[136]

Jane saw that the Tasmanian Society could supply British naturalists with Antipodean specimens and Tasmanian collectors with metropolitan recognition. Yet the matter had to be managed carefully, so that the Tasmanian Society complemented, but did not replace, carefully built networks of patronage. Their first journal made it clear that they were collecting data, not indulging in interpretation.[137] Doing so neatly reconciled the tensions between colonial collectors and metropolitan patrons while also promising to promote the "practical application" of natural history. Reciprocal gift-giving of specimens and books continued between collectors and patrons, but men like Gunn were no longer entirely dependent upon their own small libraries, the fruit of years of correspondence and unacknowledged collaboration. Now the Tasmanian Society's library, bolstered by Jane Franklin's lavish spending, made it possible for colonial collectors to describe and classify material quickly. Members sent material not only to Richardson and Hooker but also to the anatomist Richard Owen in Edinburgh—specimens that contributed to Owen's own exploration of the concept of extinction.[138] The Tasmanian Society also functioned as a correspondence hub. At every "Scientific Tea" the members shared letters from around the world and reported on the meetings in their letters to Britain and elsewhere.[139] Though they were not formal members, Jane, Eleanor, and Sophia regularly attended meetings. Eleanor was happy to stay up past midnight listening to her father read a paper by Herschel, but she noted that "some, not to say many of the gentlemen were charming us with the delightful noise of snoring; we were nevertheless much interested."[140] While they did not read papers themselves, Jane's correspondence and observations were sometimes read out by others.[141]

The absorbing question of extinction ran through the Tasmanian Society's meetings. Ideas about evolution and extinction were developing in scientific circles, fuelled by geological and fossil discoveries, new theories about the age of the earth, and augmented by explorers' reports.[142] British Arctic circles were at the core of these developments. The geologist Charles Lyell (whose *Principles of Geology* had fired Darwin's imagination on the *Beagle*), the zoologist William Buckland, the polymath William Whewell, and the anatomist Richard Owen had been friends of the Franklins for years, and eagerly corresponded with the Tasmanian Society. So did Beaufort, Herschel, and Hooker, all of whom gleaned crucial information about tides, meteorological phenomena, and botany from the Tasmanian Society's members. Australia's unique flora and fauna fascinated European naturalists with the promise of looking into the deep past, but on the island of Tasmania, plants, animals, and people were even more alluring, particularly as they appeared to be going extinct in real time. In 1841, Jane's brother-in-law John Simpkinson wrote to John Phillip Gell,

> Have you taken much interest in the Aborigines & collected any information about them? It would be a sad loss if records were not kept of their physiology & still more of their language: since as I suppose their extirpation is certain within another generation. I hope your scientific magazine will do something in this way speedily; the geology & plants can wait.[143]

The Tasmanian Society's meetings were peppered with reports on the linguistics, tool use, and physiology of Indigenous people in Tasmania, Australia, and New Zealand. Gunn prepared a report on Indigenous plants of the island and their traditional uses, meant as a practical guide to survival in the bush.[144] Dr. John Lhotsky's attempt at an Indigenous Tasmanian vocabulary was published by the RGS in 1839 and read out by Franklin at a meeting of the Tasmanian Society.[145] In response, Jane Franklin asked Dove, the catechist on Flinders Island, to prepare a grammar of some of the Indigenous languages in use on the island. This was ironic, because Dove had previously complained that they were impossible to learn.[146] He contributed a paper arguing that Indigenous Tasmanians had no means of making fire, a false assertion reproduced for well over a century as proof that they were doomed "representatives of the immensely ancient Palaeolithic period."[147] Settlers on the mainland also sent specimens for collection and discussion. Theresa Walker, Australia's first female sculptor, sent both fossils and wax models of the heads of Indigenous people in her employment in South Australia and begged for reciprocal specimens if possible.[148] These conversations, papers, and remains were tucked in among observations of unusual geology, flora and fauna, magnetic science, and tidal and astronomical observations from around Australia and New Zealand. When printed and bound, the *Tasmanian Journal* was presented as a unique contribution to a global discussion about the secrets of the deep past and the (apparently) disappearing marvels of the present. It was also presented as proof of Tasmanian civility, and by extension, the success of the Franklins' civilizing mission.

Jane Franklin intended the *Tasmanian Journal* to circulate alongside hostile settler correspondence and newspapers, both in Australasia and in Britain. Members of Arthur's circle had latched onto the Tasmanian Society, and colonial science as a whole, as further evidence of John Franklin's unfitness to govern. Some suggested he would simply be happier if he were to return to exploration, while others saw the Tasmanian Society as evidence of his unmanly domination by his bluestocking wife.[149] By the time *Erebus* and *Terror* arrived in Hobart in August 1840, the acting colonial secretary Matthew Forster was circulating a rumor that the Tasmanian Society was in fact a radical political body. Jane wrote that "it was very desirable the Platipus Journal should come out with as little delay as possible in order to prove to the public how surpassingly innocent were our lucubrations."[150] She arranged for the journal to be printed locally by the government printer, and by John Murray in Britain. She wrote to Mary, "we expect you will all patronize [it] by purchase in London," and later sent her crates full of locally printed copies, with detailed instructions about where to send them and how to dedicate them "with Sir John Franklin's compliments."[151] As the number of corresponding members increased, issues were sent to mainland Australia, New Zealand, the Cape, Europe, and Britain.[152] Copies were soon on the shelves of the libraries of the Royal Society and the RGS, sent personally by the Franklins and carried by travelers who had experienced their hospitality and heard about their troubles.[153]

In Jane Franklin's mind, James Ross's Antarctic Expedition was another opportunity for the Franklins to maintain their links to British Arctic circles. Ross's instructions were written by Sabine, Beaufort, and Herschel, charging him to seek the South Magnetic Pole and to establish magnetic observatories at St. Helena, Cape Town, and Hobart in order to chart the earth's magnetic field. Richardson worked with William Hooker to write the natural history instructions and secured a place on board for Hooker's botanist son, Joseph Dalton Hooker.[154] Long before the expedition arrived in 1840, Jane wrote to Gunn, "our journal ought to be the appointed vehicle of [Ross's] discoveries or experiments."[155] She knew that any news from the expedition would be eagerly anticipated. If copies of the *Journal* contained explorers' preliminary observations, and if it circulated alongside their private letters, it could only do her good.

Erebus and *Terror* arrived in Tasmania in August 1840. Within nine days, two hundred convicts built Rossbank Observatory on the banks of the River Derwent.[156] Franklin's nephew, Lt. Joseph Henry Kay, was placed in charge, and the whole Franklin family participated in observations. Franklin told Richardson how he loved his time spent at the observatory and the discussions he had with Ross about the prospect of locating the South Magnetic Pole.[157] Franklin had brought his Arctic magnetic observations with him and now compared them with those taken at Rossbank.[158] But, as he lamented to Sabine, "I scarcely ever examine ... the observations now in progress here without receiving some new idea which I have not leisure or means of working out."[159] Eleanor's eclectic education now included helping Kay and her father on the grueling term days, when observations were made at precise intervals. Jane asked Bock to sketch Ross, Crozier, and Franklin at the observatory, which she later sent to Sabine inside an official dispatch (Figure 3.2).[160]

The expedition's arrival turned the island into what Andrew Lambert has called a "post office of the southern hemisphere" where official and personal correspondence were blended.[161] Ross wrote to Sabine weekly, and Franklin's dispatches contained summaries of Ross's proceedings for his friends.[162] Dispatches from Britain intended for Ross also contained presents for the Franklins and the Tasmanian Society. In 1841, for example, Sabine sent a copy of his wife Elizabeth's new translation of Baron Ferdinand Petrovich von Wrangel's narrative of his 1821–3 Siberian expedition, a book which would gain new significance a decade later during the Franklin searches (see Chapter 5). For Franklin's friends in Britain, this correspondence suggested that he was out of his element as a governor of a penal colony. As Sabine wrote to Ross, "I fear poor Franklin has no very agreeable berth at Hobarton."[163] Some sympathetic letters found

Figure 3.2 Thomas Bock, *Observatory, Domain, Sir John Franklin, Captain Crozier and Captain James Ross, RN*, 1840. This was among the pieces that Jane Franklin sent back to Britain in 1843 to document the Franklins' devotion to colonial science. Original in Tasmanian Museum and Art Gallery. The Picture Art Collection/Alamy Stock Photo. Image ID: P5PD30.

their way into both British and Tasmanian papers, which Jane copied with satisfaction, reciting them back to her sister.[164]

Soon after the Antarctic Expedition arrived in Tasmania, Jane Franklin invited Ross and his "most scientific" officers to join her "Platipus Society." They attended meetings and contributed papers, though not all were willing.[165] Kay contributed a paper on terrestrial magnetism, while Hooker and the surgeon Robert McCormick presented their brand-new observations of geology, fossils, and botany of Kerguelen Island.[166] It would be long before anyone else, even Hooker's father, would learn of their findings in their letters, and longer still before they would be published. But for Hooker, colonial sociability took him away from more important tasks. He had struck up a new friendship with Gunn, who was both his father's protégé and Franklin's private secretary, and both men preferred botanizing to socializing. Hooker wrote to his father that "I hate dancing attendance at Government House," and soon after, Gunn resigned from his official position, complaining that "incessant official drudgery [had] almost knocked Botany out of my head."[167] Hooker also thought that the colonists' interest in science was only skin-deep, more pretension than curiosity. Gould's *Birds of Australia* was coming out in installments, and Hooker wrote, "Three hundred copies of Gould's most extravagant book are purchased by these colonists, solely for the pleasure of seeing the show of it on their tables."[168]

The Antarctic expedition departed for the frozen continent in November 1840 and returned in May 1841. The officers, eager to repay the colonists for their hospitality, hosted the "Glorious First of June" winter ball on board the discovery ships, recalling London's great Arctic soirees of the 1820s. Their arrival was celebrated in the local theater in *The South Polar Expedition*, whose cast of characters included the entire Franklin family. Eleanor was not allowed to attend the play, but secretly reveled in reports (perhaps gleaned from the newspapers) about how it pilloried her parents, particularly her stepmother who was portrayed drinking a bumper of wine with Captain Ross. She pointed out that the play "is said to have been ridiculous in the extreme, from its extreme dissimilarity. Sir John Franklin, for instance, had a head full of hair."[169] Later that year, Ross regaled his Sydney hosts with tales of Hobart's elegance, sophistication, and its improvement, and wrote to Jane that he believed "Tasmania must eventually become the metropolis of the Southern Empire." Jane copied Ross's letter for her father, mentioning in the same breath how she was sending copies of the *Tasmanian Journal* to Mary to distribute to "scientific individuals & the rest to Murray the publisher."[170]

Colonial science, politics, and rumor were woven into the complex webs of friendship, sociability, and obligation that linked the Arctic circles to Tasmania. Fuelled by the Franklin family's Arctic connections, the Tasmanian Society developed the colony's reputation as a scientific center in the Southern Hemisphere. Well supplied with unique and exotic contributions about the Antipodean and Antarctic regions, the Tasmanian Society and its members produced material in the *Tasmanian Journal* for a colonial and a metropolitan audience that associated Tasmania, its peoples, flora and fauna with the ancient past, and toyed with the possibility of their extinction. This was vital both for the reputations of amateur naturalists and the Franklin family, particularly as it counteracted rumors spread by hostile settlers and their periodicals. Yet visiting friends and allies also tended to reinforce some of those rumors, particularly when it came to Jane Franklin's involvement in scientific matters and her husband's poor fit as a colonial governor. The Franklins' civilizing mission, so far as it was directed toward settlers, seemed incomplete and skin-deep, and the family themselves seemed out of place.

"A Little Native Girl I Brought Up for 2 or 3 Years . . ."

Years after the Franklins left Tasmania, the chaplain Robert Crooke described Jane Franklin's boudoir as a cabinet of curiosities, containing "snakes, toads, stuffed birds and animals, weapons of savages, specimens of wood and stone, and last though not least, a juvenile lubra arrayed in bright scarlet."[171] This was, he said, the "sanctum sanctorum" of government. The "juvenile lubra" was Mithina, a little girl who was brought to Government House from Flinders Island in 1841, aged about six.[172] For Crooke, in that cabinet of curiosities, everything was out of place: the boudoir was the seat of power, occupied by a middle-aged woman, observed by a child in a red dress who ought not to have been there (Figure 3.3).

Since the late nineteenth century, Mithina's short life has been fictionalized, dramatized, and sentimentalized. Scholars, novelists, artists, and others have been drawn to the image of the little girl in her red dress, and to the frustrating lack of

Figure 3.3 Thomas Bock's portrait of Mithina, *c.* 1841. Original in the Tasmanian Museum and Art Gallery, Hobart, Tasmania. The History Collection/Alamy Stock Photo. Image ID: J435EW.

records about her. In some retellings, as in Crooke's, she is linked to Jane Franklin's unconventionality and boundary crossings. In others, she appears as a tragic lost soul, and as an emblem of an extinction that did not happen.[173] This section traces how Mithina was entangled in the struggles of others. During her time at Government House, Jane and Eleanor Franklin developed very different views about Indigenous education and acculturation, and particularly about whether or not children should be removed from their parents. These views played into their own struggles for authority with outsiders, with Mithina, and with each other. Meanwhile, Mithina's kin at Wybalenna were simply trying to hold onto their children and to maintain relationships with young people by any means necessary. Both struggles were framed by global discourses of science, humanitarianism, and improvement, though in very different ways.

Mithina was born on Flinders Island in 1835. She probably remained for some time with her mother Wongerneep/Eveline, perhaps longer than other children. Despite grieving the losses of her husband and another daughter, Wongerneep was an adept navigator of the complex dynamics at Wybalenna. Robinson's journals indicate that she often kept her distance from the settlement, spending time in the bush with her kinswomen, collecting mutton birds, eggs, and perhaps parrots for Robinson. She quickly mastered the art of sewing, and when convict servants refused to make dresses for the women of the settlement, she and her kinswomen did, earning Robinson's approval.[174] Amid ongoing conflict between the staff, some parents managed to keep their young children with them, instead of surrendering them to live with others, and this may have been the case with Mithina.[175] After her husband Towterer's death in September 1837, Wongerneep remarried Palle (Hannibal) in 1838. Mithina called him her father, but whether she stayed with him or elsewhere after her mother died in 1840 is unknown.[176]

Soon after Wongerneep died, Jane and Eleanor Franklin went on journeys that reinforced their diverging ideas about Indigenous education and acculturation. Between December 1840 and January 1841, Jane, Eleanor, and John Phillip Gell traveled to South Australia, where they visited the family of the explorer Charles Sturt and a Moravian mission. Their visit made a deep impression on Eleanor and Gell. They both noted the Moravians' efforts to preach and instruct in Indigenous languages, and on how the children at the school seemed to influence their parents.[177] Gell later argued to the Tasmanian Society that a knowledge of Indigenous languages was essential to evangelization, while Eleanor had already attended sermons in Hobart delivered in Māori. She began to correspond with Captain William Hobson, the new governor of Aotearoa New Zealand, about the need for Māori teachers and Bibles.[178] Jane Franklin thought differently. When it came to children, her overriding concern was to maintain order, control, and discipline. Eleanor knew this well. Jane had been briefly in charge of her when she was six, and John Franklin was commanding the *Rainbow*. Eleanor was deeply attached to her father, and she cried bitterly when Jane made her memorize prayers that dwelled on the dangers of the sea. Satisfied that she had broken down Eleanor's resistance, Jane wrote to John, "When left to herself and to me, she is almost all I could wish, and my influence over her is almost unbounded."[179]

Not long after their return from South Australia in early 1841, Jane traveled to Aotearoa New Zealand. She fell down the hatchway of the ship, badly injured her leg, and became dependent on missionaries to travel around the islands (usually carried in a sedan chair by Māori men). She became embedded in missionary circles engaged in complex negotiations with Māori in the aftermath of the Treaty of Waitangi.[180] Her observations confirmed her belief that the improvement of Indigenous children required severing their ties with family and community. Failure to do so, she thought, undermined the discipline of mission schools and settler homes, giving Indigenous parents too much control. When she stayed with the missionaries Robert and Susan Maunsell, she noted that they had two girls as servants whom they had "redeemed from slavery by a couple of blankets." She explained their purchase of the girls, writing, "A free girl would not submit, nor would be allowed to submit to any sort of punishment. . . . This throws a great difficulty in the way of the Missionaries who if they were to punish a child in the school in the slightest manner, must expect the child to be instantly taken away."[181] While she thought that Indigenous place names ought to be preserved, she objected to teaching and preaching in any language but English. She wrote,

> It is well known that the Missionaries of whatever denomination object to the children learning English, & endeavour as much as possible to retain their exclusive influence by dealing with the natives solely or mainly thro' their own language—I agree with Col. Wakefield & Dr. Evans that except for the object of exercising an

exclusive influence over them, this is an erroneous view of things, & that the most effectual way to civilize them & give them new ideas is to put them in possession of the language of their civilizers.[182]

She also met Gunn's friend, the botanist and missionary William Colenso, when he was printing millions of pages of Bibles and other religious texts in Māori. While she persuaded him to contribute botanical papers to the *Tasmanian Journal*, she would not listen to his arguments in favor of evangelization in Indigenous languages.[183]

It appears that John Franklin shared his wife's views, for during her absence, he attempted to remove all the Indigenous children from Flinders Island. In May 1841, he began another investigation of Wybalenna. In their report after a visit to the settlement, William Moriarty and W. F. Mitchell argued that most of the settlement's boys should be sent to sea on the colonial cutters *Eliza* and *Vansittart*, and the girls should be sent to the Orphan School. They argued that this was motivated by the "most philanthropic feelings" and suggested that "the parent will willingly endure the bereavement in exchange for Sugar, or any other equally prized luxury."[184] In June 1841, Adolphus joined the colonial cutter *Vansittart* and was paid £12 a year.[185] He was one of the few literate boys on board (the others being convict boys from Point Puer, also placed on board by Franklin), and a year later Eleanor reported that he was teaching the others to read.[186] Lynette Russell has argued that, despite its dangers, the sea offered Indigenous men and boys a greater measure of freedom than life on land.[187] It is impossible to know whether or not Adolphus saw it this way.

While aboard the *Vansittart*, Adolphus visited both Flinders Island and his own country around Robbins Island, as the ship cruised Bass Strait and visited Port Phillip. It is tempting to imagine that, as a result, he may have been able to contact his uncle Tunnerminnerwait and companions Walter Arthur and Thomas Bruny at Port Phillip. It is certain that he was entangled in ongoing violence, as the armed cutter not only rounded up convicts but also pursued the last Indigenous Tasmanian family who had eluded capture.[188] In March 1842, Franklin turned the *Vansittart* over to junior officers of HMS *Beagle* to help the *Beagle*'s survey of Bass Strait (see below).[189] Adolphus remained on board until at least 1843, when the Canadian exile Linus Miller claimed to have seen "a native lad, of the age of fourteen years, who was engaged as a cabin boy."[190]

Meanwhile, at Government House, Mithina was alternately described as a promising experiment in acculturation, and as a "remnant" of a disappearing people. She was only ever mentioned in writing by the Franklins' innermost circle: Jane Franklin, Eleanor Franklin, and John Phillip Gell. Other descriptions of her were written decades later.[191] Little is known about her early days there, except that she was also educated by Eleanor and was given a bright red dress and a small doll. Many Indigenous Tasmanian women dressed themselves in red when they could, donning red hats and shawls, and it is reasonable to suppose that Mithina's dress represented her own choice.[192] The six-year-old might already have been literate by the time she arrived, for by September 1841 she wrote to her father at Wybalenna without prompting or coaching. Eleanor copied the letter in her diary,

> I am good little girl I have pen & ink cause I am good little girl, I do love my father, I have got a doll & a shift & a petticoat I read my Father. I thank thee for sleep. I

have got red frock. Like my father to come here to see my father. I have got sore feet and shoes and stockings and am very glad, all greet huge ships tell my father [illeg] rooms.

One wonders whether the "huge ships" might have been *Erebus* and *Terror*, greeted by so many at the winter's ball in June. Eleanor added in her diary, "Said one day I do love my God. I think she is affec^tc & intelligent."[193] It is impossible to know whether or not Eleanor's own separations from her father and family made her any more sympathetic to Mithina's longing. But she does seem to have been convinced of the girl's "capacity" for civilization, which, as Zoe Laidlaw has pointed out, was understood by Evangelicals as a marker of common humanity.[194] Perhaps Mithina's doll also speaks to that recognition. Possibly obtained from a missionary's supply, the tiny doll with black skin wore a dress that is now brown with age, and decorated with bright red ribbons at the shoulders (Figure 3.4).[195]

By contrast, Jane's descriptions of Mithina come from three interactions with surgeons between July and September 1841. The first was the new commandant of Flinders Island, the second a naturalist, and the third a humanitarian. Each interaction had a different purpose, a different audience, and a different staging of Mithina. Only one of them gives any window onto Jane Franklin's own feelings about her civilizing project or her new ward. After Franklin's May 1841 inquiry, Malcolm Smith was removed as commandant and a naval surgeon, Peter Fisher, was appointed in his place.

Figure 3.4 A small doll found among Eleanor Franklin Gell's collection in the Derbyshire Record Office. It matches the description of a doll given to Mithina. Derbyshire Record Office D8760/F/OBJ/3.

When Fisher dined at Government House in July 1841, Jane "brought Mathinna in & gave him instructions." His official instructions would follow a fortnight later, but Jane had clearly drafted some or all of them in advance, and Mithina was there as a living illustration. The instructions ordered Fisher to remove the other Indigenous children at Wybalenna and to compel the adults to labor. This echoed John Franklin's belief (forged in 1821 as he starved at Fort Enterprise) that bodily suffering and physical labor were the route to salvation (see Chapter 1).[196] Fisher was unable to implement either order. Henry Reynolds has argued that a core tenet of Indigenous Tasmanian identity after the Black War was that they were a free people in exile who had been unjustly deprived of their lands and had a right to determine their futures.[197] The attempt to break up families and force them to labor like convicts ran up against both of these. Amid this conflict, Fisher sent Jane an account of Mithina, stating approximately how old she was and who her parents were, but Jane's request for further information was never answered.[198]

Within weeks, the convict ship *Asia* arrived. Its surgeon, Dr. Sinclair, had been Jane's traveling companion in the Mediterranean ten years earlier.[199] He carried recommendations from Hooker and the Richardsons, as well as letters from Mary Richardson and Mary Anne Kendall, all testifying to his character and interest in natural history. He was invited to dinner at Government House, and saw the new issue of the *Tasmanian Journal* strewn across the table, about to be dispatched to New Zealand, Sydney, the Cape, and London. A fortnight later, he returned and he and Jane discussed phrenology in Jane's drawing room. This was the place that Robert Crooke later described, either from memory or imagination, as the secret seat of Tasmanian government, in which Mithina was supposed to be a fixture. We do not know whether Mithina was there, or if Bock's phrenological study of Jane's head was alongside the busts, portraits, objects, or mortal remains she had collected and which she and Sinclair discussed. It was, to Jane's mind, just the place for an intimate scientific discussion, and that night she wrote in her diary,

> we came to the Aborigines & I entirely agreed with him in his want of sympathy with those people who think it so very shocking that these inferior races of men should be gradually disappearing from the earth to make room for a higher race—I thought it was more as specimens of natural history that they were regretted than for anything else.[200]

It was a bald statement, devoid of any pretense of sympathy. There was no maternal concern for human suffering, like that claimed by humanitarian women. There was no belief in a shared human past or future, like that of her stepdaughter and other Evangelicals. There was, however, hard evidence of Jane Franklin's belief in the inevitability of Indigenous extinction. This position was fundamentally at odds with the humanitarian mission that underlay the emerging Protectorates. As Anna Gurney had put it in the Select Committee Report on Aboriginal Tribes in 1837, "to imagine that there now exists a race of men devoted by Providence to destruction, is assuredly to libel the beneficent and merciful character of the Most High."[201] For humanitarians and many evangelical Anglicans, human beings shared a single origin and a future determined by a benevolent yet inscrutable Creator. Such a vision underpinned most British civilizing missions, and their aim to remake men, women, and children in the model of middle-class Britons. Jane Franklin, however, had evidently become convinced of the opposite—that Indigenous mortality was caused not by settler violence or introduced disease but by biological racial difference. The theological implications of this position do not seem to have distressed her.

Jane Franklin may not have agreed with many humanitarians, but she knew she needed to boost her humanitarian credentials, especially in the heady, feverish days of the Niger Expedition. In 1841, Thomas Fowell Buxton pressed the Admiralty to send an official expedition of three ships to the Niger River to establish Christian missions, to promote commerce, and to stamp out the slave trade. He was aided by Parry and others in their shared circles of humanitarians and explorers—circles which drew closer together at one of the fetes for the expedition, when the widowed Parry proposed Catherine Hoare, one of Buxton's relatives.[202] The Niger Expedition's popularity nearly eclipsed that of Ross's Antarctic expedition. Jane monitored Buxton's work as closely as possible in British newspapers and correspondence that arrived in Tasmania.[203] Parry's sympathetic letters to Franklin described his and Beaufort's support for the venture, and Mary Simpkinson described the festivities before the ships' departure, one of which she hosted.[204] "The Niger Expedition has made people so mad," Jane wrote to Ross in Sydney, "There have been dinners & balls I believe on board," she added, "& Mrs. Fry lecturing the crew." She described Mary's "African Party" attended by the officers "with the Ashantee princes & their tabor etc."[205] In her eyes, the expedition was a folly, a view shared by many others when a third of the crew died from fever and the ships returned after five months.[206]

The fact that both Fry and their Arctic friends like Parry were so deeply involved in the Niger Expedition was one more irritating reminder of Jane Franklin's obligations, and perhaps her failures. Though she had seen it in practice many times, Jane Franklin still struggled with Fry's model of public engagement rooted in maternal concern. She had left England in 1836 promising to devote herself "heart and soul" to convict women but had never yet written Fry a single word on the subject. As she had once confessed to Gunn, "The fact is I think all such ministrations as Mrs Fry's . . . to be nearly worthless."[207] As her biographer Alison Alexander has observed, Jane had little time and less interest in ameliorating the condition of convict women and was more concerned with making punishment more effective and severe, including shaving women's heads and, importantly, removing their children. Convict women, she thought, were a source of corruption, and they could only be reformed by a "right system at work for their humiliation."[208] But Jane's hand was forced when she was greeted on her return from Aotearoa New Zealand in June 1841 by the convict ship *Rajah*, Fry's personal emissary, Kezia Hayter, and by an elaborate quilt sewn by the convict women on board (now in the National Gallery of Australia). She briefly flirted with a Ladies' Committee to visit female convicts at the Cascades Female Factory and invited Hayter to live at Government House and help with Eleanor's education (and perhaps Mithina's too). Hayter, however, declined. Jane also wrote a letter to Fry that developed the theme so much on her mind—that mothers must be separated from their children to punish one and civilize the other.[209]

In September 1841, as Jane was courting Hayter, writing to Fry, dispatching the *Tasmanian Journal*, and making frank admissions to Dr. Sinclair, the convict ship *Waverly* arrived. The surgeon, Dr. Dunn, had a letter of introduction from Parry and a close association with "the good female philanthropists of England who interest themselves about female convicts."[210] Knowing that Dunn was returning to England, Jane made sure he was well provided with material that demonstrated the benefits of separating children from their parents. Just before he left, she took him on a tour of the Female Factory and introduced him to Mithina. She left the two of them alone, with Mithina chatting away, mostly in English. (Jane recorded that the little girl "continued to make him understand her in talking.")[211] When Dunn left a few days later, he was armed with an introduction to Mary Simpkinson and sheaves of papers on Jane's views on female convict discipline, the operation of the Orphan School, and his own account of Mithina which, sadly, does not survive. Neither does Mithina's impression of him— only a copy of her letter to her father, written around the same time, asking him to come and see her. Shortly thereafter, Fry's emissary, the Quaker George Washington Walker, asked the Flinders Island catechist Robert Clarke to send testimony about the Tasmanians' "capacity for improvement" to the Aborigines' Protection Society (APS) in London, which was also headed by Buxton.[212]

In October 1841, there was an Indigenous Tasmanian rebellion in the Port Phillip colony, led by Adolphus's uncle, Tunnerminnerwait. He, Truganini, and four others raided houses, burned huts, and killed two whalers, in what historians have understood as an act of retaliation sparked by the abduction of one of their comrades. It took several military expeditions and a detachment of Maconochie's "native police" to locate them. In late November 1841, they were caught and committed for trial. Kate Auty and Lynette Russell have argued that even by the legal standards of the 1840s, the trial was a sham.[213] Robinson testified that the accused were sufficiently civilized to know right from wrong, and as a result, Tunnerminnerwait and the other men were hanged, while Truganini and the women were sent back to Flinders Island, followed by the rest of the Tasmanians in Port Phillip in late 1842.[214] Jane Franklin never mentioned the uprising or executions in any of her surviving correspondence. If she realized that she had conversed several times with Truganini (whom she knew as Lallah Rookh), or that Tunnerminnerwait was Adolphus's uncle, or that she had portraits of both of them in her drawing room, she did not comment on it. For her, the rebellion was completely overshadowed by Montagu's dismissal as colonial secretary and its ramifications for the Franklins.

At the same time as the Port Phillip rebellion, John Montagu (who had returned from England in early 1841) persuaded Franklin that a doctor at Richmond, Dr. Coverdale, should be dismissed for negligence. The town petitioned Franklin to reinstate Coverdale, and Montagu accused Jane of instigating the petition. After a confrontation at Government House, Montagu was dismissed. This unleashed an explosion of rumor from the Arthur circles that targeted the Franklins and their associates, airing the most salacious and sordid material that Montagu's supporters possessed. For example, the principal of the Orphan School, Rev. Ewing, had been accused of sexual assault at the school but nevertheless had been kept at his post.[215] He was also a protégé of Jane Franklin's and a member of the Tasmanian Society. The case now surfaced in print, suggesting that the "mantle of petticoat influence" had saved Ewing from disgrace.[216] Meanwhile, Anstey and Swanston circulated rumors about Franklin's past. They possessed a Canadian letter which may have alluded to rumors of murder, cannibalism, and what George Back had told Willard Wentzel were "things that must not be known" on Franklin's 1819–22 expedition (see Chapter 1). Anstey wrote to Swanston, "That letter from Mr Williams—the Governor of one of the Hudson's Bay Company's posts—pronounced the old man, many years ago, to be a fool.—Sir George Back, at a later period declared the same aged person to be that, and something more."[217] In December, Montagu wrote a series of hostile articles about the Franklins, accusing John of imbecility and Jane of political meddling. Both Franklins later characterized these as "dastardly and impudent, though cunningly devised falsehoods."[218]

In early 1842, Montagu traveled to the Colonial Office in London to argue that he should be reinstated. He would later write, "My whole case turned upon the fact of Lady Franklin's improper interference in the business of Government."[219] He told the Colonial Under Secretary James Stephen that she was "a vindictive intermeddling woman" who had overcome "a plain Sailor and a man of sense." Stephen was convinced that she had "forfeited the immunities of her sex by meddling in Public Affairs," and that Franklin was "deficient in the authority and self-reliance required in such an Office."[220] Stephen was also engaged in a massive reform of the Colonial Office, purging private networks in a bid to centralize administration and formalize communication across the empire.[221] The networks of friendship and obligation that were central to the Franklins' struggles for authority were now, like those of many other colonial administrators, increasingly liabilities rather than assets.

In this crisis, as in so many others, Mary Simpkinson acted as her sister's envoy to the Arctic circles. Jane instructed Mary to tell Beaufort and Parry that Montagu was "trying to be [Governor] instead of Sir John, for that is in fact the truth." She gave precise instructions about what to show Beaufort, Parry, and Sabine, particularly how Mary should pitch particular Tasmanian newspaper articles. Jane also begged her to "send us every notice you see or hear of respecting [the *Tasmanian Journal*], whether good bad or indifferent." She asked Mary to make "great friends" of a Mr. and Mrs. MacLachlan who were visiting from Tasmania, and carrying Bock's painting of Franklin, Ross, and Crozier at the observatory.[222]

Both Mithina and Adolphus were also entangled in the Franklins' campaigns to shore up their reputations in England. Jane sent Mary a copy of Bock's portrait of Mithina and followed it a few weeks later with a description of the girl's transformation.[223] The second letter was prompted by the Franklins' encounter with Adolphus on board the cutter *Vansittart*. John Franklin had lent the cutter to the officers of HMS *Beagle*, who had returned to Tasmania to survey Bass Strait.[224] Adolphus had been on board for nearly a year and was rapidly becoming a good seaman, learning the ropes and keeping the watch. While Eleanor noted that he was teaching the other boys to read, Jane told Mary he was "vastly inferior . . . to Mathinna in intelligence & sweetness of expression—& is much blacker in complexion than Mathinna who appears to us to be daily growing more copper—coloured as she advances in civilization."[225]

Under the command of Lieutenant Charles Forsyth, Adolphus cruised back and forth across the strait under naval discipline. He also appears to have received naval rations of rum.[226] In addition to the survey, he was involved in an effort to rescue the Franklins when they disappeared in May 1842 during their overland journey to the island's west coast. They both referred to this journey as "our Land Expedition," and it was clearly undertaken with an eye on their metropolitan scientific circles. Accompanied by a naturalist, a surveyor, a journalist, and twenty convicts, they intended their journey to be understood as a scientific expedition with a published narrative, and Jane did try to persuade John Murray to publish the account.[227]

It is also possible that while on the *Vansittart*, Adolphus was involved in developing Indigenous networks of knowledge across Bass Strait and alongside British scientific networks. The vessel not only cruised along Tasmania's north and west coasts but also stopped at Flinders Island, went back and forth to Port Phillip, and ultimately joined the *Beagle* in Sydney. On Flinders, Adolphus and the rest of the vessel's crew observed the rule of the new commandant, Dr. Henry Jeanneret, a surgeon-naturalist from Port Arthur. Jeanneret was not only removing children from Wybalenna but also forcing the adults to labor for their rations. Someone sent this information to Walter George Arthur in Port Phillip. He later mentioned having a courier on one of the ships that visited Flinders Island regularly.[228] Walter Arthur wrote to the Quaker George Washington Walker in Hobart, who warned Harriet Jeanneret that "the aborigines have received the impression that the present mode of treatment on Flinders is rigid and severe."[229] This may be example of what Tracey Banivanua Mar identified as an Indigenous "intellectual and discursive circuitry" of the 1840s that was made possible by mobile Indigenous actors, like Adolphus.[230] When Walter Arthur and the other Tasmanians landed at Hobart in October 1842, he requested, and received, an audience with the Franklins. Arthur spoke with Jane Franklin for more than an hour. While the newspapers took note of their meeting, Jane Franklin made no record of it.[231]

In January 1843, the Franklins received a dispatch from Lord Stanley, the Secretary of State for the Colonies, exonerating Montagu and excoriating Franklin for incompetence. Unknown to the Franklins, the dispatch was already circulating among the Arthur and Derwent Bank circles. Montagu had sent copies of it and his own correspondence to his friends in Hobart, Port Phillip, and Sydney, as well as to the Athenaeum and United Service Clubs in London, to which both he and Franklin belonged.[232] It became known as "Montagu's Book," and it claimed that Jane Franklin and her "unprincipled coterie of flatterers" had been responsible for Montagu's dismissal and that the colony as a whole had been "sacrificed to female artifice."[233] Swanston made sure it was displayed at the Derwent Bank for everyone to read, but first he sent a full copy to Anstey, who was delighted by the humiliation of "the woman."[234]

The Franklins tried to suppress the "Book" in Tasmania and in London. Jane wrote to Mary about her horror of being seen in the London newspapers and the Colonial Office "in a light the most repulsive to my nature, my tastes, my habits and my principles."[235] John Franklin begged Richardson, Parry, James Ross, and Beaufort "to confer together and determine on what next steps they can take."[236] He asked Richardson to contact "any of our mutual scientific friends who continue their interest in the happiness and welfare of my self my dearest wife & daughter."[237] He asked Ross to intercede with Stanley, and (betraying the extent of Jane's knowledge of government affairs) told him to see Mary Simpkinson for details of his private, sealed dispatches to the Colonial Office. Montagu, he said, returned from England "determined to destroy Lady Franklin," adding "she cannot help being clever but that is what the party cannot bear—They think they could have got on with a simple unsuspicious & obstinate old fool like myself, but her discernment has unveiled them."[238]

Jane Franklin also turned to scientific circles for vindication. Strzelecki was in Britain promoting his narrative of his round-the-world voyage, and Jane told Mary, "he will be the brightest star in your galaxy of worthies." Jane made sure that he was well supplied with Tasmanian "curiosities" to circulate along with tales of the Franklins' woes. Mithina's portrait was among these. She asked Mary to give it to Strzelecki to have it engraved and enclosed a lock of Mithina's hair. Bock's portrait, she said, was a very good likeness, "but the figure is too large & tall—she looks there like a girl of 12, but is only 7—the attitude is exactly hers, & she always wears the dress you see her in." She made it clear, however, that the portrait was not a sentimental one, however it might appear. It was meant to testify to the Franklin family's attempts to use their home at Government House to improve the colony and its people. In doing so, she gestured to their promotion of colonial art and science, to their own victimization by the Arthur circle, and what she now saw as the folly of acculturation. "I think you will find people much interested in this portrait & the hair," she wrote to Mary, "She is one of the remnant of a people about to disappear from the face of the earth."[239] She had already given Strzelecki two other portraits of Tasmanian intermediaries, but Mithina's was intended to "show the influence of some degree of civilization upon a child of as pure a race as they, and who in spite of every endeavour, and though entirely apart from her own people, retains much of the unconquerable nature of the savage."[240]

As the Franklins' recall loomed, their correspondence began to focus on Mithina's "wildness," "disobedience," and above all, her "savagery." Eleanor wrote to her cousin Catherine in February 1843 that though Mithina "is improving . . . it will probably be a long time before she becomes quite civilized."[241] Jane told Mary that Mithina "retains much of the unconquerable nature of the savage; extreme uncertainty of will and temper, great want of perseverance and attention, little if any, self controle [sic], and great acuteness of the senses and facility of imitation."[242] Yet they refused to return her to Flinders Island. In June 1843, the catechist Robert Clarke wrote to the new colonial secretary J. E. Bicheno and asked Franklin "to grant permission to the Aboriginal 'Palle' the father of the female child now under His Excellency's protection to be brought from Flinders Island to see his child." He made it clear that this was at "their request made thro me." This was the only time that Franklin directly acknowledged Mithina's presence in Government House. Two days later, he wrote on the back of the file, "Mr Clarke to be informed that I cannot comply with his request. He is involving himself with matters which in no way belong to him."[243] A month later, Mithina was sent to the Orphan School, where she would remain for over a year.[244]

In August 1843, the Franklins learned that they had been recalled when the new governor, Sir John Eardley-Wilmot, unexpectedly arrived in Tasmania and moved into Government House. It was a humiliating experience, as the Franklins had to move out, sell many of their possessions, and scramble to secure passage to England.[245] They were comforted by their new friend, the bishop of Tasmania, Francis Nixon, who said of Jane, "if her stockings are blue, her petticoats are so long that he has never found it out."[246] When the Franklins returned to Britain, this sense of humiliation followed them. Mary Richardson wrote that Jane Franklin

> is just exactly what she was, only vexed and harassed by personal affronts w^h she cannot get above or disregard. Her mind is active and interested in the colony, but she is quite unable to bear the misrepresentation she has met with. . . . She was vexed that I did not see all as she did & thought all I said unfeeling & factious.[247]

The Franklins' Tasmanian experiences followed them to Britain, and then to the Arctic. Shortly after returning to Britain in 1844, Franklin put his name forward to lead a new polar expedition in HMS *Erebus* and *Terror* to complete the Northwest Passage and contribute to the Magnetic Crusade.[248] Beaufort and Sabine were both uncomfortable with the idea, preferring James Ross, who had much more experience. But Ross had been shattered by his recent expedition and had promised his new wife Ann never to return to the ice. Both Back and Sabine approached Ross privately, raising discreet objections to Franklin based on his age and health, but he declined. Beaufort asked Richardson and Parry for their opinions, but to his surprise, Richardson wrote that the obese 59-year-old was fit and healthy, while Parry reportedly said, "If you don't let him go, the man will die of disappointment."[249]

And so in 1844–5, John Franklin made ready for a new Arctic expedition. It was certainly an attempt to restore his reputation, but it was also a new development in the Franklin family's struggles over truth. As the Franklins prepared for John's departure, two publications circulated alongside the press coverage of the new expedition. The first was their own *Narrative of Some Passages in the History of Van Diemen's Land*.[250] The 157-page pamphlet attempted to vindicate the Franklins from the charges of "petticoat government" laid out in Montagu's "Book." It was privately printed in London, and copies were sent both to Tasmania and to the Colonial Office. The pamphlet bore John Franklin's name, but it was largely crafted by Jane, and edited by Edward and Elizabeth Sabine.[251] In his last letter to his wife from the *Erebus* in 1845, Franklin wrote that he had pressed it on all his officers, who were "struck with the moderation and yet firmness of the language."[252] The second was Strzelecki's *Physical Description of New South Wales and Van Diemen's Land*. Financed by the Franklins and the Tasmanian Society and dedicated to John Franklin, the book was hugely influential. Charles Darwin used it to revise his account of Tasmania in the second edition of the *Voyage of the Beagle*.[253] The work including Strzelecki's view that "attempts to civilize & christianize the aborigines, from which the preservation & elevation of their race was expected to result *have utterly failed*."[254]

Strzelecki had, for a time, held Mithina's portrait. By December 1844, it had been returned to Jane Franklin. Keen to rebuild her relationship with the Richardsons on the eve of John Franklin's departure, she invited their daughter Josephine to visit her. Jane promised to give the ten-year-old a pair of gloves made by Indigenous women on Flinders Island and to show her Mithina's portrait. "When you come to see me," Jane wrote, "I will show you a portrait of Mathinna Wageniss Flinders a little native girl whom I brought up for 2 or 3 years. . . . She is dressed in a scarlet frock with a black leather girdle which sets off her naked black arms & legs to great advantage."[255]

Within months, Mithina's portrait would be painted again, this time by the artist John Skinner Prout. In 1845, Prout traveled to Wybalenna with Jane Franklin's nephew, Frank Simpkinson, who was now stationed at Rossbank Observatory. Prout's portrait of Mithina was one of twenty-one portraits of Indigenous Tasmanians which are now in the British Museum.[256] Jane Franklin never mentioned that her nephew had met the "little native girl whom I brought up," nor did she ever refer to Prout's portrait, if she even knew it existed.

In 1846, while John Franklin was imprisoned in the ice off the west coast of King William Island, Walter George Arthur wrote a petition to Queen Victoria that was signed by eight respected elders on Flinders Island. The petition directly contested the narrative of extinction that Strzelecki and the Franklins had promoted. It not only articulated that the Tasmanians were a free people unjustly deprived of their land but also that they had been systematically abused by the commandant Dr. Jeanneret; that he had ruined their homes, their gardens, their church services, and their educations; and that in short, all their own efforts at "improvement" had fallen victim to his caprice.[257] In the inquiry that followed, Mithina was interviewed by Lt. Matthew Friend, in order to determine whether or not the catechist's wife had hanged a five-year-old girl, as Mithina and others maintained. As the ten-year-old Mithina told her story, she relegated the Franklins to a corner of her own brief history, saying:

> I do not know how old I am. I lived with Lady Franklin for some time. I have been under the care of Mr and Mrs Clark, when I was flogged I was placed across a table and my hands and feet were tied. I was flogged every day. I did not do my work and if I did my work, it was needle work. I made my clothes. I have no father or Mother. I think I was flogged when I ought not to have been flogged.[258]

Leonie Stevens has argued that Mithina's testimony spoke not only to the everyday violence that she experienced but also to the forms of resistance and rebellion available to Indigenous children.[259] One of the most common, and the most powerful, was to tell stories, to "gammon," to try to take control of the truth. If, as Stevens has argued, Mithina was a key member of this group of openly rebellious children, then the child was full of stories, weapons deployed in her own struggles with authority, which had little if any reference to those which Jane Franklin had attached to her.

It has been said that Tasmanian history is characterized by absence, particularly of Indigenous children taken by violence, abduction, and other disappearances.[260] As Penny Russell has argued, Mithina has come to represent hundreds of other children who vanished, leaving behind few archival traces.[261] In this chapter, I have tried to show how these children, like so many other intermediaries, were entangled in the politics of truth. They were part of stories that circulated around colonial civility, scientific research, philanthropic missions, progress, and improvement during the Franklins' administration. They were also linked into histories from the other side of the world, the obligations and connections of the Arctic circles and their families. They were connected to circuits of imperial science as both specimens and participants, whether collecting gull's eggs, working on survey ships, or being modeled and posed as specimens of a "dying race."

So far as Jane Franklin was concerned, Mithina and Adolphus were meant to be evidence of her own attempts at "improvement," including her arguments in favor of removing children from their families, her view that Indigenous extinction was inevitable, and her promotion of her husband and herself as patrons of colonial science. In her eyes, these children's lives were one small part of her own painful emergence as a woman in the public sphere. They were linked to the Antipodean experiences that left her with a suspicion of the press, a propensity to see enemies everywhere, and a better understanding of her gendered authority. When she left Tasmania, she was determined never to be pilloried again as a "man in petticoats." During the search for her missing husband, she would change how she claimed authority, grounding her public presence in a wife's sentiment, anxiety, and philanthropy rather than a woman's interest in science and improvement. Yet she could not predict how that authority would be shaped by other intermediaries with disrupted childhoods, people who would shape her own struggles over the truth.

It is much more difficult to discover how the Franklins fit into the struggles of Indigenous Tasmanians in general and Adolphus and Mithina in particular. Neither Jane Franklin nor her stepdaughter Eleanor perceived how these children were linked to emerging circuits of Indigenous imperial literacy or the complex politics at Wybalenna. It is impossible to know whether Adolphus ran messages back and forth across Bass Strait for Walter George Arthur, or how often Mithina gammoned at Wybalenna, even if it meant a flogging. Like so many other intermediaries from Baffin Island to Tasmania, they slipped in and out of view as they negotiated the perilous middle grounds of their childhoods. Both children engaged in acts of resistance, some of which registered in the archival record and some of which did not. By the 1850s they, like John Franklin, had disappeared from the written record, but not from living memory.[262]

Notes

1 *lutruwita* is the name of the main island of Tasmania in *palawa kani*, the only Indigenous language in *lutruwita* Tasmania today, and has been painstakingly reconstructed by *palawa* and *pakana* scholars. Tasmania and Van Diemen's Land were used alternately in the 1830s and 1840s, formally switching to "Tasmania" in 1856. For brevity and ease, I will use Tasmania throughout this and subsequent chapters.

2 Robert M'Cormick, *Voyages of Discovery in the Arctic and Antarctic Seas, and Round the World . . .* (London: Sampson Low, Marston, Searle, and Rivington, 1884), 200–3; Leonard Huxley, *Life and Letters of Sir Joseph Dalton Hooker, O.M, G.C.S.I., Based on Materials Collected and Arranged by Lady Hooker* (London: John Murray, 1918), 1, 2:119.

3 TA MM44/1/3, Eleanor Franklin to Catherine Franklin, May 22, 1841.

4 TA GO33/1/39, 236, see below n. 188. With respect to names and naming conventions, *palawa* and *pakana* are terms of identification used by Indigenous Tasmanian people today in *palawa kani*. Generally speaking, *palawa* refers to people now living in the south of *lutruwita*/Tasmania and *pakana* to people in the north,

including the East Coast and Bass Strait Islands. These are contemporary groups, and following advice, I use "Indigenous Tasmanians" to refer to the diverse political and linguistic groups on the islands in the period covered by this chapter. Mithina is usually called "Mathinna" following Jane Franklin's spelling, but I use the spelling suggested by the Tasmanian Museum and Art Gallery. I have left direct quotes as they were written. Since Adolphus clearly stated that he wished to be known by that name, I have respected that wish, see n. 188.

5 See Penny Russell, "Girl in a Red Dress: Inventions of Mathinna," *Australian Historical Studies* 43, no. 3 (2012): 341-62. For the Franklins as patrons of science, see Lambert, *Gates of Hell*, 61-140; Penny Russell, "Unhomely Moments: Civilising Domestic Worlds in Colonial Australia," *The History of the Family* 14 (2009): 329-39.

6 See Konishi et al., *Indigenous Intermediaries*; Shellam et al., *Brokers and Boundaries*; Schaffer et al., *The Brokered World*; Kennedy, *Last Blank Spaces*, 159-94; Lester and Laidlaw, *Indigenous Communities and Settler Colonialism*; Samuel Furphy and Amanda Nettelbeck, eds., *Aboriginal Protection and Its Intermediaries in Britain's Antipodean Colonies* (New York and London: Routledge, 2019).

7 Lyndall Ryan, *Tasmanian Aborigines: A History since 1803* (Sydney: Allen and Unwin, 2012), 3-42.

8 Patsy Cameron, *Grease and Ochre: The Blending of Two Cultures at the Colonial Sea Frontier* (Hobart: Fullers Bookshop, 2011). For the blended society of the early nineteenth century, see James Boyce, *Van Diemen's Land* (Melbourne: Black, Inc., 2010), 15-141 and also Ryan, *Tasmanian Aborigines*, 58-83.

9 Henry Reynolds, *The Other Side of the Frontier: Aboriginal Resistance to the European Invasion of Australia* (Ringwood: Penguin Books Australia, 1990); Henry Reynolds, *Fate of a Free People: A Radical Re-Examination of the Tasmanian Wars* (Ringwood: Penguin Books Australia, 1995); Boyce, *Van Diemen's Land*, 197-202; Ryan, *Tasmanian Aborigines*, 112; Benjamin Madley, "From Terror to Genocide: Britain's Tasmanian Penal Colony and Australia's History Wars," *Journal of British Studies* 47 (January 2008): 77-106.

10 Nicholas Clements, *The Black War: Fear, Sex and Resistance in Tasmania* (St. Lucia: University of Queensland Press, 2014), 1-4.

11 Henry Reynolds, *A History of Tasmania* (Cambridge: Cambridge University Press, 2012), 29; Lester, *Imperial Networks*, 106-9; PP 1831 (259), Van Diemen's Land. Copies of All Correspondence Between Lieutenant-Governor Arthur and His Majesty's Secretary of State for the Colonies, on the Subject of the Military Operations Lately Carried on Against the Aboriginal Inhabitants of Van Diemen's Land.

12 The literature here is considerable and growing. See Boyce, *Van Diemen's Land*, 261-313, Ryan, *Tasmanian Aborigines*, Clements, *Black War*; see Tom Lawson, *The Last Man: A British Genocide in Tasmania* (London: I.B. Tauris, 2014); Nicholas Dean Brodie, *The Vandemonian War the Secret History of Britain's Tasmanian Invasion* (Richmond: Hardie Grant Books, 2017). For the "History Wars", see Stuart MacIntyre and Anna Clark, *The History Wars* (Melbourne: Melbourne University Press, 2003); Ann Curthoys, "The History of Killing and the Killing of History," in *Archive Stories: Facts, Fictions, and the Writing of History*, ed. Antoinette Burton (Durham and London: Duke University Press, 2006), 351-73.

13 Lester and Dussart, *Colonization*, 67-76.

14 See Lyndall Ryan, "Historians, *Friendly Mission* and the Contest for Robinson and Trukanini," in *Reading Robinson: Companion Essays to Friendly Mission*, eds.

Anna Johnston and Mitchell Rolls (Hobart: Quintus Publishing, 2008), 147–60; Cassandra Pybus, *Truganini: Journey Through the Apocalypse* (Crows Nest: Allen & Unwin, 2020); Allison Cadzow, "Guided by Her: Aboriginal Women's Participation in Australian Expeditions," in *Brokers and Boundaries: Colonial Exploration in Indigenous Territory*, ed. Tiffany Shellam et al. (Canberra: ANU Press, 2016), 85–118; Reynolds, *Fate of a Free People*, 121–57.

15 N. J. B. Plomley, *Friendly Mission: The Tasmanian Journals of George Augustus Robinson, 1829-34*, 2nd ed. (Launceston and Hobart, Tasmania: Queen Victoria Museum & Art Gallery and Quintus Publishing, 2008). Reynolds, *Fate of a Free People*, 159; Ryan, *Tasmanian Aborigines* 219.

16 In 1830, Adolphus's uncle, Tunnerminnerwait/Pevay, met Robinson on Robbins Island and began traveling with him. Tunnerminnerwait, his older brother Wymurric and his wife Larratong, their son Timemernedic, and the rest of the Parperloihener clan, traveled to Flinders Island in 1832. A year later, Robinson captured Mithina's parents (Towterer and Wongerneep) in June 1833 at Port Davey. Clements, *The Black War*, 180–9. Ryan, *Tasmanian Aborigines*, 166–70; for a synopsis of the conflict with the Van Diemen's Land Company, see Boyce, *Van Diemen's Land*, 202–5; Ian McFarlane, "Cape Grim," in *Whitewash: On Keith Windschuttle's Fabrication of Aboriginal History*, ed. Robert Manne (Melbourne: Black Inc., 2003), 277–98; Plomley, *Friendly Mission*, 773; Pybus, *Truganini*, 304.

17 Ryan, *Tasmanian Aborigines*, 232–9; for Robinson's models, see Alan Lester, "George Augustus Robinson and Imperial Networks," in *Reading Robinson: Companion Essays to Friendly Mission*, eds. Anna Johnston and Mitchell Rolls (Hobart: Quintus Publishing, 2008), 27–39.

18 Arthur was the son of Rolepa, the Ben Lomond chief, while Thomas, David, and Peter Brune were the sons of Woorraddy, the Nuennone chief.

19 Ryan, *Tasmanian Aborigines*, 220–22, 232. See Judy Birmingham and Andrew Wilson, "Archaeologies of Cultural Interaction: Wybalenna Settlement and Killalpaninna Mission," *International Journal of Historical Archaeology* 14 (2010): 15–38; Leonie Stevens, *Me Write Myself: The Free Aboriginal Inhabitants of Van Diemen's Land at Wybalenna* (Clayton: Monash University Publishing, 2017); Grant Finlay, *'Good People Always Crackney in Heaven' Mythic Conversations in lutruwita/Tasmania* (Hobart: Fullers Publishing, 2019); Penny Van Toorn, *Writing Never Arrives Naked: Early Aboriginal Cultures of Writing in Australia* (Canberra: Aboriginal Studies Press, 2006).

20 Laidlaw, "Aunt Anna's Report"; Great Britain, *Report of the Parliamentary Select Committee on Aboriginal Tribes (British Settlements) Reprinted, With Comments, by the Aborigines Protection Society* (London: William Ball, Aldine Chambers, 1837), 13–15; Lester and Dussart, *Colonization*, 91.

21 He was supported by, among others, the testimony of the Quaker travelers George Washington Walker and James Backhouse, who had visited Flinders as part of their intercolonial "witnessing" tour at the behest of Elizabeth Fry. Penelope Edmonds, "Travelling 'Under Concern': Quakers James Backhouse and George Washington Walker Tour the Antipodean Colonies, 1832–41," *The Journal of Imperial and Commonwealth History* 40, no. 5 (December 2012): 769–88.

22 Parry, *Parry of the Arctic*, 136. DRO D8760/F/FJR/1/1/48, Franklin to Richardson, April 6, 1829; SPRI MS 438/26/491, Parry to Lady Maria Stanley, Admiralty, April 11, 1829.

23 Lyndall Ryan, "The Australian Agricultural Company, the Van Diemen's Land Company: Labour Relations with Aboriginal Landholders, 1824-1835," in *Intimacies*

of Violence in the Settler Colony: Economies of Dispossession around the Pacific Rim, eds. Penelope Edmonds and Amanda Nettelbeck (Cham, Switzerland: Palgrave-Macmillan, 2018), 25–44; SPRI MS 438/26/341, Parry to Franklin, Port Stephens, October 4, 1830.
24 Jane Franklin's time in the Mediterranean is best explored in Alexander, *Ambitions*, 29–46.
25 Daniel Simpson, "Expeditionary Collections: Haslar Hospital Museum and the Circulation of Public Knowledge, 1815-1855," in *Mobile Museums: Collections in Circulation*, ed. Felix Driver, Mark Nesbitt, and Caroline Cornish (London: UCL Press, 2021), 149–77.
26 DRO D8760/F/FJR/1/1/63, John Franklin to John Richardson, June 17, 1832.
27 RGS-IBG AP 115, Minutes of the Raleigh Dining club, 1827-54.
28 Driver, *Geography Militant*, 32–7.
29 Richard Drayton, *Nature's Government: Science, Imperial Britain, and the "Improvement" of the World* (New Haven and London: Yale University Press, 2000), 130–2.
30 As this river runs through both Dene and Inuit territory, it has multiple names today, and perhaps more in the 1830s. It is now known as the Back River.
31 SPRI MS 1503/9/4-14, John Richardson correspondence, 1832; SPRI MS 1503/9/16, Franklin to Richardson, October 6, 1832.
32 See SPRI MS1503/9/18, George Back to John Richardson, October 26, 1832; SPRI MS 395/41/2-9BL; SPRI MS395/54/1 BL, M. Maconochie to Back, March 11, 1839.
33 Hugh N Wallace, *The Navy, the Company, and Richard King: British Exploration in the Canadian Arctic, 1829-1860* (Montreal: McGill-Queen's University Press, 1980), 23–4; Laidlaw, *Protecting the Empire's Humanity*, 31–60.
34 Wallace, *Richard King*, 30.
35 Eber, *Encounters on the Passage*, 37; Fossett, *In Order to Live Untroubled*, 140–6.
36 James Heartfield, *The Aborigines' Protection Society: Humanitarian Imperialism in Australia, New Zealand, Fiji, Canada, South Africa and the Congo, 1836-1909* (New York: Columbia University Press, 2011), 15–17; Laidlaw, *Protecting the Empire's Humanity*, 31–60; Lester and Dussart, *Colonization*, 86–113.
37 DRO D8760/F/FJR/1/1/74, Franklin to Richardson, May 15, 1835.
38 Ross, *Polar Pioneers*, 165–214; John Cawood, "The Magnetic Crusade: Science and Politics in Early Victorian Britain," *ISIS* 70, no. 4 (December 1979): 492–518; Edward J. Larson, "Public Science for a Global Empire: The British Quest for the South Magnetic Pole," *ISIS* 102, no. 1 (March 2011): 34–59.
39 SPRI MS248/303/67, John Franklin to Jane Franklin, March 25, 1836. TA MM4/1/3, John Franklin to Hannah Booth, March 26, 1836; SPRI MS 248/303/68, John Franklin to Jane Franklin, April 7, 1836; see also DRO D8760/F/FJR/1/1/48, Franklin to Richardson, April 6, [1829]. Franklin had experience in diplomacy from his time on HMS *Rainbow* in the Mediterranean in addition to his time on the Barren Grounds.
40 N. J. B. Plomley, *Weep in Silence: A History of the Flinders Island Aboriginal Settlement* (Hobart: Blubber Head Press, 1987), 524, 527.
41 Penny Olsen and Lynette Russell, *Australia's First Naturalists: Indigenous Peoples' Contribution to Early Zoology* (Canberra: NLA Publishing, 2019), 102; Pybus, *Truganini*, 143; see also Stevens, *Me Write Myself*, 137–8.
42 Plomley, *Weep in Silence*, 346; Finlay, '*Good People*', 223–4; Stevens, *Me Write Myself*, 186–8.

43 Ian McFarlane, *Beyond Awakening: The Aboriginal Tribes of North West Tasmania: A History* (Launceston: Fullers Bookshop, 2008), 195; Plomley, *Weep in Silence*, 421, 436–7, 440–1, 472; Sally Dammery, *Walter George Arthur, A Free Tasmanian?* (Melbourne: Monash Publications in History, 2001), 7. Clements, *The Black War*, 117.
44 Ronald Gunn to William Hooker, February 15, 1838, in *Van Diemen's Land Correspondents: Letters from R.C. Gunn, R.W. Lawrence, Jorgen Jorgenson, Sir John Franklin and Others to Sir William J. Hooker, 1827–1849*, ed. T. E. Burns and J. R. Skemp (Launceston: Queen Victoria Museum, 1961), 71.
45 McFarlane, *Beyond Awakening*, 195–6.
46 Plomley, *Weep in Silence*, 481, 494, 498.
47 SPRI MS395/53/1, Alexander Maconochie to Back, March 14, nd.
48 Alexander, *Ambitions* 176; SPRI MS395/53, correspondence between Alexander and Mary Maconochie and George Back; AJCP M Series: Papers of Sir Walter Trevelyan, Newcastle Upon Tyne University, Series WCT 182, letters from Mary Maconochie (http://nla.gov.au/nla.obj-1508188840); AJCP M Series: M1167-M1168, Letters of George Coombe, National Library of Scotland, Fonds MSS. 7201-7515, https://nla.gov.au/nla.obj-1063077966.
49 P. R. Eldershaw, *Guide to the Public Records of Tasmania. Colonial Secretary's Office* (Hobart: Archives Office of Tasmania, 1957).
50 For Franklin's relationship with Montagu, see Craig Joel, *A Tale of Ambition and Unrealised Hope: John Montagu and Sir John Franklin* (North Melbourne: Australian Scholarly Publishing Pty Ltd., 2011). For Montagu and Forster's interests in the Derwent Bank, see Eleanor Robin, *Swanston: Merchant Statesman* (North Melbourne: Australian Scholarly Publishing Pty Ltd., 2018).
51 Kirsty Reid, *Gender, Crime and Empire: Convicts, Settlers and the State in Early Colonial Australia* (Manchester: Manchester University Press, 2007), 168–70; Edmonds, "Travelling 'Under Concern.'"
52 SPRI MS395/53/1, Alexander Maconochie to George Back, March 14, nd.
53 John Vincent Barry, "Pioneers in Criminology: Alexander Maconochie," *The Journal of Criminal Law, Criminology and Police Science* 47, no. 2 (July–August 1956): 151; Reid, *Gender, Crime and Empire*, 174.
54 *The Austral-Asiatic Review*, January 16, 1838, 4.
55 DRO D8760/F/FJR/1/1/77, John Franklin to John Richardson, August 18, 1837.
56 SPRI MS 248/174, Jane Franklin to Mary Simpkinson, October 7, 1837; Woodward, *Portrait of Jane*, 206–7; for female convicts, Alexander, *Ambitions*, 94–104.
57 Quoted in Alexander, *Ambitions*, 179.
58 TA NS1602, Thomas Anstey to Charles Swanston, February 23, 1837, March 12, 1837.
59 TA NS1602, Anstey to Swanston, November 16, 1837.
60 DRO D8760/F/FJR/1/1/77, John Franklin to John and Mary Richardson, August 18, 1837.
61 SPRI MS395/54/1/BL, Mary Maconochie to Back, April 30, nd.
62 SPRI MS395/54/1/BL, Mary Maconochie to Back, April 30, nd.
63 RGS AP 115, Minutes of the Raleigh Dining Club, February 5, 19, and March 5, 1838.
64 SPRI MS 1503/18/1, John to Mary Richardson, February 22, 1838; SPRI MS 1503/18/20, John to Mary Richardson, March 23, 1838.
65 RS16/8, Jane Franklin to Mary Simpkinson, June 21, 1838 (extracts).
66 SPRI MS 248/89; BJ, Jane Franklin diary, September 22, 1840.
67 SPRI MS395/53/1/BL, Alexander Maconochie to Back, March 14, [1839].

68 PP 1837-8 [121] Report on the State of Prison Discipline in Van Diemen's Land, &c, by Captain Maconochie.
69 Reid, *Gender, Crime and Empire*, 161-203.
70 TA NS6102, Anstey to Swanston, October 4, 1838. Others saw Maconochie's dismissal as the work of Montagu and Forster, see Morris Miller, *Pressmen and Governors: Australian Editors and Writers in early Tasmania, a Contribution to the History of the Australian Press and Literature with Notes Biographical and Bibliographical* (Sydney: Angus & Robertson, 1952), 33.
71 NA BJ 3/18, 3 November, 1838—for the Molesworth report, see Reid, *Gender Crime and Empire*.
72 Quoted in Lambert, *Gates of Hell*, 114.
73 See RGS-IBG CB2/221, John Gould correspondence from Hobart, 1834-1840.
74 Robinson in *Weep in Silence*, 605.
75 For other examples, see Plomley, *Weep in Silence*, 700.
76 See Rebecca Wood, Rebecca Wood, "Frontier Violence and the Bush Legend: The Sydney Herald's Response to the Myall Creek Massacre Trials and the Creation of Colonial Identity," *History Australia* 6, no. 3 (2009): 67.1-67.19, DOI: 10.2104/ha090067.
77 Lester and Dussart, *Colonization*, 113.
78 Plomley, *Weep in Silence*, 610.
79 Olsen and L. Russell, *Australia's First Naturalists*, 102.
80 Plomley, *Weep in Silence*, 779.
81 Ryan, *Tasmanian Aborigines*, 225-7. Lester and Dussart, *Colonization*, 107.
82 It is impossible to do justice here to the complexity of these negotiations of identity and obligation at Wybalenna. See Finlay, *'Good People'*, 62-137; Stevens, *Me Write Myself*, 71-217; Ryan, *Tasmanian Aborigines*, 219-52.
83 TA CON31/1/14, 94.
84 Laidlaw, *Colonial Connections*, 70-1.
85 SPRI MS395/54/1 BL, Mary Maconochie to Back, March 11, 1839.
86 SPRI MS 248/174, Jane Franklin to Mary Simpkinson, February 13, 1839.
87 SPRI MS 248/174, Jane Franklin to Mary Simpkinson, February 13, 1839; February 23, 1839.
88 DRO D8760/F/FJR/1/1/82, John Franklin to J. Richardson, December 5, 1840; for further details of Peter Barrow (including the Hobart brawl) see Samuel Furphy, "'Philanthropy or Patronage?: Aboriginal Protectors in the Port Phillip District and Western Australia," in *Aboriginal Protection and Its Intermediaries in Britain's Antipodean Colonies*, ed. Samuel Furphy and Amanda Nettelbeck (New York and London: Routledge, 2019), 58-76.
89 SPRI MS 395/54/1 BL, Mary Maconochie to Back, March 11, 1839.
90 SPRI MS 248/174, Jane Franklin to Mary Simpkinson, February 13 and 23, 1839.
91 Alexander, *Ambitions*, 172-4.
92 *Colonial Times*, February 12, 1839, 5; "Colonial Magistracy," *Colonial Times*, February 12, 1839, 4.
93 SPRI MS 248/174, Jane Franklin to Mary Simpkinson February 23, 1839.
94 For the importance of such envoys, see Laidlaw, *Colonial Connections* 68.
95 For the Niger expedition, see David Lambert, *Mastering the Niger: James MacQueen's African Geography and the Struggle over Atlantic Slavery* (Chicago and London: University of Chicago Press, 2013), 176 206; Andrew Porter, *Religion versus Empire? British Protestant Missionaries and Overseas Expansion, 1700-1914* (Manchester and New York: Manchester University Press, 2004), 150-2; Laidlaw, *Protecting the Empire's Humanity*, 117-24; for Parry's involvement see Parry, *Parry of the Arctic*, 213-14.

96 SPRI MS 248/88, Jane Franklin Diary, June 1840.
97 SPRI MS 248/88; BJ, Jane Franklin Diary, June 1840, August 20, 1840.
98 TNA CO 18 /24: Western Australia: Original Correspondence: Offices and Individuals: 1839: Peter Barrow.
99 TA MM44/1/3, Letters to Eleanor Franklin, {March 1839 by context}.
100 George Mackaness, ed., *Some Private Correspondence of Sir John and Lady Jane Franklin* (Sydney: Australian Historical Monographs, 1947), 1:68. For the enquiry, see Ryan, *Tasmanian Aborigines*, 240. For Smith's relationship with Anstey and Swanston, see TA NS6102.
101 Penny Russell, ed., *This Errant Lady: Jane Franklin's Overland Journey to Port Phillip and Sydney, 1839* (Canberra: National Library of Australia, 2002), 28.
102 Mar, "Imperial Literacy," 14.
103 Russell, *This Errant Lady*, 28.
104 See Olsen and Russell, *Australia's First Naturalists*, 77–8; see also Russell, *This Errant Lady*.
105 Cadzow, "Guided by Her," 85–118.
106 Allison Cadzow, "Turandurey (c. 1806–?)," Australian Dictionary of Biography, National Centre of Biography, Australian National University, https://ia.anu.edu.au/biography/turandurey-29903/text37019 (accessed September 18, 2022).
107 SPRI MS 248/86; BJ, Jane Franklin Diary, August 23, 1839.
108 *The Australian*, August 27, 1839, 2.
109 TA MM44/1/3, Letters from Eleanor Franklin to her family in England; Eleanor Franklin diary, June 4, 1838–November 13, 1839.
110 TA MM44/1/3, Eleanor Franklin diary, especially July 25 to September 25, 1839.
111 Quoted in Alexander, *Ambitions*, 129.
112 Van Toorn, *Writing*, 1–20; Ballantyne, *Webs of Empire*, 124–36; Ryan, *Tasmanian Aborigines*, 230–7; Reynolds, *Fate of a Free People*, 159–78. There were a variety of relationships with the written word, including the "littoral literacy" of sealers, traditional inscriptions like cicatrices or petroglyphs, to ritual use of captured Biblical texts, and red ochre during the war. See Finlay, *'Good People'*, 236, TA NS1612, Journal of John Scot.
113 Finlay, *'Good People'*, 229–48.
114 See Van Toorn, *Writing*, 11–14, 20; Finlay, *'Good People'*, 88–107; Stevens, *Me Write Myself*, 97–149; Ryan, *Tasmanian Aborigines*, 235.
115 Pierre Dumontier, quoted in N. J. B. Plomley, "Notes on Some of the Tasmanian Aborigines, and on Portraits of Them," *Papers and Proceedings of the Royal Society of Tasmania* 102, no. 2 (1968): 50.
116 TA SWD 28/1/1, Register of Children Admitted and Discharged from the Male and Female Orphan School, 3, 8.
117 "The Orphan School," *Colonial Times*, April 23, 1839, 4. See also Kim Pearce and Susan Doyle, *New Town, A Social History* (Hobart: Hobart City Council, 2002), 57.
118 SPRI MS 248/87; BJ, Jane Franklin diary, November 4, 1839.
119 Bronwen Douglas and Chris Ballard, eds., *Foreign Bodies: Oceania and the Science of Race, 1750-1940* (Canberra: ANU Press, 2008), 9–10, 12.
120 SPRI MS 248/87; BJ, Jane Franklin diary, December 16, 1839. Alexander, *Ambitions*, 130; Plomley, "Notes," 52. For Jane Franklin's correspondence with the Laws, see SPRI MS248/156; BJ, Jane Franklin diary, March 27, 1837.
121 Plomley, "Notes," 52; for Dumontier, see Douglas and Ballard, *Foreign Bodies*, 33–98.

122 Quoted in Alexander, *Ambitions*, 130.
123 TA NS 6102, Anstey to Swanston, January 27, 1840.
124 Robin, *Swanston*. Robin's work is the most detailed analysis of the Derwent Bank Records and the networks of its members—the papers remain largely uncataloged. The principle collection is TA NS 4979.
125 SPRI MS 248/174, Jane Franklin to Mary Simpkinson, February 23, 1839.
126 Alexander, *Ambitions*, 172–4.
127 RST 16/8, Jane Franklin to Mary Simpkinson, January 1, 1842.
128 See Alexander, *Ambitions*, and Kathleen Fitzpatrick, *Sir John Franklin in Tasmania, 1837-1843* (Melbourne: Melbourne University Press, 1947).
129 Elbourne, "The Sin of the Settler," 2–3; Lester, *Imperial Networks*, 68–9; Steven Shapin, "Placing the View from Nowhere: Historical and Sociological Problems in the Location of Science," *Transactions of the Institute of British Geographers* 23, no. 1 (1998): 5–12; Secord, "Knowledge in Transit," 654–72.
130 Endersby, *Imperial Nature*, 54–111; Eleanor Cave, "Flora Tasmaniae: Tasmanian Naturalists and Imperial Botany, 1829-1860" (PhD thesis, University of Tasmania, 2012), especially Chapter 4.
131 See Barbara T. Gates, "Those Who Drew and Those Who Wrote: Women and Victorian Popular Science Illustration," in *Figuring It Out: Science, Gender and Visual Culture*, ed. Ann B. Shteir and Bernard V. Lightman (Hanover and London: Dartmouth College Press, 2006), 192–213.
132 Stefan Petrow, "The Life and Death of the Hobart Town Mechanics' Institute 1827-1871," *Papers and Proceedings: Tasmanian Historical Research Association* 40, no. 1 (March 1993): 7–18.
133 Alexander, *Ambitions*, 64–75.
134 Louisa Anne Meredith, *My Home in Tasmania, during a Residence of Nine Years* (London: John Murray, 1852), 30.
135 Michael E. Hoare, "'All Things Are Queer and Opposite': Scientific Societies in Tasmania in the 1840s," *ISIS* 60, no. 2 (Summer 1969): 198–209. The motto of the society might also be translated as "whichever way you look at it, this is baffling." Alexander, *Ambitions*, 110.
136 Bill Jenkins, "The Platypus in Edinburgh: Robert Jameson, Robert Knox and the Place of the Ornithorhynchus in Nature, 1821–24," *Annals of Science* 73, no. 4 (October 2016): 425–41; Annaliese Claydon, "P is for Platypus," in *Animalia: An Anti-Imperial Bestiary for Our Times*, ed. Antoinette Burton and Renisa Mawani (Durham and London: Duke University Press, 2020), 140–4.
137 Hoare, "All Things," 204.
138 Richard Owen, *Report on the Extinct Mammals of Australia, and on the Geographical Distribution of Pliocene and Post-Pliocene Mammals in General* (London: British Association for Advancement of Science, 1845).
139 See Huxley, *Life and Letters*; AJCP M Series, Journal of Robert McCormick, 1840-1841, Wellcome Institute for the History of Medicine Library, File WMs.3367; AJCP M Series, Letters of John Gell to his family, 1839-1843, M377-380, Series A, File 5, http://nla.gov.au/nla.obj-90490443.
140 Quoted in Alexander, *Ambitions*, 111.
141 For example, her observations of Indigenous methods of hunting possum in NSW. See Olsen and Russell, *Australia's First Naturalists*, 77 and SLNSW TAS PAPERS 148: Papers of the Tasmanian Society for the Promotion of Natural Science, 1841-1844, 20.

142 Patrick Brantlinger, *Dark Vanishings: Discourse on the Extinction of Primitive Races, 1800-1930* (Ithaca and London: Cornell University Press, 2003), 17-44.
143 SPRI MS 248/92; BJ, Jane Franklin Diary, "Extracts of a letter of John Simpkinson to Mr Gell, dated April 14, 1841."
144 Robert C. Gunn, "Remarks on the Indigenous Vegetable Productions of Tasmania Available as Food for Man," *The Tasmanian Journal of Natural Science, Agriculture, Statistics, &c.* 1, no. 1 (1842): 35-52.
145 John Lhotsky, "Some Remarks on a Short Vocabulary of the Natives of Van Diemen Land; And Also of the Menero Downs in Australia," *The Journal of the Royal Geographical Society of London* 9 (1839): 157-62; SPRI MS 248/87; BJ, Jane Franklin Diary, November 5, 1839.
146 TA CRO 90/1/4, Thomas Dove, "Report to the Moderator of the Presbytery of Van Diemen's Land on the moral and religious features of the Aborigines of Flinders Island," July 18, 1838.
147 See Thomas Dove, "Moral and Social Characteristics of the Aborigines of Tasmania, as Gathered from Intercourse with the Surviving Remnant of Them Now Located on Flinders Island," *The Tasmanian Journal of Natural Science, Agriculture, Statistics, &c.* 1, no. 4 (1842): 247-54. See also Rebe Taylor, "The Polemics of Making Fire in Tasmania: The Historical Evidence Revisited," *Aboriginal History* 32 (2008): 1-26.
148 SPRI MS489/2, Jane Franklin to Gunn, nd. October 1839 by context; SPRI MS 248/88; BJ, Jane Franklin diary, June 30, 1840. See Jane Hylton, *Colonial Sisters: Martha Berkeley and Theresa Walker, South Australia's First Professional Artists* (Adelaide: Art Gallery Board of South Australia, 1994).
149 This was especially the case with Robert Lathrop Murray, the editor of *The Austral-Asiatic Review*. See Miller, *Pressmen and Governors*, 208.
150 SPRI MS248/89: BJ, Jane Franklin Diary, August 7, 1840.
151 SPRI MS 248/174, Jane Franklin to Mary Simpkinson, June 13, 1840.
152 Alexander, *Ambitions*, 111.
153 "Accessions to the Library. To 27th May, 1844," *The Journal of the Royal Geographical Society of London* 14 (1844): xi-xxii; "Back Matter," *Philosophical Transactions of the Royal Society of London* 134 (1844): 325-8.
154 Michael Dettelbach, "Humboldtean Science," in *Cultures of Natural History*, ed. N. Jardine, J. A. Secord, and E. C. Spary (Cambridge: Cambridge University Press, 1996), 287-304; Cawood, "The Magnetic Crusade," 492.
155 TA NS1313, Jane Franklin to Ronald Campbell Gunn, nd.
156 Ross, *Polar Pioneers*, 222.
157 DRO D8760/F/FJR/1/1/82, Franklin to Richardson, December 5, 1840; DRO D8760/F/FJR/1/1/84, Franklin to Richardson, April 13, 1841.
158 Lambert, *Gates of Hell*, 131-3.
159 NA BJ 3/18, John Franklin to Edward Sabine, March 13, 1841.
160 Woodward, *Portrait of Jane*, 229.
161 Lambert, *Gates of Hell*, 129.
162 NA BJ 3/18, John Franklin to Edward Sabine, March 13, 1841.
163 Ross showed the letter to Jane, who sent a copy to Mary. RST 16/8, Jane Franklin to Mary Simpkinson, September 7, 1840.
164 See, for example, "The Antarctic Expedition," *The Athenaeum*, April 10, 1841, which contained a letter to Sabine from Franklin, which was republished in Tasmania and commented upon by Jane Franklin.
165 SPRI MS 248/89, Jane Franklin Diary, August 24, 1840.

166 TA MM44/1/3, Eleanor Franklin Diary, October 4, 1840; J. H. Kay, "Terrestrial Magnetism," *The Tasmanian Journal of Natural Science, Agriculture, Statistics, &c.* 1 (1841): 124–36.
167 Huxley, *Life and Letters*, 106; Ronald Gunn to Sir William Hooker, October 31, 1841, in Burns and Skemp, *Van Diemen's Land Correspondents*, 91.
168 Huxley, *Life and Letters*, 107.
169 Quoted in Alexander, *Ambitions*, 115.
170 RST 16/7, Jane Franklin to John Griffin, October 12, 1841.
171 Robert Crooke, *The Convict: A Fragment of History* (Hobart: University of Tasmania Library, 1958), 45.
172 It is often claimed that Mathinna came to Government House in 1839 along with Adolphus. The fact that Mathinna had a 'lively recollection' of the Flinders commandant Malcolm Smith and his family, who did not arrive on the island until mid-1839, indicates that she did not arrive until later, as does Jane Franklin's attempt to learn about Mathinna's past in September 1841. I suspect that she did not arrive until after her mother's death in September 1840, but this cannot be proved.
173 Russell, "Girl in a Red Dress." See also Stevens, *Me Write Myself*, n. 330, Alexander, *Ambitions*, 130–8. For fictional and dramatic interpretations of Mithina's life, see Richard Flanagan, *Wanting* (New York: Atlantic Monthly Press, 2008), and also Bangarra Dance Theatre, *Mathinna*, 2008, Choreography Stephen Page. Musical score David Page. Penny Russell has a comprehensive list of interpretations in "Girl in a Red Dress," 342, n. 4.
174 Plomley, *Weep in Silence*, 302, 317, 481.
175 See Stevens, *Me Write Myself* and Finlay, '*Good People*' for the conflict, for young children living with their parents, see Plomley, *Weep in Silence*, 126.
176 Plomley, *Weep in Silence*, 843; SPRI MS248/92; BJ, Jane Franklin diary, September 10, 1841.
177 TA MM44/1/3, Eleanor Franklin to Catherine Franklin, February 6, 1841.
178 John Phillip Gell, "The Vocabulary of the Adelaide Tribe," *The Tasmanian Journal of Natural Science, Agriculture, Statistics, &c.* 1, no. 2 (1842): 109–24, TA MM44/1/3, November 12, 1839, September 22, 1841.
179 SPRI MS248/172/4, Jane Franklin to John Franklin, December 8, 1830. For Jane Franklin's views on children, see also Alexander, *Ambitions*, 30, 53, 129.
180 It is impossible to do justice to this complex topic here, but see Tony Ballantyne, *Entanglements of Empire: Missionaries, Maori, and the Question of the Body* (Chapel Hill: Duke University Press, 2014).
181 SPRI MS 248/90; BJ, Jane Franklin diary, March 29, 1841.
182 SPRI MS 248/90; BJ, Jane Franklin diary, March 6, 1841. For her views on place names, April 21, 1841.
183 For Colenso and the importance of Māori religious texts, see Ballantyne, *Webs of Empire*, 149–50. For Jane Franklin's views, see SPRI MS 248/90; BJ, Jane Franklin diary, April 28, 1841.
184 TA GO33/1/39, 179–246.
185 The Flinders commandant reported a boy being sent to Hobart in June 1841, TA GO33/1/39, 236, and in March the following year, Adolphus was reported as having been on board the *Vansittart* for about ten months. The wages for Indigenous boys were proposed by Moriarty (TA CSO5/1/287/7593) and recorded in TA CSO50/1/16-18.

186 TA MM 4/1/3, Eleanor Franklin diary, March 14, 1842; for Franklin's order, see TA CSO5/1/287/7593, William Moriarty to John Montagu, March 24, 1841.
187 Lynette Russell, *Roving Mariners: Australian Aboriginal Whalers and Sealers in the Southern Oceans, 1790-1870* (Albany: State University of New York Press, 2012).
188 See, for example, "Ship News," *The Cornwall Chronicle*, November 6, 1841, 2; *Launceston Courier*, December 13, 1841, 2; "The Natives," *Launceston Courier*, December 27, 1841, 3.
189 TA GO1/1/48, December 10, 1842. Franklin intended this to be seen as another example of his scientific patronage, but instead he was censured by the Colonial Office for exceeding his authority.
190 Linus Wilson Miller, *Notes of an Exile to Van Dieman's Land* (Fredonia: McKinstry, 1846), 363.
191 See Russell, "Girl in a Red Dress."
192 Greg Lehman, personal communication, June 24, 2022.
193 TA MM44/1/3, Eleanor Franklin diary, September 21, 1841.
194 Laidlaw, *Protecting the Empire's Humanity*, 16.
195 The doll still exists and is in the collections of the Derbyshire Record Office, at present on loan to the Tasmanian Museum and Art Gallery, DRO D8760/F/OBJ/3.
196 SPRI MS 248/91; BJ, Jane Franklin diary, July 26, 1841; SPRI MS 438/18/3, John Franklin to W. E. Parry, July 9, 1829; for Fisher's orders see TA GO33/1/39, 228.
197 Reynolds, *Fate of a Free People*, 178-84.
198 SPRI MS 248/92; BJ, Jane Franklin diary, September 3, 1841.
199 RST 16/8, Jane Franklin to Mary Simpkinson, October 12, 1841.
200 SPRI MS 248/92; BJ, Jane Franklin diary, August 21, 1841, September 10, 1841.
201 Great Britain, *Report of the Parliamentary Select Committee on Aboriginal Tribes*, ix.
202 Porter, *Religion versus Empire?* 150-2; Parry, *Parry of the Arctic*, 214; Parry recommended one of the commanders, see SPRI 438/26/604, Parry to Lady Maria Stanley, November 2, 1839.
203 See, for example, "English News," *Colonial Times (Hobart, Tas.: 1828-1857)*, January 12, 1841, 4.
204 SPRI MS 248/91; BJ, Jane Franklin diary, June 30, 1841.
205 SPRI MS248/175, Jane Franklin to James Ross, July 20, 1841. For Parry's involvement in the Niger expedition, see Parry, *Parry of the Arctic*, 197-209.
206 Porter, *Religion versus Empire?* 151-2.
207 TA NS1313, Jane Franklin to Ronald Gunn, January 14, 1839.
208 Alexander, *Ambitions*, 94-104, quote 95.
209 Ibid., See also Jane Franklin to Elizabeth Fry, August 3, 1841 in Mackaness, *Some Private Correspondence*, 22-9.
210 SPRI MS 248/174, Jane Franklin to Mary Simpkinson, October 12, 1841.
211 SPRI MS 248/92; BJ, Jane Franklin diary, September 29, 1841.
212 UTAS Quaker Collection, A9/A1/25 (6), George Washington Walker to Robert Clarke, October 29, 1841.
213 Kate Auty and Lynette Russell, *Hunt Them, Hang Them: "The Tasmanians" in Port Phillip, 1841-42* (Melbourne: Justice Press, 2016).
214 McFarlane, *Beyond Awakening*, 208-11; Pybus, *Truganini*, 163-79; Stevens, *Me Write Myself*, 210-11.
215 TA CSO8/1/2/420.

216 A Colonist, "To the Editor," *The Cornwall Chronicle*, November 6, 1841, 4.
217 TA NS6102, Anstey to Swanston, November 14, 1841.
218 John Franklin, *Narrative of Some Passages in the History of Van Diemen's Land, During the Last Three Years of Sir John Franklin's Administration of its Government* (privately printed, 1845), 28–9.
219 Quoted in Fitzpatrick, *Franklin in Tasmania*, 339.
220 Alexander, *Ambitions*, 195–6.
221 Laidlaw, *Colonial Connections*, 169–99.
222 SPRI MS 248/174, Jane Franklin to Mary Simpkinson, February 7, 9, 22, 1842.
223 RST 16/8, Jane Franklin to Mary Simpkinson, January 1, 1842.
224 John Lort Stokes, *Discoveries in Australia: With an Account of the Coasts and Rivers Explored and Surveyed during the Voyage of H.M.S. Beagle, in the Years 1837-38-39-40-41-42-43, by Command of the Lords Commissioners of the Admiralty: Also, a Narrative of Captain Owen Stanley's Visits to the Islands in the Arafura Sea* (London: T. and W. Boone, 1846); Crawford Pasco, *A Roving Commission: Naval Reminiscences* (Melbourne: George Robertson, 1897).
225 SPRI MS 248/94, Jane Franklin diary, March 11, 1842; TA MM 4/1/3, Eleanor Franklin diary, March 14, 1842.
226 An inquiry was instituted by Franklin's successor, John Eardley-Wilmot, into the uses of the *Vansittart* under Franklin's administration. See TA CON1/1/16/1442/2-3, *Vansittart*—vessel—deficiencies in stores examined—June–July 1844.
227 RST 16/8, Jane Franklin to Mary Simpkinson, April 22, 1842; David Burn, *Narrative of the Overland Journey of Sir John and Lady Franklin and Party from Hobart Town to Macquarie Harbour* (London, 1843).
228 Stevens, *Me Write Myself*, 246.
229 UTAS Quaker Collection, W9/a1/29 (11), George Washington Walker to Harriet Jeanneret, September 16, 1842.
230 Mar, "Imperial Literacy," 1–2.
231 "Local," *The Courier*, October 14, 1842, 2.
232 SPRI MS 248/316 John Franklin to James Clark Ross, July 20, 1843; Alexander, *Ambitions*, 198; Fitzpatrick, *Franklin in Tasmania*, 335, 342–3.
233 Alexander, *Ambitions* 198.
234 TA NS 6102, Anstey to Swanston, May 25, 1843, June 5, 1843.
235 Quoted in Fitzpatrick, *Franklin in Tasmania*, 343.
236 NA BJ3/18, John Franklin to Edward Sabine, January 29, 1843.
237 DRO D8760/F/FJR/1/1/85, John Franklin to John Richardson, April 20, 1843.
238 SPRI MS 248/316 John Franklin to James Clark Ross, September 13, 1843.
239 SPRI MS 248/174, Jane Franklin to Mary Simpkinson, February 13, 1843.
240 SPRI MS 248/174, Jane Franklin to Mary Simpkinson, March 8, 1843.
241 TA MM 4/1/3, Eleanor Franklin to Catherine Franklin, February 14, 1843.
242 SPRI MS 248/174, Jane Franklin to Mary Simpkinson, March 8, 1843.
243 TA CSO8/1/84/1925, June 14–19, 1843.
244 TA SWD28/1/1, Register of Children Admitted and Discharged from the Male and Female Orphan School, 75.
245 Alexander, *Ambitions* 200.
246 SPRI MS248/316, Franklin to J. C. Ross, September 13, 1843.
247 SPRI MS 1503/28/4, Mary Richardson to Mrs. Day, June 1844.
248 A. Lambert, *Gates of Hell*, 148–66.
249 Alexander, *Ambitions*, 203–5; Ross, *Polar Pioneers*, 274–6.

250 John Franklin, *Narrative of Some Passages in the History of Van Diemen's Land During the Last Three Years of Sir John Franklin's Administration of its Government* (London: Printed by Richard and John E. Taylor, 1845).
251 NA BJ3/18, John Franklin to Edward Sabine, July 5, 1845.
252 RGS SJF/7/6, John Franklin to Jane Franklin, July 1, 1845.
253 Charles Darwin, *Journal of Researches into the Natural History and Geology of the Countries Visited During the Voyage of H.M.S. Beagle Around the World Under the Command of Capt. Fitz Roy, R.N.*, 2nd edition, corrected, with additions (London: John Murray, 1845), 648.
254 Paul Edmund Strzelecki, *Physical Description of New South Wales and Van Diemen's Land* (London: Longman, Brown, Green, and Longmans, 1845), 348–50.
255 SPRI MS 1503/28/10, Jane Franklin to Josephine Richardson, December 6, 1844.
256 "Methinna, V.D.L." Portrait by John Skinner Prout, 1845, Oc2006, Drg.20, British Museum, https://www.britishmuseum.org/collection/object/E_Oc2006-Drg-20 (accessed January 20, 2023).
257 Stevens, *Me Write Myself*, 260–70.
258 TA CSO11/1/27, 93–5, Mithinna's testimony to the Friend Enquiry, October 1846.
259 Stevens, *Me Write Myself*, 305–13.
260 Kate Warner, Tim McCormack, and Fauve Kurnadi, "Pathway to Truth-Telling and Treaty: Report to Premier Peter Gutwein" (Hobart: Department of Premier and Cabinet, November 2021), https://www.dpac.tas.gov.au/__data/assets/pdf_file/0005/627242/Pathway_to_Truth-Telling_and_Treaty_251121.pdf (accessed August 27, 2022).
261 Russell, "Girl in a Red Dress," 342.
262 The catechist Robert Clark was the last person to mention Adolphus. In his census of the residents of Wybalenna, composed around October 1847, he notes that Adolphus had "gone to England," but no record of his departure has been found. Plomley, *Weep in Silence*, 886. Mithina disappears from the archival record after she was returned to the Orphan School in 1847, and then sent to the settlement at Oyster Cove in 1851. TA CSO24/280/6187, 311. For a discussion of the narratives woven around Mithina's disappearance from the archival record and speculations about her death, see Russell, "Girl in a Red Dress," 352–5.

4

"Have You Seen the Esquimaux Sketch of the Ships?"

Disappearing Ships and Inuit Maps, 1845–9

In February 1849, Sir John Richardson wrote to his wife Mary Fletcher Richardson from Fort Confidence on the shores of Great Bear Lake, weighed down by cares. He was worried about his old friend, Sir John Franklin, whose Northwest Passage expedition in HMS *Erebus* and *Terror* had disappeared four years before. The previous summer, Richardson, John Rae, and the Keewatin Inuit translators Ouligbuck and his son William Ouligbuck Jr. had searched the coastline between Mackenzie and the Coppermine Rivers but found no trace of the missing ships. It was also much colder than he had expected. The pack ice was so thick in the late summer that it seemed permanently fixed, and winter had come early. At the same time, Richardson worried about his young children left behind in Scotland. They had lost their mother, Mary Booth Richardson, four years earlier, and Richardson had just married his old friend Mary Fletcher. He also worried about politics at home, for the last news he had was of revolutions on the continent, the planned Chartist meeting on Kennington Common, and the evacuation of Queen Victoria and her children, all on the heels of a cholera epidemic. He sought solace in the Roman poet Horace, but as he wrote to Mary, "even these days of rail-roads and steam vessels and electric telegraphs I must wait longer for an answer than Horace was required to do; nor can I receive it until I have crossed a tract equal to the breadth of the whole Roman empire."[1]

Six months later, at Mittimatalik/Pond Inlet on Baffin Island, Robert Anstruther Goodsir started a letter to his family in Edinburgh. He was the surgeon on the whaler *Advice*, captained by William Penny, and they were also looking for the Franklin expedition. Goodsir's brother Harry was Franklin's surgeon in the *Erebus*, and Penny's friend Alexander M'Donald was the surgeon in the *Terror*. Unlike Richardson, they *had* just had news of the missing expedition. An Inuit hunter named "Usky" had come to Mittimatalik from the south to trade with the commercial whalers. What he had to trade was information—a map that he drew for Captain William Kerr of the *Chieftain*, showing four ships stuck in the ice. Kerr understood these to be *Erebus*, *Terror*, and the two rescue vessels under James Clark Ross, *Enterprise* and *Investigator*. The next day, Kerr, Penny, and Captain John Parker of the *Truelove* weighed anchor and headed west for Prince Regent Inlet to try to verify Usky's information. But they were stopped by heavy ice and a terrible storm, and had to return to Mittimatalik's safe harbor. Now Parker was returning to Britain in the *Truelove*, carrying the map which the whalers had already annotated with their own understandings. Goodsir wrote to his family that he feared Kerr had asked the Inuit "leading questions" and failed to understand their replies. Goodsir warned his anxious parents to be wary of the map, for "there can be no confidence placed in it whatsoever."[2] The arrival of this map and story would start a kind of arrhythmic pulse of information that, like an arrhythmic heartbeat, produced intense anxiety. At its core was the hope that the missing men were still alive—a hope that rested on the Inuit ability to travel, observe, and report where the British could not.

In-between Fort Confidence and Mittimatalik, on the icy, stony ground of King William Island, a party of forty survivors from *Erebus* and *Terror* struggled southward, dragging heavy wooden boats weighed down with curtain rods and silverware, begging for seal meat from the Netsilingmiut whom they met on their way to the mouth of Back's Fish River. Seal meat was very scarce in these terrible years, which the Netsilingmiut later remembered as "the years of horror," when caribou and seal fled from the country, the ice would not melt, blizzards and starvation set in, and many people died from exposure and hunger.[3] They shared what they could with the starving men, but they also kept them under close observation. Sometime later, the Netsilingmiut would trade that information to other hunters, who would in turn pass it on to William Ouligbuck, Jr. and John Rae. In the meantime, those survivors would have starved to death, and some would have eaten their companions. John Franklin had died and been buried somewhere (no one knows where) in June 1847, the *Erebus* was imprisoned in the ice, and the *Terror* was stuck off the south shore of King William Island. The rest of the expedition was scattered in small groups across the region.[4] In these profoundly cold years, the ice did not melt, the migrations of caribou and whales shifted, and the area around King William Island temporarily became a dead zone, on the borderlands of shifting Inuit territories and utterly outside British knowledge.[5]

In their correspondence with their families, both Richardson and Goodsir glimpsed something that would come to shape the searches for the survivors whom they believed were alive somewhere in the great white spaces of their own ignorance. It was not just the heavy pack ice that imprisoned the expedition, nor the pathos of being so close and yet so far from those they sought to save. It was something even more basic—their response to information, to how it traveled, to whether it could be trusted, and to how to act upon it. These vignettes from 1849 show us how the speed of information was changing in both Britain and Arctic North America, with steam power and the telegraph on one end, and changing patterns of subsistence and travel on the other. This dynamic created a space in which authority, expertise, and truth itself were up for grabs. Amid these pulses of silence and chatter, the Franklin women and their supporters created a compelling argument that rested on Indigenous testimony—that not only was there credible evidence that the expedition was still in existence, but that the missing men were both representatives of the imperial nation and deserving subjects of British philanthropy and therefore must not be abandoned.

Ice and Information Arrhythmia

Ice sets both the scene and the tempo of this story. Every year, millions of tons of old sea ice are driven from the Beaufort Sea into the Canadian archipelago by winds, currents, and the rotation of the earth, where it combines with the hard ice of calving glaciers and newly formed ice along the shore's edge.[6] These dynamics rendered a Northwest Passage impossible for British explorers, particularly those trying to take deep-draught vessels through Lancaster Sound. The years of the Franklin expedition and the searches for Franklin were uncommonly heavy ice years, coinciding with another period of intense cold at the end of the Little Ice Age, in which the narrow passages between islands in the Canadian archipelago were choked with thick old ice that would not melt in the summer.

The 1840s were a period of unprecedented change across the northern part of North America, principally due to the expansion of the British and Russian fur trades in Alaska and Canada and international commercial whaling in the Bering Strait and Lancaster Sound. By 1845, the Russian American Company (RAC) and the Hudson's Bay Company (HBC) had established trading posts within 300 miles of each other on the Yukon River in Alaska and Canada. Each company was anxious about the other's operations as well as those of Indigenous middlemen.[7] Several long-distance Indigenous trading networks now spanned the Western and Eastern Arctic. There were the Athapaskan-speaking Gwich'in Dene whose trading networks linked the HBC posts on the Mackenzie River to RAC posts at Michaelovsk (Saint Michael) on the Bering Strait, as well as a separate trading network linking Alaskan Iñupiaq territories across the northern coasts. Trade goods flowed east across the Bering Strait from Chukchi trading fairs in northern Asia as far as the Mackenzie River Delta, while Alaskan furs made their way west to the Chinese market at Kiakhta.[8] To complicate matters further, in 1848, an American whaler out of Hobart arrived in the Bering Strait, sparking a rush to the region by American, British, Tasmanian, and New Zealand whaleships. They flooded the region with trade goods, and heralded decades of introduced disease, resource depletion, and social upheaval.[9]

By 1848, these trade networks were linked to Canadian Inuit trails across the sea ice of the Eastern Canadian Archipelago, with Barter Island as the connection point with the Iñupiaq to the west, Gwich'in middlemen to the south, and Baffin Island to the east (see Map 1 and Map 3).[10] The increased presence of commercial whalers in Lancaster Sound, together with more peaceful relations between Inuit and Chipewyan meant that by the 1840s, a number of new trading places had emerged. Mittimatalik/Pond's Inlet and Chesterfield Inlet were among the most important, and where much of the following story takes place.[11]

The trade in goods was accompanied by a brisk traffic in information. Fur traders wanted to keep an eye on their competition; whalers were always looking to expand their grounds; and from 1848, every outsider asked about Franklin. What this meant was that as Indigenous networks expanded, stories about wandering white men became highly valuable and traveled widely.

At the same time, more Inuit were leaving their homes and traveling to Britain and America. The British whalers and the surgeons who feature in this chapter had all brought Inuit from Baffin Island and Cumberland Sound to Britain over the previous decade. Penny had been credited with opening the new whaling ground in Cumberland Sound in 1840 based on information from Inuluapik, an Inuk boy he had taken to Aberdeen for a year. Penny's surgeon, the now-lost Alexander M'Donald, had published Inuluapik's biography, while the boy's map of Cumberland Sound was published as an Admiralty chart in the same year.[12] Parker, the *Truelove*'s captain, had brought an Inuit couple back from Nyatlick (in Cumberland Straits) to Hull in 1847 in order to teach them English and to display them in an attempt to raise funds for his own philanthropic mission to Baffin Island (see below). The wife, Uckaluk, died from measles on the way home in the summer of 1848.[13]

Meanwhile in Britain, the rapidly increasing speed of communication and transportation seemed to collapse time and space. The introduction of the telegraph, the railway, the expansion of the periodical press, and the rapidity of steam printing made for a public that was saturated with information at a pace unimaginable a decade before.[14] News traveled at lightning speed along telegraph lines and was consumed by an expanding readership that patronized public libraries, and bought and distributed pamphlets, tracts, and increasingly cheap books. Yet there were still enormous blank spaces on the map of England in 1848 and beyond its shores, places where neither the telegraph nor the railway reached. As Mark W. Turner has argued, this geography contributed to a pattern of progress and pause that was characteristic of nineteenth-century life, in which the pause constituted an important space for interaction and communication.[15] This was also a constitutive feature of Arctic exploration, as each autumn was marked by the return of whale ships and naval ships whose news (often from Indigenous informants) would then circulate through the periodical press. For twenty years and more, British audiences had consumed Arctic narratives as periodical installments—what Janice Cavell has called a "connected narrative."[16] This arrhythmia fed into that anticipation. As Bayly has argued, gaps and silences could produce anxiety and "information panics" in colonial settings when it seemed as if Indigenous information orders were equal or superior to that of the British.[17] In the case of the search for the Franklin expedition, those gaps and silences took on a new character that was different from the drip-dosing of adventure in popular periodicals. Now they were coupled with confusion over the validity of Indigenous information, and it was in those meaningful pauses that the Franklin women and others negotiated their authority. As James Clark Ross's wife, Lady Anne Ross, put it, this arrhythmic pulse gave rise to "excited hopes and weary silence" in which rumors multiplied, information was processed, and meaning was created.

1845: *Erebus* and *Terror* Depart

In May 1845, HMS *Erebus* and *Terror* departed from Gravesend to chart the Northwest Passage. Steam-powered and ice-strengthened, these polar veterans had been fitted out with modern conveniences and equipment, from lead-soldered tinned food to delicate scientific instruments. In the captain's cabin of the *Erebus* sat Sir John Franklin—fifty-nine years old, obese, sorrowful, and suffering from influenza. He was surrounded in his misery by Arctic and Tasmanian mementoes. Landscapes of Fort Enterprise and Fort Franklin were on the walls, drawn by his niece Mary Anne Kendall and her husband Edward Kendall, who had died a few months earlier.[18] Jane Franklin's portrait hung on the wall, perhaps a duplicate of Thomas Bock's phrenological study of her head (see Chapter 3).[19] His bookshelves contained a library of scientific and religious works selected by his wife, and his desk was filled with old letters they had chosen from Arctic friends, colleagues, and rivals, together with many copies of the pamphlet that he, Jane, and the Sabines had written in the aftermath of "Montagu's Book." A capuchin monkey named Prince Albert, a present from Jane, cavorted around.[20]

It was in this cabin that Franklin wrote his final letters home from Disco Bay off the Greenland coast. He wrote to the bereaved Mary Anne and to Richardson, both of whom had lost their spouses in the last previous months. He reminded them of his continuing faith in the wisdom of divine providence, which he hoped would comfort them in their sorrow and his absence.[21] He wrote to his daughter and to his wife about his plans for the future and relentless worrying about the past (particularly about Tasmania), and he begged them to look after each other.[22] Then he wrote a poem down from memory, one that his first wife Eleanor had written for him as a Valentine in 1823 in which she cast herself as a Yellowknife Dene woman known as Greenstockings, who insisted that her lover return to the Arctic (see Chapter 1).[23] Whatever Franklin might have meant by sending this poem from his first wife to his second, in the imagined voice of an Indigenous woman who challenged the rival claims of the Arctic and his home on his heart, cannot be known. A few days later, the ships headed toward Lancaster Sound. A passing whaler saw them, hailed them, but had no reply. Then they disappeared, never to be seen again.

The expedition's design was supposed to ensure its success, but instead doomed it to failure. The ships were caught in the shallow ice-choked passages of the Canadian Archipelago in a particularly heavy ice year, the tinned provisions would poison the men, and the equipment would burden retreating parties on the ice.[24] The instructions had been written by Franklin, Richardson, Parry, James Ross, Beaufort, and Sabine—core members of the old Arctic circles. Franklin was to sail west into Lancaster Sound, heading southwest after Cape Walker, joining the Canadian coast after the Coppermine River. An alternative route was added at the last minute: if the southwest route was blocked, Franklin was to investigate Wellington Channel to discover whether it was the opening to an open polar sea. The interpretation of these instructions was one battleground in the contest for authority over the missing Franklin expedition.

Another struggle for authority centered on the role of commercial whalers, both within the expedition and during the rescue attempts. Unlike his subordinate officer Captain Francis Crozier (commanding the *Terror*), Franklin had little experience of ice navigation, and so he recruited whaling captains from northern England and Scotland to serve as his ice masters. Every ship-based Arctic expedition since 1818 had done so, but there had been frequent clashes between naval officers and whaling skippers.[25] This welded the maritime networks of the Davis Strait fleet to the expedition, intertwining the search for Franklin with the friendships and cross-cultural alliances of the whalers. The Admiralty and Jane Franklin looked first to the whaling fleet for assistance in 1848, assuming that lavish rewards (£20,000 from the Admiralty, £3,000 from Jane Franklin), plus their financial and emotional interest in the expedition, would encourage them to search. Yet they failed to understand the simmering resentment within the community. No whaling captain had ever been put in charge of an expedition, and many would echo Captain William Jackson, who wrote, "I do not intend going without I have command of the Vessel as I do not intend to be overruled by any Naval Commander."[26] That frustration was compounded by the fact that government support for the northern fishery had steadily declined as a result of British expansion into the Pacific, declining stocks of bowhead whales, American competition, and the promotion of the southern whale fishery in the Indian and South Pacific to the detriment of the Davis Strait fleet.[27]

Both captains and owners therefore looked askance at rewards for rescue, unless they were within their own control. Thomas Ward, the *Truelove*'s owner, wrote to the Hull town clerk that it was impossible to "volunteer any generosity" in the search for Franklin. Indeed, as he and others pointed out, whaling captains were subject to "heavy penalties & restrictions to prevent them neglecting their fishery in order to look out for rewards."[28] Nevertheless, he accepted Jane Franklin's request to administer her own reward for information about her husband.[29] Looking for *Erebus* and *Terror* meant running unaccountable risks—going deep into the pack ice, pursuing information rather than whales, and likely returning home empty, with a dissatisfied crew and angry owners. There was no reward for failure. One had to be motivated by other interests.

"Frozen Up Beyond Our Ken": Spring 1848–Summer 1849

Rumblings about rescuing *Erebus* and *Terror* began in 1847, prompted by fears that their supplies would be running low amid reports of starvation in the region. But it was unclear who exactly would conduct the search, for the Admiralty, the HBC, and the whaling fleet were all reluctant to send either ships or men. Eventually, the Admiralty consented to finance two rescue expeditions and the HBC one. James Clark Ross took HMS *Enterprise* and *Investigator* into Lancaster Sound to see if Franklin had been penned up on the eastern side of the archipelago. HMS *Herald* and *Plover* were sent under Captain Rochfort Maguire to the Bering Strait to search and coordinate with Russian authorities in Alaska.[30] Sir John Richardson's expedition was supported by the HBC. Richardson, Dr. John Rae, the Inuk translator Ouligbuck, and his son William would descend the Coppermine River (see Timeline 3 and Map 4). Ouligbuck was widely regarded as one of the most experienced Inuit men in the HBC's service, and Rae was a highly skilled Arctic traveler and HBC employee from Orkney, whose father was an old friend of Richardson's.[31] Jane Franklin tried to go with Richardson, who flatly refused to take her.[32] Scoresby explained to her, "You are now in your own place," he wrote, "in the place of duty & where you are more likely to have early news. . . . But whether or not—it is your place."[33]

In Tasmania, Jane Franklin had frequently argued that she was moved by a wife's duty and affection to take extraordinary actions on her husband's behalf. As discussed in Chapter 3, she was nevertheless often characterized, both in the colony and in Britain, as unfeminine and a poor influence on her weak-minded husband. But the same argument had a very different purchase when attached to the fate of missing British sailors five years later and on the other side of the world. Knowing that the Admiralty did not intend to send any more relief expeditions, Jane wrote to heads of state in America, France, and Russia to beg for their help. In an impassioned letter to the US president Zachary Taylor in 1849, she appealed to a spirit of "generous rivalry," "kinship," and "noble competition," as she implored the Americans to send rescue expeditions. Penny Russell has argued that she appealed to a "transnationalism of sentiment," comprised of both national self-interest and individual sympathy rooted in a common "civilized" identity, all of which depended on her gendered performance of intense anxiety and wifely devotion.[34] Jane Franklin also claimed to represent the families of the crew. In doing so, she tapped into a widespread vein of support for maritime wives, compelled to stay on shore while their husbands left home for months or years.[35]

Though Jane Franklin claimed to represent the friends and relatives of the missing, not everyone accepted her as a figurehead. In February 1849, Jane, Eleanor (newly married to John Phillip Gell), and Sophia Cracroft traveled to the northern whaling ports to advertise Jane's £3,000 reward for news of the expedition, to be administered by the *Truelove*'s owner, Thomas Ward. The tour belied the rising tensions within the family—Jane had wanted Eleanor's marriage to be put off until her father returned. When she refused, Jane summoned Sophia Cracroft to London from Guernsey to be her companion. As the search progressed, Jane and Sophia were drawn closer together and Eleanor was pushed farther away.[36] Within months, Eleanor denounced her stepmother as "slightly deranged."[37] But in early 1849, these women's northern tour was reported as the pilgrimage of a devoted wife which inspired the "daring and generous commanders of these ships in her cause."[38] But these men, too, were often motivated by their own relationships. Captain Charles Reid, whose brother Thomas was the ice master of the *Erebus*, carried supplies, cylinders enclosing messages, charts, and letters for Ross, while Captain David Kerr of the *Chieftain* and William Penny of the *Advice* both carried letters.[39] Penny had already spent two summers searching for his friend and former shipmate M'Donald on the *Terror*.[40]

In July 1849, Jane and Sophia moved to Orkney to await news from the northern whaling fleet. The *Herald* and *Plover*'s months-old dispatches reported no sign of Franklin in the Bering Strait, and no intelligence received from the Russian authorities, the whalers, or the Iñupiat.[41] Richardson's dispatches and his letters to his wife revealed that he had found no sign of his friend.[42] Nothing at all had been heard from Ross's expedition in *Enterprise* and *Investigator* which, it seemed, had also vanished. No news was grim news, and the *Athenaeum* reported in early September, "Nothing occurs to thaw the secret which, like everything else in those latitudes, seems frozen up beyond our ken."[43]

"Have You Seen the Esquimaux Sketch of the Ships?": July–October 1849

Meanwhile, people were gathering at Mittimatalik on Baffin Island. In June, the shore fast ice was still hard up on the land, and people came from as far away as the Boothia Peninsula to the west and Igloolik to the south to hunt narwhal and to meet relatives.[44]

This was where the whalers Captain William Penny of the *Advice*, Captain John Parker of the *Truelove*, and Captain David Kerr of the *Chieftain* were all fishing and trading for goods and information. On July 28, a man known as Usky went aboard the *Chieftain* with a dozen men. In broken Inuktitut, Kerr asked him if he had seen other ships entering Lancaster Sound. Their conversation was a halting mixture of Inuktitut, English, and gestures, which continued in Kerr's cabin where he asked Usky to draw him a chart. As he consulted with his relatives, Usky drew four ships separated by a peninsula. As they talked with each other, the men were producing consensus, and therefore certainty about their information.[45] Kerr, however, understood their discussion as the opposite, as uncertainty or even dissimulation. He asked pointed but guarded questions of Usky, which produced the information that two ships had passed by four years ago, and two again the previous year. All were now stuck in the ice to the west, but all were well. Kerr interpreted this information to mean that both Franklin's and Ross's expeditions were trapped in Prince Regent Inlet, were in communication with each other, and also that Usky had personally visited them. Later, it would emerge that he had never actually heard any of those things, but had inferred them from the evidence at hand.[46]

The encounter between Usky and Kerr was just one of many hundreds of similar encounters around the world. These kinds of cross-cultural communications were crucial to British geographical knowledge, relied on by both explorers in the field and armchair geographers.[47] They were also highly problematic. The ideal explorer was a trained observer, draftsman, skilled linguist, who had a bevy of scientific instruments at his command in perfect working order and was in full possession of his faculties. Such circumstances were, of course, extremely rare, and explorers had to rely on Indigenous information when they could not travel, observe, and report for themselves (which was most of the time). But how could such information—and informants—be trusted? First and foremost, understanding "native reports" generally required people to understand each other in the first place, but around the middle of the century, there was a shift in favor of direct, trained observation, as opposed to the gathering of testimony by a skilled linguist.[48] It was supposed to be easier, after all, to train an eye than a tongue, and various "hints to travelers" (of which the Royal Geographical Society (RGS) was the most prominent) hoped to direct the traveler's gaze and ensure the credibility of his observations.[49] As Felix Driver has pointed out, however, the politics of observation were contentious, as the reception of Harriet Martineau's *How to Observe—Morals and Manners* indicated, particularly its message that anyone, regardless of class, gender, or education, could be a reasonable observer.[50]

Under these circumstances, Indigenous information needed to be subjected to a barrage of tests in order to be considered "trustworthy." It needed to be given voluntarily and without promise of reward by a person whose character was already known, and to have the appearance of truthfulness. The character of the interviewer mattered, too. Did they ask leading questions? Did they understand what was said?[51] The ultimate test was corroboration by the European eye—by "ocular demonstration," though this too was subject to question, particularly if sight (or indeed, reason) was damaged.[52] The British whalers at Mittimatalik had done all of this before. Penny and Parker had both taken young Inuit to Britain to train them as interpreters, hoping to secure not only reliable go-betweens but also access to their kinship and trading networks.

The day after his exchange with Usky, Kerr told the story to Parker and Penny, but the terrible weather and ice stopped them from entering Prince Regent Inlet, and they returned to whaling.[53] Meanwhile, the *Advice*'s surgeon Goodsir was worried about the way the map had been produced. He wrote to his family that after his initial excitement, "I soon saw much to throw doubt upon [the report's] correctness and authenticity."[54] He pointed out "the extreme difficulty of extracting correct information of any kind from the Esquimaux even by those best acquainted with their habits and language," and that he feared Kerr had put "leading questions" to them which, "they are sure to answer in the affirmative." Goodsir sent his letter home by the same ship that carried the map—*Truelove*, captained by Parker and owned by Ward, whom Jane Franklin had appointed to administer her private reward.[55] At sea, Parker altered the map, adding a line labeled "Track from ship to ship," later adding fuel to the fire. In a private letter which would, like so many others, become public information, Goodsir cautioned his anxious parents that "there can be no confidence placed in [the map] whatever."[56]

For the Franklin family and for the public, the Mittimatalik map was a source of hope. Jane and Sophia were in Orkney, having tea with John Rae's mother, when the news was personally delivered to them. Parker had landed at Stromness, on the other side of the island, and one of his men ran 20 miles to inform the women that Franklin was safe. Sophia wrote to her mother, "it has pleased God to send us news of the Expedition which seems to be as authentic as it is favorable."[57] Isabella Cracroft, in turn, wrote to her daughter (John Franklin's niece) Mary Price on Norfolk Island that "you can imagine our anxiety for further intelligence on this interesting subject."[58] By the time Mary received her aunt's letter, she probably already knew about the map from the British newspapers. After four years of waiting for news, once the Mittimatalik map hit the steam-powered newspaper presses in early October, it took on a life of its own.

Within days of Kerr's landing at Stromness, the British press had proclaimed the "Safety of Sir John Franklin's Expedition," the safety of Ross's rescue mission, and rejoiced that their families' trial was over.[59] The *Morning Chronicle* assured its readers that both Franklin and Ross's ships were stuck in Prince Regent's Inlet and, "no doubt is entertained in the highest official quarters as to the authenticity of the intelligence."[60] The *Sun* rejoiced, "A gleam of news . . . has at length broken through the hitherto impervious haze of uncertainty."[61] The *Literary Gazette* published a facsimile of the map and insisted, "there is every reason to be assured of its TRUTH" (Figure 4.1).[62] The next day, Eleanor's cousin Anne Weld wrote to her, "Does not the rumour of the safety of the Expedition make your heart beat wildly? If true, I suppose my Uncle may be in England even while I write—have you seen the Esquimaux sketch of the ships?"[63] Her husband Charles was not so sure. He was the assistant secretary and librarian of the Royal Society and a frequent contributor to the *Athenaeum*.[64] Now he published an anonymous article in the *Athenaeum* which praised the "heroic confidence," of Lady Franklin, but pointed out that the map's authority "rests on the testimony of the natives. If that can be received with confidence, the safety of Sir John Franklin and his companions . . . would seem to be assured."[65] The Welds' different responses gesture to a bigger feature of this pause in the pulse of Arctic information. In that anxious moment when *everything* was speculation, then *anything* was possible. It was echoed in the "Suggestions for the Relief of Sir John Franklin" file at the Admiralty.

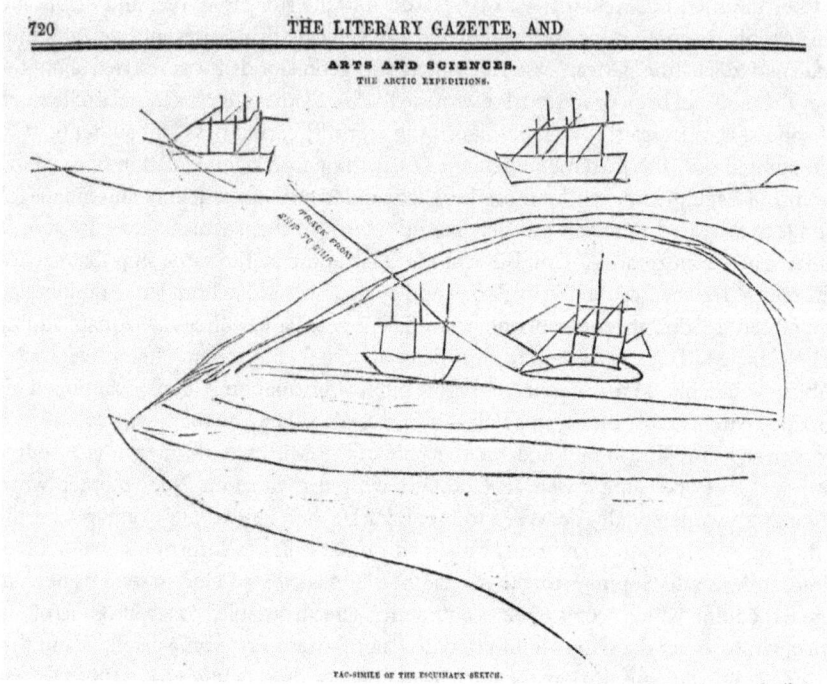

Figure 4.1 Usky's map drawn at Mittimatalik, Baffin Island, July 1849. Published as "Facsimile of the Esquimaux Sketch," with the note, "there is every reason to be assured of its TRUTH." "The Arctic Expeditions," *Literary Gazette*, October 6, 1849: 721.

It included a series of letters from George Shepherd, a civil engineer, which made detailed suggestions for ice blasting (based on experiments in the Danube). He was supported by a Commander Fleming, who wrote, "I have exhausted all my thinking powers as to how these most valuable [Gallant] Officers can be retrieved. . . . None have thought or felt more intensely than I have and continue to do (Dear Lady Franklin and other Suffering dear Ladies excepted)."[66]

The core of the old Arctic circles—Parry, Back, Beaufort, and William Scoresby—began to correspond both with John Barrow Jr. at the Admiralty and with Jane Franklin about the map. Barrow Jr.'s father, the influential Second Secretary Sir John Barrow, had died the previous year. They were concerned that the whalers might not be trustworthy observers who could properly acquire and calibrate Inuit information. The question rested not on their experience but on their "interest," particularly in the rewards offered by the Admiralty and by Lady Franklin. Parry wrote to Barrow Jr. on October 5 that it was essential to determine *exactly* how the Inuit were questioned, noting "when I wanted to obtain from them information as to the line of coast or opening in the land . . . you might, without great care, make them say almost anything."[67] Here he was remembering the spring of 1822, when Iligjaq drew her map of the coast to the north and west of the frozen-in HMS *Fury* and *Hecla* (see Chapter 2). At the time, Parry was convinced that his method of questioning and calibration produced an "accurate" map.[68] Now he emphasized that if the whalers had no similar system of determining "accuracy," then the map's value was doubtful. Determining this meant figuring out what questions had been asked and how, what relationships existed between whalers and Inuit, and who those Inuit were.

Scoresby and Back also had their doubts. Scoresby warned Barrow that the whalers' anxiety might have compromised their objectivity, for "it is natural to interpret ambiguous signs by our ideas of probable facts."[69] He suggested that their interest might have been both emotional and financial, noting that many of them had friends on the missing expedition. Back was concerned about the rough compass rose that appeared on some versions of the map, and when he found out that the *Truelove*'s owner Ward had inscribed it without reference to either magnetic or "true" north (especially important so close to the pole), he wrote, "This just makes the difference between Barrow's Strait and Regent's Inlet."[70] This was damaging, considering that Ward was administering Jane Franklin's £3,000 reward. Yet despite their concerns about the whalers' credibility, these men still generally trusted the Inuit information, not least because of their own experiences with Inuit geographical knowledge. Parry wrote to Barrow Jr. that the map "conveys to my mind hope, almost amounting to certainty, that the 4 ships are still in being."[71] Scoresby wrote that he believed in the "general accuracy of the Esquimaux" and that the report was "extremely plausible and likely."[72] Back, despite his doubts, was quoted in the *Athenaeum* asserting that he "never knew an Indian or an Esquimaux tracing to fail."[73]

At the same time, other members of the Arctic circles began to evaluate the map's trustworthiness through alternative means. This included Alexander Maconochie, Franklin's former private secretary in Tasmania, who had shaken Franklin's administration with his proposals for penal reform (see Chapter 3). In 1840, the Maconochies had gone to Norfolk Island, where Alexander was appointed as the commandant of the settlement of "secondary correction." They remained there until 1844, while Maconochie further developed the theories and practices of penal reform.[74] He and his family had returned to Britain at the same time as the Franklins, in 1844; they were replaced on Norfolk Island by John and Mary Franklin Price.[75] On his return to Britain, Maconochie had published extensively on his penal system, become the governor of a new prison at Birmingham, and had mended his fences with Jane Franklin.[76] Now, actively interested in the search and deeply frustrated by its built-in arrhythmia of information, he decided to short-circuit it by consulting clairvoyants. He consulted Emma, the famed "Bolton Clairvoyante," and sent her revelations to Jane Franklin in Orkney and to several newspapers. He signed the letters to the newspapers only "M," but both Jane and Sophia identified him as the author.[77] Sitting in a darkened room in a mesmeric trance, the young woman claimed to have spoken directly to Franklin, who, immersed in the ice, told her that the Inuit were lying. She claimed to have asked him, "Have you seen any natives? Then what makes them say you have seen them? Well, I thought so; if they could get over these heaps of ice, you could get over them also."[78]

Maconochie hoped that mesmerism could collapse time and space in the Arctic as the telegraph and railway had in Britain. As he put it, "in these days, when we make the lighting carry our messages, and the sun take our pictures, it is very difficult to draw the precise line betwixt the possible and the impossible."[79] In doing so, he gestured to a widespread problem—the thin boundaries between scientific orthodoxy and heterodoxy in which practices like mesmerism and phrenology dwelt.[80] In 1849, mesmerism could still be understood to overlap with magnetic science, though these ideas were becoming increasingly less respectable. Jane wrote to Barrow Jr. that she "not think that he wd have any objection to his friends speaking about it, but may not wish his name appended in the newspaper."[81] But Maconochie was also addressing the lack of information and the unlikelihood of getting more in the near future. These two factors made it possible for him to suggest (albeit anonymously) his unorthodox solution of employing clairvoyants, while at the same time, undermining the tenuous authority of Inuit evidence.

In the midst of frustrated suggestions for collapsing time and space through mesmerism, or annihilating icy prisons with dynamite, the press demanded a tangible archive of European journals, relics, or even a piece of wood to corroborate the Inuit report—and their absence was a cause for suspicion. On October 13, Goodsir's letter to his family from Baffin's Bay was published in the *Athenaeum*, resurrecting the idea that the whalers were untrustworthy reporters who had asked "leading questions" of the Inuit, and that the Inuit were only interested in rewards. Franklin's nephew Weld wrote a companion article in which he argued that the public's judgment had been led astray by "news [which] generally travels with the properties of an avalanche." He also questioned Inuit motives, asking why they had no tokens to prove they had visited the ships, and why Ross had not sent any messengers with them.[82] The question of Inuit credibility circulated rapidly through newspapers and magazines, and they were lent credence by Goodsir's suspicions, because he was an emotionally "interested" party with a missing brother. There was also the matter of Inuit "interest" in producing the map in the first place. On October 25 and 26, the *Hull Packet and East Riding Times* claimed that the "cunning" Inuit "have invented the statement they give of the position of Sir John Franklin and Sir James Ross, in the hope of obtaining some reward."[83]

The question of Inuit financial interest tapped into an important dynamic in the politics of truth, particularly when it came to the value of information. Expedition narratives had often painted Inuit as inveterate thieves, willing to do anything for wood, metal, and beads.[84] The stereotype developed out of a gross misunderstanding of Inuit trading practices and control of territory and resources. Regardless of where an expedition ended up, whether at a node in a long-distance trading network (like Parry at Igloolik in 1821–3) or on its fringes (like the Rosses at Kablunaaqhiuvik in 1830–1, or indeed, apparently, the wrecks of HMS *Terror* and *Erebus* in 1847–8), trade was desirable, even in a time of scarcity, and often people were more than happy to swap information for goods. That was particularly the case for wood and metal, both of which were available in different parts of the Canadian archipelago, but never in great supply. There was, however, no moral obligation for that information traded to be correct or total, especially when given to strangers. It might be fed in bits and pieces by people whom outsiders thought were authorities. Stealing also asserted authority over strangers. These were some of the ways in which Inuit were responding to a changing world with an unpredictable climate and increased trade.[85] What it meant was that those who sought to devalue Inuit information often presented them as greedy and immoral. Taken together with the gospel of progress that underlay the ice-blasting suggestions, it also meant the beginning of a racialized refrain that would continue for decades—that wherever Inuit could travel and survive, so could the British. The *Belfast News-Letter* claimed, "It is an incontestable fact that a European can sustain as much cold, hardship, hunger and all the privations of savage life . . . as well as any Esquimaux in the world, and perhaps better."[86] Such a view offered hope that did not depend on either Inuit information or on whalers or other intermediaries to interpret it.

The Arctic circles put a different spin on the question of Inuit interest, in which they questioned whalers' practices of taking young Inuit people away to train as interpreters, and speculated on the consequences. Parry wrote a memorandum in which he asked, "is it not possible that the Eskimaux was only retailing the information he had derived from ourselves, the exact purport of his conversation being mistaken in consequence of the very imperfect knowledge of the language possessed by our people?" He pointed out that because Parker and Penny had been taking Inuit back and forth to Britain for years, there were plenty of intermediaries at Mittimatalik—people who knew all about the British anxiety to find the missing ships (Figure 4.2). Parry speculated that the Inuit that Parker had taken to Britain in 1847 had monitored the news in England up to the time that Ross departed in the spring of 1848, had gone home and spread the news throughout the community at Mittimatalik, and then fed it back to whalers. The

Figure 4.2 Inuluapik was one of several young Inuit who were taken by whalers to Britain to be trained as intermediaries. He was taken by William Penny from Cumberland Sound to Aberdeen in 1839, and his maps were later published by the Admiralty. From *A Narrative of Some Passages in the History of Eenoolooapik*, by Alexander McDonald. Courtesy Science Photo Library/Alamy Stock Photo, Image ID: 2ACT4K8.

end result was, "Eskimaux in Pond's Bay <u>must</u> have known the most important facts as well as we do."[87] Parry may or may not have known that Parker had intended to found a mission with Inuit converts as missionaries. In 1847, he and Ward had taken Uckaluk and Memiadluk to a Moravian settlement at Fairfield in northern England to discuss training them as missionaries, but they had wanted to go straight home rather than stop at the Labrador training school.[88] In Parry's view, any inconsistencies could be attributed to the recirculation of rumors and fragments of facts among the people gathered at Mittimatalik, but that without further physical proof—tokens of "Wood, Metal, or Paper" from the ships themselves—the truth of the report could not be confirmed. Parry sent his memorandum to Barrow Jr. at the Admiralty, to Jane Franklin, and to Eleanor Gell.

Jane Franklin thought that she had ample experience of Indigenous intermediaries from her time in Tasmania, Australia, and New Zealand. She felt she had witnessed the "corruption" of contact between Indigenous people and whalers, sealers, convicts, or sailors, and she tended to be suspicious of intermediaries who had not been separated from their families and educated by Europeans. She was also well aware of explorers' dependence on Indigenous intermediaries and on local knowledge. She had traveled with intermediaries herself, on her overland expedition between Port Phillip and Sydney in 1839 (see Chapter 3). Her Antipodean experiences informed not only how she evaluated the authority of Indigenous people but also how she understood her own, for she was determined never again to be called a "man in petticoats."

During the search for her husband, Jane Franklin fully developed her public image as a loving wife, compelled by duty and devotion to search for her husband. Unlike in Tasmania, she did not present herself in public for the sole purpose of extending knowledge, improvement, and science. Her authority, she claimed, was rooted in sentiment, and her reason was tempered by anxiety (rather than the other way around). Her expressions of anxiety and distress in 1849 may have been purely performative, perfectly genuine, or somewhere in-between. They were both highly gendered and appropriate to their mid-Victorian moment, but they were also a part of a longer trajectory. As Philip J. Stern has argued, exploration knowledge was comprised of an "odd admixture of reason and emotion, authority and empiricism, induction and deduction, desire and faith," and was very far indeed from being either objective or rational.[89] Real, imagined, or performed, Jane Franklin's professed weakness helped make the case that she deserved both information and sympathy. As an explorer's wife, a maritime wife, and an anxious wife, she had a right not only to access information but also to gather and interpret it. In doing so, she also undermined the credibility of other relatives (notably her stepdaughter Eleanor) to do the same, arguing that they were motivated by self-interest and spite, rather than devotion and anxiety.

Jane Franklin and Sophia Cracroft frequently deployed this combination of sentiment, frailty, and reason. Jane often wrote to Barrow Jr. about how the clairvoyant reports and the Inuit reports either contradicted or supported each other, and begging to know how both were received at the Admiralty.[90] "It is thus that I <u>reason</u>," she wrote, "while yet my imagination is affected, & I derived a relative comfort I fear in observing that they all agree in one thing—that my husband is alive."[91] She frequently complained of how she could not think clearly because of her headaches and bodily weakness, and how her imagination ran in all directions at once. She told Barrow Jr. that he was her chivalrous defender, his father's heir in more ways than one. She wrote once, "I cannot tell you how deeply I feel your unwearied exertions—I am always afraid that every body will get tired at last, but you, impelled alike by principle and feeling, have made me believe you will never fail—God knows how I want such a support."[92]

In October 1849, Jane and Sophia traveled to whaling ports to interrogate the whalers in person. Along the way, they wrote detailed reports to Barrow Jr., Scoresby, and Parry. Their key questions were, whether the whalers had asked leading questions of the Inuit, and to what extent the captains had subsequently embellished the story. Jane had received a number of letters from the whaling captains before she met with them, but she found them lacking. She wrote, "the main point on which I request a precise answer, [who] began to talk about the expeditions, the whale ships or the Esquimaux—we are not likely to get any satisfactory answer to this question—I dareseay even themselves (The ships) cannot tell."[93] While they waited, the women gathered information—about the captain's reputations, their families and shipowners, and their correspondence, by seeking out their wives. Meeting with whalers' wives took the edge off the possibility of consorting with a class of maritime men seen as "uneducated, uncivilized, and fundamentally unrestrained."[94] Like other sailors, whalers were also vulnerable to the charge of being undomesticated—not tied to land, they were subject to their own rules, and prone to spinning tales.[95]

When the *Advice* arrived in Aberdeen, Jane wrote to Barrow Jr. to say that she had met with Goodsir and Penny. They first met Penny's wife Margaret, who promptly turned over all his letters. The Pennys had married in 1840 but had only actually lived together for a fraction of their nine years of marriage. Margaret Penny's life, like all whaling wives, was lived in absence and anticipation. In 1857, she would accompany her husband to Baffin Island where he began his own permanent whaling station and private colony.[96] Jane Franklin liked Margaret, and when she met Penny, decided that his character, though rough, was admirable. Jane told Barrow Jr. that Penny was "far superior to all the other whaling masters" and Sophia wrote to her mother, "we are much pleased with him. . . . He always leads the way in the very difficult navigation of the heavy Pack of ice in getting across Davis Straits."[97] After Parker of the *Truelove* arrived at Hull, the women met him too, and Jane wrote to Barrow Jr. that he "required a little cross-examination—even if I s^d be thwarted in this, you at the Admiralty will have him to yourself."[98] Soon after, they met with Robert Goodsir, and Jane wrote that he had "painfully annihilated . . . my remaining hopes abt the Esq report," telling her that though Parker had claimed that Usky had volunteered his information, in fact Kerr had asked the hunter leading questions. According to Goodsir, both Parker and Kerr were "noted for telling tales," and he added that Penny had urged Parker not to "go home & make assertions, but to be very careful what he said."[99] Based on their conversation with Goodsir, Sophia wrote to her mother that "there is no doubt that Captain Parker has made up a story. . . . We shall take good care to expose his treachery." Sophia begged her mother to write to Mary Price on Norfolk Island for "I fear you must have told her about the Esquimaux story, which must now be recalled."[100] They had been the victims of story-spinning sea captains and of dishonest natives, they wrote, and as a result, Jane's hopes were dashed and she was prostrated by headaches. Now they could only wait for Kerr to return in the *Chieftain*. Jane wrote to Scoresby about her anxiety to get "his own unprompted story, before he knows what Parker has said before him."[101]

Meanwhile, Eleanor (now twenty-five and pregnant with her first child) was equally determined to understand the map, how it had been produced, and by whom. Her claims of experience and affection were much different to her stepmother's. She had very different relationships with the men at the heart of the Arctic circles, principally Richardson, Parry, Beaufort, Back, Sabine, and James Ross. They had all known her since her infancy. Richardson had dislodged her from her crib so that he and Franklin could make midnight observations in 1824, and Beaufort had been one of her mother's pallbearers; she had danced on the deck of *Erebus* and *Terror* in Tasmania in 1841 and made observations for Sabine with Ross, and Back was one of her husband's parishioners.[102] Eleanor had also been closely involved in the education of the two Tasmanian children at Government House (see Chapter 3). Unlike her stepmother, however, she had never bombarded their friends with evidence of the family's maltreatment by Tasmanian settlers. Indeed, John and Mary Richardson's correspondence alluded to their fears that Jane Franklin might be an adverse influence on Eleanor, though they never explicitly said as much.[103]

Eleanor gathered these fragments and recollections as she set out to understand the Mittimatalik map. She claimed that, as a loving daughter, she had just as much of a right and duty to evaluate evidence and question authorities as her stepmother did. Eleanor also had a legitimate legal concern about her inheritance from her mother, which she feared (rightly) that Jane Franklin might spend without her consent. She and her husband believed that her stepmother was acting as rashly now as she had in Tasmania, and they feared the consequences. But she was also embattled, for Sophia Cracroft had taken up a role as Jane's defender. The cousins had grown up together as sisters on the islands of Guernsey and Tasmania, and had seldom been apart. Now Sophia's letters accused Eleanor of heartlessness, and of "[overlooking] the sorrow of others concerned in the Expedition and even more, the feelings of agony w^h my Uncle must be suffering."[104] Mary Simpkinson's daughter Marian begged her cousin to make peace with Jane. "You have had great provocation, as all candid people who know both sides of the question, must acknowledge," she wrote to Eleanor, but "it has been hitherto on her side, do not, by showing irritibility [*sic*] give her any advantage over you."[105]

Eleanor wrote to Beaufort's daughter Rosalind to ask for her father's opinion of the Mittimatalik map, as well as Jane Franklin's and Alexander Maconochie's use of clairvoyants to evaluate its accuracy. Rosalind replied, "Papa is much too happy and too thankful in the hopes held out by this good news to have any doubts of its truth." She added, "He has no belief in Clairvoyance and no admiration for the present sample of it—which he thinks both false and clumsy. If she is ignorant of the Subject, those about her are not."[106] Eleanor also wrote to Parry, who replied,

> With respect to the Clairvoyante I am sorry that I omitted to answer you, but I was too much occupied with the realities of the case at that time, to allow me to give one thought to what I believe to be mere delusion—for such is the impression, I am free to confess, w^h the several Accounts I rec^d from Miss Cracroft, have, upon the whole, left upon my mind.[107]

Parry also made sure that she received copies of some of the reports and memoranda about the map that he prepared and received.

Eleanor also personally met with Parker, accompanied by her husband. The account of the meeting does not survive, but despite their differences in status, they had much in common. Unlike Jane Franklin, the Gells and Parker shared an interest in the work of Moravian missions, the translation of the Bible into Indigenous languages, and the use of Indigenous missionaries. Both families experimented with the education of Indigenous people in their home, though in very different circumstances. Whether any of this was discussed is unclear, but the Gells did send a copy of the original map, some newspaper clippings, and an account of their meeting with Parker to Lady Anne Ross sometime in mid-October. Her husband was, of course, also missing. When Anne Ross replied to Eleanor, she wrote, "These excited hopes and weary silence are sadly trying in every way, bodily, mentally & spiritually." She, too, had been poring over the evidence, had been fed a steady stream of information from Scottish ports, and had been in contact with Jane Franklin. While she worried that the map had been drawn "in the hope of gain," she hoped Inuit rather than the whalers had made it, "So if from them I am still building hope upon it."[108] Anne Ross perfectly captured the central problem: hope depended on believing Inuit to be reliable and trustworthy observers, and on trusting the whalers to understand and faithfully communicate the information they received. Denying that—and reasserting social and racial hierarchies of authority—led to despair.

Ambiguous Signs and Probable Facts: November–December 1849

In November 1849, two of the three rescue expeditions returned to Britain. John Richardson returned to Haslar and left Rae behind to continue the search. More explosively, James Clark Ross returned with HMS *Enterprise* and *Investigator*. Like Richardson and Rae, Ross had encountered heavy ice, and been stuck in Port Leopold at the top of Prince Regent's Inlet for eleven months. He had sent men on sledging journeys in several directions, but they had not seen any sign of the *Erebus* and *Terror* nor of any Inuit.[109] Parry wrote to Barrow Jr. as soon as he heard of Ross's return, "I need not say how greedy I am for further intelligence. . . . How entirely the Eskimaux Reports have thus vanished! Alas! For poor dear Lady F!"[110] Jane Franklin wrote to Barrow Jr., "I have felt palsied by [Ross's] return and all its fearful consequences."[111]

The widespread disappointment at Ross's return has generally been understood to be the reason that the Admiralty dispatched a fleet of eight ships in 1850 to Lancaster Sound and the Bering Strait to continue the Franklin search.[112] This assumption ignores the power of the Mittimatalik map, which continued to command attention among Arctic circles and in the press well after Ross's return. But the Mittimatalik map did not vanish. Instead, it was transformed from an "Esquimaux rumor" to a trustworthy and verifiable piece of evidence that could launch ships.[113] In November 1849, Jane Franklin's supporters used the evidence she and Sophia supplied from the whalers to change both the meaning of the map and the quality of the received information. Fundamentally, they shifted the vulnerability of the explorers into a philanthropic cause and the sailors into deserving subjects of British humanitarianism in a way that presaged the figuring of British soldiers in the Crimea five years later.[114] Once that happened, the Mittimatalik map supported a great cause and became tantalizing evidence for Hope. The other crucial thing that they did was, effectively, to subtly change the quality of time. That long pause in-between bursts of information promised to be still longer and more frustrating as the northern winter set in. But once the map was redefined as trustworthy evidence *to be verified*, the quality of the pause changed from a long stretch of anxious waiting to a short period of frantic preparation.

In Scotland, Jane and Sophia waited for Kerr at his home port of Kirkaldy. They interviewed him on October 30, when he described the encounter at Mittimatalik in more detail. According to Kerr, Usky never claimed to have visited the ships, and had not said, "whether the two sets of ships had any communication with each other, but [Kerr] only inferred that they had." Kerr had apparently drawn the "track from ship to ship" after the fact. Jane Franklin sent her report of the conversation to Barrow Jr., along with several letters received from other whaling captains.[115] Sophia wrote to her mother that their doubts had been dispelled, and that "the Captn's [Kerr's] story has confirmed our former hopes. The story is so consistent & apparently so careful is he not to infer too much, i.e. more than was expressed that we believe that the Esquimaux have seen the ships" and then asked her to correlate it to the most recent statement of the Bolton Clairvoyante.[116] Meanwhile, Parker was called to attendance at the Admiralty, and described how he understood Inuit travel and communication networks between Baffin Island and Prince Regent Inlet. He also explained more about the circumstances of how the map had been drawn. Usky had approached Kerr first, "very anxious to express his meaning" but Kerr could not understand him. Usky had "made signs for paper" and had been taken down to the cabin, where he "immediately drew the four ships and explained by the words (familiar to the whalers) implying ships, and seasons."[117] Effectively the episode reasserted the accuracy and credibility of both Inuit communication and the whalers' reports. Inconsistencies were attributed to failures of communication, but the fact remained that Inuit had observed four ships, but had not chosen to visit them—which explained the lack of "tokens."

At the same time, James Ross was criticized for his early return in *Enterprise* and *Investigator*, and for failing to search Wellington Channel, which was the alternate route in Franklin's instructions. Some suggested that Ross had failed to search Wellington Channel because he wanted to pursue his own scientific agendas rather than hunt for Franklin, criticism which Parry dismissed as "atrocious, abusive, and ignorant."[118] A week after Ross's return, Scoresby gave an influential address at the Whitby Institute. Noting that the public sympathy "had been greatly excited by the reports of certain Esquimaux," he displayed a lithograph of the Mittimatalik map and argued that Ross's return should not put a "depressing check" on hope. He reminded his audience (many of whom were wealthy captains and shipowners with long Arctic connections) that Inuit maps "have been repeatedly proved to be remarkably characteristic of reality." The confusion around where the ships were actually located, whether they were in communication with each other, and whether Inuit had actually been on board could be explained by Kerr's anxiety to get information from his informant, and Scoresby reiterated that "it is natural to interpret ambiguous signs by our ideas of probable facts." In the end, he stated to applause, he was "still disposed to hold by . . . the Esquimaux sketch." His address used the Mittimatalik map to make an impassioned case for hope, charity, and action.[119] His oratory drew on his varied campaigns for improvement, most recently through his floating church and efforts at social reform in his parish at Bradford.[120] As Alison Winter has argued, these campaigns contributed considerably to his cultural authority in the public sphere as a man of the sea, of the ice, of science, and of the cloth.[121]

Whitby is far more isolated in the twenty-first century than it was in the mid-nineteenth century, when it was a thriving Yorkshire whaling port connected to London by sea, with wealthy captains and shipowners patronizing local literary and philosophical societies. Accordingly, Scoresby's address did not stay on the windy edge of the North Yorkshire moors. It began to be reprinted in regional newspapers across the industrial north, and at the same time, copies traveled to John Barrow Jr. and to Jane Franklin. Whether Scoresby sent these or not is unclear. John Barrow Sr. had treated him badly thirty years earlier, not only denying him the command of expeditions but also failing to credit his discoveries (see Chapter 1). As recently as 1847, Scoresby was still smarting about these slights but was willing to work with Barrow Jr. in the search for Franklin.[122] The autumn of 1849 marked the beginning of their collaboration. Barrow Jr. sent Scoresby's address to the *Morning Herald* in London and wrote to him, "we must all be up and moving."[123] Jane wrote to Scoresby a few weeks later, "Your article is much admired—only it is too short."[124]

Scoresby's address was widely influential and shifted the public discourse about the Inuit map to cast it as a credible source of hope and action. In London, the *Morning Chronicle* now felt that all their doubts about the Inuit report had been based on "mere inferences" made as the story percolated first through the whale fleet and then through the press. Usky's statement that the ships had passed by "would warrant us in believing that this was all the Esquimaux wished to communicate."[125] This was crucial. Inuit information was not seen as *ipso facto* credible or trustworthy, but it was sufficiently suggestive to demand further investigation. Ross and his crew had not had this intelligence, and therefore could not have investigated it, despite what the papers called their "philanthropic zeal."[126] The only possible solution was to send out a government expedition manned by trained officers. Despite the lack of traces, "we still rejoice in the hope that the lost ones are yet in safety," somewhere on the unknown Arctic coast.[127] At least four editorials expressed their hopes that government would call forth "every possible energy . . . to devise new means for renewing and pursuing our philanthropic task of ascertaining the fate of so many good, gallant and brave men."[128]

Backing out of such a task now was, of course, impossible. Roger Harwood, the leader writer for the *Morning Chronicle*, wrote on November 24, "As a nation, we are bound in honour to any great and worthy purpose which we have once taken up: we cannot be severed from it without losing a part of ourselves; willfully to surrender it would be baseness—to resign it on compulsion must be a pain and a grief."[129] Meanwhile, the Mittimatalik map was published again, this time superimposed over an Admiralty map of Baffin's Bay drawn by Parry and John Ross in 1818. Black lines on the map indicated the track of the *Truelove*, while red lines demarcated the extent of the ice and narrated the Inuit report. Franklin's and Ross's presumed locations were clearly marked with Xs and the caveat "by Esquimaux report" while Usky's sketch was inset at the bottom but turned so that Ward's compass rose pointed in the wrong direction.[130]

In December 1849, at Jane's urging, Scoresby wrote a series of articles in the *Morning Herald* that were subsequently published in a pamphlet in January. In them he argued that there were "grounds of reasonable hope" that the explorers were still alive and that abandoning them would "stultify the impulses of humanity." These articles were notable for two reasons: first, in the way that Scoresby continued to harness humanitarian impulse to Arctic rescue; and second, in the way that he utterly erased the Mittimatalik map from its earlier, prominent position. In them, Scoresby argued that national honor lay in spontaneous sympathy and zealous action in the absence of (European) evidence.[131] Scoresby's key point was that Franklin and his men "are the legitimate objects of a national duty and care" because they were sent out on government service, "and not only is this a Government expedition, and therefore national, but by the general interest given to its objects, and the universal sympathy yielded to its perils, by the British public, *we* as the people, *have recognized it as our own*" (emphasis original).[132] In short, Scoresby argued, the missing sailors were deserving, legitimate objects of philanthropy, and to insist on their rescue was both humane and patriotic. He also took care to point out that the glory should not be restricted to the Navy, but that there were whalers "well known to possess both the inclination and the ability to take a share in an exploration of this kind," men full of "zeal and perseverance," who had not yet been "fairly tried" in the Arctic Service.[133] Scoresby's articles were bolstered by a lengthy discussion of the nature of the ice dynamics in Lancaster Sound and Baffin Bay and extracts taken from published and unpublished journals. He outlined detailed, apparently well-informed plans for ice traveling, arrangement of parties, and the use of modern technologies like kites and balloons to gather information. In doing so, he placed the responsibility for gathering information exclusively in the hands of the British. Whereas in November, the Inuit map was the basis of hope, by January, it had vanished from public discourse.

The philanthropic argument fell on fertile ground. As Cavell has argued in her study of the print culture of polar exploration, over the previous thirty years, a "connected narrative" had developed that linked polar explorers' persons, successes, and failures to a developing concept of what it meant to be British. That powerful harnessing of polar exploration to a national narrative also made it vulnerable to radical reinterpretation in the volatile climate of 1848 and afterward. The Admiralty's perceived reluctance to continue the search, combined with both the amplified rhetoric of the press and the identification of middle and working-class reading publics with the explorers, developed into a new belief that public opinion alone could bring to light a great "dereliction of duty" on the part of the Admiralty, and force a recalcitrant government to act.[134] Entangled with that nationalist narrative was a humanitarian narrative that a responsible government was honor-bound to alleviate the suffering of its vulnerable (and deserving) subjects. It was a narrative buried deep in humanitarian governance, but unlike Captain Parker's request for humanitarian aid for starving Inuit in Baffin Bay in 1847 (or indeed, aid for famine-stricken Ireland), the notion of starving Englishmen in the Arctic ice prompted action.

The "Suggestions for the Relief of Sir John Franklin" file at the Admiralty documents a sudden deluge of letters in November and December of 1849.[135] Men volunteered out of the blue to join any relief expedition, like the 22-year-old medical student Robert Cox, who begged the Lords to let him go on this "mission of philanthropy," writing, "when a fellow creature is in distress any individual has a right to succour him & had I the means I myself would lead an expedition to the North Pole in quest of the missing voyagers."[136] Another who feared that "the anxiety of poor Lady Franklin must be deeply aggravated" offered to join the "Esquimaux tribes at the pole to scour the ice thoroughly in all possible directions."[137] Richardson declined this latter idea, pointing out that any such journey would require taking women and children, stopping to catch seals, and would be restricted to the Inuit tracks and trails that already existed. Moreover, he added, "as soon as a scarcity of provisions began to be felt the European party would be left to shift for themselves." If such a thing were contemplated, Richardson added, it was best done through the people who were coming and going from Mittimatalik.[138]

Most of the letters and plans were convinced that technology could penetrate the ice and rescue the missing men without the need for Indigenous information or support. A man who heard Scoresby's lecture at Whitby sat down the next day to draw up a plan for a flying ship suspended by three balloons, a plan which Captain Hamilton denounced as "a complicated scheme [that is] purely ridiculous."[139] Other plans included fitting ships with steam-driven circular saws in the prow; a railway engineer's model for an amphibious proto-snow machine (on the premise that "Ice forms its own Railway, as you can stear [sic] to any point"); messages printed on gutta percha and delivered by balloon; the release of ten thousand carrier pigeons; the development of a "Franklinean Dispatch Carrier" (a hot air balloon that dropped messages from exploding grenades); and many more plans that involved a combination of rockets, balloons, and ice blasting. The latter received its own file.[140] Almost to a man, they argued, like Scoresby, that it was a humanitarian duty to rescue Franklin and his men. As a Cornish schoolmaster wrote, "it is the duty of every one who can think on any means likely to be useful in restoring our lost countrymen, to do so, as their object was to extend our geographical knowledge, and thus confer a general boon on all mankind."[141]

Jane and Sophia returned to London from Scotland in November 1849. Jane used her power of attorney over her husband's finances (and her stepdaughter's inheritance from her mother) to equip her own expedition in the *Prince Albert*. Parker, Penny, and Kerr all volunteered to command it, along with at least two other whaling captains.[142] She chose instead a man with no polar experience whatever, but who had demonstrated devotion to her in Tasmania—Charles Forsyth. He had been one of the *Beagle*'s officers who had been temporarily placed in command of the *Vansittart* in 1842 (see Chapter 3).[143] Jane seemed to have considered Penny as his second, but the latter repeatedly told her that he was unwilling to serve on an expedition with naval officers unless he was under a "joint and equal command."[144] Instead, she pressed Beaufort to consider Penny for a naval command, writing to Scoresby that "I want him to go his own way to work with a set of whalers—he is a man of the most undoubted perseverance."[145] Her primary concern was to validate the Mittimatalik map, and Forsyth was sent to examine the region of Boothia and Prince Regent Inlet, where Usky seemed to have placed Ross's relief expedition and the missing ships.

The Franklin family were deeply divided over the new expedition. Mary Simpkinson had recently suffered a stroke and was partly paralyzed, but this did not prevent her from helping her sister, often inviting Jane and Sophia to stay. Her daughter Marian Simpkinson wrote to Eleanor, "I hope Government will be induced to send to Behring's Straits, but I am afraid my aunt will do a great deal of mischief, her violence and strong feeling and her strange way of viewing everything will be very likely to frustrate any attempt she may make to have another ship sent out." She dreaded having Jane and Sophia come to stay with them, but wrote, "I suppose [Sophia] and my aunt are inseparable." Her objections were drowned out by her mother Mary, who Marian reported "does not care if I sleep on the ground, these are her words, rather than not gratify every wish of Aunt F's."[146]

In response to public pressure and Jane Franklin's influence, Beaufort drew up a plan to send out a rescue fleet in 1850. The Bering Strait was considered to be the most important location, since James Ross thought that Franklin was west of any navigable point in Lancaster Sound. Yet Lancaster Sound (and implicitly, the Inuit report) was by no means neglected. Beaufort argued that steam-powered vessels should be used to investigate whether Franklin had followed his instructions and gone up Wellington Channel. The use of steam, he pointed out, was essential to erase the anxious silence. "Only useless expenditure and reiterated disappointment will attend the best efforts of sailing vessels," he argued, "leaving the lingering survivors of the lost ships as well as their relatives in England in equal despair." He incorporated several of the suggestions from the public: ice-blasting equipment, circular saws, and balloons for dispatching messages. In addition, he proposed that Penny be allowed to command a separate detachment to investigate Jones Sound with sailing ships, arguing that "his local knowledge, his thorough acquaintance with all the mysteries of ice navigation, and his well-known skill and resources seem to point him out as a most valuable auxiliary."[147]

Parry, Richardson, and Back were all invited to comment on the proposal. Back and Parry agreed on dispatching steamers, and Parry agreed that the search would be incomplete without searching Wellington Channel. He advised that Penny's "intelligence, zeal, and long experience in ice navigation appear to me to entitle his opinion to their Lordship's consideration."[148] Richardson reiterated his belief that life was sustainable at high latitudes and insisted that official expeditions should be coordinated both with the trading activities of the HBC and the RAC as well as with the Inuit. Hope, he pointed out, was to be located in the Inuit and Iñupiaq trading network between the Mackenzie River and the Bering Strait, in which "intelligence of any interesting occurrence is conveyed along the coast." He also suggested that both the HBC and the Russians should be encouraged to offer rewards for information, pointing out that evidence like the existing map "forbid us to lose hope."[149] Parry summed up the case by stating, "the time has not yet arrived, when the attempt ought to be given up as hopeless" and pointed out that if they acted now, " the Country at large" would be satisfied that they made every effort "so long as the most distant hope remains of ultimate success."[150] Over the course of the winter, the Lords of the Admiralty were reluctantly persuaded by the arguments of the polar officers, the public, and the Franklin family to send a new expedition, because, "it appears to be our bounden duty to continue our search after our Missing Expedition, and to use every feasible means at our disposal for their recovery."[151] Admiral Cowper was, however, hesitant to expose any more men "to the risks of penetrating that vast unknown region without anything but guesses to guide them."[152]

The new rescue expeditions consisted of eight ships, whose tracks spanned the North American Arctic (see Timeline 3 and Map 4). HMS *Enterprise* and *Investigator* were sent to the Bering Strait to search the northern coast of Alaska and to dispatch overland expeditions into the HBC territories. Meanwhile, Captain Horatio Austin was put in charge of the search from Lancaster Sound. A veteran of Parry's 1824–5 voyage, Austin commanded HMS *Resolute* and was ordered to investigate every possible route Franklin could have taken from Lancaster Sound—north up Wellington Channel, west to Melville Island, or southwest via Cape Walker (Figure 4.3). Austin was accompanied by naval commanders and crews aboard HMS *Assistance* (Captain Erasmus Ommanney), and two screw steamers, the *Pioneer* (Lt. Sherard Osborn) and the *Intrepid* (Lt. Bertie Cator). There were also two American naval ships, *Advance* and *Rescue*, and two private expeditions, one of which was Lady Franklin's *Prince Albert*, and the other in the *Felix*, led by Sir John Ross and backed by the HBC.[153] Finally, Penny was placed in command of a naval expedition with the newly christened HMS *Lady Franklin* and HMS *Sophia*. The *Lady Franklin*'s figurehead was, appropriately enough, Hope leaning on an anchor.[154]

Figure 4.3 Broadside Linen Poster, "Captain Austin's Expedition in Search of Sir John Franklin: *Intrepid, Resolute, Assistance, Pioneer*." Mr. Green's signal balloon was one of many suggestions sent to the Admiralty in the autumn of 1849 in response to the Mittimatalik map. W.L. Crowther Library, State Library of Tasmania.

The autumn of 1849 set a pattern that would characterize the remainder of the Franklin search. Both naval and whaling ships would continue to depart in the spring and return in the autumn, bringing with them stories, maps, and very occasionally, a relic of the lost expedition. These pieces of evidence might be observed or collected *in situ*, and frequently they were extracted from Indigenous informants. Inuit intelligence drawn from the extensive (and expanding) Indigenous trading networks across the North American Arctic testified to the fact that Indigenous people could travel, observe, and report where the British could not. The flow of information had a built-in arrhythmia. When that combined with the already unsettled nature of geographical authority, Indigenous testimony, and vernacular knowledge, a space was opened for the women of the Franklin family to claim a gendered authority to access and interpret geographical data. Drawing on both new and old Arctic circles, they were able to reframe Arctic rescue as government's philanthropic duty.

Notes

1 SPRI MS 1503/39/6, John Richardson to Mary Richardson, February 1849.
2 TNA ADM 7/189/13, Robert Goodsir to his family, copy by Sophia Cracroft, August 21, 1849.
3 Fossett, *In Order to Live Untroubled*, 148–9.
4 Eber, *Encounters on the Passage*, 74–83.
5 Fossett, *In Order to Live Untroubled*, 139–66, and Jean L. Briggs, *Never in Anger: Portrait of an Eskimo Family* (Cambridge, MA: Harvard University Press, 1970), 12–15 for Inuit accounts of these years.
6 See National Snow and Ice Data Center, "Sea Ice," https://nsidc.org/learn/parts-cryosphere/sea-ice, accessed 21 July, 2023.
7 Bockstoce, *Furs and Frontiers*, 179–224. See also Shepherd Krech III, "The Eastern Kutchin and the Fur Trade, 1800-1860," *Ethnohistory* 23, no. 3 (Summer 1976): 213–35.
8 Bockstoce, *Furs and Frontiers*, 143.
9 John Bockstoce, *Whales, Ice and Men: The History of Whaling in the Western Arctic* (Seattle and London: University of Washington Press, 1986), 21–6, 93–102.
10 David Morrison, "The Copper Inuit Soapstone Trade," *Arctic* 44, no. 3 (September 1991): 239–46; Matthew W. Betts, "The Mackenzie Inuit Whale Bone Industry: Raw Material, Tool Manufacture, and Trade," *Arctic* 60, no. 2 (June 2007): 129–44.
11 Smith, "Chipewyan, Cree and Inuit," 133–56; George Wenzel, "Clyde Inuit Settlements and Community: From Before Boas to Centralization," *Arctic Anthropology* 45, no. 1 (2008): 1–21; Dorothy Harley Eber, *When the Whalers Were Up North: Inuit Memories from the Eastern Arctic* (Norman: University of Oklahoma Press, 1996), 3–16.
12 Alexander McDonald, *A Narrative of Some Passages in the Life of Eenoolooapik, A Young Esquimaux, Who Was Brought to Britain in 1839 in the Ship "Neptune" of Aberdeen; An Account of the Discovery of Hogarth's Sound: Remarks on the Northern Whale Fishery and Suggestions for its Improvement, &c &c* (Edinburgh: Fraser & Co., 1841). See also H. G. Jones, "The Inuit as Geographers: The Case of Eenoolooapik," *Etudes/Inuit/Studies* 28, no. 2 (2004): 57–72.

13 TNA ADM 7/189/13, W. E. Parry Memorandum to Barrow, Haslar, Gosport, October 25, 1849; *Truelove: From War to Whaler* (Hull City Council, 2008). http://www.hullcc.gov.uk/museumcollections/collections/storydetail.php?irn=196&master=425 (accessed May 19, 2011).
14 J. Secord, *Victorian Sensation*, 41–76.
15 Mark W. Turner, "Periodical Time in the Nineteenth Century," *Media History* 8, no. 2 (2002): 194.
16 Cavell, *Tracing the Connected Narrative*, 3.
17 C. A. Bayly, "Knowing the Country: Empire and Information in India," *Modern Asian Studies* 27, no. 1 (1993): 4; Bayly, *Empire and Information*, 165–71.
18 NMM FRN 1/28, John Franklin to Mary Anne Kendall, Whale Fish Islands, July 12, 1845. Kendall was meant to accompany Franklin as First Lieutenant.
19 RST 16/8, Jane Franklin to Mary Simpkinson, June 21, 1838 (extracts).
20 Woodward, *Portrait of Jane*, 253.
21 DRO D8760/F/FJR/1/1/91, John Franklin to John Richardson, July 7, 1845; NMM FRN 1/28, John Franklin to Mary Anne Kendall, July 12, 1845.
22 DRO D8760/F/FEG/1/1/15, John Franklin to Eleanor Franklin, July 6, 1845.
23 The letter is identified in the RGS-IBG archives as having been sent from the *Erebus*. It is in John Franklin's hand and evidently written from memory, for several stanzas are switched around, and some words replaced. See Chapter 1. RGS-IBG SJF/7/5, "Miss Greenstockings to her faithless admirer."
24 Savours, *Search for the North West Passage*, 270–81.
25 See, for example, SPRI MS 1199/1/1-2, Parry, Private Journal HMS *Alexander*, 1818, Official Journal, HMS *Hecla*, 1819–20.
26 WM SCO 778, Box N, William Jackson to William Scoresby, Hull, March 25, 1851.
27 John Bockstoce, "From Davis Strait to Bering Strait: the Arrival of the Commercial Whaling Fleet in North America's Western Arctic," *Arctic* 37, no. 4 (December 1984): 530.
28 TNA ADM 7/188/3, Thomas Barkhurst to Thomas Thompson, January 13, 1849.
29 "Reward Offered by Lady Franklin," March 20, 1848, in Erika Behrisch Elce, ed., *As Affecting the Fate of my Absent Husband: Selected Letters of Lady Franklin Concerning the Search for the Lost Franklin Expedition, 1848-1860*. (Montreal and Kingston: McGill-Queen's University Press, 2009), 64.
30 Savours, *Search for the North West Passage*, 186–9.
31 See HBCA B.42/a/151-157, 179, 185; B.157/a/1; B.186/b/34; B.200/a/26, 141; B.200/b/13-17; B.239/a/141; B.239/b/104b; B.239/c/3 Richardson's family had kept up a friendship with the Raes for years. See SPRI MS 248/281/1, SPRI MS 1503/18; Ian Bunyan et al., *No Ordinary Journey: John Rae, Arctic Explorer, 1813-1893* (Edinburgh: National Museums of Scotland/Montreal and Kingston: McGill-Queen's University Press, 1993).
32 Parry, *Parry of the Arctic*, 221.
33 WM SCO 778, Box N, William Scoresby to Jane Franklin, April 29, [1847?].
34 Penny Russell, "Wife Stories: Narrating Marriage and Self in the Life of Jane Franklin," *Victorian Studies* (Autumn 2005): 35–57; Penny Russell, "Citizens of the World? Jane Franklin's Transnational Fantasies," in *Transnational Lives: Biographies of Global Modernity, 1700-Present*, ed. Desley Deacon, Penny Russell, and Angela Woollacott (New York: Palgrave-Macmillan, 2010), 195–208.
35 Norling, *Captain Ahab Had a Wife*, 142–50.
36 Woodward, *Portrait of Jane*, 264; Alexander, *Ambitions*, 211–12.

37 *Chambers's Edinburgh Journal*, "Gossip from London," April 14, 1849, 232 for the tour; DRO D8760/F/FEG/1/38/3, Eleanor Gell to Mrs. Majendie, nd (late June/early July, 1849 by context) for the "slightly deranged" quote.
38 "Arctic Expedition – Lady Franklin," *Caledonian Mercury*, February 19, 1849, 2.
39 TNA ADM 7/188/3, Charles Reid to Captain Hamilton, March 21, 1849; SPRI MS 116/63/56, William Penny to Jane Franklin, March 6, 1849; OA D 23/7/15/5, David Kerr to Lady Franklin, March 21, 1849.
40 W. G. Ross, *This Distant and Unsurveyed Country: A Woman's Winter at Baffin Island, 1857–58* (Montreal and London: McGill-Queen's University Press, 1997), xxxi.
41 TNA ADM 7/189/3-10.
42 SPRI MS 1503/38-39, John Richardson Correspondence, 1848–9; NA ADM 7/188/17, Report of Sir John Richardson.
43 *The Athenaeum*, "Our Weekly Gossip," September 8, 1849, 913.
44 David S. Lee and George W. Wenzel, "Narwhal Hunting by Pond Inlet Inuit: An Analysis of Foraging Modes in the Floe-Edge Environment," *Etudes/Inuit/Studies* 28, no. 2 (2005): 133–57.
45 For the importance of consensus with respect to geographical information, see Aporta, "Trail as Home," 131–46.
46 ADM 7/189/13, "Memorandum of Capt Parker's attendance at Admiralty."
47 Lawrence Dritsas, "Expeditionary Science: Conflicts of Method in Mid-Nineteenth Century Geographical Discovery," in *Geographies of Nineteenth Century Science*, ed. David N. Livingstone and Charles W. J. Withers (Chicago and London: University of Chicago Press, 2011), 255–77.
48 Dane Kennedy has finely illustrated this tension between the linguistic knowledge of the Orientalist and the direct observation by the explorer in his examination of the White Nile Controversy in 1857–9. See Dane Kennedy, *The Highly Civilized Man: Richard Burton and the Victorian World* (Cambridge, MA and London: Harvard University Press, 2005), 108–16.
49 Driver, *Geography Militant*, 56.
50 Ibid., 61–2.
51 Dritsas, "Expeditionary Science," 270–2; Adrian S. Wisnicki, "Charting the Frontier: Indigenous Geography, Arab-Nyamwezi Caravans, and the East African Expedition of 1856-59," *Victorian Studies* 51, no. 1 (Autumn 2008): 103–37.
52 Charles W. J. Withers, "Mapping the Niger, 1798-1832: Trust, Testimony, and 'Ocular Demonstration' in the Late Enlightenment," *Imago Mundi* 56, no. 2 (2004): 170–93; Kennedy, *Highly Civilized Man*, 112.
53 TNA ADM 7/189/13, "Memorandum of Capt Parker's attendance at Admiralty."
54 [C. R. Weld] "The Arctic Expeditions," *The Athenaeum*, October 13, 1849, 1038.
55 "Reward Offered by Lady Franklin," March 20, 1848, in Elce, *As Affecting the Fate*, 64.
56 TNA ADM 7/189/13, Robert Goodsir to his family, copy by Sophia Cracroft, August 21, 1849.
57 SPRI MS 248/247/13, Sophia Cracroft to Isabella Cracroft, October 2, 1849.
58 TA NS 1004/1/11, Isabella Cracroft. to Mary Franklin Price, November 13, 1849.
59 "Safety of Sir John Franklin's Expedition," *Times*, October 6, 1849, 3.
60 "News of Sir John Franklin's Expedition," *The Morning Chronicle*, October 5, 1849, 5.
61 "Safety of Sir John Franklin," *The Sun*, October 5, 1849, in ADM 7/188/13.
62 "The Arctic Expeditions," *Literary Gazette*, October 6, 1849, 720–1.

63 DRO D8760/F/FEG/1/49/4, Anne Weld to Eleanor Gell, 7 October, 1849.
64 Anita McConnell, "Weld, Charles Richard (1813–1869)," *Oxford Dictionary of National Biography*, Oxford University Press, January 2006 (accessed March 19, 2013). doi:10.1093/ref:odnb/28982.
65 [C. R. Weld] "The Arctic Expeditions," *Athenaeum*, October 6, 1849, 1012.
66 TNA ADM 7/608, Commander R. H. Fleming to Captain Hamilton, October 19, 1849.
67 TNA ADM 7/189/13, W. E. Parry to John Barrow, Jr., Holyhead, October 5, 1849.
68 Bravo, *Accuracy of Ethnoscience*, esp,. 6–11.
69 TNA ADM 7/189/13, William Scoresby to John Barrow, Jr., Whitby, October 9, 1849.
70 TNA ADM 7/189/13, George Back to Captain Hamilton, Ramsgate, October 18, 1849.
71 TNA ADM 7/189/13, W. E. Parry to John Barrow, Jr., Holyhead, October 7, 1849.
72 TNA ADM 7/189/13, William Scoresby to John Barrow, Jr., Whitby, October 9, 1849.
73 "The Arctic Expeditions," *The Athenaeum*, October 13, 1849, 1038.
74 John Vincent Barry, *Alexander Maconochie of Norfolk Island: A Study of a Pioneer in Penal Reform* (Melbourne: Oxford University Press, 1958).
75 John Vincent Barry, *The Life and Death of John Price: A Study of the Exercise of Naked Power* (London and New York: Melbourne University Press, 1964).
76 Alexander Maconochie, *On the Management of Transported Criminals* (London: C. Whiting, 1845); Alexander Maconochie, *Crime and Punishment : The Mark System Framed to Mix Persuasion with Punishment, and Make Their Effect Improving, yet Their Operation Severe* (London: J. Hatchard, 1846); Alexander Maconochie, *Norfolk Island* (London: J. Hatchard, 1847); Alexander Maconochie, *Secondary Punishment: The Mark System* (London: John Ollivier, 1848). For the Maconochies' relationships with the Franklins, see TA NS 1004/1/8, Eleanor Franklin to Mary Franklin Price, February 10, 1847.
77 "The Bolton Clairvoyant," *Preston Guardian*, October 6, 1849, 2; "Sir John Franklin and the Bolton Clairvoyante," *Lloyd's Weekly Newspaper*, October 7, 1849, 10; "The Bolton Clairvoyante Again – Sir John Franklin's Expedition," *Belfast News-Letter*, October 9, 1849, 1. ADM 7/189/13, Jane Franklin to John Barrow, Jr., October 7, 1849; SPRI MS 248/247/21, Sophia Cracroft to Isabella Cracroft, October 25, 1849.
78 "Sir John Franklin: Further Revelations by the Bolton Clairvoyante," *Hull Packet and East Riding Times*, October 26, 1849, 5; "The Bolton Clairvoyante and Sir John Franklin," *Newcastle Courant*, October 26, 1849, 2.
79 [Maconochie] "The Bolton Clairvoyante," 3.
80 Alison Winter, "The Construction of Orthodoxies and Heterodoxies in the Early Victorian Life Sciences," in *Victorian Science in Context*, ed. Bernard Lightman (Chicago and London: University of Chicago Press, 1997), 24–50; Alison Winter, "'Compasses All Awry': The Iron Ship and the Ambiguities of Cultural Authority in Victorian Britain," *Victorian Studies* (Autumn 1994): 69–98.
81 TNA ADM 7/189/13, Jane Franklin to John Barrow, Jr., October 7, 1849.
82 [C. R. Weld] "The Arctic Expeditions," *The Athenaeum*, October 13, 1849, 1038.
83 "Sir John Franklin: Further Revelations by the Bolton Clairvoyante," *Hull Packet and East Riding Times*, October 26, 1849, 5.
84 These stereotypes were articulated and challenged by Richard King at the Ethnological Society. Richard King, "On the Physical Characters of the Esquimaux," *Journal of the Ethnological Society of London* 1 (1848): 45–59; R. King, "On the

Intellectual Character of the Esquimaux," *Journal of the Ethnological Society of London* 1 (1848): 127–53; R. King, "On the Industrial Arts of the Esquimaux," *Journal of the Ethnological Society of London* 1 (1848): 277–300. For the contest between the Ethnological and Anthropological Societies, see George W. Stocking, Jr., *Victorian Anthropology* (London: Collier Macmillan Publishers, 1987), 249–54.

85 See Burch, *Alliance and Conflict*, 19, 20, 119; Bockstoce, *Furs and Frontiers*, 132–4.
86 "Sir John Franklin and His Company," *Belfast News-Letter*, October 16, 1849, 1.
87 ADM 7/189/13, Parry to Barrow, October 25, 1849.
88 Ross, *This Distant and Unsurveyed Country*, xxxv.
89 Philip J. Stern, "Exploration and Enlightenment," in *Reinterpreting Exploration: The West in the World*, ed. Dane Kennedy (Oxford and New York: Oxford University Press, 2014), 69.
90 TNA ADM 7/189/13, Jane Franklin to John Barrow, Jr, Peterhead, October 7, 1849.
91 TNA ADM 7/189/13, Jane Franklin to John Barrow Jr., Kirkcaldy, October 20, 1849.
92 TNA ADM 7/189/13, Jane Franklin to John Barrow, undated [1849].
93 TNA ADM 7/189/13 Jane Franklin to John Barrow Jr, October 24, 1849.
94 Ballantyne, *Webs of Empire*, 124.
95 Most of the scholarship on the nineteenth century is concerned with the navy rather than the fishing or merchant fleets, but see Mary A. Conley, *From Jack Tar to Union Jack: Representing Naval Manhood in the British Empire, 1870-1918* (Manchester: Manchester University Press, 2009); Isaac Land, *War, Nationalism and the British Sailor, 1750-1850* (New York and London: Palgrave Macmillan, 2009).
96 Ross, *This Distant and Unsurveyed Country*.
97 TNA ADM 7/189/13, Jane Franklin to John Barrow, October 20–24, 1849; SPRI MS 248/247/21, Sophia Cracroft to Isabella Cracroft, Dundee, October 25, 1849.
98 TNA ADM 7/189/13, Jane Franklin to John Barrow Jr., Kirkcaldy, October 20, 1849.
99 Ibid.
100 SPRI MS 248/247/21, Sophia Cracroft to Isabella Cracroft, Royal Hotel, Dundee, October 25, 1849.
101 WM SCO 819 Box P, Jane Franklin to William Scoresby, Kirkcaldy, October 24, 1849.
102 Back is identified as Gell's parishioner in RGS-IBG CB4, Murchison Correspondence, Sophia Cracroft to Roderick Murchison, November 2, 1853.
103 SPRI MS 1503/18/1, J. Richardson to M. Richardson, February 22, 1838; SPRI MS 1503/18/20, J. Richardson to M. Richardson, March 23, 1838; SPRI MS 1503/28/4, Mary Richardson to Mrs. Day, June 1844.
104 SPRI MS 248/247/17, Sophia Cracroft to Isabella Cracroft, October 15, 1849.
105 DRO D8760/F/FEG/1/44/11, Marian Simpkinson to Eleanor Gell, [October 1849].
106 DRO D8760/F/FEG/1/49/4, Rosalind Beaufort to Eleanor Gell, October 6, 1849.
107 DRO D8760/F/FEG/1/50/2, W. E. Parry to Eleanor Gell, December 5, 1849.
108 DRO D8760/F/FEG/1/51/3, Lady Anne Ross to Eleanor Gell, November 1, 1849.
109 Oddly, they did not bring any dogs with them, though Ross and his mate Abernethy had learned how to drive dogs from both Iglulingmiut and Netsilingmiut. As his descendant M. J. Ross points out, if Ross had brought dogs to Port Leopold, he might have significantly altered the course of British naval polar exploration, which subsequently relied almost exclusively on man-hauling. Or perhaps not. See Ross, *Polar Pioneers*, 307.
110 TNA ADM 7/189/13, W. E. Parry to Barrow, November 5, 1849.
111 TNA ADM 7/189/13, Jane Franklin to John Barrow, "Sunday Night."

112 Savours, *Search for the North West Passage*, 190–2; Cavell, *Tracing the Connected Narrative*, 184; Ross, *Polar Pioneers*, 315–20; Lambert, *Gates of Hell*, 189.
113 "Our Weekly Gossip," *Athenaeum*, 1149, November 3, 1849, 1110–11.
114 Anita Rupprecht, "*Wonderful Adventures of Mrs Seacole in Many Lands* (1857): Colonial Identity and the Geographical Imagination," in *Colonial Lives: Across the British Empire: Imperial Careering in the Long Nineteenth Century*, ed. David Lambert and Alan Lester (Cambridge: Cambridge University Press, 2006), 176–203.
115 TNA ADM 7/189/13, Jane Franklin to John Barrow Jr., Kirkcaldy, October 30, 1849.
116 SPRI MS 248/247/22, Sophia Cracroft to Isabella, Catherine and Elizabeth Cracroft, November 1, 1849.
117 Ibid.
118 Cavell, *Tracing the Connected Narrative*, 184.
119 WM SCO 778, Box N, "Outline of an Address at the Soiree of the Whitby Institute, Nov. 6, 1849"; "Sir John Franklin's Expeditions," *Manchester Times*, November 14, 1849, 8.
120 Bravo, "Geographies of Exploration and Improvement," 512–38; Stamp and Stamp, *William Scoresby*, 140–61, 186–99.
121 Winter, "Compasses All Awry," 69–98.
122 Stamp and Stamp, *William Scoresby*, 203.
123 WM SCO 778 Box N, John Barrow to William Scoresby, November 12, 1849.
124 WM SCO 819 Box P, Jane Franklin to William Scoresby, December 1, 1849.
125 "Sir John Franklin's Expedition," *The Morning Chronicle*, November 10, 1849, 3.
126 "Sir John Franklin's Expedition," *Daily News*, November 10, 1849, 3; "Sir John Franklin's Expedition," *Morning Chronicle*, November 10, 1849, 3; In ADM 7/188/13, *Standard*, "Sir John Franklin's Expedition," November 10, 1849; *Morning Herald*, "Sir John Franklin's Expedition," November 10, 1849.
127 "Sir John Franklin's Expedition," *Daily News*, November 10, 1849, 3.
128 Ibid.; "Sir John Franklin's Expedition," *Morning Chronicle*, November 10, 1849, 3; In ADM 7/188/13, *Standard*, "Sir John Franklin's Expedition," November 10, 1849; *Morning Herald*, "Sir John Franklin's Expedition," November 10, 1849.
129 *Morning Chronicle*, November 24, 1849, 4.
130 A copy of the map is at SPRI MS 395/96/16/d BL.
131 William Scoresby, *The Franklin Expedition: or, Considerations on Measures for the Discovery and Relief of our Absent Adventurers in the Arctic Regions* (London: Longman, Brown, Green, and Longmans, 1850), 11.
132 Ibid., 15.
133 Ibid., 46–7.
134 Cavell, *Tracing the Connected Narrative*, 170–1.
135 TNA ADM 7/608, "Suggestions for the Relief of Sir John Franklin."
136 TNA ADM 7/608, Richard Cox to the Lords of the Admiralty, November 6, 1849.
137 TNA ADM 7/608, Mr. Fawsett to the Lords of the Admiralty, November 8, 1849.
138 TNA ADM 7/608, Richardson to Sir F. Baring, evaluating the plan of Mr. Fawsett.
139 TNA ADM 7/608, Mr. Jones to the Lords of the Admiralty, Hilda Cottage, Whitby, November 9, 1849.
140 TNA ADM 7/608, "Suggestions for the Relief of Sir John Franklin."
141 TNA ADM 7/608, Mr. John Moore West, Castle Cottage, Liskeard, December 15, 1849.
142 TNA ADM 7/608, John Graville to Jane Franklin, Hull, December 14, 1849.

143 TNA ADM 7/608, Commander Forsyth to Lady Franklin, December 16, 1849.
144 SPRI MS 116/63/59, William Penny to Jane Franklin, Bolmun, December 26, 1849.
145 WM SCO 819 Box P, Jane Franklin to William Scoresby, December 1, [1849].
146 DRO D8760/F/FEG/1/44/5, Marian Simpkinson to Eleanor Gell, nd. [December 1849 by context].
147 TNA ADM 7/188/9, Memorandum of Sir Francis Beaufort.
148 TNA ADM 7/188/6, W. E. Parry to John Parker, Esq., December 2, 1849.
149 TNA ADM 7/188/17, Report of Sir John Richardson's Expedition. Richardson's opinion was also published alongside an account of Scoresby's address in "The Arctic Expedition," *Caledonian Mercury*, November 22, 1849, 2.
150 TNA ADM 7/188/6, W. E. Parry to John Parker, Esq., December 2, 1849.
151 TNA ADM 7/188/6, Remarks on the Opinions of Sir Edw Parry, Sir Geo Back, Captain Beechey, & Sir John Richardson, as to the Expediency of Adopting Further Measures for the Relief of Sir John Franklin.
152 Ibid.
153 Savours, *Search for the North West Passage*, 193–203.
154 Ibid., 194.

5

"The Argument from Negative Evidence"
The Many Lives of the Open Polar Sea, 1850–3

In June 1850, in the Greenland town of Sisimiut/Holsteinsborg, a young man named Adam Beck sought work as an interpreter. He was a Kalaallit-Danish man of twenty-nine who had been educated by Moravian missionaries, was literate in Kalaallisut, bilingual in Danish, and an excellent fiddler.[1] Young men like Beck had long found work as interpreters on whalers and discovery ships, and he had certain expectations of his pay, his duties, and his treatment when he was hired by Sir John Ross for the *Felix*, an Hudson's Bay Company (HBC)-funded Franklin rescue expedition. When he joined the *Felix*, however, he found that her crew of Peterhead whalers were violently drunk. The master had drunk himself into a "state of insanity," the mate was "furious with drink," and according to Beck, three of the whalers threw him overboard "either to make a game of me, or with serious designs on my life."[2] Further north, in HMS *Lady Franklin*, the whaling captain William Penny also acquired an interpreter at Upernavik, the Danish sub-governor Carl Petersen.[3] It was the beginning of a long year.

On August 13, five Royal Navy ships under the command of Captain Horatio Austin—HMS *Lady Franklin*, HMS *Sophia*, HMS *Assistance*, HMS *Pioneer*, and HMS *Intrepid*—joined the *Felix* and Jane Franklin's private expedition in the *Prince Albert*. They anchored off Savissivik/Cape York. On shore, they saw a small family group of Inughuit—people whom Ross had dubbed the "Arctic Highlanders" on his last visit in 1818. They still had only limited contact with outsiders, and Beck was nervous. He had grown up hearing stories of northern Inuit being murderers, while the Inughuit told stories about eastern cannibals who would someday cross the country and devour them.[4] Beck and the Inughuit family bridged mutual fear, suspicion, and linguistic barriers, and one of them, a teenage boy named Qalasirssuaq, came on board the *Assistance*. Others called him Kallihirua. The *Assistance*'s captain Erasmus Ommanney would dub him Erasmus York. Years later, he would sign his letters to his godmother Eleanor Gell as "Kalli."[5] On board the *Prince Albert*, Beck told the steward what he had understood from Qalasirssuaq and his relations: that four years earlier, two ships had been trapped in the ice at a place called Omanek, the officers wore epaulettes on their shoulders, and local people had killed the crews and burned the ships.[6] Peterson confronted Beck and called him a liar. The *Intrepid* was sent to investigate and found that HMS *North Star* had overwintered further north in 1849–50, and caused a deadly epidemic.[7] On the way, the *Intrepid* paused and her crew ransacked Inughuit graves for curiosities, including the grave of Qalasirssuaq's father, as his weeping son begged them to stop.[8] Satisfied that Beck's tale had been explained, the fleet headed west into Lancaster Sound with both Qalasirssuaq and Beck, the one unwilling, the other unnerved. Before they headed into the pack, Beck wrote an account (in his own dialect of Kalaallisut) of what he had understood from Qalasirssuaq and his kin, which Ross enclosed in his dispatch home.[9]

One week later, at the base of Wellington Channel in Lancaster Sound, the squadron reassembled and met an American rescue expedition, the USS *Advance* and USS *Rescue*. It was here that Ommanney and a party of officers found the first "relics" of the Franklin expedition at Cape Reilly—bits of wood, some ragged clothing, naval stores, and empty meat tins. They were given to the *Prince Albert*'s commander, Charles Forsyth, who left for England to report to Lady Franklin. A few days later, a party found the remains of Franklin's 1845–6 camp on Beechey Island, including the graves of three of his crew, mountains of tin cans, and a pair of cashmere gloves weighed down with a stone to keep them from blowing away (Figure 5.1). Yet there were no written records—nothing to indicate how long the ships had stayed, when they had left, or where they had gone. Sherard Osborn of the *Pioneer* wrote, "everyone felt that there was something so inexplicable in the non-discovery of any record, some written evidence of the intentions of Franklin and Crozier on leaving this spot, that each of us kept returning to again search over the ground."[10]

Within a few weeks, the American ships were caught in the moving pack ice and dragged up Wellington Channel. In spring, they would be dragged back out again.[11]

Figure 5.1 Elisha Kent Kane, "Beechey Island—Franklin's first winter quarters," in E. K. Kane, *The U.S. Grinnell expedition in search of Sir John Franklin: a personal narrative* . . . (New York: Harper and Brothers, 1853). Sourced from Wikimedia Commons.

The British ships escaped this fate but were pushed together near Beechey Island and overwintered together in the long Arctic night. On the *Assistance*, Qalasirssuaq learned English and swapped his skin clothes for naval slops. Beck maintained that he had truthfully reported what he had been told by Qalasirssuaq and his kin, and as a result, he was accused of theft and drunkenness and threatened with violence.[12] Meanwhile, Penny was convinced that Franklin had ascended Wellington Channel, and in the spring of 1851, he tried to follow. He was forced to turn back just as he sighted open water beyond a barrier of ice.[13] When he returned, he asked Austin for a steamer to return to the top of the channel, but Austin refused. Several stormy discussions followed, and Austin finally demanded that Penny write down his views. In a brief note, written in the heat of the moment and demonstrating the dangers of sarcasm in official reportage, Penny wrote: "Wellington Channel requires no further search; all has been done in the power of man to accomplish and no trace can be found. What else can be done?"[14] Having witnessed the American ships being pulled by the ice first up Wellington Channel, and then back down and out into Baffin's Bay, Austin ordered the naval ships to return home. Ross followed in the *Felix*, convinced that Franklin must have perished in Baffin's Bay as Beck had reported. He stopped at Upernavik, where Beck made another sworn deposition before a Danish magistrate. Beck laid out not only what he had heard at Savissivik but also how he had been persecuted. The magistrate's wife translated the document, and Ross included it with his official report.[15]

There were, then, three interwoven strands of evidence about Franklin's possible fate in the autumn of 1851: Beck's depositions, the Beechey Island relics, and Penny's sighting of the open water at the top of Wellington Channel. All of them seemed to contradict each other, and even themselves. One suggested that Franklin's crews had perished, possibly in Baffin's Bay, while the other suggested that they might have gone up Wellington Channel—or not. The state of the ice prevented following up any of these leads, though the fate of the Americans in the *Advance* and *Rescue* seemed to indicate that any or all of those scenarios might be true.

In London, a new Arctic circle, centered on Jane Franklin, came together to interpret the heterogeneous archive of Wellington Channel. Derived from connections from the Franklins' imperial lives rather than from John Franklin's naval career, this circle formulated an "argument from negative evidence": that the missing expedition had ascended Wellington Channel and were trapped behind a barrier of ice in an open polar sea where there was plentiful animal life. There was still time to rescue them, but only if the Admiralty quickly dispatched a steamer to break through the ice. The idea that there might be a vast area of open water circulating around the North Pole dated back at least to the Renaissance, but was revived during the searches for Franklin.[16] Over the course of 1851–2, the men and women of this circle defined the exploration of an imaginary open polar sea as a national, philanthropic, and scientific cause. Support for it was cast as evidence of civility and opposition to it as evidence of moral and professional failure. It was a surprisingly flexible and mobile cause. In Britain, Janice Cavell has argued, the open polar sea articulated with the "fluid and never fully resolved" relationship between the explorers and the nation. Both middle- and working-class periodicals began to present the search for the Franklin expedition as a crusade in which "only the voice of the people could compel bureaucrats to continue the search." By 1851, a diverse host of political interests, including Irish nationalists, Radicals, Tories, and Liberals were happy to link the search with their own agendas.[17] As Michael Robinson has argued, the open polar sea also appealed to a diverse array of American interests, from those filled with patriotic fervor, to those inspired by Jane Franklin's tragic devotion, to scientists interested in the circulation of ocean currents.[18] In Tasmania, as this chapter will demonstrate, settlers dovetailed the idea with their battle for self-government and their new status as an Arctic whaling port.

This chapter charts the origins and some of the trajectories of the "argument from negative evidence." The politics of truth at its heart were shaped by a circle of humanitarians, whaling captains, journalists, and explorers, including Anna Gurney, Sarah Bowdich Lee, William Kennedy, and Alexander Kennedy Isbister. The rescue of Franklin offered humanitarians like Gurney a new cause, as imperial humanitarianism fragmented and diversified in the wake of Buxton's death in 1845, and as the advent of settler self-governance threatened to undo the work of humanitarian "protection" in the colonies.[19] She and Lee drew on their long experiences of politics, science, publishing, and exploration to help Jane Franklin.[20] Indigenous literacy and testimony were core to the controversy, both through Adam Beck's depositions and through the work of Jane Franklin's supporters, the Métis men Kennedy and Isbister. Both men drew on their Arctic experiences, political activism, and opposition to the HBC's monopoly as they offered Jane Franklin their assistance. Drawing on experiences derived from their diverse imperial lives, these women and men asserted Jane Franklin's rights, moral authority, and version of the "truth" through petitions, memorials, and the press.[21] Their reasons for doing so were varied and seldom clearly articulated. Yet each of them came to invest in what was increasingly identified as the philanthropic project of Arctic rescue.

"The Deplorable Story of the Esquimaux" and the "Argument from Negative Evidence"

In October 1850, Charles Forsyth returned to London in Lady Franklin's *Prince Albert* with the first relics of the Franklin expedition from Cape Reilly—bits of rope, wooden fragments, and animal bones. At the same time, Ross's report and Beck's first deposition were published in the *Times*.[22] Ross summarized Beck's testimony about the ships being pillaged and burned on the Greenland coast, but the editors also printed the untranslated text and invited "some learned philologists to solve the problem."[23] Jane Franklin wrote to William Scoresby that the "deplorable story of the Esquimaux" had at first "made me very uneasy" but that both she and Sophia felt that the Cape Reilly relics "at once demolished the Esquimaux story."[24] It was the first drop of information from the area around Beechey Island; the stories of open water, ice barriers, and steamers would not arrive for another year. Yet at this early stage, the return of the *Prince Albert* and Beck's testimony brought together three experienced critics of empire: Anna Gurney, William Kennedy, and Alexander Kennedy Isbister.

It was the *Times*'s invitation to translate Beck's deposition that caught Anna Gurney's attention. Confined to a wheelchair by polio, Gurney had devoted herself to scholarship and philanthropy for most of her life. In 1836–7, she had been the secret author of the *Report from the Select Committee on Aborigines*, which T. F. Buxton had referred to as "Aunt Anna's Report" and which had promoted "protection" as the solution for settler-Indigenous conflict in the empire (see Chapter 3).[25] While the Franklins were in Tasmania, Gurney had continued her humanitarian work as she also turned her attention to other causes. These included her own philological, botanical, and geological research, as well as relief programs for destitute sailors.[26] She also helped Buxton prepare for the Niger Expedition in 1841, designed to thwart the slave trade and facilitate Christian missions. It had failed spectacularly; nearly one-third of the British crew had died of fever, and the expedition returned to Britain within five months. Its failure is often linked to the midcentury disintegration of British humanitarianism, with Buxton dying disappointed in 1845, and his followers feeling rudderless in his absence.[27] Yet the expedition had its afterlives and among them were the entanglement of the Buxtons, Gurneys, and Frys with the Arctic circles, particularly through Sir William Edward Parry. He had acted as an adviser on steam navigation for the expedition, and later married Gurney's cousin Catherine Hoare, whom he had met at an expedition dinner.[28] Parry had also helped Gurney's nephew, Samuel Gurney Cresswell, join HMS *Resolute*, which in 1850 was searching for Franklin north of the Bering Strait.[29]

Gurney had studied Inuktitut, using missionary dictionaries, and she now translated Beck's deposition and sent it to Parry, who sent it to Barrow.[30] She also printed a circular addressed to whaling captains, asking them to determine where (and if) the massacre at "Omanek" had taken place. Parry circulated this to Barrow and to Captain Hamilton, the Secretary of the Admiralty, asking that it be distributed "with something like official Sanction."[31] Jane was irritated, writing to the *Prince Albert*'s new commander William Kennedy that "this enquiry has been instituted at request of Miss Gurney, who means well, but the consequences will be lamentable—we shall have all sorts of fictions & foolish stories brought home—are not the relics of Cape Reilly enough ... & say something to counteract this."[32]

Jane's dismissal of Beck's evidence and Gurney's efforts did not mean that she universally rejected Indigenous knowledge—far from it. Her new commander, William Kennedy, was a Métis ex-fur trader with an old connection to Arctic circles. His father, Alexander Kennedy, had sheltered Richardson and Hepburn at Cumberland House in 1820, while his mother, Aggathas (a Swampy Cree woman), had prepared snowshoes, moccasins, and food for the expedition. In 1825, at age eleven, Kennedy had been taken away to his father's people at St. Margaret's Hope, Orkney—a small, tight-knit community not far from twelve-year-old John Rae's home. Both boys were constantly shooting, boating, and preparing for later employment in the fur trade countries.[33] Between 1833 and 1846, Kennedy was employed by the HBC in Inuit territories in Ungava and Labrador, but he also criticized company rule, particularly its trade in alcohol. He resigned in 1846 and lobbied against the company's monopoly in Rupert's Land.[34] In 1850, when he read about the Mittimatalik map and James Ross's early return, he traveled at his own expense to Britain and offered his services to Jane Franklin.

Kennedy's removal from his mother and his Orcadian education echoed Jane's views—that Indigenous children must be separated from their parents, particularly their mothers, educated in isolation, and not permitted to return home until they were fully transformed (see Chapter 3). Yet with Kennedy, she was also intrigued and attracted by his lingering ambivalence, his in-betweenness—what Zoe Laidlaw has called a "layered identity."[35] She later wrote to Murchison,

> The Indian character is strongly developed in Mr K's face & now & then in his character when the wrongs of his maternal race are brought to his memory—At these times, he wants only, as I tell him, the tomahawk in hand, & the single lock on the scalp to be the personification of an Indian warrior. At all others, he is the gentlest & most humble minded of good Christians, but in every phase of character, faithful, generous, devoted & true.[36]

Dissatisfied with Forsyth's early return, Jane offered the *Prince Albert* to Kennedy. He accepted, proposing to head into Lancaster Sound and turn south from Cape Walker, heading toward the Canadian mainland. This was, in fact, the direction in which *Erebus* and *Terror* had been dragged by the moving pack ice, but no one knew that yet. As Jane and Sophia gave Kennedy unfettered access to their Arctic library, they also made use of his biography, his expertise, and his use of Indigenous technology. They told officials and family members how he had resigned from the HBC because of his disgust at the "degradation & cruelty pervading their system." They described his expertise with Inuit kayaks, his temperance principles, and his preference for men who had experience working with Inuit.[37] Jane also suggested to him that he engage "an Esquimaux or half caste Dane at any of the settlements in Davis Strait," and specifically mentioned Inuluapik, the boy whom Penny had brought back several years before (see Chapter 4).[38] Kennedy departed in June 1851, with Franklin's old comrade John Hepburn (recently returned from Tasmania) on board and the French naval lieutenant Joseph Rene Bellot as his second-in-command, along with a long list of names to be inscribed on new locations, including Gurney, Scoresby, and La Trobe (after both Charles La Trobe, the governor of Victoria, and his brother Peter, a Moravian bishop, see below).[39]

In September 1851, Austin's squadron returned. Penny and Austin were quarrelling bitterly, and Ross was carrying Adam Beck's additional depositions. Ross immediately published his belief that Franklin's ships had left Cape Reilly in the summer of 1846 and had "been wrecked on the east coast of Baffin's Bay, and, in short, that the report of Adam Beck is in every respect true."[40] The account caused a sensation, particularly because it was coupled with the fate of the American ships, *Advance* and *Rescue*. Their experience of being dragged up Wellington Channel and then back out seemed to confirm the plausibility of Beck's account, and suggested that the remains of the lost expedition might be found on the Greenland coast. Together, Beck's testimony, Ross's support, and the Americans' experience were explosive. Sophia noted with irritation that Anna Gurney "actually interpreted the signs of haste in quitting Beechey Bay, to an attack upon our people by the Esquimaux, by whom they might have been overpowered!"[41] As the metropolis hummed with people bound for the Great Exhibition, Lt. Sherard Osborn wrote to Sophia to ask, "if he can do anything to set aside Adam Beck's story w^h is flying ab^t everywhere." A flurry of visitors descended to offer their help in denouncing the "despairing story." Jane's sister Fanny Majendie came, promising to write to the editor of the *Nautical Standard*, while Franklin's sister Hannah Booth called, "much excited—wd write to Times."[42] When Penny's surgeon Dr. Sutherland visited, Sophia "impressed upon him the necessity of everywhere, publicly & privately denouncing the wicked fabrications of old Ross & the absurd fallacies wh were entertained in Omnibuses, on Railways."[43]

The tangled lines of Sophia's and Jane's journals and letterbooks document how the "argument from negative evidence" was assembled in the autumn of 1851 in response to the Wellington Channel controversy. It was comprised of four essential parts: First, that neither Beck, nor his testimony, nor anyone who supported his testimony could be trusted. Second, that the relics of Beechey Island proved that *Erebus* and *Terror* had ascended Wellington Channel in the spring of 1846, even though they had left no record behind. Third, the open water at the top of Wellington Channel indicated an open polar sea behind the barrier of ice, where it was likely that there was plentiful animal life. Fourth, this evidence ought to compel the Admiralty to dispatch a steamer to break through the pack ice and enter the open polar sea without delay. Sophia Cracroft and Jane Franklin did not, however, assemble the argument alone. They were aided by many others within their newly developed Arctic circle, whose motivations were as complex and diverse as their own biographies. This chapter focuses on two: Sarah Bowdich Lee and Alexander Kennedy Isbister.

In January 1851, Jane Franklin mentioned "Mrs Lee" in a letter to William Scoresby, writing that she had proposed to "Mrs Lee (formerly Bowdich) to write a book for general readers, on the Arctic regions similar to her African & Australian Wanderings."[44] They had known each other in circles of polite science in the 1820s, when the *Magazine of Natural History* described Sarah Bowdich as "a lady of the most amiable disposition and elegant manners, and of great and various acquirements" (see Chapter 2).[45] Her extraordinary career has long fascinated both historians of science and literary scholars.[46] As her biographer Mary Orr has observed, the well-connected young widow skillfully negotiated female propriety and gendered scientific authority.[47] In the 1820s, while living with Baron Cuvier, she became close friends with the founder of the Aborigines' Protection Society (APS), Dr. Thomas Hodgkin. Both she and her first husband exerted a powerful influence on Hodgkin's thinking about African leadership in "civilization" projects.[48] After her husband's death in Africa in 1825, she wrote Cuvier's biography, became friends with Alexander von Humboldt, and was widely recognized as an ichthyologist, an ornithologist, and a gifted artist. Though she originally wrote and published "for survival," first to fund her and her husband's work, and then to support their children after his death, she continued to publish well after her 1828 remarriage to Robert Lee, an assizes clerk.[49] Like many other female popularizers of science in the mid-nineteenth century, she established herself as a religious and ethical guide to the human and natural world.[50] As Orr has noted, she was particularly adept in "dressing her learning in the female modesty of potential error," presenting her own scientific findings while begging indulgence for her imperfect understanding.[51]

Lee also had firsthand experience of equipping and promoting expeditions. In addition to her own expeditions with her first husband between 1815 and 1824, she appears to have been involved in the Niger Expedition alongside Gurney and Parry. She was recognized as an authority on the Asante within geographical social circles, and Buxton and Parry used her African narratives to prepare for the expedition. Mary Simpkinson mentioned her presence at Niger Expedition gatherings in her letters to Jane Franklin in 1840. No doubt Lee's fluency in Arabic, her charisma and her conversation made her another of Mary's bright stars. When John Phillip Gell saw her at a geographical gathering at Sir Robert Inglis's in 1849, he called her "my lively friend Mrs Lee, once a great traveller in Africa."[52] By 1851, Sarah Bowdich Lee had an intimate knowledge of the world of publishing, substantive humanitarian and scientific credentials, and global connections. Moreover, she was a person of enormous energy, imagination, and skill.[53]

Alexander Kennedy Isbister was William Kennedy's 29-year-old nephew. Born at Cumberland House in 1822, he began working for the HBC as a teenager, helping to establish Fort MacPherson in 1840–1 and exploring the Peel River area. Frustrated with his limited opportunities as a Métis man in the HBC, he left to attend university at Aberdeen and Edinburgh when he was twenty. Between 1846 and 1850, he campaigned against the HBC from London, simultaneously building up his authority as a traveler, a scientist, and a reformer and became one of the APS's key informants. In 1847, he facilitated a petition to Parliament from the Métis population of Red River against company rule, arguing that it thwarted rather than facilitated "civilization," traded in spirits, prevented free trade, and contributed to widespread starvation.[54] With assistance from Hodgkin and the APS, Isbister presented the petition to Parliament (using the name of Alexander Koonaubay Isbister), while his uncle William Kennedy also corresponded with Hodgkin, asserting that the HBC was actively thwarting the "civilization" of the Saulteaux.[55] After the petition's failure, Isbister began writing ethnological papers on the peoples and the region around Great Slave Lake and the Mackenzie River.[56] His ethnological and political arguments complemented each other—that all parties would benefit from Indigenous independence, sovereignty, and control over trade.[57]

Laidlaw has argued that layered identities both enabled and restricted Indigenous interlocutors in London, and that the careful establishment of credentials (especially scientific and geographical credentials) was vital for people like Isbister, allowing him to modulate between different positions as an "authentic" native, an "acculturated" Christian, or someone in-between.[58] By 1850, Isbister had established himself as an Arctic authority, a thorn in the side of the HBC, a critic of government policy, a humanitarian and a vital contributor to the APS, a reformer, a journalist, and a public intellectual who published regularly with the *Athenaeum*, the *Morning Chronicle*, the *Colonial Intelligencer*, and elsewhere.[59] Isbister's biographer treats the period between 1851 and 1856 as an interlude, and his involvement with the Franklin search as minimal.[60] However, Jane Franklin's and Sophia Cracroft's diaries and correspondence indicate that he was among their most vital supporters. Eloquent and experienced, Isbister became their intermediary, adviser, and envoy with the press.[61]

Isbister and Lee were key members of the overlapping circles that came together in response to Adam Beck's testimony and the Beechey Island relics in 1851, including relatives, whalers, journalists, surgeons, bureaucrats, and explorers. They relied heavily on the *Morning Chronicle* and the *Athenaeum*, calling the former the "organ of the Arctic Question."[62] The *Chronicle*'s editor John Douglas Cook and subeditor

Philip Harwood dropped by the Franklin house constantly between September and December of 1851, publishing many anonymous letters by this new Arctic circle.[63] It was in the *Morning Chronicle* that Sophia developed what her cousin Charles Weld called "the argument from negative evidence" in early September 1851. Drawing on personal conversations, field correspondence, and their own extensive Arctic library, she wrote two anonymous articles arguing that Franklin and his men were trapped behind a barrier of ice in Wellington Channel, and that life was sustainable at such high latitudes.[64] She returned repeatedly to Penny's discovery of open water beyond the ice barrier in Wellington Channel, with driftwood and "enormous numbers" of animals. "Now, with signs so indisputably hopeful," she wrote, "will any one say that Sir John Franklin's party are not still living?"[65] She supported Penny's evidence with John Rae's correspondence, particularly his description of how he and his party had, "by our own exertion, in a country previously totally unknown to us, obtained the means of subsistence for twelve months. Why may not Sir John Franklin's party do the same?"[66] She also drew on Russian sources, particularly Elizabeth Lieves Sabine's 1840 translation of Baron Ferdinand Petrovich Wrangel's narrative of his 1821–4 Siberian expedition, in which he described seeing open water and a multitude of animal life off the north coast. She may have been pushed toward Wrangel by Elizabeth Sabine's mother, Mrs. Lieves, who sometimes worked late into the night alongside Jane and Sophia and slept at their home.[67] Taken together, Sophia argued, Rae and Wrangel had proven that life was sustainable at high latitudes. She made this argument to any willing listener, often pulling out a copy of Wrangel's narrative or Rae's letters in support.[68]

Sir John Ross, however, kept Beck's testimony in circulation when he wrote in *Lloyd's Weekly* that "the report of Adam Beck is in every respect true."[69] Harwood left the *Morning Chronicle*'s office to warn Sophia that it "had appeared as a matter of news in the Evg. Edition of Chronicle and wd be repealed on Monday."[70] The credibility of Indigenous informants was often linked to Europeans who vouched for them, and so Franklin's supporters focused on dismantling Ross's character.[71] In an anonymous article in the *Chronicle* two days later, Sophia attacked Ross's "fertile imagination" and "ingenious creations" arguing that his testimony "drove Sir John Franklin and his crew back into the dreadful bay, on purpose to be murdered."[72] She encouraged Sarah Bowdich Lee to speak to one of her contacts at Somerset House to "[bring] forward Sir John Ross's villainy."[73] With Sophia's endorsement, Weld wrote an article for the *Athenaeum* suggesting that Ross was using Beck's story for his own self-promotion and demanded that the Admiralty contradict it or be guilty of a dereliction of duty.[74] Meanwhile, Jane recorded that she was "writing to & fro Mrs Lee abt Adam Beck."[75]

Over the following weeks, as London swelled with crowds bound for the Crystal Palace, Lee, Isbister, Gurney, Weld, and others wrote scores of letters and articles that cast the search up Wellington Channel as both rational and a moral imperative. As they did so, they also paired the image of the lost men with a critique of the government and the Admiralty in particular. Isbister had visited Sophia after her articles ran in the *Chronicle* and said that he "could get at both Chronicle and Herald and might he be allowed to address letters to them. Of course without any acknowledged or implied cooperation with my aunt."[76] In the *Athenaeum*, weekly articles by either or both Weld and Isbister urged the Admiralty to immediately dispatch Penny with a steamer to Wellington Channel.

Weld argued that that it was certain Franklin had ascended Wellington Channel because there was no *credible* evidence to the contrary, and argued that "There is not an hour to lose if this last chance is to be tried."[77] Another article, possibly by Isbister, pointed out that Beck's tale contradicted previous reports (including by Ross) that the Inughuit were peaceful, and hinted that Ross's credibility was further diminished because his expedition was financed by the HBC.[78] Lee also wrote a letter to the *Daily News* (signed "Arcticus") that suggested she was an Arctic officer. She claimed that there was abundant evidence of the expedition's "safety and prosperity in an advanced part of Lancaster Sound." The absence of records, she argued, pointed not to a sudden, helpless "drifting out" in the pack ice, but rather a rapid response to the clearing of ice in Wellington Channel. She warned that if the Admiralty failed to give Penny a steamer to return that season, "this Arctic question, which they like so little, will be an incubus on their bosoms for years to come. The very uncertainty in which it may be left will give it an undying vitality."[79]

As they developed "argument from negative evidence" in print, the same circles also organized a petition to complement it. Petitions were, at midcentury, an old political tool used by a new swathe of interlocutors.[80] In the 1840s, British women were vital contributors to mass petition movements against slavery, the Corn Laws, and the Poor Law Amendment, legitimating their public activity as the natural outgrowth of their feminine roles as guardians of morality.[81] Petitions were also a key tool of Indigenous political engagement, part of what the late Tracey Banivanua Mar called a new "imperial literacy" in which communities linked by circuits of commerce, missionaries, and colonial policy adapted these vehicles of protest to their own circumstances.[82] The Wellington Channel campaign was linked, albeit tentatively, to both of these movements, through Isbister's experience with the Red River petition of 1847 and through Gurney's and Lee's decades of humanitarian campaigning. It is unclear which of them first proposed the idea of the petition (or whether it came from Jane Franklin or Sophia Cracroft) but by September 1851, the campaign was in full swing.

With Sarah Bowdich Lee's help, Sophia drafted the headings of several petitions. Though the language varied, the message was the same: all the *credible* evidence pointed to Wellington Channel as Franklin's "certain route," and therefore the Admiralty must dispatch a steamer to reach Wellington Channel. Each petition contrived to make the belief in an open polar sea a reflection of character—whether that was chivalrous support of Lady Franklin, philanthropic zeal to rescue missing countrymen, or bitter disappointment with the Admiralty for failure to do either. Isbister urged Jane and Sophia to be both swift and careful, and above all, not to be directly associated with the campaign. Sophia wrote in her journal that he advised her, "now is the moment for pressing [the petitions] upon the public," but also warned against "the disadvantage of my Aunt's [Jane Franklin] being supposed to promote it."[83] The women took care to launder petitions through third parties, asking friends and relatives to send them on to regional towns, scientific bodies, and newspapers.[84] Lee forwarded petitions to her contacts and deposited them with her publishers, and also gathered signatures herself in shops in Southampton Row and Paddington. Anna Gurney organized at least two petitions in Norfolk which were signed by the Buxton and Gurney families. Mary Anne Kendall walked her petition around the naval community of Gosport, while her mother Sarah Kay and sister

Emily were responsible for another at Greenwich.[85] Jane's sister Fanny Majendie sent petitions to her contacts in scientific and social circles.[86] Franklin's sister Mrs. Booth was responsible for organizing a petition in Franklin's hometown of Spilsby.[87] Isbister also apparently organized a petition, but it is unclear which one.[88] Barrow Jr., meanwhile, kept Sophia appraised of how the petitions were being received at the Admiralty, suggested new contacts through whom they could be channeled, and sent accounts of the petitions to more newspapers.[89] Though Sophia was gratified by signatures from men and women of rank, she pushed the petitions as a popular phenomenon, for "numbers were of more consequence . . . than mere station," and suggesting that "distinguished" petitions be supplemented by others "with the signatures of the Tradesmen."[90]

In all, eighty-nine petitions were received at the Admiralty. There were so many, in fact, that the Admiralty's clerks simply stopped replying to them and merely filed them, sometimes without the date they were received.[91] Some were enormous, fitting with difficulty into the bound Admiralty files. Many memorials were organized by town councils, learned societies, and universities.[92] Others were arranged by parish, town, or neighborhood.[93] Still others were left open in coffee houses for anyone to sign, as they were in the whaling port of Dundee. A few were organized by occupation; the employees of the Great Western Railway Company submitted one, while another was enigmatically signed "The Artizans of London."[94] All of them accepted the speculative interpretation of the voiceless relics of Beechey Island, rejected Adam Beck's depositions, urged the Admiralty to dispatch a steamer under Penny's command to Wellington Channel, and many denounced both Austin and the Lords of the Admiralty for dereliction of duty. Several also articulated specific local concerns. The petition from Dundee, for example, reflected the whaling port's long-held frustration with the government (sometimes expressed through petitions) over tariffs and the perception that the Southern Fishery was given preferential treatment over the Davis Strait Fishery. For example, when Penny had brought Inuluapik to Scotland in 1839, whaling shipowners had petitioned the Admiralty to send an expedition to survey Cumberland Sound and confirm the teenage boy's geographical information. The Admiralty declined, though it did publish Inuluapik's charts.[95] Now the Dundee paper argued "it becomes almost a local duty that every gentleman in this town should lend his influence in overcoming the hesitations of the Admiralty, especially as Captain Penny has given admirable proof of his zeal, intrepidity and ability to command such an expedition."[96] When the Dundee petition arrived at the Admiralty, it accused the Lords of the Admiralty of "dereliction of duty."[97]

Whether they came from London artisans, Scottish whalers, or Irish scientific societies, the Wellington Channel petitions all claimed that the government was neglecting its duty of care to missing sailors and their families. They all dangled the possibility of the triumph of progress, industry, steam power, discovery, and philanthropy in an open polar sea, a potent mixture in the autumn of 1851. They were not solely inspired by Isbister and Lee, but were linked both rhetorically and methodologically to the humanitarian projects and political causes that both supported, particularly as the petitions also held the imperial state to account for moral failures and broken promises. The optical effect was of mass mobilization and intense political disaffection around a single, polarizing question—how could the "truth" of the missing expedition be discovered, and by whom? That was the question that the Arctic Committee was tasked with answering in the autumn of 1851.

"Utterly Unworthy of Credit": The Arctic Committee, October–December 1851

The petition campaign and the "argument from negative evidence" were both attempts to influence the Admiralty's Arctic Committee, which convened in October 1851 to "inquire into and report on the conduct of the officers entrusted with the command of the late expeditions in search of Sir John Franklin."[98] Clive Holland has argued that the committee was "in effect conducting a trial" and to a certain extent this was true.[99] Its members were all naval officers, including the three Arctic veterans Parry, Back, and William Frederick Beechey, engaged in two separate but related enquiries. The first was, as Holland observed, a *de facto* court-martial of Penny and Austin, as the committee tried to ascertain whether or not they had been justified in returning to England, whether their disagreement had compromised the search, and whether Penny had requested (and been denied) a steamer to search Wellington Channel. The stakes attached to the second set of problems were still greater. Was it prudent or necessary to send another expedition, and if so, to which quarter? Was there reason to believe that the ice in Wellington Channel was permeable? If so, had Franklin gone up it? If he had, was long-term survival possible at such a high latitude? Was there legitimate evidence of an "open polar sea" into which Franklin could be followed? Could the Cape Reilly relics be reconciled with Adam Beck's testimony about what he had been told by Qalasirssuaq and his kin, and if not, which was more believable? How, in short, were Indigenous and vernacular testimony to be weighed, did their significance change when they were written down, and what was their value in the absence of an expedition's written archive?

Jane and Sophia were convinced that the committee was innately hostile to them because of its connections to Franklin's comrades in the old Arctic circles. They had relied on the members of the Arctic circles, especially Beaufort, Parry, Sabine, and Richardson, for many years, but they were always struggling to maintain these connections. Their reliance on clairvoyants, their familial struggles (especially with Eleanor Gell), and their own long personal histories often made this difficult (see Chapter 4). Parry and Beaufort seemed to be their most steadfast supporters, yet neither was available to them while the committee was sitting (see below). Richardson was not sitting on the committee, but his opinion carried weight, and he often discussed matters with his neighbor Parry at Gosport.[100] Both Jane and Sophia wrote to him often, expressing mutual affection and begging for advice.[101] Yet Richardson seemed cool, seldom communicating with them except through Franklin's niece Mary Anne Kay Kendall (who was also his neighbor), and was unconvinced by the "argument from negative evidence."[102] The women were also nervous about George Back's presence on the committee, complaining that he was untrustworthy and resentful. Sophia dubbed him the "wicked Sir G. Back" and wrote to Scoresby that he was on the committee "to the regret of all most deeply interested in their work."[103] These frosty relationships cut off important channels of informal influence.

In her attempt to win Richardson over, Jane offered him £500 in compensation for the life insurance policy he had forfeited to search for Franklin in 1848. To do so, she opened her husband's will. She then discovered that she had been misusing her power of attorney over Franklin's affairs to spend Eleanor Gell's inheritance from her mother. Jane's nephew Frank Simpkinson was Franklin's executor, and when he and the Gells learned that she had opened the will, there was a stormy confrontation followed by serious financial concerns for Jane Franklin. Though she did not yet know it, Jane's aged father disinherited her in favor of Frank Simpkinson, angry about her lavish spending on the expeditions and her misuse of Eleanor's money.[104]

As the committee began its meetings in October, a letter of Jane's to the American millionaire Henry Grinnell was published with severe consequences. Jane wrote to Grinnell of her despair at the Admiralty's inaction but assured him that Beaufort, Barrow, and Hamilton were "at their posts" to push the Wellington Channel route from within the Admiralty. She claimed that her health and her resolve were failing, and urged Grinnell to send a private expedition to the polar sea. She wrote, "to you will belong all the virtue and credit of continuing the search when our countrymen fail."[105] The effect of the letter was threefold. The first was to imply that the Admiralty was thwarting British enterprise, philanthropy, and destiny. The second was to promote further sympathy for a woman in physical and financial distress. The third was to see some Admiralty officials accused of ungallant behavior and others exposed to accusations of "petticoat influence." Jane and Sophia tried to suppress the letter, but failed and it was published widely.[106] It meant that Parry cut them off, "saying he c^d not have any personal commun^n with us at present."[107] Jane continued to try to contact him, but they did not hear from him directly for nearly a month.[108] After the committee adjourned, Parry told them that the letter had been included in the papers for the committee's review and, "he had said . . . that he was going to see my aunt that day—but when this unfortunate letter appeared, some of them said that he had better not go to her!"[109]

Unable to influence the committee from within, Jane and Sophia had Penny articulate their position. They had decided to make him and his conflict with Austin the personification of the populist element of the "argument from negative evidence." Penny was cast as an experienced and loyal sailor whose noble impulses had been thwarted by Austin. Their supporters circulated this association of Penny with "the public" and Austin with the Admiralty both privately and in print. Weld, for example, wrote an article in the *Athenaeum* in which he claimed, "the public will never acquit Capt. Austin of a fearful neglect of his duty . . . and Capt. Austin, it may well be supposed, will never be able to forgive himself," if it later emerged that any member of the expedition might have been saved by going up Wellington Channel.[110] Sophia also wrote to Mary Anne Kendall "explaining the meaning of Penny's words" in his dispatches, asking her to make his case within naval social circles at Portsmouth.[111] Mary Anne reported that "They call her a 'Pennyite'" which Sophia characterized as "a vulgar faction term, but said how cd she be other than for him, when he is all for further search, Austin declares there shall be no more."[112] As Cavell has noted, this argument took root across not only the middle-class periodicals that Jane Franklin influenced but also a swathe of working-class periodicals in which Penny was held up as an Arctic hero for the common man.[113]

The problem with having Penny articulate the "argument from negative evidence" was that he had triggered the committee through his letter to Austin, in which he wrote, "Wellington Channel requires no further search." He was placed in an impossible position, forced simultaneously to defend and contradict himself. Penny, like many other whaling captains, tended to avoid writing for the public and practiced what Ballantyne has called "littoral literacy," characterized by a specific form of "useful knowledge" relative to the environment in which he worked, the records that he kept for his employers, and his correspondence with his wife Margaret, who like other Arctic wives was the keeper of his archive (Figure 5.2).[114] Later, the *Lady Franklin*'s surgeon Peter Sutherland wrote, "Without rhetoric and unsophisticated, his arguments fell to the ground before men whose lives had ever been closely associated with figures."[115] When the Admiralty released Penny's letters to the press, he and Margaret traveled to London together. When they arrived, Sophia and Jane presented Penny with a letter they had written to the Admiralty under his name. According to Sophia, he was "delighted" and copied and signed it in their presence. The letter contained a new assertion that Penny had urged Austin to "Go up Wellington Channel, Sir, and you

Figure 5.2 Stephen Pearce, *William Penny*, 1851. One of several portraits owned at one time by Lady Jane Franklin, on her death, this was donated by Sophia Cracroft to the National Portrait Gallery. Art Collection 3/Alamy Stock Photo. Image ID: HYEAX0.

will do good service to the cause," which no one had ever heard him say.[116] Sophia and Jane thought it was essential to their argument, but it may have amounted to perjury.[117]

Over the following weeks, Sophia and Jane wrote or outlined most of Penny's testimony and reviewed his evidence every evening, writing notes in the margins to "set him right."[118] Pressured by both opponents and supporters, Penny's decisions, conduct, and character were minutely examined every day, and he became exhausted, angry, and apathetic.[119] The women often relied on his wife to mediate. Jane described Margaret Penny as a woman of "great discretion & good sense," and Sophia wrote once that, when she was going to amend Penny's notes from the day's hearings, they were "much struck with his wife's clear sense & simplicity & her influence over him."[120] Earlier, he had sent his dispatches to Margaret as a safekeeping measure, writing, "My Conduct is now Publick property and if any one <u>dare</u> to assail it my beloved will not be silent."[121] Now, she produced these documents, including what Sophia described as "a torn & worn out letter of Sir John Ross to her husband" which ended in "a wicked insinuation."[122]

Penny was anxious and defensive when the hearings began. As he started making the case Sophia had outlined, he stopped and asked, "Do you understand? As they say I sometimes put in a word that completely changes the sense of a sentence."[123] When he was asked to explain why he had written that the channel required no further search, he explained that he and Austin had been arguing for hours, and "I told him everything that had taken place about the Wellington Channel," he said, "which would have been worth fifty letters from me."[124] Austin maintained that Penny had been both unreasonable and incomprehensible. "I could not reason with Captain Penny," he stated, "I could not get anything that was satisfactory. It was a sort of rambling conversation of which I could make nothing."[125] Matters were made worse when the letter that Sophia had written for Penny, in which he claimed he had told Austin to search Wellington Channel, was read out by the chairman in front of both men. Austin denied that any such exchange had happened, and called Penny a liar on record. Shortly afterward, Barrow said that Penny "ought to feel as if every member of the Committee . . . were in fact trying to convict him."[126]

While Penny's and Austin's evidence was weighed against each other, so were Beck's and Qalasirssuaq's testimonies about their exchange at Savissivik, in which the story of the burning of the ships and the death of the crews had been told. The tension between their written and oral communications was set up as a conflict between "acculturated" and "authentic," "pure" and "corrupted," "half-caste" and "full-blood," and the shifting credibility attached to all those categories applied to Indigenous people. Beck had not come to Britain, but Qalasirssuaq (now known as "Erasmus York") had, and was presented to the committee as a "pure Esquimaux" who, unlike Beck, was untainted by the outside world.

When expeditions failed or disappeared, surviving guides were in a terribly precarious position, with their testimony and experience ranged against an often-partial expedition archive.[127] A few years earlier, an Indigenous Australian guide known as Jacky Jacky had been one of the few survivors of Edward Kennedy's expedition to the Australian Cape York in Queensland. As Maria Nugent has shown, he took great care to preserve the expedition's archive, burying Kennedy's body, instruments, papers, and possessions, positioning himself as a faithful servant and a trustworthy witness.[128] Beck's credibility, in contrast, was undermined both by his mixed background and by his written challenge to the missing expedition's only archive—the voiceless relics of Beechey Island. As his depositions were laid before the committee, Austin's sailors testified that he was an unreliable drunkard, and Austin described him as "about the worst description of a civilized savage I ever saw."[129] Ross was the only one who vouched for Beck's character, partly because he thought Inuit were incapable of lying, partly because he was an educated Christian, and finally because he had been threatened "very severely."[130]

Ross's support was predicated on the threats that were part of a landscape of intimidation on Arctic discovery vessels, on which interpreters often found that silence meant safety. The Kalaallit interpreter Hans Hendrik later recalled constant accusations of stealing and lying on the two Franklin relief expeditions that he served on, persecution by sailors, and threats of corporal punishment and extreme isolation. This was often the case when, as in Adam Beck's case, their testimony was likely to make an expedition either stay out longer (and face more danger) or go home early (and get paid less).[131] As Ipiirvik (the brother-in-law of Inuluapik, Penny's interpreter in 1839–40) once cautioned Hendrik, when conflict arose, silence was always the best policy, reminding him, "we poor natives must be very careful with regard to ourselves."[132] Nineteenth-century Inuit usually tried to avoid conflict where possible and defined aggression broadly. Adults who spoke harshly, hastily, and angrily were considered irrational, childlike, and unpredictable, and the routine brutality on British whaling and naval ships would have been very shocking. While it is not possible to know whether or not interpreters experienced *ilirasuktuq* (the feeling of *ilira*—not quite fear, but the feeling that it is wise to yield), as Routledge notes, it is reasonable to suppose that this emotion—or something like it—was common, and was particularly evident when people tried hard to please and accommodate volatile outsiders.[133]

These histories of intimidation and silence lay behind both Beck's and Qalasirssuaq's experiences, but in different ways. Qalasirssuaq had gone on board the *Assistance* in 1850 and still had not returned home. After the desecration of his father's grave, he had asked to be returned to his mother and siblings but was taken instead to Beechey Island. In the *Assistance*'s shipboard newspaper, one of the officers claimed that though "slow to learn the English language, [he] has yet by his constant cheerfulness and good humour, and willingness to make himself useful, become a great favourite," and that his maps have "invariably proved perfectly correct."[134] They brought him to London, took him to the Great Exhibition, and his portrait, showing him dressed in Navy slops, was published on the front page of the *Illustrated London News* (Figure 5.3).[135] As Routledge has observed, these kinds of long sojourns could be damaging for young Inuit people, who were cut off from the networks of people, animals, traditions, stories, and knowledge, which were key to developing core Inuit values of tolerance, generosity, persistence, adaptability, and respectfulness.[136]

Qalasirssuaq came before the Arctic Committee in November 1851, accompanied by Ommanney, the Moravian missionary Christian Beck (no relation to Adam), and the Moravian bishop Peter La Trobe.[137] The purpose was to find out exactly what he and his relatives had told Adam Beck at Savissivik. His testimony was translated first into

Figure 5.3 Portrait of Qalasirssuaq, "The Esquimaux Erasmus York." Illustration for *The Illustrated London News*, 25 October 1851. Look and Learn/Illustrated Papers Collection/Bridgeman Images, LIP1102358.

German, and then into English. Under questioning, he admitted that he had told Adam Beck "a number of things, chiefly about the country," that he had heard of shipwrecks a long time ago, and that he had never heard anything about any murders. He was reluctant to discuss Adam Beck's character, apart from stating that he was a liar.[138] Adam Beck and John Ross had always claimed that Penny's interpreter Petersen had bullied Qalasirssuaq into silence, but this was not entered into the evidence, and the Moravian missionary remarked that "after the Esquimaux fashion, Erasmus was very reluctant to speak out."[139]

Qalasirssuaq's testimony was ranged against one of Adam Beck's depositions (the other, containing the information about the burned ships and dead men, had not been translated by La Trobe's interpreters, who had difficulty understanding it).[140] Beck's first deposition recounted Qalasirssuaq's descriptions of his country, its geography, and its animal life. This kind of contextual information was highly important, for Inuit utilize a complex and multidimensional spatial orientation; finding one's way requires close observation of topography, wind direction, ice formation, animal movements, and constellations.[141] These subtle observations were normally narrated in meaningful sequences that could help orient oneself within an animate landscape.[142] However, not only did the committee fail to understand its significance, but it also provided fuel for Jane Franklin's supporters to ridicule Beck as a fabulist. The *Morning Chronicle* reproduced the deposition on December 8. The subeditor Roger Harwood wrote that "the public mind has been much agitated for the last year and a half by the report of this awful catastrophe, given upon the authority of Adam Beck," and printed the following paragraph, taken from what Qalasirssuaq was purported to have told Adam Beck:

> While I have been here there have been many ships. There were also many people upon the land. On the islands there were but few native people. A good many show themselves when pleased.... There were birds, such as eider fowl.... There were also other little birds, that look white, that are found in the country, and also ravens—little ravens and great ravens—and various birds mixed together ... there is a little bird with red at the top of the head. The people here are few. And this is written by me from my heart.[143]

In doing so, Harwood presented the testimony of both Indigenous men as unthreatening and irrelevant, adding, "We recommend an attentive perusal of this document to the Honourable Hudson Bay Company, and to—*Punch*."[144] Sophia wrote that it constituted "the truly exquisite finale of the Adam Beck story," and thanked Harwood.[145] A person calling themselves "*Risum Teneatis*" (translated as "can you help laughing?") wrote to the *Chronicle* mocking the "exquisite fairy tale" of the "venerable Adam Beck" and expressing incredulity that the Admiralty had wasted so much time on the matter.[146] The same day, Jane Franklin visited Mrs. Lieves and "read the 2 Adam Beck articles ... much amused," but was disappointed to find that Mrs. Lieves had already told the story at dinner.[147]

In mid-November, Sophia had been confident that the "argument from negative evidence," the petitions, and Penny's testimony would sway the Arctic Committee. She noted with delight that Parry said, "many things had come out & been said of w^h we could know nothing—little imagining, good man, how much we really do know, & when & how certain strings have been pulled."[148] Yet the committee's findings, handed down on December 5, 1851, took them by surprise. Austin was found blameless in not searching farther up Wellington Channel, and Penny was judged to have only thought of the idea when he returned to England and "found everybody disappointed." The committee concluded that "some desultory conversation ... appears to have taken place" on the subject of a steamer, but gave it no weight.[149] Based on the relics of Cape Reilly, the committee cautiously recommended that another expedition be dispatched the following spring. In 1852, the Admiralty sent Sir Edward Belcher with five ships to search Wellington Channel. The *Resolute* and *Intrepid* would be abandoned in 1853, as would the *Assistance* and *Pioneer* in 1854. In the western Arctic, HMS *Investigator* was also lost in the pack ice in 1853 after two years imprisoned at Melville Island. Lt. Samuel Gurney Cresswell (Anna Gurney's nephew) and Captain Robert McClure completed the first European traverse of the Northwest Passage on foot in 1853, bringing the *Investigator*'s sick and wounded from Melville Island toward Beechey Island, where they were picked up by Belcher's one remaining ship (see Map 4 and Timeline 3).[150]

Publicly accused of lying by Austin and belittled by the final report of the committee, Penny felt as if his career and his character had been shattered. Sophia recorded that Penny visited them in January 1852, just before he returned to Aberdeen. She wrote that he said:

he was tired of dancing attendance, spoke haughtily & unkindly of having followed our advice even at the sacrifice of his own interests. . . . I told him that a day wd come, when he wd think more kindly of his friends and be sorry for many things he had thought of them. He said, "perhaps so". . . . He did not however return.[151]

Penny wrote to Barrow Jr., "I entered upon this search with the ardour of a generous . . . seaman. My God what is the return, that I have met with: Robbed of everything but my integrity that they cannot rob me off [sic]. It is hard indeed."[152]

Adam Beck's credibility was also shattered, both in Britain and in Greenland. Years later, Jane Franklin would still refer to him as a "mendacious half-caste Esquimaux" who had undermined her search for her husband.[153] In 1860, the American explorer Charles Francis Hall interviewed Beck in Upernavik. Hall wrote, "Even here his name is blackened by the public notoriety given him abroad as the man who fabricated falsehoods relative to the destruction of two ships . . . and the violent deaths of the officers and men supposed to refer to Sir John Franklin's expedition." He had fallen into poverty and was unable to feed his wife and children, and Hall reported that he had "lost all self-respect, for all shun him." Yet Beck continued to insist that, despite extensive abuse, he had accurately reported what he had been told.[154] The aspersions cast on his character did not fade with time. In 2009, John Franklin's biographer Andrew Lambert never mentioned Beck by name, referring only to his "horror story" as "one of many frauds perpetrated on men like Ross, men who were willing to suspend disbelief."[155]

After 1851, Jane Franklin supported two private expeditions to the polar sea. The first was an overland expedition proposed by Lieutenant Bedford Pim, who wanted to cross Siberia by dogsled. Jane Franklin gave him £300, but the Imperial Russian Geographical Society pointed out that Pim was virtually guaranteed to fail and the expedition went nowhere.[156] The second was proposed by a merchant marine captain, Donald Beatson, who wanted to enter the polar sea from the Bering Strait in a screw steamer. Jane and Sophia organized a subscription to fund Beatson, as they had with the *Prince Albert*. Anna Gurney favored Pim's plan, but according to Sophia, "Mrs Lee has sent [Anna Gurney] M Beatson's paper and begged her, instead of supporting Lieut Pim by subscription . . . to transfer the assistance to Mr Beatson."[157] Jane obtained a screw steamer, the *Isabel*, and began equipping it for the journey, but Beatson's proposed expedition never went forward. She gave the steamer to the naval captain Edward Augustus Inglefield to take to the far north of Greenland, in part to check up on Adam Beck's story (see below). These expeditions opened up yet another dimension of the open polar sea, this time in Tasmania, where "argument from negative evidence" recombined with the campaign against transportation.

Transporting the Open Polar Sea—The Tasmanian Search for Franklin

From 1851, the idea of the open polar sea acquired a firm hold on the public imagination in Britain, America, and Australia. As the petitions to the Admiralty had demonstrated, the combination of philanthropy, steam power, and government critique articulated easily with local conditions. In America, Elisha Kent Kane (the medical officer of the *Advance*) and Grinnell both reproduced the "argument from negative evidence" in the autumn of 1851, appealing to a diverse array of groups in antebellum America.[158] But in Tasmania, colonists latched onto the open polar sea as one of several means to demonstrate their respectability, liberality, and philanthropy in the context of the larger struggle against transportation and for self-government. Dane Kennedy has argued that when the Burke and Wills expedition went missing in the Australian interior a decade later, it offered colonists a "potent means of mobilizing the public sympathies and sense of allegiance to the colonial state and the imperial enterprise."[159] In 1852, however, support for Jane Franklin and the open polar sea was used to both criticize the colonial state and to define a Tasmanian identity. This was made possible, in part, by a peculiarly Antipodean arrhythmia—the circulation of British, colonial, and missionary press; private correspondence; and Arctic intelligence from Tasmania's own whaling fleet in the Bering Strait. In Tasmania, that arrhythmic pulse of Arctic information collided with settler politics, in particular their quest for new political rights and opposition to humanitarian projects.[160] It is significant, therefore, that one of the tools Tasmanian settlers used to secure their legitimacy as fully fledged imperial citizens was the rescue of Franklin, a campaign laden with humanitarian language and associations, and labeled as a philanthropic project for a liberal nation.

By 1850, Jane Franklin had acquired a transnational reputation as an icon of devoted femininity. She had been in the public eye for two years, begging the Admiralty for her husband's rescue, organizing her own expeditions, and approaching foreign powers for help. In impassioned letters to the US president Zachary Taylor in 1849, she had appealed to national pride, a spirit of "generous rivalry" and "kinship" and of "noble competition," invoked her emotional fragility and wifely devotion, the heroism of her husband and his sailors, and the spectacle of a shared philanthropic cause that both superseded and facilitated imperial rivalry.[161] She portrayed herself as both Arctic expert and devoted wife, which, as Erica Behrisch Elce has argued, enabled her to claim a moral high ground from which she could criticize the Admiralty and excuse her own presence in the public sphere.[162] This status derived from two modes of women's public authority: the maternal conscience of the philanthropist and the veiled expertise of the woman of science. They did not wholly insulate her from accusations of undue influence, but they tempered and contextualized it in a way that she had not managed in Tasmania (see Chapter 3). Now, sympathetic articles painted a portrait of a woman bankrupting herself out of wifely devotion, not only denying herself a comfortable and respectable old age but also embracing physical suffering (headaches, weakness, and fatigue) exacerbated by bad news and betrayal. Over time, a strange convergence developed between Jane Franklin's campaign to rescue her husband and the Tasmanian settlers' campaign to end transportation and secure self-government. Each not only cast themselves as victims of an unfeeling government but also found both moral certainty and unthinkable possibility in blank spaces and the absence of information.

The Tasmanian anti-transportation campaign is far too complex to do justice to here. It was one of the most important political events of a generation, part of what Hilary M. Carey has called a "noisy trans-colonial hue and cry" that linked Australia and the Cape Colony.[163] Briefly, from 1844, settlers argued that probation and transportation were corrupting the colony and leading to an epidemic of violence and vice, in particular homosexuality.[164] Tasmania still received the bulk of the empire's convicts, and free colonists objected both to paying for the probation system and to the limitations it imposed on their free institutions—for self-government would never be granted to a penal colony. Beginning in 1844, anti-transportationists began to depict themselves in both British and Australian newspapers as parents and family men compelled to action by the moral collapse that surrounded them, which was facilitated by a remote and unfeeling imperial government.[165] Chief among these were tales of sexual deviance, especially widespread homosexuality. Stories of sin were alluded to by daring ellipses in both Tasmanian and British newspapers, where Tasmania was declared a modern-day Sodom. Franklin's replacement, Sir John Eardley-Wilmot, was dismissed amid rumors of his own immorality, and temporarily replaced by Charles La Trobe, the brother of the Moravian bishop Peter La Trobe. During his brief tenure, La Trobe wrote a damning report on the probation system, which included the "prevalence of unnatural crime" at probation stations, and concluded that homosexuality was a "stigma on the whole colony."[166] Kirsty Reid has argued that there was little evidence to support these charges; nevertheless, they persisted and grew in both colonial and metropolitan contexts, fuelled by unquantifiable suggestions, rumors, and fears.[167]

Settlers also claimed that they and their families were endangered by the surviving Indigenous Tasmanians, after their petition to Queen Victoria and subsequent enquiry led to the abandonment of Wybalenna in 1847. Briefly, in 1846, Walter George Arthur and others composed a petition that both asserted their sovereignty and contested the terms of their indefinite detention.[168] Requesting that Dr. Henry Jeanneret be removed from his position as commandant, Arthur argued that his countrymen were treated like slaves and that the settlement itself prevented their "improvement."[169] This rhetoric reflected, in large part, his immersion in networks of Pacific missionary periodicals, Tasmanian newspapers, and humanitarian correspondence.[170] It also echoed a theme that Adele Perry has identified in Canada and the West Indies, in which mixed-race elites distinguished themselves from both slaves and other Indigenes as they articulated "their own ambivalent location within the connecting sinews and thick local histories of empire and rule."[171] William Kennedy and Alexander Isbister's activism in Rupert's Land and in London used similar rhetoric and strategies, and also shared a similar vision of the future, of stable communities with politically enfranchised and "respectable" Indigenous landholders.[172] In short, both constituted part of what Mar has called the "observable tip" of broader phenomenon of Indigenous "imperial literacy" in the 1840s.[173] When the petition from Flinders Island was received in London, Earl Grey urged the new governor, William Denison, to "extinguish this controversy" by returning the survivors of Wybalenna to the mainland, arguing that they were bound for extinction anyway.[174] When Denison announced the closure of Wybalenna, some colonists saw it as further evidence of a "diabolical" government determined to destroy their families and futures. The Launceston *Examiner* declared that when transportation was taken together with the Irish Famine, the Poor Laws, and the Indigenous return to the Tasmanian mainland, "the wickedness of the Government is so great, so manifold, that no one voice can denounce it all."[175] In this way, the petition's testament to the survival of the Indigenous Tasmanian community came to be wrapped into a narrative of their extinction and also entangled in settler narratives of their victimization by government.[176]

Meanwhile, Tasmanian horizons were expanding northward through its own whaling fleet (which came, in time, to incorporate several Indigenous Tasmanian men, including Walter Arthur).[177] Hobart had long been an important southern whaling port, and it was from Hobart in 1848 that American whaling captain Thomas Roys departed for the Bering Strait, where he found bowhead whales in abundance.[178] These whales were the cornerstone of life in large, semisedentary Iñupiat whaling communities on Alaska's northwest coast, whose physical and spiritual sustenance depended on the whale hunt.[179] Roys's wildly successful voyage sparked a mad rush of whalers to the Bering Strait.[180] Though generally referred to as "Yankee whaling," this was also a British, Tasmanian, and Aotearoa New Zealand whaling operation. Between 1848 and 1852, scores of ships left Hobart for the Bering Strait, many with wives and children on board. Their crews may have included Indigenous Tasmanians alongside Māori, Hawaiians, convicts, and escaped African-American slaves.[181]

As their whalers pushed into the North Pacific and Arctic and as their newspapers claimed victimization at the hands of the British government, many settlers laid claim to philanthropy, humanity, and liberality—in particular through the Royal Society of Tasmania (which had recently united with the Franklins' Tasmanian Society).[182] Governor Denison used the Royal Society to organize Tasmania's massive contribution to the Great Exhibition, comprised of hundreds of submissions—more than any other Antipodean colony.[183] They also received donations for their own growing collections, which included an extraordinary array of both Arctic and Tasmanian "curiosities." Shipowners, captains, and even ship chandlers donated items, including a walrus skull, Iñupiaq clothing, a sealskin-covered *umiaq* (which was paddled around the pond at the Botanical Gardens), and what appear to be a selection of grave goods from the grave of an *umialik* (an Iñupiaq captain of a whaling crew, a person of great moral and spiritual standing).[184] In 1852, Charles La Trobe donated a collection of rock specimens from Franklin's winter quarters at Cape Reilly, though whether he obtained them from his brother Peter or from Jane Franklin is impossible to tell.[185] The Franklin's friend and protégé Dr. Joseph Milligan was also the society's secretary, and donated many objects and observations obtained from Indigenous Tasmanians resettled at Oyster Cove, where he was the superintendent. As he collected spears, waddies, and stories, he also facilitated a trade in body parts, asking, on one occasion, for any "well authenticated specimens of Crania" which he could forward to Joseph Barnard Davis, who was developing a method to use the forms of human skulls to date British archaeological sites.[186] Objects, bodies, exhibitions, and stories from both ends of the earth (and many places in between) combined at the society's meetings and in its proceedings to portray settlers as men devoted to science, progress, and improvement in Tasmania and across the Pacific.[187]

At the same time, colonists, feeling themselves to be in the midst of an historic struggle to purify and liberate themselves, began to rewrite their own histories and to memorialize the Franklins as misunderstood benefactors of Tasmanian science and philanthropy. The man who was the face and voice of the anti-transportationists, the Rev. John West, published *The History of Tasmania* in 1852, in which he wrote that Franklin's administration was "disinterested," his piety "ardent," and his conscience "scrupulous," and that Franklin had appreciated the "general character" and "moral worth" of settlers. He argued that Jane Franklin's "masculine intellect and adventurous spirit led some to ascribe to her more than the usual authority of her sex and station but whenever apparent, her influence was exercised on the side of religion, science, and humanity."[188] Also in 1852, John Murray published Louisa Ann Meredith's *My Home in Tasmania*, one of her several books of popular natural history aimed at a metropolitan audience.[189] Its early chapters invoked Jane Franklin as a woman unfairly treated by colonists. "The coarse and unmanly attacks made in some of the public papers on Lady Franklin, whose kindness and ability, even if not appreciated at their full value, ought at least to have met with gratitude and respect, were most disgraceful."[190] It may have helped that Meredith's son-in-law was Franklin's nephew, Captain Joseph Henry Kay, who was still manning Rossbank Observatory more than a decade after James Clark Ross had left him there.[191]

In Tasmanian newspapers, the search for *Erebus* and *Terror* was commonly said to "unite the civilized world."[192] Jane Franklin was described as a "most estimable lady," and a "devoted wife," with a "most touching cause," and the search as a "noble object."[193] Articles from British newspapers elevated the rescuers as examples of chivalric manhood, and reproduced suggestions and experiments in the wake of the Mittimatalik map, as well as clairvoyant reports commissioned by Jane Franklin and Alexander Maconochie (see Chapter 4). Grinnell's privately financed expeditions were also noted as a "noble instance of American philanthropy and heroism".[194] Additionally, odd scraps of intelligence gleaned by Tasmanian whalers were published in the newspapers. For example, in 1851, the *Examiner* published reports from Yupik hunters (via Russian translators) that Franklin's party had been massacred on the Yukon River, and later published an account from the Hobart whaler *Emu* of "two vessels being frozen up in the ice, with many people on board."[195]

These accounts were embedded in a stream of private correspondence from Britain detailing the "argument from negative evidence." Joseph Henry Kay and his brother William Porden Kay received regular dispatches from their cousin Sophia Cracroft, who made extensive notes on letters sent and received. They also received news from their sister Mary Anne Kendall in Gosport, as well as from Edward Sabine and Eleanor Gell.[196] Bishop Nixon and his wife received regular dispatches from Sophia, Jane, and the Gells among others.[197] John Hepburn wrote to his friend John Mitchell from Point Puer about his own hopes and fears about Kennedy's expedition in the *Prince Albert* in 1851.[198] Ronald Campbell Gunn was managing Jane Franklin's property in Tasmania, and Jane and Sophia wrote to him often about the state of the search, usually because they needed money.[199] On Norfolk Island, Mary Franklin Price was kept appraised of Inuit intelligence, ships' departures and returns, and both familial and expeditionary dramas.[200] Other naval officers once attached to *Erebus*, *Terror*, or the *Beagle*, along with the families of both missing and searching explorers, also received information from Britain.[201] Tasmanians would also have gotten news from Arctic veterans in person, many of whom came south on whalers or in search of gold. Penny's second mate in the *Lady Franklin*, John Leiper, died in Hobart in 1852 "owing to a disease brought on by untiring zeal and severe privations endured in the late search for Sir John Franklin," according to his death notice.[202] William Parker Snow, the first mate in the *Prince Albert* under Forsyth, also headed for Victoria as a gold-seeker, meaning to make his fortune and so finance a new search.[203]

In 1852, as Tasmania began losing its young men to the Victorian goldfields, the Kay brothers began to approach prosperous settlers for donations to Beatson's expedition and appealing to their enterprise, benevolence and philanthropy.[204] Beatson's plan to search the Bering Strait with a steamer was published in May 1852, together with the notice that a subscription list had already been opened at the Royal Society's rooms.[205] A further £1,800 was needed to dispatch the ship, and it was noted that Beaufort, Barrow, Lord Ellesmere, Murchison, Collinson, and Kellet had subscribed, alongside Lady Franklin's contribution of £600.[206] Accounts of the subscription were published alongside articles that Reid describes as "apocalyptic" from the anti-transportation movement, which claimed that the penal colony was on the precipice of being "struck down by a righteous divine vengeance."[207]

The Franklin Fund, as it came to be known, was never presented as an explicitly anti-transportation cause. Indeed, many on both sides of the transportation debate subscribed to it. Yet it certainly aligned with a desire to portray the colony and its residents as civilized, even as Governor Denison lamented that "one third of the whole free male population has already deserted" the colony for the Victorian goldfields.[208] In July, the Kays opened the fund to the public in order to "enlist the unanimous sympathy of the whole colony."[209] Articles rehashed the "Argument from Negative Evidence" as it had appeared over the last six months in the Tasmanian newspapers; that the relics of Cape Reilly and Beechey Island indicated that Franklin had ascended Wellington Channel and entered a mysterious polar sea where provisions were plentiful; that Jane Franklin had "cast her all upon the waters"; and that zealous colonists could now both alleviate her misfortunes and testify to their lasting regard for the Franklin family.[210] The same banks where, nine years earlier, the colonists could read "Montagu's Book" with its claims of unwomanly interference by Jane Franklin were now opened for subscriptions to her privately financed expedition. The expedition was identified as an opportunity for Tasmanian settlers to participate in a global philanthropic cause, rather than narrowly defined local and insular concerns.[211] Generous contributions would rank settlers against the governments of the United States and Russia, and, the *Colonial Times* claimed, "would be spoken of in every circle of polite and commercial men, and accepted as proof of our unity in heart and in spirit with the great people from which we sprung."[212]

In September, the full list of subscribers to the Franklin Fund was printed in the local newspapers. It included many members of the Royal Society, prominent anti-transportationists and government loyalists alike.[213] At the same time, the Legislative Council offered an address to Lady Franklin. Thomas Gregson (whom she had once accused of being part of a "vast conspiracy" against her) commented that it would be a subject of deep reproach to the colony if they did not sympathize with Franklin's fate. "Don't let it be said that, while so much had been done, the colony did not entertain the most lively solicitude for his safety," Gregson said.[214] Shortly thereafter, Joseph Kay wrote two letters to Jane Franklin to accompany the donations. One expressed the donors' "unbounded admiration" and "deepest sympathy" for her "corroding cares." The other was private and contained an explicit *quid pro quo*. As Kay offered her the money, he added that "the Settlers of VDL are one of the most liberal set of men in the world," but that the colony's "detestable penal character" meant that

> it never obtains its share of favourable notice . . . [in] the Public Press of England. . . . If you can command the columns of the "Times" . . . the opportunity is such a legitimate one for paying them a compliment, and it is astonishing how useful a favourable notice of their good qualities may be to the Colony in an indirect manner.[215]

Jane Franklin did not disappoint. She wrote to the Tasmanian Legislative Council that their sentiments had "excited the attention and touched the hearts of the people of England."[216] Beatson could not command the *Isabel*, though she was fully equipped, and so Jane Franklin dispatched her to the west coast of Greenland under Captain Inglefield—effectively, to refute the testimony of Adam Beck and to try to enter the polar sea.[217] Inglefield's voyage, in an unusually open ice year, enabled him to sail much further than anyone expected, into Smith Sound and, he thought, the polar sea. He then sailed south again, entered Lancaster Sound and reached Beechey Island. One night, he and his surgeon Peter Sutherland (also Penny's surgeon and defender on HMS *Lady Franklin*) secretly excavated the grave of 25-year-old able seaman Joshua Hartnell. After opening his coffin, they rapidly reburied the frozen body, fearing the "superstitious feelings of the sailors."[218]

After the *Isobel*'s return, Jane Franklin sent a copy of the narrative, *A Summer Search for Sir John Franklin, with a Peep into the Polar Basin*, to Tasmania, with a note that she intended to rename the vessel *Tasmania* and send her back to the Bering Strait. Though she did not rename the *Isobel*, she did reequip it under William Kennedy's command.[219] However, Kennedy's 1853 voyage was scuppered by both the Californian and the Australian gold rushes. He was unable to procure crew in the Orkneys because so many young men had already headed for Victoria's goldfields.[220] In Valparaiso, the crew mutinied and it became impossible for the ship to proceed. Kennedy was effectively marooned, increasingly depressed and embarrassed as he waited for instructions. In early 1854, he chartered the *Isobel* and sailed along the Chilean coast with a local crew. He wrote to Barrow that he was ready to proceed to the Arctic during the 1854 season, though he despaired of finding crew, for "the scum of California and Australia are here" in Chile. He added, bleakly, "The cold, the cold of Valparaiso, how infinitely more terrible than that of the Arctic regions, the first reaches my soul; the last can but take the skin off my face."[221]

In her pioneering study of mid-nineteenth-century Indigenous "imperial literacy," Tracey Banivanua Mar identified what she called "an emerging intellectual and discursive circuitry" of humanitarian ideas in the 1840s.[222] The Wellington Channel campaign might be seen as one facet of this phenomenon. After all, it was sparked by one Indigenous man, Adam Beck, and elaborated by another, Alexander Isbister, men who were alternately visible and invisible, credible and untrustworthy, depending on their location and objectives, deploying and downplaying their identities amid a hardening racial rhetoric at midcentury. Qalasirssuaq was caught in the middle and far from home.

Looked at another way, the Wellington Channel campaign might be seen as the legacy of painful lessons from the Franklins' imperial lives: the usefulness of humanitarian rhetoric and organization, the power of the press, the perils of what happened when women exceeded their gendered authority. The campaign to search the open polar sea might also be seen as another dimension of women's participation in the midcentury public sphere and the ways in which they sought to influence public discourse, government policy, and geographical agendas. It might also be seen as a counterweight to arguments about the faltering power of the humanitarian movement, or perhaps as a long afterlife of T. F. Buxton's failed Niger Expedition a decade earlier. In 1853, Charles Dickens mocked busybody humanitarians in *Bleak House* through Mrs. Jellyby, who privileged her African philanthropy over the needs of her own neglected children. Yet he was also deeply sympathetic to the philanthropic arguments developed by Jane Franklin's circles and would deploy some of them a year later in his "Lost Arctic Voyagers" essays in *Household Words* (see Chapter 6). The Wellington Channel controversy might be seen as evidence of a new dimension of settler politics, as colonists adapted a geographical fiction on the opposite side of the world to suit their own political agendas. It was, of course, all of these things. The imagined open polar sea revolved around the uneven, dynamic, and contested intelligence produced by Arctic exploration, ultimately testifying to the power of silence in which an "argument from negative evidence" could circulate amid a cacophony of conflicting voices.

Within a decade of Adam Beck's testimony, there would be an explosion of Kalaallit writing in the Greenlandic newspaper, *Atuagagdliutit, nalinginarmik tusaruminasassumik*

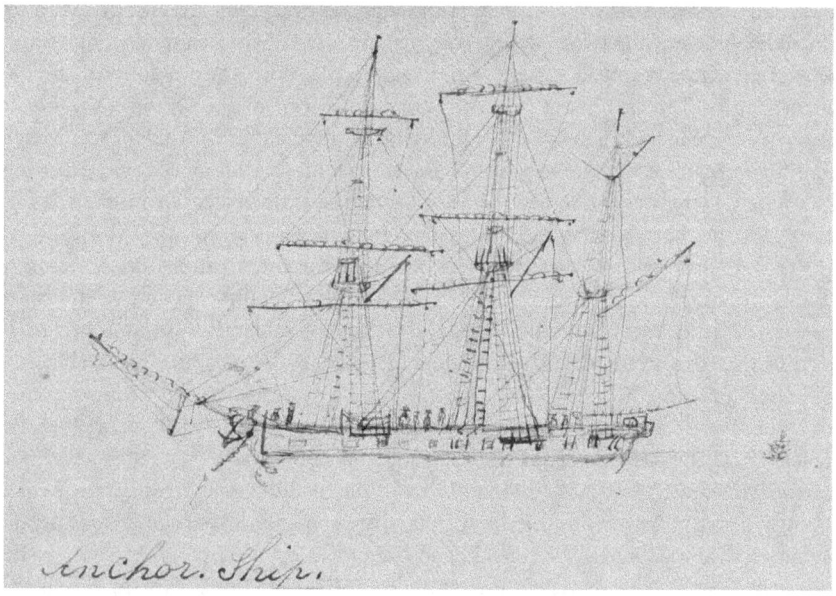

Figure 5.4 Qalasirssuaq's drawing of the "Anchor Ship" in a letter addressed to Eleanor Gell and signed "Kalli," St. Augustine's College (Canterbury), May 11, 1853. Derbyshire Record Office, D8760/F/OBJ/5.

univkat, in which Indigenous schoolteachers, seal hunters, and others urged people to give up "European dainties and articles of clothing," and contracting debts with white traders like Carl Petersen (Penny's unscrupulous interpreter). As one seal hunter put it, "The Greenlanders have great need of acquiring an approximate idea of their home affairs."[223] Adam Beck lived to see this phenomenon, but Qalasirssuaq did not. In 1853, Qalasirssuaq was baptized Erasmus Kallihirhua York. Eleanor Franklin Gell became his godmother, and Erasmus Ommanney his godfather. He corresponded with Eleanor, sending her illustrated letters from the missionary college in Canterbury. He tried to return home via the Moravian missionary school in Labrador, but he caught a fever and died in 1856. The Gells helped finance his privately printed biography, and Eleanor kept "Kalli's" letters and drawings, as she did Mithina's pin cushion and doll (Figure 5.4).[224] It is impossible to know if she kept these objects as mementos or curiosities, how often she touched or displayed them, or whether she called them "relics" like the fragments of wood and metal associated with her father's missing expedition. We cannot know how she remembered these two young Indigenous people from opposite ends of the earth, nor how or whether those memories were bound up with those of her missing father.

Notes

1. SPRI MS 1008, John Ross to Archibald Barclay. Secretary of Hudson's Bay Company, June 30, 1850.
2. Ross, *Polar Pioneers*, 327; PP 1852c (1449) Arctic Expeditions. Further Correspondence and Proceedings connected with the Arctic Expedition, no. 11, 136.
3. PP 1852j (390) Arctic Expedition. Copy of Further Correspondence which has been transmitted to the Admiralty between Admiral Sir John Ross and the Danish Inspector-General, touching the fate of the expedition under Sir John Franklin. Enclosure to No. 6, 8.
4. For accounts of such tales, see SPRI MS1199/1, William Edward Parry, private journal, HMS *Alexander*, August 10, 1818, 22. Wilhelm A. Graah, *Narrative of an Expedition to the East Coast of Greenland, Sent by the Order of the King of Denmark, in Search of the Lost Colonies* . . . , trans. G. Gordon Macdougall (London: John W. Parker, 1837), 31.
5. Savours, *Search for the North West Passage*, 197; DRO D8760/F/OBJ/5, Letters, writing and drawings by Erasmus Augustine Kallihirua.
6. Ross, *Polar Pioneers*, 328; David Woodman, *Unravelling the Franklin Mystery: Inuit Testimony* (Montreal: McGill-Queen's University Press, 1991), 56–8. John Smith, the steward on the *Prince Albert*, had been employed at Churchill and understood Inuktitut, SPRI MS 248/106 BJ, Lady Franklin and Sophia Cracroft, Letter Book, January 17–March 1851; SPRI MS 248/107 BJ, Jane Franklin, Sophia Cracroft, Letter Book, March–May 1851.
7. HC PP 1852 (390), Enclosure to No. 6, 8; PP 1852 [1449], No. 11, 136.
8. Craciun, "The Franklin Relics in the Arctic Archive," 16.
9. ADM 7/192/4, John Ross to the Secretary of the Admiralty, August 22, 1850.
10. Quoted in Savours, *Search for the North West Passage*, 203.
11. Michael F. Robinson, "Reconsidering the Theory of the Open Polar Sea," in *Extremes: Oceanography's Adventure at the Poles* (Maury Workshop on the History of Polar Oceanography IV), ed. Keith R. Benson and Helen Rozwadowski (Sagamore Beach: Science History Publications, 2007), 15–29.

12 HC PP 1852c [1449], no. 11, 136; Ross, *Polar Pioneers*, 327; SPRI MS 116/63/115, William Penny to Margaret Penny, Assistance Bay, April 13, 1851; SPRI MS 116/63/116, William Penny to Margaret Penny, May 8, 1851.
13 Clive Holland, "The Arctic Committee of 1851: A Background Study, Part 1," *Polar Record* 20, no. 124 (1980): 3–17.
14 "The Arctic Searching Expeditions," *Times*, October 6, 1851, 7.
15 TNA ADM 7/192/4, Sir John Ross's Expedition.
16 Robinson, "Reconsidering the Theory," especially 16–21.
17 Cavell, *Tracing the Connected Narrative*, 169, 173.
18 Robinson, "Reconsidering the Theory."
19 See Lester, *Imperial Networks*, 113; Lester and Dussart, *Colonization*, 226–75; Laidlaw, *Protecting the Empire's Humanity*, 9–11, 175–333.
20 Elizabeth Elbourne, "Imperial Politics in a Family Way: Gender, Biography and the 1835–36 Select Committee on Aborigines," in *Frontier, Race, Nation: Henry Reynolds and Australian History*, ed. Bain Attwood and Tom Griffiths (Melbourne: Australian Scholarly Publishing, 2009), 111–35.
21 Ravi de Costa, "Identity, Authority and the Moral Worlds of Indigenous Petitions," *Comparative Studies in Society and History* 48, no. 3 (July 2006): 669–98 for the moral authority of petitions.
22 "The Arctic Expedition," *The Times*, October 1, 1850, 8.
23 *Times*, October 2, 1850, 8.
24 WM, SCO 819 Box P, Jane Franklin to William Scoresby, 21 Bedford Place, October 14, 1850.
25 Laidlaw, "Aunt Anna's Report"; Lester and Dussart, *Colonization*, 86–104.
26 Elbourne, "Imperial Politics," 131–2.
27 Porter, *Religion Versus Empire*, 151.
28 See Chapter 3, and also Parry, *Parry of the Arctic*, 197–209, 213–14.
29 Dominick Harrod, ed., *War, Ice and Piracy: The Remarkable Career of a Victorian Sailor, the Journals and Letters of Samuel Gurney Cresswell* (London: Chatham Publishing, 2000), 98–101; Hutchinson, *Sir John Franklin's Erebus and Terror*, 118.
30 TNA ADM 7/192/22, W. E. Parry to John Barrow, Jr., February 24, 1851.
31 TNA ADM 7/192/22, W. E. Parry to Barrow, February 24, 1851.
32 MA MG2 C1/40, Jane Franklin to William Kennedy, March 19, 1851.
33 MA MG1 D1/5, Alexander Kennedy to his sons Alexander and Phillip, February 1, 1832; SPRI MS 248/106; BJ, Jane Franklin and Sophia Cracroft, 1851 Letterbook, February 3, 1851; Bunyan et al., *No Ordinary Journey*, 1–11.
34 Edward Charles Shaw, "Kennedy, William," in *Dictionary of Canadian Biography*, vol. 11 (University of Toronto/Universite Laval, 2003), http://www.biographi.ca/en/bio/kennedy_william_11E.html (accessed November 28, 2021).
35 Zoe Laidlaw, "Indigenous Interlocutors: Networks of Imperial Protest and Humanitarianism in the Mid-Nineteenth Century," in *Indigenous Networks: Mobility, Connections and Exchange*, ed. Jane Carey and Jane Lydon (London: Routledge, 2014), 114–39.
36 BL add. Ms 46126, Jane Franklin to Roderick Murchison, November 4, 1852.
37 SPRI MS 248/106; BJ, Jane Franklin and Sophia Cracroft, Letterbook, 1851, February 3–5, 1851.
38 MA MG2 C1, Jane Franklin to William Kennedy, nd [1851 by context].
39 Ibid.

40 "The Arctic Expedition," *The Times*, October 4, 1851, 6; "Search for Sir John Franklin" *Lloyd's Weekly*, Iss. 462, September 28, 1851, 7.
41 SPRI MS 248/241 BJ, Sophia Cracroft Journal, September 23, 1851.
42 SPRI MS 248/241 BJ, September 29–October 1, 1851.
43 SPRI MS 248/241 BJ, October 17, 1851.
44 WM SCO819 Box P, Jane Franklin to William Scoresby, January 7, 1851.
45 Orr, "Fish with a Different Angle," 209.
46 Bernard Lightman, *Victorian Popularizers of Science: Designing Nature for New Audiences* (Chicago, IL and London: University of Chicago Press, 2007), 95–166; Ann B. Shteir, "Elegant Recreations? Configuring Science Writing for Women," in *Victorian Science in Context*, ed. Bernard Lightman (Chicago: University of Chicago Press, 1997), 236–55; Norcia, *X Marks the Spot*, 78–84; Orr, "Pursuing Proper Protocol"; Mary Orr, "Women Peers in the Scientific Realm: Sarah Bowdich Lee's Expert Collaborations with Georges Cuvier, 1825–1833," *Notes and Records* 69 (2015): 37–51; Mary Orr, "The Stuff of Translation and Independent Female Scientific Authorship: The Case of Taxidermy . . . anon. (1820)," *Journal of Literature and Science* 8, no. 1 (2015): 27–47.
47 Orr, "Pursuing Proper Protocol," 280.
48 Laidlaw, *Protecting the Empire's Humanity*, 104–5.
49 Orr, "Women Peers"; Donald deB. Beaver, "Writing Natural History for Survival – 1820-1856: The Case of Sarah Bowdich, Later Sarah Lee," *Archives of Natural History* 26, no. 1 (1999): 19–31.
50 Lightman, *Victorian Popularizers*, 100.
51 Orr, "Pursuing Proper Protocol," 277–85. See also Lightman, *Victorian Popularizers*, 102–3.
52 SPRI MS 248/88, June 30, 1840. SPRI MS 248/92; BJ, August 23, 1841 referring to letter of April 6, 1841; Lambert, *Mastering the Niger*, 188; AJCP M 377-380—Papers of the Gell and Franklin families, Series A/File 4/Letters of John Gell to his sister Elizabeth Gell, 18 January 1849, https://nla.gov.au/nla.obj-904903567/view (accessed March 15, 2022). For Inglis's support of Jane Franklin, see Cavell, *Tracing the Connected Narrative*, 188.
53 See especially Orr, "Women Peers."
54 Alexander K. Isbister, *A Few Words on the Hudson's Bay Company: With a Statement of the Grievances of the Native and Half-caste Indians, Addressed to the British Government through their Delegates now in London* (London: C. Gilpin, c. 1846).
55 Laidlaw, *Protecting the Empire's Humanity*, 271–2. Barry Cooper has an extensive discussion of the petition and the circumstances around it, see Cooper, *Alexander Kennedy Isbister: A Respectable Critic of the Honourable Company* (Ottowa: Carleton University Press, 1988), 107.
56 Alexander K. Isbister, "Some Account of Peel River, North America," *Journal of the Royal Geographical Society* 15 (1845): 332–45; "On the Chippewyan Indians," *Transactions of the British Association for the Advancement of Science* (1847): 119–22.
57 Cooper, *A Respectable Critic*, 38.
58 Laidlaw, "Indigenous Interlocutors."
59 Cooper, *A Respectable Critic*, 172 n 54, 182, 223.
60 Cooper, *A Respectable Critic*, 234.
61 Laidlaw, *Protecting the Empire's Humanity*, 278. Isbister particularly focused on Scottish journals in early 1851, see MA MG2 C1 6 William Kennedy to James Bremner, nd, copy by Sophia Cracroft.

62 SPRI MS 248/162, Sophia Cracroft Journal, September 20 and 27, 1851; WM SCO 819 Box P, Jane Franklin to William Scoresby, October 16, 1851.
63 SPRI MS 248/162 BJ, September 20–28, 1851; WM SCO 819 Box P, Jane Franklin to William Scoresby, October 16, 1851.
64 Sophia had either drafted these articles herself or outlined them for Harwood—in any event, her diary records that both Cook and Harwood met with her and promised a leading article on the subject. SPRI MS 248/241 BJ, Sophia Cracroft Journal, September 12–13, 1851.
65 "The Arctic Expedition," *Morning Chronicle*, September 13, 5.
66 Quoted in [C. R. Weld] "The Arctic Searching Expeditions," *The Athenaeum*, October 4, 1851, 1046–7.
67 DRO D8760/F/FKA/3/5, Jane Franklin to Frances Kay, April 9, [nd].
68 SPRI MS 248/241 BJ, October 1, 1851.
69 "Search for Sir John Franklin," *Lloyd's Weekly*, Iss. 462, September 28, 1851, 7.
70 SPRI MS 248/241 BJ; Sophia Cracroft Journal, September 28, 1851.
71 See Withers, "Mapping the Niger," 170–93; Dritsas, "Expeditionary Science"; Wisnicki, "Charting the Frontier," 103–37; Bravo, "Ethnographic Navigation," 199–235.
72 [Sophia Cracroft] "The Arctic Searching Expeditions," *Morning Chronicle*, October 6, 1851, 5. Jane forwarded the article to Cook, as she noted in her journal. SPRI MS 248/162, October 4–5, 1851.
73 SPRI MS 248/241 BJ, October 4, 1851.
74 [C. R. Weld] "The Arctic Searching Expeditions," *The Athenaeum*, October 4, 1851: 1046–7.
75 SPRI MS 248/241 BJ, September 30–October 1, 1851.
76 SPRI MS 248/241 BJ, September 24, 1851.
77 [C.R. Weld] "Our Weekly Gossip," *The Athenaeum*, September 27, 1851, 1022.
78 [A.K. Isbister?] "The Arctic Searching Expeditions," *The Athenaeum*, October 11, 1851: 1069–70.
79 [Sarah Bowdich Lee] Arcticus, "The Search for Sir John Franklin," *Daily News*, September 22, 1851, 6. This is identified as Lee's work in SPRI MS 248/162, September 19, 1851.
80 De Costa, "Identity," 670–4.
81 Henry Miller, "Popular Petitioning and the Corn Laws, 1833–46," *English Historical Review* 127, no. 527 (August 2012): 882–919; Paul A. Pickering, Jean Dunbabin, and J. S. Rowett, "'And Your Petitioners &c': Chartist Petitioning in Popular Politics 1838–48," *English Historical Review* 116, no. 466 (April 2001): 368–88; Clare Midgely, "Antislavery and Feminism in Nineteenth Century Britain," *Gender & History* 5, no. 3 (1993): 343–62; Sarah Richardson, *The Political Worlds of Women: Gender and Politics in Nineteenth Century Britain* (Abingdon: Routledge, 2013).
82 Mar, "Imperial Literacy."
83 SPRI MS 248/241 BJ, September 24, 1851.
84 SPRI MS 248/241 BJ, October 18, 19, 23, 1851.
85 SPRI MS 248/241 BJ, October 31, 1851.
86 SPRI MS 248/241 BJ, October 18, 1851; ADM 6/11, Petition from the Inhabitants of Marlborough, November 29, 1851.
87 SPRI MS 248/241 BJ, November 20, 1851; she did not sign it, but her husband, F. W. Booth, the vicar of Friskney, did. TNA ADM 7/611, Petition from residents of Lincolnshire and Dublin, December 3, 1851.

88 SPRI MS 248/241 BJ, October 20, 1851.
89 SPRI MS 248/241 BJ, October 19, 1851; October 23, 1851.
90 SPRI MS 248/241 BJ, November 25, 28, 1851.
91 TNA ADM 7/611.
92 TNA ADM 7/611, Memorial of the Provost, Magistrates, Clergy, and Inhabitants of the City of St. Andrews, October 21, 1851 to the Lords Commissioners of the Admiralty.
93 TNA ADM 7/611: Petition from the Inhabitants of Yarmouth, October 18, 1851.
94 TNA ADM 7/611, Petition from the Employees of the Great Western Railway Co, October 30, 1851; Petition "From Artizans in the City of London," November 24, 1851.
95 W. Gillies Ross, *Hunters on the Track: William Penny and the Search for Franklin* (Montreal and London: McGill-Queen's University Press, 2019), 16–17.
96 "Another Proposed Arctic Expedition," *Lloyd's Weekly*, October 12, 1851, 5.
97 TNA ADM 7/611, "Memorial signed by the inhabitants of Dundee."
98 PP 1852 [1435] Arctic Expeditions. Report of the committee appointed by the Lords Commissioners of the Admiralty to inquire into and report on the recent Arctic expeditions in search of Sir John Franklin, together with the minutes of the committee, and papers connected with the subject.
99 Holland, "The Arctic Committee of 1851: A Background Study, Part 1," 4.
100 Parry and Richardson examined the Beechey Island "relics" together PP 1851 (97) Arctic Expeditions, No. 7, C-D. For their friendship, see SPRI MS 1508/38/1-59; see also SPRI MS 438/26/639, W. E. Parry to Lady Maria Stanley, September 29, 1851, and Fletcher, *Autobiography*, 296.
101 SPRI MS 248/241 BJ, 16 September, September 24, October 8, 1851; SPRI MS 1503/44/11, Sophia Cracroft to John Richardson, 21 Bedford Place, October 10, 1851.
102 SPRI MS 248/241 BJ, September 24, 1851.
103 WM SCO 819 Box P Sophia Cracroft to William Scoresby, n.d.; SPRI MS 248/241 BJ, Sophia Cracroft Journal, October 15, 1851; October 19, 1851; October 27, 1851.
104 Woodward, *Portrait of Jane*, 280–2; Alexander, *Ambitions*, 237–8.
105 "The Arctic Committee," *Daily News*, October 28, 1851, 3.
106 These are only some of the places in which it appeared: "The Arctic Committee," *Caledonian Mercury*, October 30, 1851, 3; "The Arctic Committee: Letter from Lady Franklin," *The Era*, November 2, 1851, 2; "Lady Franklin and the Artic (sic) Expedition," *Lloyd's Weekly*, November 2, 1851, 3.
107 SPRI 248/241 BJ, October 29, 1851.
108 SPRI MS 248/162, November 2, 1851; SPRI 248/241 BJ, November 12, 1851.
109 SPRI 248/241 BJ, November 20, 1851.
110 [C. R. Weld] "The Arctic Searching Expeditions," *The Athenaeum*, October 4, 1851, 1046–7; SPRI MS 248/241 BJ, October 4, 1851.
111 SPRI MS 1503/44/11, Sophia Cracroft to John Richardson, 21 Bedford Place, October 10, 1851.
112 SPRI 248/241 BJ, October 13, 1851.
113 Cavell, *Tracing the Connected Narrative*, 193–201, quote 197.
114 Ballantyne, *Webs of Empire*, 126, 131–3; for whalers' correspondence with their wives and families, see Norling, *Captain Ahab Had a Wife*, 165–261; Norling, "'How Frought with Sorrow,'" 422–46.
115 Quoted in Holland, "The Arctic Committee of 1851: A Background Study, Part 1," 9.
116 HC PP 1852 [1435], Enclosure No. 29, William Penny to the Secretary of the Admiralty, October 10, 1851, lviii.

117 SPRI 248/241 BJ, September 16, 1851.
118 SPRI 248/241 BJ, October 28, 1851; PP 1852 [1435] October 31, 1851, 60–2.
119 For Penny's perspective on the committee, see Ross, *Hunters on the Track*, 364–79; see also Holland, "The Arctic Committee of 1851" parts I and II, and also SPRI 248/241 BJ, *passim*.
120 SPRI 248/241 BJ, October 29, 1851.
121 SPRI MS 116/63/115, Wm Penny to Margaret Penny, Assistance Bay, April 13, 1851.
122 SPRI 248/241 BJ, Sophia Cracroft Journal, October 30, 1851.
123 HC PP 1852 [1435], October 27, 1851, 1.
124 Ibid., 8.
125 HC PP 1852 [1435], October 29, 1851, 34.
126 SPRI 248/241 BJ, Sophia Cracroft Journal, November 1, 1851.
127 Kennedy, *Last Blank Spaces*, 159–94.
128 Maria Nugent, "Jacky Jacky and the Politics of Aboriginal Testimony," in *Indigenous Intermediaries: New Perspectives on Exploration Archives*, ed. Shino Konishi, Maria Nugent, and Tiffany Shellam (Canberra: ANU Press, 2015), 67–84.
129 HC PP 1852 [1435], October 29, 1851, 27; November 4, 1851, 97.
130 HC PP 1852 (390). Arctic Expedition. Copy of Further Correspondence which has been transmitted to the Admiralty between Admiral Sir John Ross and the Danish Inspector-General. Lewis Platon to John Ross, February 6, 1852.
131 Hans Hendrik, *Memoirs of Hans Hendrik, the Arctic Traveller, Serving Under Kane, Hayes, Hall and Nares, 1853–1876, Written By Himself*, ed. Prof. Dr. George Stephens, trans. Dr. Henry Rink (London: Trubner & Co. 1878), 32–3, 42, 49, 57.
132 Hendrik, *Memoirs*, 57. For Ipiirvik and his wife, Tookoolitoo or "Hannah" (both of whom worked with Charles Frances Hall on Franklin relief expeditions and traveled to Britain and to America), see Routledge, *Do You See Ice?* 35–76.
133 Routledge, *Do You See Ice?* 61–2, 90–4; Thrush, "The Iceberg and the Cathedral."
134 *Arctic Miscellanies: A Souvenir of the Late Polar Search* (London: Colburn and Co., 1852), 327. For a broader discussion of this newspaper, see Hester Blum, *The News at the Ends of the Earth: The Print Culture of Polar Exploration* (Durham and London: Duke University Press, 2019), 91–137.
135 *Arctic Miscellanies*, 89–93; "The Great Exhibition," *Times*, October 11, 1851, 5.
136 Routledge, *Do You See Ice?*, 45.
137 HC PP 1852 [1435], November 8, 1851, 135. ADM 7/192/4, Peter La Trobe to E. P. Elsner, January 30, 1851; SPRI 248/241 Sophia Cracroft Journal, October 12, 1851.
138 HC PP 1852 [1435], November 8, 1851, 137.
139 Ibid.
140 Ibid., 138. The Moravian interpreters could not work out if Beck had described the people at Cape York as "murderers" or "people." Indeed, it might have been both, and colored by Beck's own expectations—Hans Hendrik also mentioned being afraid of northerners, as were other southern Kalaallit interpreters on European expeditions between 1818 and 1840, see note 4.
141 Aporta, "The Sea, the Land," 163–80; John MacDonald, *The Arctic Sky: Inuit Astronomy, Star Lore, and Legend* (Toronto: Royal Ontario Museum and Nunavut Research Institute, 1998).
142 Claudio Aporta, "New Ways of Mapping: Using GPS Software to Plot Place Names and Trails in Igloolik (Nunavut)," *Arctic* 56, no. 4 (2003): 325. See also David Woodward and G. Malcolm Lewis, eds., *The History of Cartography*, vol. 2, bk. 3,

Cartography in the Traditional African, American, Arctic, Australian, and Pacific Societies (Chicago: University of Chicago Press, 1998), 1–10.
143 "Alleged Murder of Sir John Franklin and the Crews of the Erebus and Terror in Baffin's-Bay – Deposition of Adam Beck," *Morning Chronicle*, December 9, 1851, 3.
144 Ibid.
145 SPRI 248/241 BJ, December 8, 1851.
146 Risum Teneatis, "Adam Beck's Story," *Morning Chronicle*, December 10, 1851, 5.
147 SPRI MS 248/162, [December 10, 1851].
148 SPRI 248/241 BJ Sophia Cracroft Journal, November 20, 1851.
149 HC PP 1852 [1435], Report of the Arctic Committee, iii, see also Clive Holland, "The Arctic Committee of 1851: A Background Study, Part 2," *Polar Record* 20, no. 125 (1980): 105–18.
150 Savours, *Search for the North West Passage*, 264–7.
151 Quoted in Holland, "The Arctic Committee Part 2," 117.
152 BL add ms 35306, William Penny to John Barrow, nd [December 1851/January 1852 by context].
153 Jane Franklin to the Lords of the Admiralty, February 24, 1854, in Elce, ed., *As Affecting the Fate*, 105.
154 Charles Francis Hall, *Life with the Esquimaux: A Narrative of Arctic Experience in Search of Survivors of Sir John Franklin's Expedition from May 29, 1860 to September 13, 1862* (London: Sampson Low, Son and Marston, 1864), 66–7.
155 Lambert, *Gates of Hell*, 202.
156 RGS JMS/17/18 PIM, Bedford Pim, Outline of a plan for a further search after the (remains of the Franklin) Expedition.
157 SPRI MS 248/241 BJ, November 22, 1851.
158 Robinson, "Reconsidering the Theory."
159 Kennedy, *Last Blank Spaces*, 243.
160 Lester and Dussart, *Colonization*, 225–75.
161 Russell, "Citizens of the World? Jane Franklin's Transnational Fantasies," 195–208.
162 Elce, *As Affecting the Fate*, 12–13.
163 Hilary M. Carey, *Empire of Hell: Religion and the Campaign to End Convict Transportation in the British Empire, 1788*-1875 (Cambridge: Cambridge University Press, 2019), 220. See also Alison Alexander, *Tasmania vs the British Empire: The Battle to End Convict Transportation* (Hobart: Forty South Press, 2022); Reid, *Gender, Crime and Empire*, 204–54; Reynolds, *A History of Tasmania*, 119–36.
164 Franklin had opposed probation from the beginning. Fitzpatrick, *Franklin in Tasmania*, 229.
165 Reid, *Gender Crime and Empire*, 211.
166 See Boyce, *Van Diemen's Land*, 237–40.
167 Reid, *Gender, Crime and Empire*, 204-246.
168 For a detailed discussion of the petition, see Stevens, *Me Write Myself*, 260–331.
169 For the "compact," see Lester, *Imperial Networks*, 115, for the refusal to be associated with slaves or convicts, see Reynolds, *Fate of a Free People*, 7–16; Van Toorn, *Writing*, 2–3, 119–22.
170 Stevens, *Me Write Myself*, 253–57; UTAS Library S&RMC, W7/34, 2, Quaker Collection, Robert Clark to George Washington Walker, April 3, 1846.
171 Perry, *Colonial Relations*, 78.
172 Stevens, *Me Write Myself*, 284–5, De Costa "Identity," see also Lester and Laidlaw, *Indigenous Communities and Settler Colonialism*.

173 Mar, "Imperial Literacy," 1.
174 "His Excellency the Lieutenant Governor's Speech," *Guardian, or, True Friend of Tasmania*, July 24, 1847, 2; TNA CO 280/195, AJCP Reel 544, 302, 305.
175 "The New Reign of Terror," *Launceston Examiner (Tas.: 1842-1899)*, September 25, 1847, 4.
176 TNA CO 280/195, AJCP Reel 544, 302, 305.
177 See L. Russell, *Roving Mariners*.
178 The best survey remains Susan Chamberlain's unpublished PhD thesis, *The Hobart Whaling Industry, 1830-1900*. La Trobe University, 1988. See also Bockstoce, *Whales, Ice and Men*, 22-4.
179 Tom Lowenstein, *Ancient Land, Sacred Whale: The Inuit Hunt and Its Rituals* (London: Bloomsbury, 1993); Ernest S. Burch, Jr, *The Iñupiaq Eskimo Nations of Northwest Alaska* (Fairbanks: University of Alaska Press, 1998).
180 The presence of the "Greenland" whales was understood as a hopeful sign for the rescue of Franklin and evidence of an open polar sea. "The Arctic Ocean," *The Hobart Town Advertiser*, May 8, 1849, 4. "Whale Fishery in the Arctic Ocean," *Colonial Times*, July 3, 1849, 4.
181 In 1851, for example, the log of the Hobart whaler *Litherland* indicates that they spoke with at least seven whalers from Hobart in Bering Sea. TA CRO82/1/3, Log, Litherland (barque), to Bering Strait, Capt. Davis, owner Charles Seal, December 27, 1850-November 7, 1851; TA CUS36/1/497, departure record for the *Litherland*, CUS36/1/190, departure record for the *Emu*. For multiethnic crews, see Russell, *Roving Mariners*; for convicts (especially Americans) on American whaling vessels, see Cassandra Pybus and Hamish Maxwell-Stewart, *American Citizens, British Slaves: Yankee Political Prisoners in an Australian Penal Colony, 1839-1850* (Carlton South: Melbourne University Press, 2002), 160-1, 170-1.
182 Burns and Skemp, *Van Diemen's Land Correspondents*, 111-12.
183 Alexander, *Tasmania*, 159, 167-73.
184 Royal Society of Tasmania, "Proceedings of the Monthly Meetings of The Royal Society for February to December 1852," *Papers and Proceedings of the Royal Society of Tasmania* 2, no. 2 (1853): 308-9; Royal Society of Tasmania, 'Proceedings of the Monthly Meetings of The Royal Society for January to December, 1853', *Papers and Proceedings of the Royal Society of Tasmania* 2, no. 3 (1854): 490. For the ritual significance of these objects, see Jean-Loup Rousselot, William W. Fitzhugh and Aron Crowell, "Maritime Economies of the North Pacific Rim," in *Crossroads of Continents: Cultures of Siberia and Alaska*, ed. William W. Fitzhugh and Aron Crowell (Washington, DC and London: Smithsonian Institution Press, 1988), 163-9.
185 Royal Society of Tasmania, "Proceedings of the Monthly Meetings of the Royal Society for February to December 1852," 482.
186 Ibid., 335; for J. B. Davis's collaboration with Thomas Bateman, see Deborah Harlan, "Thomas Bateman, *Crania Britannica*, and Archaeological Chronology," *European Journal of Archaeology* 21, no. (June 1, 2017): 1-21.
187 J. Milligan to W. J. Hooker, August 18, 1849, in Burns and Skemp, *Van Diemen's Land Correspondents*, 112-13.
188 John West, *A History of Tasmania, with Copious Information Respecting the Colonies of New South Wales, Victoria, South Australia &c., &c., &c.* ed. A. G. L. Shaw (London and Sydney: Angus & Robertson Publishers, 1971), 174.
189 For a description of Meredith's work, see Gates, "Those Who Drew and Those Who Wrote," 194-8.

190 Meredith, *My Home in Tasmania*, 30.
191 TA NS123/1/126, Joseph Henry Kay, letters to John and Maria Meredith, 1849-1871; TA NS37, Records of the Rossbank Observatory, John Walker's Mill, Bank of VDL and the Derwent Bank.
192 *Launceston Examiner*, November 24, 1852, 5.
193 "Lady Franklin," *Launceston Examiner*, June 27, 1849, 6; "Latest from England," *The Hobart Town Advertiser*, March 8, 1850, 4. "The Arctic Expedition," *The Hobart Town Advertiser*, August 14, 1849, 3; "The Arctic Expedition," *The Courier*, October 6, 1849, 2.
194 "British Press," *The Courier*, March 16, 1850, 4; "Sir John Franklin," *The Britannia and Trades' Advocate*, July 18, 1850, 4; "English and Foreign Extracts," *Colonial Times*, August 13, 1850, 4; "The Grinnell Exploring Expedition," *The Hobart Town Advertiser*, October 1, 1850, 2.
195 "Latest News of Sir John Franklin," *Colonial Times*, April 11, 1851, 3; "Miscellaneous," *Launceston Examiner*, November 12, 1851, 3.
196 SPRI MS 248/228 BJ, Sophia Cracroft, Notes on Letters Sent, 1844-1856; TA NS123/1/126, Joseph Henry Kay, Letters to John and Maria Meredith, 1849-1871.
197 TA NS3/1/5, Miscellaneous letters, Bishop Nixon, 1842-1850.
198 TA NS3016, Letters of John Hepburn to John Mitchell, 1851-1853.
199 SPRI MS 248/228 BJ, Sophia Cracroft, Notes on Letters Sent, 1844-1856.
200 TA NS 1004, Correspondence of Mary and John Price.
201 SPRI MS 248/228 BJ; TA NS 3677/1/3, James Clark Ross to Alexander John Smith, October 7, 1852; Pascoe, *A Roving Commission*, 229, 271, 278–9.
202 "Family Notices," *The Courier*, August 7, 1852, 2. Ross, *Hunters on the Track*, 208, 306.
203 See Snow's account of his journey to Victoria in "Search for Franklin by Behring's Straits," *The Courier*, March 31, 1853, 2.
204 ALMFA, Joseph Henry Kay, Letter, 1852, June 22, H. M. Observatory, Hobart Town, to John Dobson.
205 "Further Search for Sir John Franklin," *The Courier*, May 22, 1852, 2. It was reprinted several times in Hobart and in Launceston.
206 "Another Expedition for Sir John Franklin," *Colonial Times*, June 22, 3.
207 Reid, *Gender, Crime and Empire*, 211.
208 William Denison, *Varieties of Vice Regal Life*, ed. Richard Davis and Stefan Petrow (Sandy Bay: Tasmanian Historical Research Association, 2004), 181–3.
209 *The Hobart Town Advertiser*, July 2, 1852, 2.
210 *The Hobart Town Advertiser*, July 2, 1852, 2; "Sir John Franklin," *The Courier*, July 3, 1852, 2.
211 "To the Editor of the Tasmanian Colonist," *The Tasmanian Colonist*, July 5, 1852, 2.
212 "Sir John Franklin," *Colonial Times and Tasmanian*, July 6, 1852, 2.
213 "List of Subscriptions in Aid of Capt. Beatson's Expedition which has Proceeded in Search of Sir John Franklin," *The Courier (Hobart, Tas: 1840-1859)*, August 21, 1852, 4.
214 "Legislative Council," *The Courier*, September 25, 1852, 3.
215 DRO D8760/F/FLJ/1/5, J. H. Kay to Jane Franklin, October 1, 1852.
216 SPRI MS 248/2-6/2, Jane Franklin to the Honorable the Legislative Council of Van Diemen's Land, London, May 6, 1853.
217 "Local Intelligence: The Franklin Fund," *Colonial Times*, November 23, 1852, 2.
218 Owen Beattie and John Geiger, *Frozen in Time: The Fate of the Franklin Expedition*, 5th ed. (Vancouver and Berkeley: Greystone Books, 2014), 62, 178–90.

219 SPRI MS 248/110, Copies of letters written and received, and notes, on expeditions in search of Sir John Franklin by Lady Franklin, Sophia Cracroft, February 7 to April 3, 1853.
220 SPRI MS 248/110, March 11, 1853.
221 Quoted in William Barr, "'The Cold of Valparaiso': The Disintegration of William Kennedy's Second Franklin Search Expedition, 1853–1854," *Polar Record* 34, no. 190 (1998): 203–18. See also the Kennedy, Cracroft and Franklin correspondence in MA MG2 C1.
222 Mar, "Imperial Literacy," 1–2.
223 Henry Rink, *Danish Greenland: Its People and Its Products*, ed. Robert Brown (London: Henry S. King, 1877), 259.
224 Thomas Boyles Murray, *Kalli, The Esquimaux Christian: A Memoir* (New York: General Protestant Episcopal Sunday School Union and Church Book Society, 1861); DRO D8760/F/OBJ/3, Mithina's doll; D8760/F/OBJ/5, drawing of the Anchor ship and polar bear in letter from "Kalli," St. Augustine's College [Canterbury], May 11, 1853; Eleanor's Iroquois doll is on loan to the National Maritime Museum, Greenwich, NMM Object ID AAA3777.

6

Full Circles

Relics, Stories, and Silences

When John Franklin's ships entered their winter harbor at Beechey Island in 1845, it was the beginning of an extraordinarily hard few years. Temperatures fluctuated, the ice receded in some areas and accumulated in others, the summers were short and cold, and the winters severe and colder, and animals behaved erratically. Stories of starvation and desperation were retold for many years among the Netsilingmiut and the Utkusiksalingmiut at the mouth of the Back River.[1] When *Erebus* and *Terror* were abandoned off the coast of King William Island in 1848, they became new local resources, helping some people to survive. When their spars, wood, metal, and other objects entered Inuit economies, they were linked to stories of the strange people to whom they had once belonged, and the experiences of desperation that they shared with many Inuit. Some of these objects were later traded to *qallunaat*, who returned to their own homelands with stories gathered and translated by other Inuit interpreters, acquiring more meanings along the way.

These repurposed relics, with their shared histories of suffering and survival, demonstrated the power of silence, how it could be filled up by stories and rumors, generate more, and perpetuate itself at the same time. As they responded to the relics, people from many backgrounds wove and rewove evidence into new stories, laying claim to their own credibility and undermining that of others as they sought to define the "truth" and who could tell it. Both explorers' families and Indigenous people were central to this process, looking into the past and anticipating the future, trying to ensure that stories woven out of silence were durable, if not exactly permanent. As the Netsilingmiut had remade the fragments of the *Erebus* and *Terror*, explorers' families and supporters also repurposed old stories into new narratives that would survive them in biographies and archives. This concluding chapter traces some of those efforts of the Arctic circles to define what was truth and what was fiction, to elaborate and circulate what they believed and hoped to be true, and how those echoes and silences are heard in the present.

Years of Horror: 1845–54

In 1845, there were good relationships between the Ugjulingmiut of King William Island and the Adelaide Peninsula, and their neighbors, the Utkusiksalingmiut of the Back River, the Arvilingjuarmiut of Pelly Bay, and the Netsilingmiut of the Boothia Peninsula.² They were among the most isolated groups within the Canadian archipelago, though they did have trading and kinship links to their neighbors. But things changed quickly after 1845. There were years without summer, when seals and caribou left their usual haunts. The years 1846–8 were particularly bad. Netsilingmiut hunters would later recall that they "never knew such very cold weather—there was no summer between two winters."³ Several generations later, people at Great Fish River remembered a "year of horror," of blizzards, extreme cold, starvation, and cannibalism.⁴ These years badly unsettled the region. The Netsilingmiut of the Boothia Peninsula had helped the Rosses to survive in the early 1830s, and had been salvaging wood and metal from the wreck of the *Victory* for many years, helping them to gain just a little bit of an edge.⁵ As the climate grew more severe, the Netsilingmiut began to expand their territory, pushing the Ugjulingmiut away from King William Island and further to the south, toward the mouth of the Back River and into Utkusiksalingmiut territory.⁶ The survivors of the Franklin expedition were also heading for the Back River, and both advancing and retreating Inuit groups kept them under close surveillance. Sometimes they helped the *qallunaat*, but more often they kept prudently away, investigating their camps only after most of the *qallunaat* had died.⁷ Stories circulated for generations about the strange behavior of the men who were so filthy, helpless, and strange, and seemed as if they were not fully human.⁸ Sometime after 1848, both Ugjulingmiut and Netsilingmiut investigated HMS *Erebus* and *Terror* before they sank. Like the *Victory*, these wrecks enabled Netsilingmiut to survive the unstable and severe years that followed, holding onto and expanding their territory. By the mid-1850s, Netsilingmiut had settled along the eastern shores of King William Island, and according to Francis McClintock, each family held something—wood, metal, silver, or cloth—from the wreckage of Franklin's expedition.⁹

The Orcadian explorer John Rae and the Keewatin Inuk translator William Ouligbuck Jr. both made their careers amid this larger crisis. Rae had been employed by the Hudson's Bay Company (HBC) since 1833; had lived among fur trade families in Orkney in his childhood (including the Kennedys and Isbisters); and had worked with Métis, Cree, Ojibwe, Chipewyan, and Inuit during his long career. He was a skilled traveler and physician, known for his readiness to adopt useful Indigenous or European technology (from snowshoes to "Halkett's Boat Cloak," a traveling cloak which was also an inflatable boat), methods which had earned him the Royal Geographical Society (RGS) Founder's Gold Medal in 1852. William Ouligbuck's father, Ouligbuck Sr., had been trained as an interpreter on the second Land Arctic Expedition (LAE) in 1825–7, and he and the Inuk interpreter Tattannoeuck/Augustus worked together for many years at Churchill and York Factory until Tattannoeuck's death in 1833, after which Ouligbuck served as Dease and Simpson's interpreter in the HBC's attempt on the Northwest Passage in 1839 (see Chapter 2 and Timeline 2).¹⁰ He tried to bring his son William into the same kind of work. William had a highly mobile childhood, between expeditions and forts, during which he learned to speak English fluently (Rae claimed "more correctly than one-half of the lower classes in England or Scotland") in addition to Cree.¹¹ But he was also rebellious. Rae privately complained that he was prone to bouts of "sulkiness," "falsehood and misconduct," and described him in 1848 as "one of the greatest rascals unhung."¹²

During the Ouligbuck family's association with Rae, stories of starvation were never far away and were often deeply personal. Their Keewatin kin, to the north of Churchill, suffered terribly during the subsistence crises of the 1830s and 1840s. The elder Ouligbuck frequently traveled back and forth from Churchill to camps with extra dogs and provisions, sometimes bringing starving people into Churchill. On their expedition with Rae in 1846, they were stretched for food, but not so badly as the Ugjulingmiut and the Franklin survivors to the west. They heard about the unrest and hunger around Boothia and King William Island through trading partners. In particular, they were told that the Netsilingmiut were becoming increasingly hostile toward strangers, and to be very careful and not to trespass on their territory. In 1848–9, the Ouligbucks joined Rae and Richardson again on their Franklin search, but when they returned to Churchill, they found that their kin north of Whale Cove were starving.[13] In 1852, the elder Ouligbuck died, but his son continued to work for Rae as a guide and a translator.

When Rae and William Ouligbuck advanced toward Boothia again in 1853, they were again told stories that hinted at the ruptures, violence, and unpredictability of the region to the west. It is impossible to know with certainty, but it seems likely that William Ouligbuck interpreted this intelligence in light of what he knew already—that hungry times were causing serious instability and that it was prudent to be cautious. In the spring of 1854, near the Boothia Peninsula, they encountered a small group of Netsilingmiut who discouraged them from traveling further west. One man, known to them as Innookpoozhezhuk, later approached them wearing a gold cap band that Rae recognized as from a naval officer's cap. This man had a number of articles—cutlery, medals, knives, wood—which were clearly British. Over several days they had many exchanges, out of which a story emerged that the articles had come through the trading networks, but had originated with a group of about forty *qallunaat* who had starved to death at the mouth of the Back River some years before. Rae purchased some of the material and wrote a report for the HBC, who sent it to the Admiralty, who leaked it to the press on October 24, 1854. It included the following passage: "from the contents of the kettles, it is evidence that our wretched countrymen were driven to the last dread alternative—cannibalism—as a means of prolonging existence."[14] Years later, Innookpoozhezhuk would go himself to the place where the dead men's camp was, and describe in detail to the American explorer Charles Francis Hall the evidence of cannibalism—boots filled with cooked flesh, bones broken for the marrow, skulls with holes in them—later confirmed by an archaeological expedition in the 1990s.[15] But in 1854, such stories would be understood by some as unconfirmed hearsay, and by others as slander.

"A Domesticity of Blood and Blubber": Relics and Reputations

When Rae's news arrived in Britain in October 1854, it was immediately wrapped up with other narratives of war, disease, senseless suffering, and bureaucratic bungling. The Crimean War had begun nearly a year earlier, and had largely put a stop to official naval expeditions. In January 1854, the Admiralty had removed the names of the officers on the *Erebus* and *Terror* from the active duty list, effectively acknowledging their deaths. The Gells put on mourning and asked for Franklin's will to be proved.

Jane Franklin put on pinks and greens in what Francis Spufford has called a "sartorial protest" and wrote to William Kennedy and Alexander Isbister that Eleanor was an "unnatural daughter."[16] The public had little appetite for further Arctic expeditions—though there was enthusiasm for William Penny's scheme to establish a shore whaling station on Baffin Island to evangelize Inuit and to alleviate British dependence on Russian whale oil.[17] Sir Edward Belcher's Arctic Squadron returned in September, leaving five ships behind in the ice, and Belcher faced a court-martial. October 1854 brought news on the electric telegraph of the siege of Sebastopol, the Crimean plague of cholera, and the Charge of the Light Brigade. Rae's report was printed alongside a letter detailing the mortality at the hospital in Scutari, and the dead of the expedition were enrolled alongside those of soldiers in the Crimea, "brave men battling against fearful odds, and dying in the performance of their duty."[18] William Simpkinson wrote to Eleanor Gell, "would to Heaven that all this senseless murdering & slaughtering were over! I am sorry Sebastopol was ever attempted . . . [it] was not worth all this misery—only worthy of Red Indians or Esquimaux."[19]

The "relics," meanwhile, were placed on display in the Painted Hall at the Royal Naval College at Greenwich, where Horatio Nelson's shattered body and, more recently, the Duke of Wellington's corpse had lain in state (Figure 6.1).[20] Illustrated weeklies published huge reproductions of silver spoons with Franklin and Crozier's crests, Franklin's medals, a bone-handled knife scratched with the name of able seaman James Hickey.[21] But the relics were also perplexing. The literary scholar Adriana Craciun argues that they were exceedingly difficult for Victorians to categorize. On the one hand, they were treated and understood as sacred, as relics of those who were martyrs to science, but they were also understood as anthropological displays and commercial objects. Items designed to carry British civilization and commerce to the ends of the earth had been adapted and repurposed by Inuit for their own survival when their original owners had perished, and so the question always hung in the air—to whom

Figure 6.1 "The Franklin Relics" originally published in the *Illustrated London News*, November 4, 1854. Universal History Archive/Universal Images Group via Getty Images.

did they belong? Could and should they be categorized? And what did they say about narratives of progress and improvement?[22]

Among this uneasiness, there grew considerable doubt about the Inuit who had traded the items, and questions quickly arose about how they came by the artifacts, whether it was through trade or by violence, and why they had been modified. Accusations of theft and murder accompanied questions about whether Inuit (including Ouligbuck) had "secret knowledge" of the disaster, kept back for their own purposes, and circulating beyond the reach of British intelligence. It was a kind of speculation made possible by distant glimpses of Inuit trade networks and regional instability, viewed through a prism of midcentury racial anxiety. A letter to the *Times* signed "Medicus" suggested that "it is more reasonable to suppose that our men were murdered, and that the possessors of the plate were themselves the authors of the foul deed."[23] The *Athenaeum* stated that Inuit "have no sense of truth. Like all savages, they lie without scruple."[24] This marked a key departure from the ambivalent authority that had been granted to Inuit testimony over the previous few years. After all, although Usky's testimony in 1849 and the map he drew at Mittimatalik were unsupported by relics, six naval ships had been sent in 1850 to check up on his statements. In 1851, the voiceless relics from Beechey Island stood in tension with Adam Beck's collected testimony about burned ships on Greenland's west coast. Neither was rejected out of hand, and in fact Beck's testimony was so potent that it required massive campaigning and the elaboration of the idea of the "open polar sea" to suppress it, and several expeditions to disprove it. In both cases, Arctic veterans drew on their long experience of dependence on Inuit and Dene maps and asserted that they "never knew an Indian or an Esquimaux tracing to fail."[25]

The different relationship to this Netsilingmiut testimony came down, partly, to hardening attitudes at midcentury that would become still more ossified after the Sepoy Mutiny of 1857. It also reflected a growing disenchantment with imperial humanitarianism and its objects of compassion, especially after the failure of the Niger Expedition in 1841 (see Chapter 5). The Arctic circles around Jane Franklin picked up on and effectively repurposed both of these developments, despite (or because) some of them belonged to these increasingly marginalized and criticized groups. Drawing on tactics and language they had developed over decades, from their experience as social reformers (Scoresby), humanitarian activists (Gurney), science writers and explorers (Bowdich Lee), and Indigenous activists (Isbister), they had made the absent men of the Franklin expedition into deserving subjects of British philanthropy. They had also helped Jane Franklin remake her public image, from a "man in petticoats" who meddled in Tasmanian colonial politics, into a loving wife who was compelled to adopt a public role in Britain by the Admiralty's failures in the Arctic. It was a narrative that celebrated mid-Victorian domestic ideals of chivalrous manhood and devoted femininity, ideologies of progress and improvement, self-help, Christianity, and civilization. It was successful and contagious, involving the British public in Jane Franklin's private drama, wrapping them up in anxiety and speculation in the pauses between pulses of information. This included the Tasmanian settlers who had once excoriated Jane as a "man in petticoats," and now sought to share in the glow of that narrative, as they cast themselves as virtuous, vulnerable, and devoted to both the pursuit of knowledge and the protection of their families.

The touchstone for the British reaction to Rae's report has long been Charles Dickens's "Lost Arctic Voyagers" essays in *Household Words*. In a series of articles (which some authors have suggested were prompted by Jane Franklin), Dickens developed Arctic exploration as an exemplar of British domestic virtue which could not and must not be sullied. He saw the Netsilingmiut testimony of cannibalism as a direct threat, a potential collapse of civilization into savagery.[26] This was not an isolated event. Rather, it was part of a trajectory of Dickens's writing that not only criticized humanitarianism abroad at the expense of philanthropy at "home" but was also deeply unnerved by the specter of civilizational contamination in the heart of the empire. T. J. Tallie has argued that for Dickens, the highly visible presence of Indigenous people in London threatened the idea of the city as an imperial center that was inherently "separate and above Indigenous existence."[27] From his reactions to Ojibwe performers and emissaries in 1843, Zulu dancers in 1853, and the Indian Mutiny in "The Perils of Certain English Prisoners" in 1857, a continuous theme stretched across Dicken's writing that characterized the hardening racial discourse of this extended midcentury moment—that the "noble savage" was, as he wrote in 1853, "something highly desirable to be civilised off the face of the earth . . . cruel, false, thievish, murderous; addicted more or less to grease, entrails, and beastly customs."[28]

In "The Lost Arctic Voyagers," Dickens reprised and rehearsed these polemics, arguing that English sailors, and especially officers, were incapable of cannibalism. He bolstered this with some of the most gruesome extracts from Franklin's narrative of his first disastrous expedition, emphasizing Franklin's profound suffering from starvation, and how he found comfort and sustenance in religion. Indigenous people like Michel Teroahaute, he argued, were certainly capable of reaching the "last resource," and though he discussed at length how Richardson had executed Michel, he did not mention how Richardson and Hepburn had both admitted to accidental cannibalism.[29] He was particularly concerned with what Rae's report would do to the memory of Franklin, arguing that "the noble conduct and example of such men . . . outweighs by the weight of the whole universe the chatter of a gross handful of uncivilised people, with a domesticity of blood and blubber."[30] He also took a swipe at the imperial humanitarians, writing,

> There are pious persons who, in their practice, with a strange inconsistency, claim for every child born to civilization all innate depravity, and for every savage born to the woods and wilds all innate virtue. We believe every savage to be in his heart covetous, treacherous, and cruel; and we have yet to learn what knowledge the white man—lost, houseless, shipless, apparently forgotten by his race, plainly famine-stricken, weak, frozen, helpless and dying—has of the gentleness of Esquimaux nature.[31]

Even as he attacked humanitarian optimism, Dickens reprised the humanitarian argument developed by Arctic circles over the previous eight years: the missing men were vulnerable and deserving subjects, and the Admiralty was obliged to rescue them, having sent them out in the service of science and empire. But above all, the "Lost Arctic Voyagers" essays indulged in the kind of speculation that had become very familiar during the Franklin searches, in which Britons tried to reckon with information from Indigenous sources who traveled widely in places they could not reach, that circulated in blank spaces they could only fill up with their own imaginations.

Rae responded to Dickens in the same journal, arguing that William Ouligbuck was a skilled multilingual interpreter who spoke English better than most Englishmen, and that in any event, Rae was skilled at detecting deception. Despite his doctor's training, he claimed, as William Penny had before him, that he was a man of action unaccustomed to wars of words, still less so with a writer like Dickens.[32] Yet he was still widely criticized for his lack of feeling, as he had been a few weeks earlier when he made a testy public rejoinder to an explorer's relative in the *Times*.[33] Jane and Sophia suggested that Rae's sudden fame had changed him, from a hearty, capable, unassuming man to a self-interested fortune-seeker. Having long depended on his dispatches to support their own authority, Sophia now wrote to Scoresby that Rae would not brook criticism or discussion, saying, "I must honestly tell you, that [Rae's] head appears to be completely turned by being for the moment a lion. He is not like the same man, and seems to think that no one has a right to make even a representation for the sake of fair argument, & getting at the truth."[34]

"They Forged the Last Link with Their Lives": Memories and Monopolies

The suspicion of Rae's report and the Netsilingmiut testimony it contained is often attributed to Rae's employment with the HBC, and his background as an Orcadian. It has been argued that his credibility was seriously undermined by the fact that he lived closely with Indigenous people, used Indigenous methods of travel, had Indigenous companions, and came to their defense.[35] His ostracism from the polar fraternity after 1854 is attributed to both his misfortune in being the first to hear Inuit stories of British cannibalism, to friction between the HBC and the Royal Navy in polar exploration that dated back to Franklin's first expedition, and to English distrust of Orcadians.[36] These things are certainly true, but like so much else about the Franklin archive, the attention we pay to them—particularly to their role in the drama around the missing expedition—tends to obscure other actors and motives. This last case study looks at how criticism of Rae was linked to criticism of the HBC monopoly, how both criticisms intertwined with Jane Franklin's own attempts to secure a monopoly over her husband's memory, and what roles men like William Kennedy and Alexander Kennedy Isbister, who were both Indigenous and Orcadian, played in that process.

After Rae's report, two questions hung in the air: what role should the HBC and its agents play in solving the mystery and securing Franklin's memory, and what role should they play in the future governance of Britain's North American territories? These were accompanied by the question of who should receive rewards for the discovery of the Northwest Passage and for the discovery of Franklin's fate. These linked questions illustrate the ongoing collision between Indigenous interlocutors, vernacular agents like fur traders and whalers, humanitarian networks, colonial governance, and the memory-making of explorers' families. They show how the ambiguous authority of both Indigenous actors and explorers' families played out amid the absence of records from the expedition, and how both were wrapped up in one of the great fictions of Franklin's memory—that he or his men had discovered the Northwest Passage, and, as his old companion John Richardson put it, "forged the last link with their lives." At the same time, the arguments in favor of more rescue expeditions, many of which rested on the notion that the British could easily survive and thrive in the Arctic, now became entangled with official discourse around the future of Rupert's Land and the Barren Grounds, and whether Indigenous people and Britons could or should live there, together or apart.

In 1855, the HBC sent an expedition under Chief Factor James Anderson down the Back River to verify the Netsilingmiut testimony collected by Ouligbuck and Rae. Jane Franklin was keen to retrieve records and establish timelines, yet she did not want this duty to fall to the HBC or to its officers. She argued that a new expedition should be led by a naval officer because of its "peculiar and almost sacred character" that required the expedition leader to act as chief mourner in lieu of the explorers' relatives. Part of those funereal duties, she argued, was "searching for & collecting and keeping inviolate those official records of the Expedition so interesting to the public, and the private letters & papers so precious to their surviving friends." This person, she argued should be "one in whom we can place entire trust, rather than a distant stranger!"[37] Anderson sent Jane Franklin highly detailed accounts from the field about his disintegrating birchbark canoes and his aggressive questioning of Inuit to determine whether they had seen books, bodies, graves, or ships.[38] Such detailed and dramatic reports would have been prime currency in the sociable worlds of polite science of Jane Franklin's youth, and would certainly have accorded both author and recipient a degree of credibility and authority. But to Jane and Sophia, Anderson's reports only confirmed his lack of zeal. Sophia wrote to Richardson after receiving one dispatch that "it is a very disappointing account, and one which we were certainly not prepared for" and that they had read it to John Hepburn who "was much struck with the desponding tone."[39] Sophia wrote to Scoresby that though they never expected much from the expedition, "we were not prepared to find disaster & utter failure predicted even before they started, by the very Commander himself."[40]

In 1855, Captain Robert McClure stepped forward to claim the parliamentary award for completing the Northwest Passage on foot in 1853 together with Samuel Gurney Cresswell. John Richardson wrote a letter to the *Times* in response, arguing that the priority of discovery lay with "the 40 determined men whose bones are blanching near the mouth of the Great Fish River." Drawing on the Netsilingmiut evidence and Franklin's correspondence, Richardson placed the survivors in the blank space on the map between the territory covered by earlier overland expeditions, long before McClure and Cresswell traversed their passage far to the north.[41]

Jane and Sophia went to the *Times* to get extra copies of Richardson's letter to circulate among their contacts.[42] Jane wrote to Richardson, "I have always secretly felt exactly as you have expressed respecting the discovery of a NW passage which must have been made by those who were found in the neighbourhood of the Gt Fish River, but I felt it was for others to recognize & not for me to bring forward."[43] Sophia wrote to Kennedy that there was wide support for "my Uncle's claim" to the passage. She wrote, "I need not say that we have always felt that it was so, ever since Rae returned, but felt that it was not for us to seek . . . justice" and that "it is considered very bad in McClure to maintain his own claim w^h was no longer tenable after Rae's return."[44] A few months later, Jane asked Richardson to expand on his views by writing a biography of Franklin for the *Encyclopaedia Britannica*. Sophia sent him an enormous collection of materials about his friend's life (including the pamphlet *Some Passages in the History of Van Diemen's Land*, which the Franklins had written to exculpate themselves from the charge of "petticoat government" in Tasmania).[45]

In his biography, Richardson praised Franklin's "cheerful buoyancy of mind . . . sustained by religious principle of a depth known only to his most intimate friends even in the most gloomy times." In Tasmania, he argued, Franklin had exhibited "independent political principles," "strict honor and integrity," "benevolence of character," and had promoted colonial science; and he bemoaned the factionalism of settlers and the Arthur clique as "hostile" and "subversive." In memory of his closest friend, he rehearsed the principal elements of an "authorized" biography that, like published narratives, dispensed with the ambiguities of polar travel and colonial governance, power struggles with Indigenous authorities like Akaitcho, and reliance on Indigenous intelligence and pathways. However, those ambiguities and struggles were still present, for Richardson did not question the credibility of the Netsilingmiut testimony gathered by Rae. Indeed, he made it the cornerstone of his argument that Franklin's crew had discovered the Northwest Passage. Franklin himself, he argued, could not have survived so long, and there were no reports of an older man among the survivors. Moreover, he pointed out, Franklin would never have willingly headed for the Barren Grounds, writing, "no one knew better than he the fatal result of an attempt to cross that wide expanse of barren ground lying between the mouth of the Great Fish River and . . . Great Slave Lake." The only reason someone would head toward such an inhospitable region, he speculated, was to complete the Northwest Passage, which he argued they had done, and so "forged the last link with their lives."[46] Jane and Sophia scooped up at least fifty copies of the article, which they sent throughout England, to Tasmania, and to the United States.[47] Meanwhile, in New York, Samuel Morse published a map entitled "Chart showing the Recent Search for the North-West Passage" (Map 4). Bristling with names and places associated with the Franklin search, along with the tracks of Royal Navy and American expeditions, the map was also decorated with scenes of death, like the graves at Beechey Island. A discreet dot between the mouth of the Back River and the Adelaide Peninsula marked the spot where Netsilingmiut testimony placed the survivors, labeled, "Here it is supposed Franklin & his party perished in 1850."[48]

In 1856, Anderson's expedition returned, without having found any documents from the expedition. However, the Netsilingmiut testimony Anderson had gathered confirmed Rae's original report. Soon afterward, Rae attempted to claim the Admiralty's £10,000 reward for the discovery of Franklin's fate. In response, Alexander Isbister composed a pamphlet entitled "Arctic Rewards and their Claimants" in which he combined Jane Franklin's criticisms and his own into a resounding critique not only of Rae's claims to the reward but also of the HBC's administration in general. In doing so, he rehearsed arguments that he and his uncles William and Roderick Kennedy would use a year later in their submissions to the Select Committee on the HBC.

In his pamphlet, Isbister argued that Rae was ineligible for a reward because he had failed to follow up and confirm the Netsilingmiut testimony by traveling to the site of the disaster.[49] He argued that Rae had been misled by Ouligbuck, "who had doubtless seen and learned more at the camp than he chose to communicate," and that he should have interviewed the Inuit personally.[50] He quoted an interview in a Toronto newspaper with one of Rae's other Indigenous companions, the Ojibwe man Thomas Mistegan. Mistegan had gone to the Netsilingmiut camp and later reported that he had been told that "perhaps one or two of the men may still be alive and amongst the Esquimaux" and also that "the ship was a great godsend to these people; and they now all have good sleds spears, canoes etc of oak wood."[51]

Isbister then turned to a criticism of the HBC whose "jealously guarded territory embraced the entire field of coast upon which the imperilled parties would take refuge." The HBC, he argued, was "unfettered, encouraged, nay, enjoined" to solve the mystery, but had only produced Anderson's "meager and unsatisfactory report" confirming Rae's original conclusions. Isbister not only argued that "the evidence of one HB *employe* fails in establishing that of the other" but charged the company with a systemic failure of philanthropy.[52] He argued that the HBC could have simply sent an expedition to the mouth of the Mackenzie, the Coppermine, and the Back Rivers each year, and so perhaps saved the expedition's stragglers. They were, he said, "freely and liberally supplied with public money for the execution of so sacred a trust, urged by every motive of humanity and honour to fulfil." The result, he said, was "A paltry expedition of 3 birchbark canoes . . . and few meagre driblets of apocryphal information from a camp of Esquimaux women, communicated by signs and eked out by imagination." He added, "The Esquimaux are the sole authorities on which Dr. Rae does or can rely—sole discoverers and sole depositaries [sic] of all the information we possess; and in the name of common justice, if they can but free themselves from the charge of murder, let the reward go to them, if anywhere."[53] Sophia recommended that Isbister should take out notices in the newspapers that should recommend the perusal of "a very able pamphlet on the subject, called Arctic Rewards and their claimants."[54]

Isbister reprised some of his key arguments against the HBC a year later in his testimony to the Select Committee, particularly the charge that the company and its agents were morally unfit as civilizers. As Adele Perry has argued, the Select Committee was convened not only to evaluate 200 years of the HBC's monopoly but also to design the specificities of the dispossession of Indigenous people to make way for white settlement.[55] The Aborigines' Protection Society (APS), including Isbister and Dr. Richard King, advocated for the annexation of Rupert's Land to Canada as the "best remedy for Company rule," one that would open the territory up to settlement.[56] Perry considers the Select Committee to be evidence of Isbister's labors and successes, from his early pamphlets about the company to his presentation of the Red River petition against the monopoly in 1847.[57] Laidlaw points out that it was also a family affair, spurred by William Kennedy's efforts on his return to Red River from Valparaiso in 1855 to champion Salteaux rights. He organized a deposition from the powerful

Anishinaabe chief Peguis, and a petition of 600 signatures from Red River Métis against company rule.[58]

The committee might also be considered as an outgrowth of Isbister's work on the Franklin search. Between 1850 and 1857, while within Jane Franklin's orbit, Isbister was at the center of his own nexus of information, blending his observations of white settlement, penal colonies, and the HBC together with the popular arguments made in support of Franklin rescue expeditions. At the height of the Tasmanian agitation to end transportation in 1850, for example, he had argued that the Barren Grounds ought to replace Tasmania and become a British Siberia.[59] The harsh climate would not only prevent convict escape, he argued, but, as Franklin had shown on his first expedition, it could transform men's souls. He targeted the region between Chipewyan and Inuit territories, the parts of the Barren Grounds understood to be an uninhabited no-man's-land (largely because of Franklin and Richardson's narratives). Isbister praised the Russian system of penal colonization, as one in which convicts were exiled, reformed, and extended the boundaries of the nation. But this could not be done under the supervision of a commercial company, he argued. It required the state's oversight to prevent abuses of Indigenous people and convicts, and so avoid a recurrence of the violence that had occurred in Tasmania twenty years before.[60]

Isbister was the only person who identified himself as an Indigenous man who testified in person to the committee. The others included the Arctic explorers Rae, Richardson, Back, King, and Governor George Simpson. They were asked to reflect upon not only their experiences with the HBC since 1819 but also the degree to which the HBC was committed to the improvement, relief, and civilization of Indigenous people. They were also asked whether there were feasible alternatives to the fur trade in Rupert's Land, including fisheries, whaling, and agriculture. This turned on access to the interior from northern waters, the navigability of the northern coasts for deep-draught ships, and the predictability and habitability of the climate in high latitudes—all questions that had been at the forefront of the Franklin search since 1848, but had also been central to exploration and Indigenous geopolitics in the region since Akaitcho brought them to the negotiating table with Franklin in 1820.

The testimony split into two groups, with Isbister and King forming one, and Rae, Richardson, and Back the other. Isbister and King argued that the HBC monopoly was inherently opposed to "improvement" and "civilization," preferring to keep Indians in a state of subservience and dependent upon alcohol, ammunition, and firearms. Both also argued that Rupert's Land was habitable and rich with opportunities for improvement, pointing to geological research on its rich alluvial ore deposits. In doing so, they frequently alluded to the arguments made for Franklin's probable survival in an open polar sea, both in terms of whether life could be sustained in high latitudes and whether or not Englishmen could thrive in the same country as Indians and Inuit. Their point was a vision of a shared future, in which Métis people could be in control of their own destiny and perhaps lead their own colonization of the lands to their north. It was a version, perhaps, of the Creole class in Russian America, the children of Siberian *promyshlenniki* (fur hunters) and Indigenous women who now comprised much of the colony's administrative staff, missionaries, priests, and some of its naval officers and explorers.[61] But it was at odds, as Perry has pointed out, with the commissioners' belief in the "known fact that the brown race disappears in proportion to the coming of the white race."[62] They never invoked the Tasmanian example explicitly, but it always lurked in the background of such statements as a specter of presumed extinction.

Rae, Richardson, and Back were more circumspect about whether the region could or should support colonization, whether by Britons or by Métis. As they gave their evidence, they all had to reflect on the starvation they had experienced and witnessed during their journeys at the end of the Little Ice Age. Rae said that "no person would go [to the boreal forest] to settle unless he were paid for it, and paid well."[63] Richardson reflected on his experiences of hunger during his first two expeditions with Franklin, questioned whether any Indigenous people in the region would be persuaded to embrace agriculture, and praised the HBC for alleviating famine.[64] Back's argument was that the Indians would be "almost decimated" without the HBC's intervention, and thought that the Indians had become dependent upon ammunition, which made them dependent upon the company, which put them at risk of starvation if ammunition was in short supply.[65]

Isbister's and Kennedy's advocacy before the Select Committee was one further glimpse of both men's complex positions as Indigenous activists and Arctic experts. As the terms of Canadian settlement and government changed and the power of the HBC shifted, both men wrestled with the implications of settler colonialism and Indigenous rights, Kennedy in Red River and Isbister in London. But their testimony, as well as that of the other Arctic explorers to the Select Committee in 1857, shows how the Franklin story was becoming entangled with Canadian governance and how that entanglement was partly shaped, and in very different ways, by Indigenous interlocutors. The questions and answers of the old explorers recalled histories of starvation, but the stories they chose to tell (or perhaps the stories they chose to remember) were of starving Yellowknives approaching HBC forts, not of starving Britons being rescued by Yellowknives. Both occurred, both were wrapped up in the ecological, political, and human disasters of the 1820s, but now one was leveraged above the other and linked to memories of Franklin.

Cairns, Statues, Archives, and Silences

In 1857, as Isbister, Rae, Richardson, and Back delivered their testimony to the Select Committee, Jane Franklin dispatched the *Fox* under the command of the naval captain Leopold McClintock. His instructions were to find the spot south of Cape Walker where, she claimed, she had always known the missing expedition to be located. In her instructions to McClintock, Jane wrote,

> I trust it may be in your power to confirm directly or inferentially the claims of my husband's expedition to the earliest discovery of The Passage, which, if Dr Rae's report be true (and the Government of our country has accepted (& rewarded it as such) these martyrs in a noble cause achieved at their last extremity after 5 long years of labour & Suffering, if not at an earlier period.[66]

In 1859, McClintock returned with a scrap of paper found in a cairn on King William Island, as well as a new collection of relics. Cairns are memory aids and navigational devices, important way markers that are, together with *inuksuit*, part of an animate landscape and a living archive in the Arctic. Many cairns and *inuksuit* had been demolished by Franklin searchers looking for records, but this cairn had been built by James Clark Ross in 1832 and contained a message scrawled on twice, once in May 1847 and again in April 1848 (Figure 6.2). It gave a very brief history of the ships' movement—that they had wintered at Beechey Island, ascended Wellington Channel, circumnavigated Cornwallis Island, and in 1846 had been caught in the pack ice from which they could not escape. Franklin had died in June 1847, and in April 1848 (as the first rescue expeditions were dispatched) the survivors under Crozier and James Fitzjames had headed for the mouth of the Back River. If Richardson and Rae had been able to travel slightly further east in 1848, they might have found the survivors, or perhaps their bodies. Not far away from the cairn, McClintock came across a whaleboat containing two skeletons in European clothes, several religious books, and a Bible and a copy of the gently comic novel, *The Vicar of Wakefield*. He collected many relics and interviewed several Netsilingmiut, one of whom told him that the explorers had "fallen down and died as they walked along." His discovery of a skeleton, face down on the gravel at Cape Herschel on King William Island, tended to confirm this. The skeleton had a barely legible journal underneath it, written mostly in code, and now known as the Peglar Papers.[67]

Janice Cavell has argued that McClintock's return seemed to put a period to the narrative that the Admiralty had abandoned Franklin to his fate. In his wildly popular narrative, *The Voyage of the 'Fox' in the Arctic Seas*, McClintock reiterated Richardson's argument that the men had "forged the last link" in the Northwest Passage, that there was no evidence of cannibalism, and that they had faced death with pious resignation, as Franklin and Richardson had at Fort Enterprise in 1821. While McClintock's return seemed to represent a closing of the narrative (and indeed was reported in the newspapers as "the end of an epic"), it was, in fact, the opposite.[68] As Craciun has argued, the circulation and consumption of both McClintock's narrative and the relics he brought back proved both uncomfortable and unstoppable. In particular, the stereoscopic slides of McClintock's relics circulated globally, outside both the halls of institutions and Jane Franklin's editorial control, removed into "middle-class homes, to be enjoyed or ignored like any other *bric-a-brac*" (Figure 6.3).[69] The disembodiment of the relics was particularly distressing, as the only stand-ins for the absent (and dismembered) bodies of the dead. Craciun argues that the disarticulation, circulation, and consumption of the slides presented an uncomfortable parallel to the circulation of Indigenous artifacts and body parts, a trade with which Jane Franklin was very familiar, and in which many Arctic explorers had also participated.[70] Moreover, the fact that so little writing was discovered remained both deeply frustrating and intensely unsettling. As Craciun puts it, all that was there was "the mute remains of shit and bones."[71]

In the eyes of the public, McClintock's discoveries confirmed Jane Franklin's claim to an intimate and authoritative knowledge of her husband's plans.[72] Intertwined with celebrations of her perseverance, fortitude, and "indomitable love" was the notion that

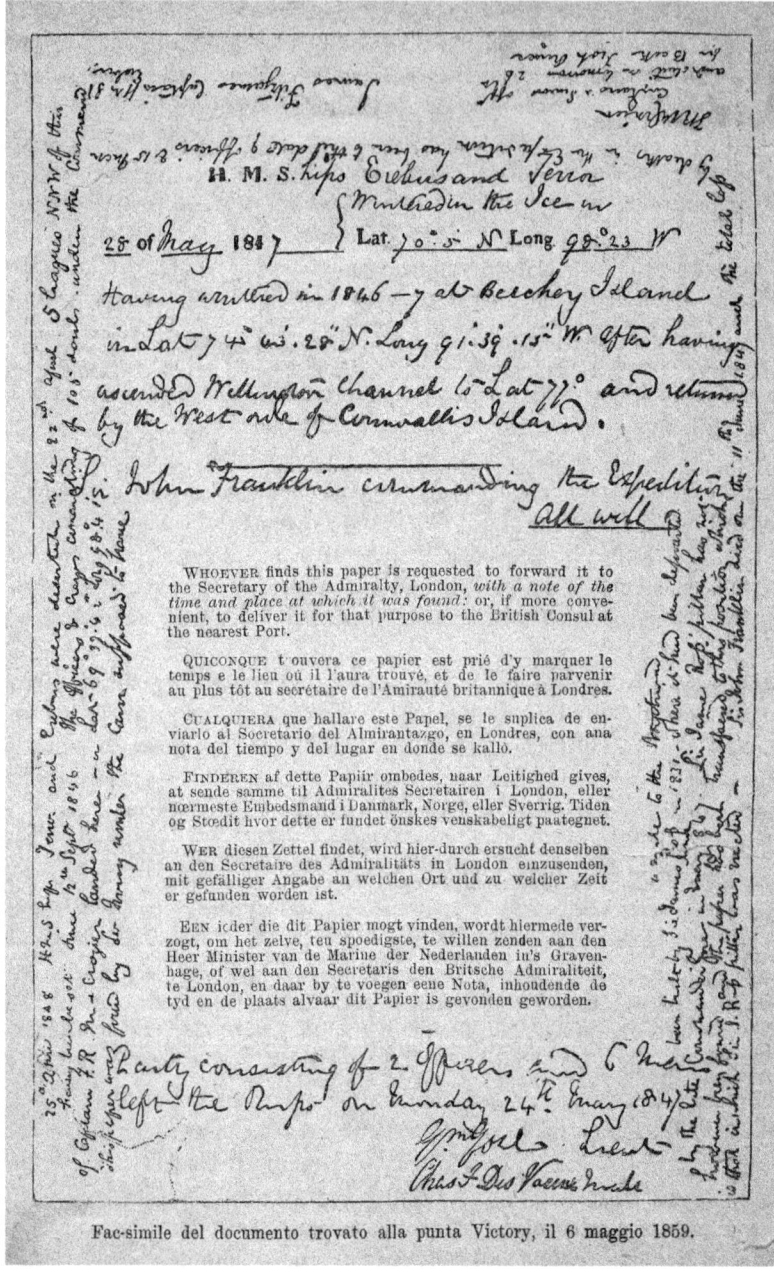

Figure 6.2 Victory Point Cairn record, found by the expedition of Leopold McClintock on King William Island, May 6, 1859. Getty Images, DEA PICTURE LIBRARY/Contributor 11466992.

Figure 6.3 A portrait photograph of Captain Leopold McClintock with a few of the Franklin relics. One of a set of stereoscopic slides that circulated around the world. This particular set ended up in Tasmania. Tasmanian Archives, Jack Thwaites Collection, NS1155/1/20/15.

her wifely devotion had informed her geographical knowledge. These qualities were represented as the highest kind of mid-Victorian feminine heroism, particularly as she had faced obstacles not only from the Arctic ice but also from her own government. Captain Sherard Osborn, who had discovered the graves at Beechey Island in 1850, wrote in the periodical *Once a Week* that "this energetic, self-reliant woman . . . [carried] out by private means what ignorance, rather than ill-will, prevented the Admiralty from executing."[73] As a result, in 1860, she received the first Gold Medal that the RGS would bestow on a woman (which she shared with McClintock), for her "noble and self-sacrificing perseverance in sending out, at her own cost, several searching expeditions, until at length the fate of her husband has been finally ascertained."[74] The Gold Medal testified, in large part, to the success of her Arctic circles in transposing humanitarian women's language of conscience into a geographical key. But in claiming all that moral authority and prescient, intimate knowledge, Jane Franklin eclipsed the labors of all those members of the Arctic circles upon whom she had depended, from Sophia Cracroft, to Mary Anne Kendall, Anna Gurney, Sarah Bowdich Lee, William Scoresby, Alexander Kennedy Isbister, and Charles Weld, among many others. Her stepdaughter, Eleanor Franklin Gell, did not live to see the presentation—she died of scarlet fever in the same year.

Amid a culture of extravagant mourning, the biographies, archives, and statues of Franklin functioned as shrines and graves for a missing body that could not be buried. Jane arranged for statues to be cast of her husband (as a much slimmer man than he was when he departed). One was erected in 1867 at Waterloo Place, not far from Nelson's Column and adjacent to the Athenaeum Club (which Franklin once felt he could not enter because of the rumors spread by John Montagu about "petticoat government" in Van Diemen's Land). Another was unveiled in Franklin's hometown of Spilsby, and another was commissioned by Tasmanian settlers. (Jane Franklin took her grandson to see it being cast.)[75] The statue was shipped out to Tasmania at enormous expense to sit at the center of the site of old Government House, now Franklin Square, where it still stands. In 1875, just two weeks before Jane Franklin died, a plaque was erected to John Franklin in Westminster Abbey. Unlike the plaque, the statue in Hobart was never officially unveiled.[76] For over a century, it has served as a perch for millions of seagulls.

Jane Franklin also developed a gallery of Arctic portraits that mixed with her cabinet of curiosities. Visitors to her home—and there were many, including the missionary David Livingstone, the reporter Henry Morton Stanley, and Queen Emma of Hawaii—would have seen portraits of Franklin, Kennedy, and Penny arranged among busts of Indigenous Tasmanians. Bock's portraits of Indigenous Tasmanians (including, perhaps, Mithina's) went into the best bedroom.[77] Most of these would later be donated by Sophia to the National Portrait Gallery, though Bock's work would end up in the British Museum, and Mithina's portrait made its way to the Tasmanian Museum and Art Gallery. After Jane Franklin's death, Sophia went blind editing her aunt's papers and passed them along to the author H. D. Traill for his biography of her uncle, which was published in 1896.[78] Its publication coincided with a new wave of polar expeditions to Antarctica, and a new cast of polar heroes and martyrs who would ultimately have their stories hitched to Franklin's during the "Heroic Age" of British exploration. It came to be part of a British narrative of tragic heroism that did not just accommodate but rather celebrated failure.[79]

Ultimately, Sophia's sister Emma Lefroy inherited Jane Franklin's papers, which Sophia had edited over many years. Her editing was severe. Some of the originals were cut apart, others had postage stamps placed over passages, and many were copied out in Sophia's hand. It was, perhaps, her most enduring protection of her aunt and uncle. It might also help to explain why there are so few journals of Jane Franklin's for the period of the Franklin searches.[80] Eleanor Gell, Mary Fletcher Richardson, Catherine Gurney Parry, and Mary Anne Kendall also kept (and edited) their own archives for the purpose of writing biographies. Before she died in 1860, Eleanor managed to obtain her parents' correspondence, her mother's poetry, and her father's correspondence with John Richardson. These were held, along with Eleanor's own Tasmanian journals and correspondence, at the family home at Hopton Hall in Derbyshire, together with Mithina's doll and pin cushion, Kalli's letters and artwork, and the Iroquois doll that her father had given Eleanor when she was three years old. Later, the papers and objects made their way to the Derbyshire Record Office. Mary Fletcher Richardson and Catherine Parry both hoarded their husbands' correspondence, asking relatives and friends to write biographies. Both of these collections ended up alongside Franklin's at the Scott Polar Research Institute at Cambridge.[81] Mary Ann Kendall's papers, which detailed the world of scientific sociability of the 1820s, were donated to the National Maritime Museum in Greenwich. And in Hobart, the official records of the Franklins' reform projects, colonial discord, and scientific endeavors ultimately rubbed shoulders with microform copies of both the Scott Polar Research Institute and the Derbyshire Record Office collections, bringing Jane, Sophia, and Eleanor together in the Tasmanian Archives.

Yet this is, by many measures, only the beginning of a story, because the absence that encouraged the preservation of these women's and families' archives—the absence of *Erebus* and *Terror*'s journals and papers—has never been filled. McClintock's return, as

Russell Potter has shown, began a cycle of adventurers (beginning with the American Charles Francis Hall) heading north to secure more Inuit information, more relics, more bones, in an attempt to solve the Franklin mystery.[82] From the 1990s, Franklin began to become the object of sustained criticism with a spate of novels, lectures, films and revisionist histories, notably by Margaret Atwood, Pierre Berton, Richard Flanagan, and Ruby Wiebe.[83] These focused not only on his unfitness to command and ignorance of Indigenous knowledge but also on the adaptability of the mythology that had emerged around him and the missing expedition. At the same time, a new round of explorers began collecting and collating Indigenous testimony with a view to solving the mystery and locating the wrecks of *Erebus* and *Terror*. David Woodman published two important books that brought together his own research with testimony from Inuit elders, followed by Dorothy Harley Eber's valuable histories.[84] At the beginning of the twenty-first century, the Canadian government began officially looking for the wrecks as part of an attempt to assert control over the Northwest Passage, reenacting the concerns of the 1820s about Russian infiltration of what was British, was now Canadian, and had always been Inuit, space.

In her lectures on Canadian literature, Margaret Atwood suggests that stories like those of the Franklin expedition "hold a curious fascination both for those who tell them and for those who hear them; they are handed down and reworked, and storytellers come back to them time and again . . . discovering new and different meanings each time the story, or a part of it, is given a fresh incarnation."[85] They are rewoven into the fabric of nations, each time with different meanings. Stephanie Barczewski has argued that the British narrative of heroic failure around Franklin came to play an important role in the self-definition of an imperial nation, that it presented an alternative narrative of empire that emphasized vulnerability in order to rationalize British dominance and misgovernment. While Barczewski recognizes the role of women like Jane Franklin as defenders of their husband's reputations and legacies, she understands their role to be rooted in conjugality and domesticity.[86] I understand it differently—as part of a much broader contest over authority and trustworthiness that arose within a kaleidoscope of intimate circles, developed over many years and across imperial spaces, all of whom had their eyes on different prizes. Franklin has become a part of several national stories linked by the British Empire—Canada, Britain, Australia—which are deeply connected, interdependent, in a constant state of motion.[87] We understand these histories better when we see them together.

The Franklins continue to be, as they were in their lifetimes, entangled in the politics of truth, and so do the objects aggregated and dispersed because of their associations with them. Those "relics" are remixed, resituated, and reinterpreted in local contexts across the globe. This process has continued since the discovery of the wrecks of *Erebus* and *Terror* in 2014 and 2016. These discoveries and excavations were remarkable achievements by any stretch of the imagination, using a combination of Inuit testimony and modern technology. They were not, however, entirely without dissonance, particularly over the ownership of the wrecks and their relics, which were located in the self-governing Inuit province of Nunavut. This tension, and the redisplay of the "relics" at Greenwich in the National Maritime Museum's *Death in the Ice* exhibition in 2017, seemed in some ways to echo the discomfort of the 1850s over their ownership and how they should be understood. The discovery and the excavation of the wrecks were presented not only as a story of cross-cultural collaboration in the exhibition but also as one of appropriate mourning. The exhibition brought together exhaustive research on the ships themselves, the experience of daily life, the biographies of the crew, the difficulty of travel, and the creeping cold. It was cast as an opportunity to remember many of the forgotten men of the expedition whose stories had been overshadowed by Franklin's, ordinary people who died terrible deaths, who left families behind, whose descendants still sorrow. Quotidian objects made up much of the exhibition, things like shoes, timepieces, the barnacle-encrusted bell of the *Erebus*, some of which were traded by Inuit in the nineteenth century and had been modified into new tools, some of which were recovered from archaeological expeditions on land, some of which were brought up from the deep. They were exhibited as specimens, but also as objects of reflection, connection, and longing.[88]

The discovery of *Erebus* and *Terror* was linked, inevitably, to the lingering desire for written records of the expedition—either to supplement or to supplant Inuit testimony. Perhaps the continuing search for journals and papers in the underwater spaces of the ships demonstrates the ongoing tension about what constitutes the truth and who gets to tell it. The literary scholars Russell Potter and Adriana Craciun both see the search for Franklin—and the need for written records—as a modern participation in a Victorian drama. It is not so much a reenactment as an ongoing, unconscious rehearsal of a never-finished cult of mourning.[89] The searching is haunted by a sense of incompleteness that attends the ambiguity of Inuit authority and archives, also inherited from the Victorians—the feeling that Inuit accounts are peripheral, are not anchored in time and place, that stories of disaster are told by others, and that a powerful silence lies at their heart. This attitude echoes the larger conflict between Western and Indigenous archives and ways of knowing, remembering, interpreting, and retelling, in which Indigenous voices are so often understood as silent or absent.[90] Historians who work with these archives often find themselves as unsure and untrustworthy intermediaries, trying to persuade others of their goodwill and honesty while crafting an original narrative. As David Turnbull has put it, "The nature of the go-between is like that of the contemporary historian, who as a teller of narratives, a crosser of boundaries, is also something of a jester or a trickster."[91]

As the final draft of this book was being completed, a new exhibition opened at the Tasmanian Museum and Art Gallery in Hobart. "*taypani milaythina-tu*: Return to Country" was many years in the making. Curated by Indigenous Tasmanian scholars and artists, descendants of the survivors of Wybalenna and the blended families of Bass Strait, the exhibition's development went hand in hand with a struggle to locate and repatriate ancestral remains in museums around the world, but mainly in Britain and Europe. The exhibition displayed new artwork from twenty Indigenous artists, alongside a number of ancestral objects loaned by British and European institutions. The purpose was to bring cultural objects back to country, albeit temporarily "on loan," to allow ongoing engagement with "exiled objects" and to create new ones. Among them were items from the Derbyshire Record Office, including Mithina's doll and pincushion—startlingly tiny—which were displayed in a room devoted to painful reflections on forced adoption, assimilation, and disconnection from country.

The exhibition also included objects from the Franklins' private collections, like a model of a reed canoe and the busts and portraits that once decorated Jane Franklin's boudoir in Hobart, and later her best bedroom in London. Franklin Square is few minutes' walk away where John Franklin's statue is now accompanied by a sculpture of the ribs of the *Erebus*, keeled over on its side, with a sculpture of a reed canoe at its heart, a scaled-up model of one collected by the Franklins on Flinders Island. It is accompanied by voices of contemporary Indigenous people reflecting on the Franklins' legacy in Tasmania.

There are many intersections and parallels between the "Death in the Ice" and "*taypani milaythina-tu*" exhibitions, for both were made out of disaggregated archives with silences at their hearts. Ostensibly, they tell similar stories—of generations of longing, partial returns, truths to be told, work yet to do, wrongs to be righted. They are linked by practices of exploration and colonialism, and they are both manifestations of the complex, fraught, and intimate ways in which Indigenous people, explorers, and families shaped archives, and also of the silences and occlusions within them. Yet they come from very different geographies and different painful histories, with vastly different politics of truth behind them.

Arctic Circles is another attempt to weave stories together that have long been told separately. Like so many others, I too have been drawn by what I have seen as blank spaces, gathered up fragments around the missing Franklin expedition, and repurposed them into something new. I have been beckoned, as much as anyone else, into what I thought was a great silence, and have been dizzied by the tales that emerged. Over time, I have realized that it is the Franklin archive itself, and the ways in which it has been made, which drew me in. Those records, stories, and silences exist because of the struggles of men and women, both British and Indigenous, to define what was and was not true, to determine who did and did not have the authority to speak, and to remake memories and relics. These are stories of knowledge-making which are unequal and fraught, and have been both braided together and prized apart by intimacy, confusion, and suspicion. They are still linked. *taypani milaythina-tu* and "Death in the Ice" remind us that they are living stories, both anchored in places and unmoored from them, and as powerful in the present as they were in the past. If we are to continue to tell them, then we must reckon with the struggles over truth that lie at their heart.

Notes

1 Fossett, *In Order to Live Untroubled*, 139–66.
2 Ibid., 144.
3 Charles Francis Hall, *Narrative of the Second Arctic Expedition Made by Charles F. Hall His Voyage to Repulse Bay, Sledge Journeys to the Straits of Fury and Hecla and to King William's Land, and Residence among the Eskimos during the Years 1864–69*. Edited by J. E. Nourse (Cambridge: Cambridge University Press, May 2014), 589, 591.
4 Fossett, *In Order to Live Untroubled*, 140.
5 Eber, *Encounters on the Passage*, 37–63.
6 Fossett, *In Order to Live Untroubled*, 146–8.

7 Eber, *Encounters on the Passage*, 64–107.
8 Dorothy Harley Eber, "Rumours of Franklin: The Strength of the Inuit Oral Tradition," *Beaver* 76, no. 3 (June/July 1996): 10.
9 Potter, *Finding Franklin*, 106–12; Eber, *Encounters on the Passage*, 84–107; Fossett, *In Order to Live Untroubled*, 150–1.
10 HBCA B.42/a/155 Churchill Journal, 1827-28; B. 42/a/57, Churchill Journal, 1829-1830; B.38/a/7, Fort Chimo Post Journal, 1836-9; B.157/a/1: Peel River Post Journal, 1840-1; B.200/b/13, McKenzie River Correspondence Book, 1840-41; B.200/a/26: Fort Simpson Journal, 1841-2; B.200/b/16: Mackenzie River Correspondence Book, 1842-43; B.200/b/17, McKenzie River Correspondence Book, 1843-44.
11 John Rae, "Lost Arctic Voyagers," *Household Words*, December 23, 1854, 248.
12 John Rae to William McTavish, London, November 26, 1852, in John Rae, *John Rae's Correspondence with the Hudson's Bay Company on Arctic Exploration, 1844-1855*, ed. A. M. Johnson et al. (London: Hudson's Bay Record Society, 1953), 239.
13 Fossett, *In Order to Live Untroubled*, 158–9, 160.
14 "The Arctic Expedition," *Times*, October 23, 1854, 8.
15 Potter, *Finding Franklin*, 25, 32–3.
16 Spufford, *I May be Some Time*, 119; Woodward, *Portrait of Jane*, 286; MA MG2 C1/5 Jane Franklin to William Kennedy, February 16, 1854.
17 "The New Davis Straits Fishery," *The Times*, September 1, 1854, 5.
18 Quoted in Cavell, *Tracing the Connected Narrative*, 205.
19 DRO D8760/F/FEG/1/41/1, William Simpkinson to Eleanor Gell, December 4, 1854.
20 The *Illustrated London News* published their reproduction of the relics directly opposite an account of the late Duke's funeral. "The Franklin Relics," *Illustrated London News*, November 4, 1854, 433.
21 *Lady's Newspaper*, "The Fate of Sir John Franklin," October 28, 1854, 257–8.
22 Craciun, "The Franklin Relics."
23 Medicus, Letter to the Editor, *Times*, November 1, 1854, 9.
24 *The Athenaeum*, "The Fate of Franklin," October 28, 1854, 1305.
25 "The Arctic Expeditions," *The Athenaeum*, October 13, 1849, 1038.
26 Charles Dickens, "Lost Arctic Voyagers," *Household Words*, December 2, 1854, 364. For the speculations about Jane Franklin's involvement, see Spufford, *I May Be Some Time*, 123–7; Ken McGoogan, *Fatal Passage: The Story of John Rae, the Arctic Hero Time Forgot* (New York: Carroll & Graf Publishers, 2002), 220–9; Ken McGoogan, *Lady Franklin's Revenge: A True Story of Ambition, Obsession and the Remaking of Arctic History* (Toronto: HarperCollins Publishers Ltd., 2005), 340–1. For a more measured assessment, see Cavell, *Tracing the Connected Narrative*, 204–18; Janice Cavell, "Publishing John Franklin's Fate," *Book History* 16 (2013): 155–84. See also Ian R. Stone, "'The Contents of the Kettles': Charles Dickens, John Rae, and Cannibalism on the 1845 Franklin Expedition," *Dickensian* 83, no. 1 (1987): 7–15.
27 Tallie, "Indigeneity, Movement, and Disrupting the Global Nineteenth Century," 188–225.
28 Charles Dickens, "The Noble Savage," *Household Words*, June 11, 1853. See Tallie "Indigeneity, Movement, and Disrupting"; Yangjung Lee, "From Silver-Store to 'all over the world': The Transimperial Entanglements of 'The Perils of Certain English Prisoners,'" *Victorian Studies* 64, no. 3 (Spring 2022): 377–400.
29 Charles Dickens, "Lost Arctic Voyagers" *Household Words*, December 2, 1854, 364.
30 Charles Dickens, "Lost Arctic Voyagers" *Household Words*, December 9, 1854, 393.

31 Dickens, "Lost Arctic Voyagers," December 2, 1854, 362.
32 Rae, "Lost Arctic Voyagers."
33 For an excellent discussion, see Cavell, *Tracing the Connected Narrative*, 204–18.
34 WM, SCO 819 Box P, Sophia Cracroft to William Scoresby, November 7, 1854.
35 This is the core argument of McGoogan, *Fatal Passage*; for how that argument has taken its own passage into the Franklin canon, see Potter, *Finding Franklin*, 83–97. See also Bunyan et al., *No Ordinary Journey*.
36 McGoogan, *Fatal Passage*, see also Hill, *White Horizon*, 114–50.
37 SPRI MS 248/212/8, Letter to the Lords of the Admiralty, November 29, 1854.
38 SPRI MS 248/113 BJ, Jane Franklin and Sophia Cracroft's Letter Book, 1855-58, "Principal points in Mr Anderson's Letter from Fort Resolution, Slave Lake, 17th Sept '55, rec'd at Paris, 1856," 15.
39 SPRI MS 1503/50/40, Sophia Cracroft to John Richardson, November 15, 1855.
40 WM, SCO 819 Box P, Lady Franklin Correspondence. Sophia Cracroft to William Scoresby, November 12, 1855.
41 Sir John Richardson, "Arctic Voyages," *Times*, June 23, 1855, 5.
42 SPRI MS1503/50/27, Sophia Cracroft to John Richardson, nd.
43 SPRI MS 1503/50/19, Jane Franklin to John Richardson, June 27, 1855.
44 MA MG2 C1/5/8, Sophia Cracroft to William Kennedy, nd [summer/fall, 1855].
45 SPRI MS1503/50/45, Beatrice Richardson to John Booth Richardson, November 29, 1855; MS1503/50/47, Sophia Cracroft to John Richardson, November 30, 1855; MS 1503/50/48, Sophia Cracroft to John Richardson, December 1, 1855.
46 *Encyclopedia Britannica Online*, s. v. "Sir John Richardson on Sir John Franklin," http://www.britannica.com/EBchecked/topic/1994314/Sir-John-Richardson-on-Sir-John-Franklin (accessed January 25, 2015). Originally published 1856.
47 SPRI MS1503/50/55, Jane Franklin to John Richardson, December 29, 1855.
48 Charles Morse, "Chart Showing the Recent Search for the North-West Passage also the Coast Explored in Search of Sir John Franklin Between the Years 1848 and 1854. (inset) Discoveries in the North Wellington Channel by Lt. DeHaven in Sept. 1850 and by Capt. Penny and his Parties in May, June and July 1851," in *Morse's General Atlas of the World. Containing Seventy Maps, Drawn And Engraved From The Latest And Best Authorities* (New York: D. Appleton & Company, 1856).
49 Jane Franklin rehearsed this argument to Murchison, see BL add ms 46126, Jane Franklin to Roderick Murchison, January 26, 1856.
50 [Alexander Kennedy Isbister], *Arctic Rewards and their Claimants* (London: T. Hatchard, 1856), 8–9.
51 Ibid., 14.
52 Ibid., 18.
53 Ibid., 24–5.
54 MA MG2 C1/100, Sophia Cracroft and Jane Franklin to A.K. Isbister, June 25, 1856.
55 Adele Perry, "Designing Dispossession: The Select Committee on the Hudson's Bay Company, Fur-Trade Governance, Indigenous Peoples and Settler Possibility," in *Indigenous Communities and Settler Colonialism: Landholding, Loss and Survival in an Interconnected World*, ed. Alan Lester and Zoe Laidlaw (Basingstoke: Palgrave Macmillan, 2015), 158–9.
56 Laidlaw, *Protecting the Empire's Humanity*, 273.
57 Perry, "Designing Dispossession," 162.
58 Ibid., 164.

59 Alexander Kennedy Isbister, "A Proposal for a New Penal Settlement, in Connexion with the Colonization of the Uninhabited Districts of British North America" (London: Trelawney Saunders, 1850).
60 Ibid., 4-5, 7-8, 11-12. Isbister's vision reflected the Russian *intelligentsia* imaginings of the Amur River delta, as a place where a future Russia free of serfdom might emerge. See Mark Bassin, *Imperial Visions: Nationalist Imagination and Geographical Expansion in the Russian Far East, 1840- 1865* (Cambridge and New York: Cambridge University Press, 1999).
61 The literature on the Creole class is considerable, but see Vinkovetsky, *Russian America*, especially 127-53; Gwenn A. Miller, "'The Perfect Mistress of Russian Economy': Sighting the Intimate on a Colonial Alaskan Terrain, 1784-1821," in *Haunted by Empire: Geographies of Intimacy in North American History*, ed. Ann Laura Stoler (Chapel Hill: Duke University Press, 2006), 297-322; Annaliese Jacobs, "Empire at the Floe Edge: Western Empires and Indigenous People in the Bering Sea and Arctic Ocean, c. 1820-1900," in *The Routledge History of Western Empires*, ed. Robert K. Aldrich and Kristen McKenzie (Abingdon: Routledge, 2013), 136-50.
62 Question of John Roebuck, Testimony of J. H. Lefroy, Great Britain, *Report from the Select Committee on the Hudson's Bay Company, Together with Proceedings of the Committee, Minutes of Evidence, Appendix and Index* (London: House of Commons, 1857), 23, quoted in Perry, "Designing dispossession," 167.
63 Testimony of Dr John Rae, Great Britain, *Report from the Select Committee*, 27.
64 Testimony of Sir John Richardson, Great Britain, *Report from the Select Committee*, 156-8.
65 Testimony of Sir George Back, Great Britain, *Report from the Select Committee*, 188.
66 RGS-IBG CB4 1851-60, Lady Jane Franklin and Sophia Cracroft letters to R. I. Murchison. Lady Franklin to Captain McClintock, Aberdeen, June 29, 1857.
67 Potter, *Finding Franklin*, 40-1.
68 Cavell, *Tracing the Connected Narrative*, 230-44, especially 238.
69 Craciun, "The Franklin Relics," 13.
70 Ibid.
71 Craciun, *Writing Arctic Disaster*, 79.
72 "The Arctic Mystery," *The Athenaeum*, September 24, 1859, 398.
73 Sherard Osborn, "The Search for Sir John Franklin," *Once a Week* 1, no. 19 (November 5, 1859): 383.
74 "Presentation of the Gold Medals to Lady Franklin and Captain Sir F. L. McClintock," *Journal of the Royal Geographical Society of London* 30 (1860): xciv.
75 NMM REY/2 Reynolds Bequest, Catalogue of Engravings known to exist of Franklin, Richardson, Parry etc; DRO D8760/F/GPL/2/1, Recollections of Lady Franklin by Phillip Lyttleton Gell.
76 TA, Research File, "Franklin Square."
77 Woodward, *Portrait of Jane*, 326; DRO D8760/F/GPL/2/1, Recollections of Lady Franklin by Phillip Lyttleton Gell.
78 Traill, *Life of Sir John Franklin, R. N.*
79 Max Jones, *The Last Great Quest*. Barczewski, *Heroic Failure and the British*, 59-84.
80 Alison Alexander has also noted the censorship of Jane's archive, see Alexander, *Ambitions*.
81 Parry, *Parry of the Arctic*; McIlraith, *Life of Sir John Richardson*; Mary Fletcher Richardson tried to get John Murray to publish the biography of her husband, writing, "The book has been prepared very much in the hope that it might become a useful

one for boys, having a Mixture of the heroic, as well as the practical, and Christian." NLS John Murray Archive, MS.41017, Mary Fletcher Richardson to John Murray, October 24, 1867 and October 26, 1867.
82 Potter, *Finding Franklin*.
83 Margaret Atwood, *Strange Things: The Malevolent North in Canadian Literature* (London: Virago Press, 2004); Pierre Berton, *The Arctic Grail: The Quest for the Northwest Passage and the North Pole, 1818-1909* (New York: Viking, 1998); Rudy Wiebe, *A Discovery of Strangers* (Toronto: A. A. Knopf Canada, 1994); Flanagan, *Wanting*.
84 Woodman, *Unravelling the Franklin Mystery*; David C. Woodman, *Strangers Among Us* (Montreal: McGill-Queen's University Press, 1995); Eber, *Encounters on the Passage*.
85 Atwood, *Strange Things*, 13.
86 Barczewski, *Heroic Failure and the British*, 16.
87 Antoinette Burton, "Who Needs the Nation? Interrogating 'British' History," *Journal of Historical Sociology* 10, no. 3 (September 1997): 227–48.
88 Hutchinson, *Sir John Franklin's Erebus and Terror*.
89 Potter, *Finding Franklin*; Craciun, "The Franklin Relics."
90 Jennifer S. H. Brown and Elizabeth Vibert, eds., *Reading Beyond Words: Contexts for Naïve History*, 2nd ed. (Toronto and London: University of Toronto Press, 2009); Adele Perry, "The Colonial Archive on Trial: Possession, Dispossession, and History in Delgamuukw v. British Columbia," in *Archive Stories: Facts, Fictions, and the Writing of History*, ed. Antoinette Burton (Durham and London: Duke University Press, 2005), 325–50.
91 David Turnbull, "Boundary-Crossings, Cultural Encounters and Knowledge Spaces in Early Australia," in *The Brokered World: Go-Betweens and Global Intelligence*, ed. Simon Schaffer, et al. (Canton: Science History Publications, 2009), 388.

Bibliography

Archival Sources

Australian Joint Copying Project (AJCP)
British Library (BL)
Derbyshire Record Office (DRO)
Hudson Bay Company Archives (HBCA)
Manitoba Archives (MA)
Mitchell Library, State Library of New South Wales (ML)
National Library of Scotland (NLS)
National Maritime Museum, United Kingdom (NMM)
Orkney Archive, Kirkwall (OA)
Royal Geographical Society with the Institute of British Geographers (RGS-IBG)
Royal Society of Tasmania, Hobart (RST)
Scott Polar Research Institute, Cambridge (SPRI)
State Library of New South Wales (SLNSW)
Tasmanian Archives, Hobart (TA)
The National Archives (TNA), United Kingdom
University of Tasmania Library, Special and Rare Manuscript Collections (UTAS)
Whitby Museum (WM)

Newspapers and Periodicals

The Athenaeum
The Austral-Asiatic Review
The Australian
Belfast News-Letter
Caledonian Mercury
Chambers's Edinburgh Journal
The Colonial Times
The Edinburgh Philosophical Journal
The Encyclopaedia Britannica Online, (1856)
The Era
Haddingtonshire Courier
Hereford Journal
Hobart Town Courier
Household Words
Hull Packet and East Riding Times
The Illustrated London News
Journal of the Ethnological Society of London

Journal of the Royal Geographical Society of London
Lady's Newspaper
Launceston Courier
Leeds Mercury
The Literary Gazette
Lloyd's Weekly Newspaper
The Mirror of Literature, Amusement and Instruction
Morning Chronicle
Morning Herald
Morning Post
Newcastle Courant
Northhampton Mercury
Once a Week
Papers and Proceedings of the Royal Society of Tasmania
Philosophical Transactions of the Royal Society of London
Preston Guardian
The Sun
The Tasmanian Journal of Natural Science, Agriculture, Statistics, &c.
The Times of London
Transactions of the British Association for the Advancement of Science
The True Colonist

Government Publications

HC PP 1831 (259) *Van Diemen's Land. Copies of All Correspondence Between Lieutenant-Governor Arthur and His Majesty's Secretary of State for the Colonies, on the Subject of the Military Operations Lately Carried on Against the Aboriginal Inhabitants of Van Diemen's Land.*
HC PP 1836 (538) *Report from the Select Committee on Aborigines (British Settlements).*
HC PP 1837-8 (669) *Report from the Select Committee on Transportation, Together with Minutes of Evidence.*
HC PP 1852a (1435) *Great Britain. Parliament. House of Commons. Arctic Expeditions. Report of the committee appointed by the Lords Commissioners of the Admiralty to inquire into and report on the recent Arctic expeditions in search of Sir John Franklin, together with the minutes of the committee, and papers connected with the subject.*
HC PP 1852c (1449) *Great Britain. Parliament. House of Commons. Arctic Expeditions. Further Correspondence and Proceedings connected with the Arctic Expedition.*
HC PP 1852j (390) *Great Britain. Parliament. House of Commons. Papers in connection with the late Arctic expeditions, or with any which may be in preparation.*
HC PP 1857 (224) (260) Report from the Select Committee on the Hudson's Bay Company.

Books and Articles (pre-1900)

[Anonymous]. *A Brave Man and His Belongings*. Privately Published, [n.d., circa 1874].
Arctic Miscellanies: A Souvenir of the Late Polar Search. London: Colburn and Co., 1852.

Back, George. *Arctic Artist: The Journal and Paintings of George Back, Midshipman with Franklin, 1819–1822*. Edited by C. Stuart Houston. Kingston and Montreal: McGill-Queen's University Press, 1994.

Bellot, Joseph Rene. *Memoirs of Lieutenant Joseph Rene Bellot*. London: Hurst and Blackett, 1855.

[Bowdich, Sarah]. *Taxidermy: Or, the Art of Collecting, Preparing and Mounting Objects of Natural History for the Use of Museums and Travellers*. London: Longman, Hurst, Rees, Orme and Brown, 1820.

Burn, David. *Narrative of the Overland Journey of Sir John and Lady Franklin and Party from Hobart Town to Macquarie Harbour*. London, 1843.

Burns, T. E. and J. R. Skemp. *Van Diemen's Land Correspondents: Letters from R.C. Gunn, R.W. Lawrence, Jorgen Jorgenson, Sir John Franklin and Others to Sir William J. Hooker, 1827-1849*. Launceston: Queen Victoria Museum, 1961.

Crooke, Robert. *The Convict: A Fragment of History*. Hobart: University of Tasmania Library, 1958.

Darwin, Charles. *Journal of Researches into the Natural History and Geology of the Countries Visited During the Voyage of H.M.S. Beagle Around the World Under the Command of Capt. Fitz Roy, R.N.* 2nd ed., corrected, with additions, 648. London: John Murray, 1845. https://archive.org/details/journalofresearc00darw_2 (accessed August 27, 2022).

Denison, William, *Varieties of Vice-Regal Life*. Edited by Richard Davis and Stefan Petrow. London: Longmans, Green, & Co., 1870.

Dove, Thomas. "Moral and Social Characteristics of the Aborigines of Tasmania, as Gathered from Intercourse with the Surviving Remnant of Them Now Located on Flinders' Island." *The Tasmanian Journal of Natural Science, Agriculture, Statistics, &c.* 1, no. 4 (1842): 247–54.

Fletcher, Eliza Dawson. *Autobiography of Mrs. Fletcher of Edinburgh: With Letters and Other Family Memorials*. Edited by Lady Mary Fletcher Richardson. Edinburgh: Edmonston and Douglas, 1875.

Fox, Caroline. *Memories of Old Friends: Being Extracts from the Journals and Letters of Caroline Fox, from 1835-1871*. Edited by Horatio Noble Pym and John Stuart Mill. London: Smith, Elder & Co., 1883.

Franklin, John. *Journey of a Second Expedition to the Shores of the Polar Sea, in the Years 1825, 1826 and 1827*. London: John Murray, 1828.

Franklin, John. *Narrative of a Journey to the Shores of the Polar Sea, in the Years 1819-20-21-22*. 3rd ed. London: John Murray, 1824.

Franklin, John. *Narrative of Some Passages in the History of Van Diemen's Land, During the Last Three Years of Sir John Franklin's Administration of Its Government*. London: Printed by Richard and John E. Taylor, 1845.

Franklin, John. *Sir John Franklin's Journals and Correspondence: The First Arctic Land Expedition, 1819–1822*. Edited by Richard C. Davis. Toronto: The Champlain Society, 1995.

Franklin, John. *Sir John Franklin's Journals and Correspondence: The Second Arctic Land Expedition, 1825–1827*. Edited by Richard C. Davis. Toronto: The Champlain Society, 1998.

Fry, Elizabeth Gurney. *Memoir of the Life of Elizabeth Fry, with Extracts from her Journal and Letters*. Edited by Katherine Fry and Rachel Elizabeth Fry Cresswell. Vol. 1. London: C. Gilpin, J. Hatchard & Co., 1848.

Gell, Edith Mary. *John Franklin's Bride: Eleanor Anne Porden*. London: John Murray, 1930.

Glascock, William Nugent. *The Naval Sketchbook, or, the Service Afloat and Ashore with Characteristic Reminiscences and Opinions*. London: Henry Colburn, 1831.

Graah, Wilhelm A. *Narrative of an Expedition to the East Coast of Greenland, Sent by the Order of the King of Denmark, in Search of the Lost Colonies*. Translated by G. Gordon Macdougall. London: John W. Parker, 1837.

Great Britain. *Report of the Parliamentary Select Committee on Aboriginal Tribes (British Settlements) Reprinted, With Comments, by the Aborigines Protection Society*. London: William Ball, Aldine Chambers, 1837.

Gunn, Robert C. "Remarks on the Indigenous Vegetable Productions of Tasmania Available as Food for Man." *The Tasmanian Journal of Natural Science, Agriculture, Statistics, &c.* 1, no. 1 (1842): 35–52.

Hall, Charles Francis. *Life with the Esquimaux: A Narrative of Arctic Experience in Search of Survivors of Sir John Franklin's Expedition from May 29, 1860 to September 13, 1862*. London: Sampson Low, Son and Marston, 1864.

Hall, Charles Francis. *Narrative of the Second Arctic Expedition Made by Charles F. Hall His Voyage to Repulse Bay, Sledge Journeys to the Straits of Fury and Hecla and to King William's Land, and Residence among the Eskimos during the Years 1864–69*. Edited by J. E. Nourse. Cambridge: Cambridge University Press, May 2014.

Hendrik, Hans. *Memoirs of Hans Hendrik, the Arctic Traveller, Serving Under Kane, Hayes, Hall and Nares, 1853–1876, Written By Himself*. Edited by Prof. Dr. George Stephens, translated by Dr. Henry Rink. London: Trubner & Co., 1878.

Hood, Robert. *To the Arctic by Canoe, 1819–1821: The Journal and Paintings of Robert Hood, Midshipman with Franklin*. Edited by C. Stuart Houston. Montreal and London: McGill-Queens University Press, 1974.

Hood, Thomas. *The Poetical Works of Thomas Hood: With a Memoir of the Author*. New York: James Miller, 1873.

Huxley, Leonard. *Life and Letters of Sir Joseph Dalton Hooker, O.M, G.C.S.I., Based on Materials Collected and Arranged by Lady Hooker*. Vols. 1 and 2. London: John Murray, 1918.

Isbister, Alexander Kennedy. *A Few Words on the Hudson's Bay Company: with A Statement of the Grievances of the Native and Half-caste Indians, Addressed to the British Government through their Delegates Now in London*. London: C. Gilpin, 1846.

Isbister, Alexander Kennedy. *A Proposal for a New Penal Settlement, in Connexion with the Colonization of the Uninhabited Districts of British North America*. London: Trelawney Saunders, 1850.

[Isbister, Alexander Kennedy]. *Arctic Rewards and their Claimants*. London: T. Hatchard, 1856.

Isbister, Alexander Kennedy. "On the Chippewyan Indians." *Transactions of the British Association for the Advancement of Science* (1847): 119–22.

Isbister, Alexander Kennedy. "Some Account of Peel River, North America." *Journal of the Royal Geographical Society* 15 (1845): 332–45.

Kay, J. H. "Terrestrial Magnetism." *The Tasmanian Journal of Natural Science, Agriculture, Statistics, &c.* 1 (1841): 124–36.

King, Richard. "On the Industrial Arts of the Esquimaux." *Journal of the Ethnological Society of London* 1 (1848): 277–300.

King, Richard. "On the Intellectual Character of the Esquimaux." *Journal of the Ethnological Society of London* 1 (1848): 127–53.

King, Richard. "On the Physical Characters of the Esquimaux." *Journal of the Ethnological Society of London* 1 (1848): 45–59.

A Lady. *A Peep at the Esquimaux; Or, Scenes on the Ice, To Which is Annexed, A Polar Pastoral.* London: H. R. Thomas, 1825.

Lea, Alice, ed. *Some Unpublished Letters of Sir John Franklin, Sir John Richardson and Others, Written During the Expeditions to North-West Canada for the Purpose of Explorations, 1819–22 and 1825–27.* Toronto: Women's Canadian Historical Society Transactions, 1918.

Lhotsky, John. "Some Remarks on a Short Vocabulary of the Natives of Van Diemen Land; And Also of the Menero Downs in Australia." *The Journal of the Royal Geographical Society of London* 9 (1839): 157–62.

Lyon, George Francis. *The Private Journal of Captain G. F. Lyon, of H.M.S. Hecla, During the Recent Voyage of Discovery under Captain Parry.* London: John Murray, 1824.

Maconochie, Alexander. *Crime and Punishment: The Mark System Framed to Mix Persuasion with Punishment, and Make Their Effect Improving, yet Their Operation Severe.* London: J. Hatchard, 1846.

Maconochie, Alexander. *Norfolk Island.* London: J. Hatchard, 1847.

Maconochie, Alexander. *On the Management of Transported Criminals.* London: C. Whiting, 1845.

Maconochie, Alexander. *Secondary Punishment: The Mark System.* London: John Ollivier, 1848.

McDonald, Alexander. *A Narrative of Some Passages in the Life of Eenoolooapik, A Young Esquimaux, Who Was Brought to Britain in 1839 in the Ship "Neptune" of Aberdeen; An Account of the Discovery of Hogarth's Sound: Remarks on the Northern Whale Fishery and Suggestions for Its Improvement, &c &c.* Edinburgh: Fraser & Co., 1841.

McIlraith, John. *Life of Sir John Richardson.* London: Longman, Green and Co., 1868.

M'Cormick, Robert. *Voyages of Discovery in the Arctic and Antarctic Seas, and Round the World. . .* London: Sampson Low, Marston, Searle, and Rivington, 1884.

Meredith, Louisa Anne. *My Home in Tasmania, during a Residence of Nine Years.* London: John Murray, 1852.

Miller, Linus Wilson. *Notes of an Exile to Van Dieman's Land.* Fredonia: McKinstry, 1846.

Mitford, Mary Russell. *The Life of Mary Russell Mitford, as Related in a Selection from her Letters to her Friends.* Edited by Alfred Guy L'Estrange. Vol. 2. London: Richard Bentley, 1870.

Owen, Richard. *Report on the Extinct Mammals of Australia, and on the Geographical Distribution of Pliocene and Post-pliocene Mammals in General.* London: British Association for Advancement of Science, 1845.

Parry, William Edward. *Journal of a Second Voyage for the Discovery of a North-West Passage from the Atlantic to the Pacific: Performed in the Years 1821-22-23, in His Majesty's Ships Fury and Hecla, under the Orders of Captain William Edward Parry.* London: John Murray, 1824.

Pasco, Crawford. *A Roving Commission: Naval Reminiscences.* Melbourne: George Robertson, 1897.

Porden, Eleanor Anne. *The Arctic Expeditions. A Poem.* London: John Murray, 1818.

Rae, John. *John Rae's Correspondence with the Hudson's Bay Company on Arctic Exploration, 1844–1855.* Edited by A. M. Johnson, E. E. Rich, R. J. Cyriax, and J. M. Wordie. London: Hudson's Bay Record Society, 1953.

Richardson, John. *Arctic Ordeal: The Journal of John Richardson, Surgeon-Naturalist with Franklin, 1820–1822.* Edited by C. Stuart Houston. Kingston and Montreal: McGill-Queen's University Press, 1984.

Ross, John. *On Intemperance in the Royal Navy*. London: Tweedie, 1852.
Sauer, Gordon C., ed. *John Gould, the Bird Man: Correspondence, with a Chronology of His Life and Works*. Vol. 2. Mansfield Centre: Maurizio Martino, 1998.
Scoresby, William. *Memorials of the Sea: Sabbaths in the Arctic Regions, or, Testimonies of Nature and Providence to the Divine Institution and Perpetuity of the Sabbath*. 2nd ed. [1st ed. 1830]. London: Longman, Brown, Green, and Longmans, 1850.
Scoresby, William. *The Franklin Expedition: Or, Considerations on Measures for the Discovery and Relief of our Absent Adventurers in the Arctic Regions*. London: Longman, Brown, Green, and Longmans, 1850.
Stokes, John Lort. *Discoveries in Australia: With an Account of the Coasts and Rivers Explored and Surveyed during the Voyage of H.M.S. Beagle, in the Years 1837-38-39-40-41-42-43, by Command of the Lords Commissioners of the Admiralty; Also, a Narrative of Captain Owen Stanley's Visits to the Islands in the Arafura Sea*. London: T. and W. Boone, 1846.
Traill, H. *Life of Sir John Franklin, R. N.* London: John Murray, 1896.
West, John. *A History of Tasmania, with Copious Information Respecting the Colonies of New South Wales, Victoria, South Australia &c., &c., &c.* Edited by A. G. L. Shaw. London and Sydney: Angus & Robertson Publishers, 1971.

Secondary Sources

Alberti, Samuel J. M. M. "Conversaziones and the Experience of Science in Victorian England." *Journal of Victorian Culture* 8, no. 2 (Autumn 2003): 208–30.
Alexander, Alison. *Tasmania vs the British Empire: The Battle to End Convict Transportation*. Hobart: Forty South Press, 2022.
Alexander, Alison. *The Ambitions of Jane Franklin, Victorian Lady Adventurer*. Sydney: Allen & Unwin, 2013.
Allen, David. "Tastes and Crazes." In *Cultures of Natural History*, edited by N. Jardine, J. A. Secord, and E. C. Spary, 394–407. Cambridge: Cambridge University Press, 1996.
Aporta, Claudio. "New Ways of Mapping: Using GPS Software to Plot Place Names and Trails in Igloolik (Nunavut)." *Arctic* 56, no. 4 (2003): 321–7.
Aporta, Claudio. "The Sea, the Land, the Coast, and the Winds: Understanding Inuit Sea Ice Use in Context." In *SIKU: Knowing Our Ice: Documenting Inuit Sea Ice Knowledge and Use*, edited by Igor Krupnik, Claudio Aporta, Lena Kielson Holm, Shari Gearheard, Gita J. Laidler, and Michael Bravo, 163–80. Dordrecht: Springer, 2010.
Aporta, Claudio. "The Trail as Home: Inuit and their Pan-Arctic Network of Routes." *Human Ecology* 37 (2009): 131–46.
Atwood, Margaret. *Strange Things: The Malevolent North in Canadian Literature*. London: Virago Press, 2004.
Auty, Kate and Lynette Russell. *Hunt Them, Hang Them: 'The Tasmanians' in Port Phillip, 1841–42*. Melbourne: Justice Press, 2016.
Ballantyne, Tony. *Entanglements of Empire: Missionaries, Maori, and the Question of the Body*. Chapel Hill: Duke University Press, 2014.
Ballantyne, Tony. *Orientalism and Race: Aryanism in the British Empire*. New York: Palgrave-Macmillan, 2002.
Ballantyne, Tony. *Webs of Empire: Locating New Zealand's Colonial Past*. Wellington: Bridget Williams Books, 2012.

Ballantyne, Tony and Antoinette Burton, eds. *Bodies in Contact: Rethinking Colonial Encounters in World History*. Durham and London: Duke University Press, 2005.

Ballantyne, Tony and Antoinette Burton. *Moving Subjects: Gender, Mobility and Intimacy in an Age of Global Empire*. Urbana and Chicago: University of Illinois Press, 2009.

Barczewski, Stephanie. *Heroic Failure and the British*. New Haven and London: Yale University Press, 2016.

Barr, William. *From Barrow to Boothia: The Arctic Journal of Chief Factor Peter Warren Dease, 1836–1839*. Montreal: McGill-Queen's University Press, 2002.

Barr, William. "'The Cold of Valparaiso': The Disintegration of William Kennedy's Second Franklin Search Expedition, 1853–1854." *Polar Record* 34, no. 190 (1998): 203–18.

Barry, John Vincent. *Alexander Maconochie of Norfolk Island: A Study of a Pioneer in Penal Reform*. Melbourne: Oxford University Press, 1958.

Barry, John Vincent. "Pioneers in Criminology: Alexander Maconochie." *The Journal of Criminal Law, Criminology and Police Science* 47, no. 2 (July–August 1956): 145–61.

Barry, John Vincent. *The Life and Death of John Price: A Study of the Exercise of Naked Power*. London and New York: Melbourne University Press, 1964.

Bassin, Mark. *Imperial Visions: Nationalist Imagination and Geographical Expansion in the Russian Far East, 1840–1865*. Cambridge and New York: Cambridge University Press, 1999.

Bayly, C. A. *Empire and Information: Intelligence Gathering and Social Communication in India, 1780–1870*. Cambridge Studies in Indian History & Society. Cambridge and New York: Cambridge University Press, 1996.

Bayly, C. A. "Knowing the Country: Empire and Information in India." *Modern Asian Studies* 27, no. 1 (1993): 3–43.

Beardsley, Martyn. *Deadly Winter: The Life of Sir John Franklin*. London: Chatham Publishing, 2002.

Beaver, Donald deB. "Lee, Sarah (1791–1856)." In *Oxford Dictionary of National Biography*. Oxford University Press, 2004 (accessed May 1, 2013). doi: 10.1093/ref:odnb/16310.

Beaver, Donald deB. "Writing Natural History for Survival, 1820–1856: The Case of Sarah Bowdich, later Sarah Lee." *Archives of Natural History* 26 (1999): 19–31.

Beer, Gillian "Travelling the Other Way." In *Cultures of Natural History*, edited by N. Jardine, J. A. Secord, and E. C. Spary, 323. Cambridge: Cambridge University Press, 1996.

Bell, Morag, Robin Butlin, and Michael Heffernan, eds. *Geography and Imperialism, 1820–1940*. Manchester: Manchester University Press, 1995.

Berton, Pierre. *The Arctic Grail: The Quest for the Northwest Passage and the North Pole, 1818–1909*. New York: Viking, 1998.

Betts, Matthew W. "The Mackenzie Inuit Whale Bone Industry: Raw Material, Tool Manufacture, and Trade." *Arctic* 60, no. 2 (June 2007): 129–44.

Birket-Smith, Kaj. *The Caribou Eskimos: Material and Social Life and Their Cultural Position. Descriptive Part*. Translated by W. E. Calvert. Report of the Fifth Thule Expedition, 1921-24. Vol. 5, pt. 1. Copenhagen: Gyldendalske Boghandel, 1929.

Birmingham, Judy and Andrew Wilson. "Archaeologies of Cultural Interaction: Wybalenna Settlement and Killalpaninna Mission." *International Journal of Historical Archaeology* 14 (2010): 15–38.

Blom, Ida, Karen Hagemann, and Catherine Hall, eds. *Gendered Nations: Nationalisms and Gender Order in the Long Nineteenth Century*. London and New York: Bloomsbury, 2000.

Blum, Hester. *The News at the Ends of the Earth: The Print Culture of Polar Exploration*. Durham and London: Duke University Press, 2019.

Bockstoce, John. "From Davis Strait to Bering Strait: The Arrival of the Commercial Whaling Fleet in North America's Western Arctic." *Arctic* 37, no. 4 (December 1984): 528–32.

Bockstoce, John. *Furs and Frontiers in the Far North: The Contest Among Native and Foreign Nations for the Bering Strait Fur Trade*. New Haven and London: Harvard University Press, 2009.

Bockstoce, John. *Whales, Ice and Men: The History of Whaling in the Western Arctic*. Seattle and London: University of Washington Press, 1986.

Bossy, Denise Ileana. "Shattering Together, Merging Apart: Colonialism, Violence and the Remaking of the Native South." *William and Mary Quarterly*, 3rd ser, 71, no. 4 (October 2014): 611–31.

Boyce, James. *1835: The Founding of Melbourne and the Conquest of Australia*. Melbourne: Black, Inc., 2011.

Boyce, James. *Van Diemen's Land*. Melbourne: Black, Inc., 2010.

Brantlinger, Patrick. *Dark Vanishings: Discourse on the Extinction of Primitive Races, 1800–1930*. Ithaca: Cornell University Press, 2003.

Bravo, Michael. "Ethnographic Navigation and the Geographical Gift." In *Geography and Enlightenment*, edited by David Livingston and Charles W. J. Withers, 199–235. Chicago and London: University of Chicago Press, 1999.

Bravo, Michael. "Geographies of Exploration and Improvement: William Scoresby and Arctic Whaling, 1782–1922." *Journal of Historical Geography* 32 (2006): 512–38.

Bravo, Michael. *The Accuracy of Ethnoscience: A Study of Inuit Cartography and Cross-Cultural Commensurability*. Manchester Papers in Social Anthropology, no. 2. Manchester: Manchester University Press, 1996.

Briggs, Jean L. *Never in Anger: Portrait of an Eskimo Family*. Cambridge, MA: Harvard University Press, 1970.

Brodie, Nicholas Dean. *The Vandemonian War: The Secret History of Britain's Tasmanian Invasion*. Richmond: Hardie Grant Books, 2017.

Brown, Jennifer S. H. *Strangers in Blood: Fur Trade Company Families in Indian Country*. Norman: University of Oklahoma Press, 1980.

Brown, Jennifer S. H. and Elizabeth Vibert, eds. *Reading Beyond Words: Contexts for Naïve History*. 2nd ed. Toronto and London: University of Toronto Press, 2009.

Brown, Joan C. *Poverty Is Not a Crime: The Development of Social Services in Tasmania, 1803–1900*. Hobart: Tasmanian Historical Research Association, 1972.

Browne, Janet. *Charles Darwin: The Power of Place*. Vol. 2. Princeton and Oxford: Princeton University Press, 2002.

Buettner, Elizabeth. *Empire Families: Britons and Late Imperial India*. Oxford: Oxford University Press, 2004.

Bunyan, Ian, Jenni Calder, Dale Idiens, and Bryce Wilson, *No Ordinary Journey: John Rae, Arctic Explorer, 1813–1893*. Edinburgh: National Museums of Scotland/Montreal and Kingston: McGill-Queen's University Press, 1993.

Burch, Ernest S., Jr. *Alliance and Conflict: The World System of the Iñupiaq Eskimos*. Lincoln and London: University of Nebraska Press, 2005.

Burch, Ernest S., Jr. *The Iñupiaq Eskimo Nations of Northwest Alaska*. Fairbanks: University of Alaska Press, 1998.

Burnett, D. Graham. *Masters of All They Surveyed: Exploration, Geography and a British El Dorado*. Chicago and London: Chicago University Press, 2001.

Burton, Antoinette, ed. *Archive Stories: Facts, Fictions, and the Writing of History*. Durham and London: Duke University Press, 2005.
Burton, Antoinette. "Archive Stories: Gender in the Making of Imperial and Colonial Histories." In *Gender and Empire*, edited by Phillipa Levine, 281-93. Oxford and New York: Oxford University Press, 2004.
Burton, Antoinette. *Burdens of History: British Feminists, Indian Women, and Imperial Culture, 1865-1915*. Chapel Hill and London: University of North Carolina Press, 1994.
Burton, Antoinette. *Dwelling in the Archive: Women Writing House, Home and History in Late Colonial India*. Oxford: Oxford University Press, 2003.
Burton, Antoinette. "Who Needs the Nation? Interrogating 'British' History." *Journal of Historical Sociology* 10, no. 3 (September 1997): 227-48.
Cadzow, Allison. "Guided by Her: Aboriginal Women's Participation in Australian Expeditions." In *Brokers and Boundaries: Colonial Exploration in Indigenous Territory*, edited by Tiffany Shellam et al., 85-118. Canberra: ANU Press, 2016.
Cadzow, Allison. "Turandurey (c. 1806-?)." In *Australian Dictionary of Biography*. National Centre of Biography, Australian National University. https://ia.anu.edu.au/biography/turandurey-29903/text37019 (accessed September 18, 2022).
Calder, Graeme. *Levee, Line and Martial Law: A History of the Dispossession of the Mairremmener People of Van Diemen's Land, 1803-1832*. Launceston: Fullers Bookshop, 2010.
Cameron, Emilie. *Far Off Metal River: Inuit Lands, Settler Stories, and the Making of the Contemporary Arctic*. Vancouver and Toronto: UBC Press, 2015.
Cameron, Patsy. *Grease and Ochre: The Blending of Two Cultures at the Colonial Sea Frontier*. Launceston: Fullers Bookshop, 2011.
Carey, Hilary M. *Empire of Hell: Religion and the Campaign to End Convict Transportation in the British Empire, 1788-1875*. Cambridge: Cambridge University Press, 2019.
Carey, Jane and Jane Lyon, eds. *Indigenous Networks: Mobility, Connections and Exchange*. New York and London: Routledge, 2014.
Carter, Christopher. "'The Sea Fryseth Not': Science and the Open Polar Sea in the Nineteenth Century." *Earth Sciences History* 32, no. 2 (October 2013): 235-51.
Cavell, Janice. "Lady Lucy Barry and Evangelical Reading on the First Franklin Expedition." *Arctic* 63, no. 2 (June 2010): 1-10.
Cavell, Janice. "Publishing John Franklin's Fate." *Book History* 16 (2013): 155-84.
Cavell, Janice. "Representing Akaitcho: European Vision and Revision in the Writing of John Franklin's Narrative of a Journey to the Shores of the Polar Sea. . ." *Polar Record* 44, no. 228 (2008): 25-34.
Cavell, Janice. "The Hidden Crime of Dr. Richardson." *Polar Record* 43, no. 2 (April 2007): 155-64.
Cavell, Janice. *Tracing the Connected Narrative: Arctic Exploration in British Print Culture, 1818-1860*. Toronto and London: University of Toronto Press, 2008.
Cawood, John. "The Magnetic Crusade: Science and Politics in Early Victorian Britain." *Isis* 70, no. 4 (December 1979): 492-518.
Claydon, Annaliese. "P is for Platypus." In *Animalia: An Anti-Imperial Bestiary for Our Times*, edited by Antoinette Burton and Renisa Mawani, 140-4. Durham and London: Duke University Press, 2020.
Clements, Nicholas. *The Black War: Fear, Sex and Resistance in Tasmania*. St. Lucia: University of Queensland Press, 2014.

Cohn, Bernard. *Colonialism and Its Forms of Knowledge.* Princeton: Princeton University Press, 1996.

Collignon, Béatrice. *Knowing Places: The Inuinnait, Landscapes, and the Environment.* Translated by Linna Weber Müller-Wille. Edmonton: Canadian Circumpolar Institute Press, 2006.

Conley, Mary A. *From Jack Tar to Union Jack: Representing Naval Manhood in the British Empire, 1870–1918.* Manchester: Manchester University Press, 2009.

Cooper, Barry. *Alexander Kennedy Isbister: A Respectable Critic of the Honourable Company.* Ottowa: Carleton University Press, 1988.

Cooper, Frederick and Anna Laura Stoler, eds. *Tensions of Empire: Colonial Cultures in a Bourgeois World.* Berkeley: University of California Press, 1997.

Craciun, Adriana. "The Franklin Relics in the Arctic Archive." *Victorian Literature and Culture* 42, no. 1 (March 2014): 1–31.

Craciun, Adriana. *Writing Arctic Disaster: Authorship and Exploration.* Cambridge Studies in Nineteenth-Century Literature and Culture. Cambridge and New York: Cambridge University Press, 2016.

Creighton, Margaret and Lisa Norling, eds. *Iron Men and Wooden Women: Gender and Seafaring in the Atlantic World.* Baltimore: The Johns Hopkins University Press, 1996.

Cruikshank, Julie. *Do Glaciers Listen? Local Knowledge: Colonial Encounters, and Social Imagination.* Vancouver and Toronto: University of British Columbia Press, 2005.

Curthoys, Ann. "The History of Killing and the Killing of History." In *Archive Stories: Facts, Fictions, and the Writing of History,* edited by Antoinette Burton, 351–73. Durham and London: Duke University Press, 2005.

Dammery, Sally. *Walter George Arthur, A Free Tasmanian?* Melbourne: Monash Publications in History, 2001.

Darwin, John. "Imperialism and the Victorians: The Dynamics of Territorial Expansion." *The English Historical Review* 112, no. 447 (June 1997): 614–42.

Daschuk, James. *Clearing the Plains: Disease, Politics of Starvation, and the Loss of Indigenous Life.* 2nd ed. Regina: University of Regina Press, 2019.

David, Robert G. *The Arctic in the British Imagination, 1818–1914.* Manchester and New York: Manchester University Press, 2000.

Davidoff, Leonore and Catherine Hall. *Family Fortunes: Men and Women of the English Middle Class, 1780–1850.* Rev. ed. London and New York: Routledge, 2002.

Davis, Richard C. "Fact and Fancy in History and Biography: The Case of Greenstockings." *Polar Record* 37, no. 200 (2001): 5–12.

Davis, Richard C. "'. . . Which an Affectionate Heart Would Say': John Franklin's Personal Correspondence, 1819-1824." *Polar Record* 33, no. 186 (1997): 189–212.

Deacon, Desley, Penny Russell, and Angela Woollacott, eds. *Transnational Lives: Biographies of Global Modernity.* New York: Palgrave Macmillan, 2010.

de Costa, Ravi. "Identity, Authority and the Moral Worlds of Indigenous Petitions." *Comparative Studies in Society and History* 48, no. 3 (July 2006): 669–98.

Demuth, Bathsheba. *Floating Coast: An Environmental History of the Bering Strait.* New York and London: W.W. Norton & Company, 2020.

Dening, Greg. *Mr Bligh's Bad Language: Passion, Power and Theatre on the Bounty.* Cambridge: Cambridge University Press, 1992.

Denison, William. *Varieties of Vice-Regal Life.* Edited by Richard Davis and Stefan Petrow, 181–3. Sandy Bay: Tasmanian Historical Research Association, 2004.

Dettelbach, Michael. "Humboldtean Science." In *Cultures of Natural History,* edited by N. Jardine, J. A. Secord, and E. C. Spary, 287–304. Cambridge: Cambridge University Press, 1996.

Devine, Heather. *The People Who Own Themselves: Aboriginal Ethnogenesis in a Canadian Family, 1660–1900*. Calgary: University of Calgary Press, 2013.
Dirks, Nicholas. *Castes of Mind: Colonialism and the Making of Modern India*. Princeton: Princeton University Press, 2001.
Douglas, Bronwen and Chris Ballard, eds. *Foreign Bodies: Oceania and the Science of Race, 1750–1940*. Canberra: ANU Press, 2008.
Drayton, Richard. *Nature's Government: Science, Imperial Britain, and the "Improvement" of the World*. New Haven and London: Yale University Press, 2000.
Dritsas, Lawrence. "Expeditionary Science: Conflicts of Method in Mid-Nineteenth Century Geographical Discovery." In *Geographies of Nineteenth Century Science*, edited by David N. Livingstone and Charles W. J. Withers, 255–77. Chicago and London: University of Chicago Press, 2011.
Driver, Felix. *Geography Militant: Cultures of Exploration and Empire*. Oxford and Malden: Blackwell Publishers, 2001.
Driver, Felix and Lowri Jones. *Hidden Histories of Exploration: Researching the RGS-IBG Collections*. London: Royal Holloway, University of London and the Royal Geographical Society–Institute of British Geographers, 2009.
Eber, Dorothy Harley. *Encounters on the Passage: Inuit Meet the Explorers*. Toronto and London: University of Toronto Press, 2008.
Eber, Dorothy Harley. "Rumours of Franklin: The Strength of the Inuit Oral Tradition." *Beaver* 76, no. 3 (June/July 1996): 4–14.
Eber, Dorothy Harley. *When the Whalers Were Up North: Inuit Memories from the Eastern Arctic*. Norman: University of Oklahoma Press, 1996.
Edmonds, Penelope. "Travelling 'Under Concern': Quakers James Backhouse and George Washington Walker Tour the Antipodean Colonies, 1832–41." *The Journal of Imperial and Commonwealth History* 40, no. 5 (December 2012): 769–88.
Edmonds, Penelope and Michelle Berry. "Eliza Batman's House: Unhomely Frontiers and Intimate Overstraiters in Van Diemen's Land and Port Phillip." In *Intimacies of Violence in the Settler Colony: Economies of Dispossession around the Pacific Rim*, edited by Penelope Edmonds and Amanda Nettelbeck, 115–37. Cham, Switzerland: Palgrave MacMillan, 2018.
Edney, Matthew. *Mapping an Empire: The Geographical Construction of British India, 1765–1843*. Chicago: University of Chicago Press, 1997.
Elbourne, Elizabeth. "Imperial Politics in a Family Way: Gender, Biography and the 1835–36 Select Committee on Aborigines." In *Frontier, Race, Nation: Henry Reynolds and Australian History*, edited by Bain Attwood and Tom Griffiths, 111–35. Melbourne: Australian Scholarly Publishing, 2009.
Elbourne, Elizabeth. "Indigenous Peoples and Imperial Networks in the early Nineteenth Century: The Politics of Knowledge." In *Rediscovering the British World*, edited by Phillip Buckner and R. Douglas Francis, 59–85. Calgary: University of Calgary Press, 2006.
Elbourne, Elizabeth. "The Sin of the Settler: The 1835-36 Select Committee on Aborigines and Debates Over Virtue and Conquest in the Early Nineteenth-Century British White Settler Empire." *Journal of Colonialism and Colonial History* 4, no. 3 (2003) (accessed 27 September 2013). doi: 10.1353/cch.2004.0003.
Elce, Erika Behrisch, ed. *As Affecting the Fate of my Absent Husband: Selected Letters of Lady Franklin Concerning the Search for the Lost Franklin Expedition, 1848–1860*. Montreal and Kingston: McGill-Queen's University Press, 2009.
Eldershaw, P. R. *Guide to the Public Records of Tasmania*. Colonial Secretary's Office. Hobart: Archives Office of Tasmania, 1957.

Endersby, Jim. *Imperial Nature: Joseph Hooker and the Practices of Victorian Science*. Chicago and London: Chicago University Press, 2008.

Fabian, Johannes. *Out of Our Minds: Reason and Madness in the Exploration of Central Africa*. Berkeley and London: University of California Press, 2000.

Finlay, Grant. *'Good People Always Crackney in Heaven' Mythic Conversations in lutruwita/Tasmania*. Hobart: Fullers Publishing, 2019.

Finn, Margot. "Women, Consumption, and Coverture in England, c. 1700–1860." *The Historical Journal* 39, no. 3 (1996): 703–22.

Fisch-Davis, Heather. *Loss and Cultural Remains in Performance: The Ghosts of the Franklin Expedition*. New York: Palgrave Macmillan, 2012.

Fitzpatrick, Kathleen. *Sir John Franklin in Tasmania, 1837–1843*. Melbourne: Melbourne University Press, 1947.

Fortescue, Michael. *From the Writings of the Greenlanders – Kalaallit atuakkiaannit*. Fairbanks: University of Alaska Press, 1990.

Fossett, Renee. *In Order To Live Untroubled: Inuit of the Central Arctic, 1550–1940*. Winnipeg: The University of Manitoba Press, 2001.

Frost, Lucy and Colette McAlpine, eds. *From the Edges of Empire: Convict Women from Beyond the British Isles*. Hobart: Convict Women's Press, 2015.

Fullagar, Kate and Michael A. McDonnell, eds. *Facing Empire: Indigenous Experiences in a Revolutionary Age, 1760–1840*. Baltimore: John Hopkins University Press, 2018.

Furphy, Samuel. "Philanthropy or Patronage?: Aboriginal Protectors in the Port Phillip District and Western Australia." In *Aboriginal Protection and Its Intermediaries in Britain's Antipodean Colonies*, edited by Samuel Furphy and Amanda Nettelbeck, 58–76. New York and London: Routledge, 2020.

Gates, Barbara T. "Those Who Drew and Those Who Wrote: Women and Victorian Popular Science Illustration." In *Figuring It Out: Science, Gender and Visual Culture*, edited by Ann B. Shtier and Bernard Lightman, 192–213. Hanover and London: Dartmouth College Press, 2006.

Geiger, John and Alanna Mitchell. *Franklin's Lost Ship: The Historic Discovery of HMS Erebus*. Toronto: HarperCollins, Ltd., 2015.

Gibson, James R. *Otter Skins, Boston Ships and China Goods: The Maritime Fur Trade of the Northwest Coast, 1785–1841*. Montreal: McGill-Queen's University Press, 2001.

Gillespie, Beryl C. "Changes in the Territory and Technology of the Chipewyan." *Arctic Anthropology* 13, no. 1 (1976): 6–11.

Girling, Richard. *The Man Who Ate the Zoo: Frank Buckland, Forgotten Hero of Natural History*. London: Vintage, 2017.

Gleadle, Kathryn and Sarah Richardson, eds. *Women in British Politics, 1760–1860: The Power of the Petticoat*. London: Palgrave Macmillan, 2000.

Gough, Julie, Dave mangenner Gough, Lauren Gower, Mary Knights, Greg Lehman, Neika Lehman, Joseph Pugliese, Zoe Rimmer, and Margaret Woodward. *Tense Past*. Hobart: Tebrikunna Press, 2021.

Grant, Shelagh D. *Arctic Justice: On Trial for Murder, Pond Inlet, 1923*. Montreal and London: McGill-Queen's University Press, 2002.

Hall, Catherine. *Civilising Subjects: Metropole and Colony in the English Imagination, 1830–1867*. Chicago and London: University of Chicago Press, 2002.

Hall, Catherine. *Macauley and Son: Architects of Imperial Britain*. New Haven and London: Yale University Press, 2012.

Harlan, Deborah. "Thomas Bateman, *Crania Britannica*, and Archaeological Chronology." *European Journal of Archaeology*, 21, no. 1 (June 2017): 1–21.

Harman, Kristyn. *Cleansing the Colony: Transporting Convicts from New Zealand to Van Diemen's Land*. Otago: Otago University Press, 2017.

Harrod, Dominick, ed. *War, Ice and Piracy: The Remarkable Career of a Victorian Sailor, the Journals and Letters of Samuel Gurney Cresswell*. London: Chatham Publishing, 2000.

Harvey, Joy. "Darwin's 'Angels': The Women Correspondents of Charles Darwin." *Intellectual History Review* 19, no. 2 (2009): 197–210.

Hay, Douglas. "Property, Authority and the Criminal Law." In *Albion's Fatal Tree: Crime and Society in Eighteenth-Century England*, edited by Douglas Hay, Peter Linebaugh, John G. Rule, E.P. Thompson, and Cal Winslow, 2nd ed. 17–63. London and New York: Verso, 2011.

Heartfield, James. *The Aborigines' Protection Society: Humanitarian Imperialism in Australia, New Zealand, Fiji, Canada, South Africa and the Congo, 1836–1909*. New York: Columbia University Press, 2011.

Helm, June and Beryl C. Gillespie, "Dogrib Oral Tradition as History: War and Peace in the 1820s." *Journal of Anthropological Research* 37, no. 1 (Spring 1981): 8–27.

Hill, Jen. *White Horizon: The Arctic in the Nineteenth-Century British Imagination*. Albany: State University of New York Press, 2008.

Hoare, Michael E. "'All Things are Queer and Opposite': Scientific Societies in Tasmania in the 1840s." *ISIS* 60, no. 2 (Summer 1969): 198–209.

Holland, Clive. "The Arctic Committee of 1851: A Background Study, Part 1." *Polar Record* 20, no. 124 (1980): 3–17.

Holland, Clive. "The Arctic Committee of 1851: A Background Study, Part 2." *Polar Record* 20, no. 125 (1980): 105–18.

Holland, Julian. "Kater, Henry (1777–1835)." In *Oxford Dictionary of National Biography*. Oxford University Press, 2004 (accessed May 1, 2013). http://doi:10.1093/ref:odnb/15186.

Hunt, Margaret. "Women and the Fiscal Imperial State." In *A New Imperial History: Culture, Identity and Modernity in Britain and the Empire, 1660–1840*, edited by Kathleen Wilson, 29–47. Cambridge: Cambridge University Press, 2004.

Hutchinson, Gillian. *Sir John Franklin's Erebus and Terror Expedition: Lost and Found*. London and New York: Bloomsbury, 2017.

Hylton, Jane. *Colonial Sisters: Martha Berkeley and Theresa Walker, South Australia's First Professional Artists*. Adelaide: Art Gallery Board of South Australia, 1994.

Jacobs, Annaliese. "Empire at the Floe Edge: Western Empires and Indigenous People in the Bering Sea and Arctic Ocean, c. 1820–1900." In *The Routledge History of Western Empires*, edited by Robert K. Aldrich and Kristen McKenzie, 136–50. Abingdon: Routledge, 2013.

Janowitz, Ann. "Amiable and Radical Sociability: Anna Barbauld's 'Free Familiar Conversation'." In *Romantic Sociability: Social Networks and Literary Culture in Britain, 1770–1840*, edited by Gillian Russell and Clara Tuite, 62–81. Cambridge and New York: Cambridge University Press, 2002.

Jenkins, Bill. "Neptunism and Transformism: Robert Jameson and Other Evolutionary Theorists in Early Nineteenth-Century Scotland." *Journal of the History of Biology* 49 no. 3 (Fall 2016): 527–57.

Jenkins, Bill. "The Platypus in Edinburgh: Robert Jameson, Robert Knox and the Place of the Ornithorhynchus in Nature, 1821–24." *Annals of Science* 73, no. 4 (October 2016): 425–41.

Joel, Craig. *A Tale of Ambition and Unrealised Hope: John Montagu and* Sir *John Franklin*. North Melbourne: Australian Scholarly Publishing Pty Ltd., 2011.

Jones, H. G. "The Inuit as Geographers: The Case of Eenoolooapik." *Etudes/Inuit/Studies* 28, no. 2 (2004): 57–72.
Jones, Max. *The Last Great Quest: Captain Scott's Antarctic Sacrifice*. Oxford and New York: Oxford University Press, 2003.
Keighren, Innes M., Charles W. J. Withers, and Bill Bell, *Travels Into Print: Exploration, Writing and Publishing with John Murray, 1773–1859*. Chicago and London: University of Chicago Press, 2015.
Keith, Lloyd, ed. *North of Athabasca: Slave Lake and Mackenzie River Documents of the North West Company, 1800–1821*. (Rupert's Land Record Society Series). Vol. 6. Montreal and Kingston: McGill-Queen's University Press, 2001.
Kennedy, Dane. *The Highly Civilized Man: Richard Burton and the Victorian World*. Cambridge, MA and London: Harvard University Press, 2005.
Kennedy, Dane. *The Last Blank Spaces: Exploring Africa and Australia*. Cambridge, MA and London: Harvard University Press, 2013.
Kennedy, Dane, ed. *Reinterpreting Exploration: The West in the World*. Oxford and New York: Oxford University Press, 2014.
Konishi, Shino, Maria Nugent, and Tiffany Shellam, eds. *Indigenous Intermediaries: New Perspectives on Exploration Archives*. Canberra: ANU Press, 2015.
Krech, Shepherd, III. "Disease, Starvation and Northern Athapaskan Social Organization." *American Ethnologist* 5, no. 4 (November 1978): 710–32.
Krech, Shepherd, III. "The Eastern Kutchin and the Fur Trade, 1800–1860." *Ethnohistory* 23, no. 3 (Summer 1976): 213–35.
Laidlaw, Zoe. "'Aunt Anna's Report': The Buxton Women and the Aborigine's Select Committee." *Journal of Imperial and Commonwealth History* 32, no. 2 (May 2004): 1–28.
Laidlaw, Zoe. *Colonial Connections, 1815–1845: Patronage, the Information Revolution and Colonial Government*. Manchester: Manchester University Press, 2005.
Laidlaw, Zoe. "Indigenous Interlocutors: Networks of Imperial Protest and Humanitarianism in the Mid-Nineteenth Century." In *Indigenous Networks: Mobility, Connections and Exchange*, edited by Jane Carey and Jane Lydon, 114–39. London: Routledge, 2014.
Laidlaw, Zoe. *Protecting the Empire's Humanity: Thomas Hodgkin and British Colonial Activism, 1830–1870*. Cambridge: Cambridge University Press, 2021.
Lamb, Jonathan. *Preserving the Self in the South Seas, 1680–1840*. Chicago and London: University of Chicago Press, 2001.
Lambert, Andrew. *The Gates of Hell: Sir John Franklin's Tragic Quest for the North West Passage*. New Haven and London: Yale University Press, 2009.
Lambert, David. *Mastering the Niger: James MacQueen's African Geography and the Struggle over Atlantic Slavery*. Chicago and London: University of Chicago Press, 2013.
Lambert, David and Alan Lester, eds. *Colonial Lives Across the British Empire: Imperial Careering in the Long Nineteenth Century*. Cambridge: Cambridge University Press, 2006.
Lambert, David and Alan Lester. "Geographies of Colonial Philanthropy." *Progress in Human Geography* 28, no. 3 (2004): 320–41.
Land, Isaac. *War, Nationalism and the British Sailor, 1750–1850*. New York and London: Palgrave Macmillan, 2009.
Larson, Edward J. "Public Science for a Global Empire: The British Quest for the South Magnetic Pole." *ISIS* 102, no. 1 (March 2011): 34–59.
Lawson, Tom. *The Last Man: A British Genocide in Tasmania*. London: I.B. Tauris, 2014.

Leask, Nigel. *Curiosity and the Aesthetics of Travel Writing, 1770–1840*. Oxford: Oxford University Press, 2002.
Lee, David S. and George W. Wenzel. "Narwhal Hunting by Pond Inlet Inuit: An Analysis of Foraging Modes in the Floe-Edge Environment." *Etudes/Inuit/Studies* 28, no. 2 (2005): 133–57.
Lee, Yangjung. "From Silver-Store to 'All over the World': The Transimperial Entanglements of 'The Perils of Certain English Prisoners.'" *Victorian Studies* 64, no. 3 (Spring 2022): 377–400.
Lester, Alan. "George Augustus Robinson and Imperial Networks." In *Reading Robinson: Companion Essays to Friendly Mission*, edited by Anna Johnston and Mitchell Rolls, 27–39. Hobart: Quintus Publishing, 2008.
Lester, Alan. "Humanitarians and White Settlers in the Nineteenth Century." In *Missions and Empire. Oxford History of the British Empire, Companion Series*, edited by Norman Etherington, 64–85. Oxford: Oxford University Press, 2005.
Lester, Alan. *Imperial Networks: Creating Identities in Nineteenth Century South Africa and Britain*. London: Routledge, 2001.
Lester, Alan and Fae Dussart, *Colonization and the Origins of Humanitarian Governance: Protecting Aborigines Across the Nineteenth-Century British Empire*. Cambridge: Cambridge University Press, 2014.
Lester, Alan and Zoe Laidlaw, eds. *Indigenous Communities and Settler Colonialism: Landholding, Loss and Survival in an Interconnected World*. Basingstoke: Palgrave Macmillan, 2015.
Liebersohn, Harry. *The Travelers' World: Europe to the Pacific*. Cambridge, MA and London: Harvard University Press, 2006.
Lightman, Bernard. *Victorian Popularizers of Science: Designing Nature for New Audiences*. Chicago and London: University of Chicago Press, 2007.
Lightman, Bernard, ed. *Victorian Science in Context*. Chicago and London: University of Chicago Press, 1997.
Lincoln, Margarette. *Naval Wives and Mistresses*. London: The National Maritime Museum, 2011.
Loomis, Chauncey. "The Arctic Sublime." In *Nature and the Victorian Imagination*, edited by U. C. Knoepflmacher and G. B. Tennyson, 95–112. Berkeley and Los Angeles: University of California Press, 1977.
Lowenstein, Tom. *Ancient Land, Sacred Whale: The Inuit Hunt and Its Rituals*. London: Bloomsbury, 1993.
MacDonald, Charlotte. "Intimacy of the Envelope: Fiction, Commerce and Empire in the Correspondence of Friends Mary Taylor and Charlotte Bronte, c. 1845–55." In *Moving Subjects: Gender, Mobility and Intimacy in an Age of Global Empire*, edited by Tony Ballantyne and Antoinette Burton, 89–109. Urbana and Chicago: University of Illinois Press, 2009.
MacDonald, John. *The Arctic Sky: Inuit Astronomy, Star Lore, and Legend*. Toronto: Royal Ontario Museum and Nunavut Research Institute, 1998.
MacIntyre, Stuart and Anna Clark. *The History Wars*. Melbourne: Melbourne University Press, 2003.
Mackaness, George, ed. *Some Private Correspondence of Sir John and Lady Jane Franklin*. vol. 1. Sydney: Australian Historical Monographs, 1947.
MacLaren, I. S. "John Barrow's Darling Project (1816–1846)." In *Arctic Exploration in the Nineteenth Century: Discovering the Northwest Passage*, edited by Frederic Regard, 19–36. London: Pickering and Chatto, 2013.

MacLeod, M. A. and R. Glover. "Franklin's First Expedition As Seen By the Fur Traders." *Polar Record* 15, no. 98 (1971): 669–82.
Madley, Benjamin. "From Terror to Genocide: Britain's Tasmanian Penal Colony and Australia's History Wars." *Journal of British Studies* 47 (January 2008): 77–106.
Mar, Tracey Banivanua. *Decolonisation and the Pacific: Indigenous Globalisation and the Ends of Empire*. Cambridge and New York: Cambridge University Press, 2016.
Mar, Tracey Banivanua. "Imperial Literacy and Indigenous Rights: Tracing Transoceanic Circuits of a Modern Discourse." *Aboriginal History* 37 (2013): 1–28.
Martin, Keavy. *Stories in a New Skin: Approaches to Inuit Literature*. Winnipeg: University of Manitoba Press, 2012.
Masson, Louis-Rodrigue, ed. *Les Bourgeois de la Compagnie du Nord-Ouest: Récits de voyages, lettres et rapports inédits relatifs au Nord-Ouest Canadien*. New York: Antiquarian Press, 1960.
Maxwell-Stewart, Hamish. "Transportation from Britain and Ireland, 1615–1875." In *A Global History of Convicts and Penal Colonies*, edited by Claire Anderson, 183–210. London: Bloomsbury Academic, 2018.
McCalman, Iain. *Darwin's Armada: Four Voyages and the Battle for the Theory of Evolution*. New York: W. W. Norton & Co, Inc., 2009.
McConnell, Anita. "Weld, Charles Richard (1813–1869)." In *Oxford Dictionary of National Biography*. Oxford University Press, January 2006 (accessed March 19, 2013). doi:10.1093/ref:odnb/28982.
McFarlane, Ian. *Beyond Awakening: The Aboriginal Tribes of North West Tasmania: A History*. Launceston: Fullers Bookshop, 2008.
McFarlane, Ian. "Cape Grim." In *Whitewash: On Keith Windschuttle's Fabrication of Aboriginal History*, edited by Robert Manne, 277–98. Melbourne: Black, Inc., Agenda, 2003.
McGoogan, Ken. *Fatal Passage: The Story of John Rae, the Arctic Hero Time Forgot*. New York: Carroll & Graf Publishers, 2002.
McGoogan, Ken. *Lady Franklin's Revenge: A True Story of Ambition, Obsession and the Remaking of Arctic History*. Toronto: Harper Collins Publishers Ltd., 2005.
Midgley, Clare. "Anti-Slavery and Feminism in Nineteenth Century Britain." *Gender & History* 5, no. 3 (1993): 343–62.
Midgley, Clare. "Female Emancipation in an Imperial Frame: English Women and the Campaign Against Sati (Widow-Burning) in India, 1813–1830." *Women's History Review* 9, no. 1 (2000): 95–121.
Midgley, Clare. *Women Against Slavery: The British Campaigns, 1780–1870*. London and New York: Routledge, 1995.
Miller, E. Morris. *Pressmen and Governors: Australian Editors and Writers in early Tasmania, a Contribution to the History of the Australian Press and Literature with Notes Biographical and Bibliographical*. Sydney: Angus & Robertson, 1952.
Miller, Gwenn A. "'The Perfect Mistress of Russian Economy': Sighting the Intimate on a Colonial Alaskan Terrain, 1784-1821." In *Haunted by Empire: Geographies of Intimacy in North American History*, edited by Ann Laura Stoler, 297–322. Chapel Hill: Duke University Press, 2006.
Miller, Henry. "Popular Petitioning and the Corn Laws, 1833–46." *English Historical Review* 127, no. 527 (August 2012): 882–919.
Morrison, David. "The Copper Inuit Soapstone Trade." *Arctic* 44, no. 3 (September 1991): 239–46.
Mowat, Farley. *People of the Deer*. New York: Carroll & Graf Publishers, 1975.

Neatby, Leslie. *The Search for Franklin*. Toronto and Edmonton: M. G. Hurtig, 1970.
Nelson, Richard K. *Make Prayers to the Raven: A Koyukon View of the Northern Forest*. Chicago and London: University of Chicago Press, 1986.
Nichols, Irby C. and Richard A. Ward. "Anglo-American Relations and the Russian Ukase: A Reassessment." *Pacific Historical Review* 41, no. 4 (November 1972): 444–59.
Norcia, Megan. *X Marks the Spot: Women Writers Map the Empire for British Children, 1790-1895*. Athens: Ohio University Press, 2010.
Norling, Lisa. "Ahab's Wife: Women and the American Whaling Industry, 1820–1870." In *Iron Men, Wooden Women: Gender and Seafaring in the Atlantic World, 1700-1920*, edited by Margaret S. Creighton and Lisa Norling, 70–91. Baltimore: Johns Hopkins University Press, 1996.
Norling, Lisa. *Captain Ahab Had a Wife: New England Women and the Whalefishery, 1720-1870*. Chapel Hill and London: University of North Carolina Press, 2000.
Norling, Lisa. "'How Frought with Sorrow and Heartpangs': Mariners' Wives and the Ideology of Domesticity in New England, 1790–1880." *The New England Quarterly* 65, no. 3 (September 1992): 422–46.
Nugent, Maria. "Jacky Jacky and the Politics of Aboriginal Testimony." In *Indigenous Intermediaries: New Perspectives on Exploration Archives*, edited by Shino Konishi, Maria Nugent, and Tiffany Shellam, 67–84. Canberra: ANU Press, 2015.
O'Leary, John "Speaking the Suffering Indigene: 'Native' Songs and Laments, 1820–1850." *Kunapipi* 31, no. 1 (2009): 47–59.
Olsen, Penny and Lynette Russell, *Australia's First Naturalists: Indigenous Peoples' Contribution to Early Zoology*. Canberra: NLA Publishing, 2019.
Orr, Mary. "Fish with a Different Angle: *The Freshwater Fishes of Great Britain* by Mrs Sarah Bowdich (1791-1856)." *Annals of Science* 71, no. 2 (2014): 206–40.
Orr, Mary. "Pursuing Proper Protocol: Sarah Bowdich's Purview of the Sciences of Exploration." *Victorian Studies* 49, no. 2 (Winter 2007): 277–85.
Orr, Mary. "The Stuff of Translation and Independent Female Scientific Authorship: The Case of *Taxidermy*… anon. (1820)." *Journal of Literature and Science* 8, no. 1 (2015): 27–47.
Orr, Mary. "Women Peers in the Scientific Realm: Sarah Bowdich Lee's Expert Collaborations with Georges Cuvier, 1825–1833." *Notes and Records* 69 (2015): 37–51.
Outram, Dorinda. "On Being Perseus: New Knowledge, Dislocation, and Enlightenment Exploration." In *Geography and Enlightenment*, edited by David N. Livingstone and Charles W. J. Withers, 281–94. Chicago and London: University of Chicago Press, 1999.
Parry, Ann. *Parry of the Arctic: The Life Story of Admiral Sir Edward Parry, 1790-1855*. London: Chatto & Windus, 1963.
Pearce, Kim and Susan Doyle. *New Town, A Social History*. Hobart: Hobart City Council, 2002.
Perry, Adele. *Colonial Relations: The Douglas-Connolly Family and the Nineteenth-Century Imperial World*. Cambridge and New York: Cambridge University Press, 2015.
Perry, Adele. "Designing Dispossession: The Select Committee on the Hudson's Bay Company, Fur-Trade Governance, Indigenous Peoples and Settler Possibility." In *Indigenous Communities and Settler Colonialism: Landholding, Loss and Survival in an Interconnected World*, edited by Zoe Laidlaw and Alan Lester, 158–72. Basingstoke: Palgrave Macmillan, 2015.
Perry, Adele. *On the Edge of Empire: Gender, Race and the Making of British Columbia, 1849-1871*. Toronto and London: University of Toronto Press, 2001.

Perry, Adele. "The Colonial Archive on Trial: Possession, Dispossession, and History in Delgamuukw v. British Columbia." In *Archive Stories: Facts, Fictions, and the Writing of History*, edited by Antoinette Burton, 325–50. Durham and London: Duke University Press, 2005.

Petrow, Stefan. *Policing in a Penal Colony: Governor Arthur's Police System in Van Diemen's Land, 1826–1836*. Urbana: University of Illinois Press, 2000.

Petrow, Stefan. "The Life and Death of the Hobart Town Mechanics' Institute 1827–1871." *Papers and Proceedings: Tasmanian Historical Research Association* 40, no. 1 (March 1993): 7–18.

Pickering, Paul A., Jean Dunbabin, and J. S. Rowett. "'And Your Petitioners &c': Chartist Petitioning in Popular Politics 1838–48." *English Historical Review* 116, no. 466 (April 2001): 368–88.

Piker, Joshua. "Lying Together: The Imperial Implications of Cross-Cultural Untruths." *The American Historical Review* 116, no. 4 (October 2011): 964–86.

Plomley, Norman James Brian. *Friendly Mission: The Tasmanian Journals of George Augustus Robinson, 1829–34*. 2nd ed. Launceston and Hobart: Queen Victoria Museum & Art Gallery and Quintus Publishing, 2008.

Plomley, Norman James Brian. "Notes on Some of the Tasmanian Aborigines, and on Portraits of Them." *Papers and Proceedings of the Royal Society of Tasmania* 102, pt. II (1968): 47–54.

Plomley, Norman James Brian. *Weep in Silence: A History of the Flinders Island Aboriginal Settlement*. Hobart: Blubber Head Press, 1987.

Podruchny, Carolyn. *Making the Voyageur World: Travelers and Traders in the North American Fur Trade*. Lincoln and London: University of Nebraska Press, 2006.

Porter, Andrew. *Religion versus Empire? British Protestant Missionaries and Overseas Expansion, 1700–1914*. Manchester and New York: Manchester University Press, 2004.

Potter, Russell A. *Arctic Spectacles: The Frozen North in Visual Culture, 1818–1875*. Seattle and London: University of Washington Press, 2007.

Potter, Russell A. *Finding Franklin: The Untold Story of a 165-Year Search*. Montreal and Kingston: McGill-Queen's University Press, 2016.

Pratt, Mary Louise. *Imperial Eyes: Travel Writing and Transculturation*. London: Routledge, 1992.

Prochaska, F. K. "Women and English Philanthropy, 1790–1830." *International Review of Social History* 19, no. 2 (December 1974): 426–45.

Pybus, Cassandra. *Truganini: Journey Through the Apocalypse*. Crow's Nest: Allen & Unwin, 2020.

Pybus, Cassandra and Hamish Maxwell-Stewart. *American Citizens, British Slaves: Yankee Political Prisoners in an Australian Penal Colony, 1839–1850*. Carlton South: Melbourne University Press, 2002.

Qikigtani Truth Commission. "Community Histories 1950–1975: Igloolik." Iqaluit, Nunavut: Inhabit Media, 2013.

Rawnsley, Willingham Franklin. *The Life, Diaries, and Correspondence of Jane, Lady Franklin, 1792–1875*. London: E. Macdonald, Ltd., 1923.

Reedy-Maschner, Katherine L. and Herbert D. G. Maschner, "Marauding Middlemen: Western Expansion and Violent Conflict in the Subarctic." *Ethnohistory* 46, no. 4 (Fall 1999): 704–43.

Reid, Kirsty. *Gender, Crime and Empire: Convicts, Settlers and the State in Early Colonial Australia*. Manchester: Manchester University Press, 2007.

Reidy, Michael S. *Tides of History: Ocean Science and Her Majesty's Navy*. Chicago and London: University of Chicago Press, 2008.
Rendall, Jane. "Women and the Public Sphere." *Gender and History* 11, no. 3 (November 1999): 475–88.
Reynolds, Henry. *Fate of a Free People: A Radical Re-Examination of the Tasmanian Wars*. Camberwell and London: Penguin Books, 2004.
Reynolds, Henry. *A History of Tasmania*. Cambridge: Cambridge University Press, 2012.
Reynolds, Henry. *The Other Side of the Frontier: Aboriginal Resistance to the European Invasion of Australia*. Ringwood: Penguin Books Australia, 1990.
Reynolds, Henry. *Truth-Telling: History, Sovereignty, and the Uluru Statement*. Sydney: NewSouth Publishing, 2021.
Richardson, Sarah. *The Political Worlds of Women: Gender and Politics in Nineteenth Century Britain*. Abingdon: Routledge, 2013.
Ritchie, Leslie. "'Expectations of Grease & Provisions': The Circulation and Regulation of Fur Trade Foodstuffs." *Eighteenth-Century Life* 23, no. 2 (1999): 124–42.
Roberts, Strother. "Trans-Indian Identity and the Inuit 'Other': Relations between the Chipewyan and Neighboring Aboriginal Communities in the Eighteenth Century." *Ethnohistory* 57, no. 4 (Fall 2010): 597–624.
Robin, Eleanor. *Swanston: Merchant Statesman*. North Melbourne: Australian Scholarly Publishing Pty Ltd., 2018.
Robinson, Michael F. "Reconsidering the Theory of the Open Polar Sea." In *Extremes: Oceanography's Adventure at the Poles* (Maury Workshop on the History of Polar Oceanography), edited by Keith R. Benson and Helen Rozwadowski, 15–29. Sagamore Beach: Science History Publications, 2007.
Ross, M. J. *Polar Pioneers: John Ross and James Clark Ross*. Montreal and London: McGill-Queen's University Press, 1994.
Ross, W. Gillies. *Hunters on the Track: William Penny and the Search for Franklin*. Montreal and London: McGill-Queens University Press, 2019.
Ross, W. Gillies. *This Distant and Unsurveyed Country: A Woman's Winter at Baffin Island, 1857-58*. Montreal and London: McGill-Queens University Press, 1997.
Rothschild, Emma. *The Inner Life of Empires: An Eighteenth-Century History*. Princeton and Oxford: Princeton University Press, 2011.
Rousselot, Jean-Loup, William W. Fitzhugh, and Aron Crowell. "Maritime Economies of the North Pacific Rim." In *Crossroads of Continents: Cultures of Siberia and Alaska*, edited by William W. Fitzhugh and Aron Crowell, 151–81. Washington, DC and London: Smithsonian Institution Press, 1988.
Routledge, Karen. *Do You See Ice? Inuit and Americans at Home and Away*. Chicago and London: University of Chicago Press, 2018.
Rupprecht, Anita. "Wonderful Adventures of Mrs Seacole in Many Lands (1857): Colonial Identity and the Geographical Imagination." In *Colonial Lives Across the British Empire: Imperial Careering in the Long Nineteenth Century*, edited by David Lambert and Alan Lester, 176–203. Cambridge: Cambridge University Press, 2006.
Russell, Gillian. "An 'Entertainment of Oddities': Fashionable Sociability and the Pacific in the 1770s." In *A New Imperial History: Culture, Identity and Modernity in Britain and the Empire, 1660–1840*, edited by Kathleen Wilson, 48–70. Cambridge: Cambridge University Press, 2004.
Russell, Gillian and Clara Tuite, eds. *Romantic Sociability: Social Networks and Literary Culture in Britain, 1770–1840*. Cambridge and New York: Cambridge University Press, 2002.

Russell, Lynette. *Roving Mariners: Australian Aboriginal Whalers and Sealers in the Southern Oceans, 1790–1870*. Albany: State University of New York Press, 2012.

Russell, Penny. "Citizens of the World? Jane Franklin's Transnational Fantasies." In *Transnational Lives: Biographies of Global Modernity, 1700- Present*, edited by Desley Deacon, Penny Russell, and Angela Woollacott, 195–208. New York: Palgrave-Macmillan, 2010.

Russell, Penny. "Girl in a Red Dress: Inventions of Mathinna." *Australian Historical Studies* 43, no. 3 (2012): 341–62.

Russell, Penny. *This Errant Lady: Jane Franklin's Overland Journey to Port Phillip and Sydney, 1839*. Canberra: National Library of Australia, 2002.

Russell, Penny. "Unhomely Moments: Civilising Domestic Worlds in Colonial Australia." *The History of the Family* 14 (2009): 329–39.

Russell, Penny. "Wife Stories: Narrating Marriage and Self in the Life of Jane Franklin." *Victorian Studies* 48, no. 1 (Autumn 2005): 35–57.

Ryan, Lyndall. "Historians, *Friendly Mission* and the Contest for Robinson and Trukanini." In *Reading Robinson: Companion Essays to Friendly Mission*, edited by Anna Johnston and Mitchell Rolls, 147–60. Hobart: Quintus Publishing, 2008.

Ryan, Lyndall. *Tasmanian Aborigines: A History since 1803*. Sydney and Melbourne: Allen and Unwin, 2012.

Ryan, Lyndall. "The Australian Agricultural Company, the Van Diemen's Land Company: Labour Relations with Aboriginal Landholders, 1824–1835." In *Intimacies of Violence in the Settler Colony: Economies of Dispossession around the Pacific Rim*, edited by Penelope Edmonds and Amanda Nettelbeck, 25–44. Cham, Switzerland: Palgrave-MacMillan, 2018.

Said, Edward W. *Orientalism*. London: Routledge, 1978.

Salmond, Anne. *The Trial of the Cannibal Dog: The Remarkable Story of Captain Cook's Encounters in the South Seas*. New Haven and London: Yale University Press, 2003.

Savours, Ann. *The Search for the North West Passage*. New York: St. Martin's Press, 1999.

Schaffer, Simon, Lissa Roberts, Kapil Raj, and James Delbourgo, eds. *The Brokered World: Go-Betweens and Global Intelligence*. Canton: Science History Publications, 2009.

Secord, Anne. "Botany on a Plate: Pleasure and the Power of Pictures in Promoting Early Nineteenth-Century Scientific Knowledge." *Isis* 93, no. 1 (March 2002): 28–57.

Secord, Anne. "Corresponding Interests: Artisans and Gentlemen in Natural History Exchange Networks." *British Journal for the History of Science* 27 (1994): 383–408.

Secord, James A. "Edinburgh Lamarkians: Robert Jameson and Robert E. Grant." *Journal of the History of Biology* 24, no. 1 (Spring 1991): 1–18.

Secord, James A. "How Scientific Conversation Became Shop Talk." In *Science in the Marketplace: Nineteenth-Century Sites and Experiences*, edited by Aileen Fyfe and Bernard Lightman, 23–59. Chicago and London: University of Chicago Press, 2007.

Secord, James A. "Knowledge in Transit." *ISIS* 95 (2004): 654–72.

Secord, James A. "Scrapbook Science: Composite Caricatures in Late Georgian England." In *Figuring It Out: Science, Gender and Visual Culture*, edited by Ann B. Shteir and Bernard Lightman, 164–91. Hanover: Dartmouth College Press, 2006.

Secord, James A. *Victorian Sensation: The Extraordinary Publication, Reception, and Secret Authorship of Vestiges of the Natural History of Creation*. Chicago and London: University of Chicago Press, 2000.

Shapin, Steven. "Placing the View from Nowhere: Historical and Sociological Problems in the Location of Science." *Transactions of the Institute of British Geographers* 23, no. 1 (1998): 5–12.

Shaw, Edward Charles. "Kennedy, William." In *Dictionary of Canadian Biography*, vol. 11. University of Toronto/Université Laval, 2003, http://www.biographi.ca/en/bio/kennedy_william_11E.html (accessed November 28, 2021).

Shellam, Tiffany, Maria Nugent, Shino Konishi, and Alison Cadzow, eds. *Brokers and Boundaries: Colonial Exploration in Indigenous Territory*. Acton: ANU Press and Aboriginal History, Inc., 2016.

Shteir, Ann B. *Cultivating Women, Cultivating Science: Flora's Daughters and Botany in England 1760–1860*. Baltimore: The John's Hopkin's University Press, 1996.

Shteir, Ann B. "Elegant Recreations? Configuring Science Writing for Women." In *Victorian Science in Context*, edited by Bernard Lightman, 236–54. Chicago: University of Chicago Press, 1997.

Simpson, Daniel. "Expeditionary Collections: Haslar Hospital Museum and the Circulation of Public Knowledge, 1815–1855." In *Mobile Museums: Collections in Circulation*, edited by Felix Driver, Mark Nesbitt, and Caroline Cornish, 149–77. London: UCL Press, 2021.

Sivasundarum, Sujit. *Nature and the Godly Empire: Science and Evangelical Mission in the Pacific, 1795–1850*. Cambridge: Cambridge University Press, 2005.

Sleeper-Smith, Susan, ed. *Rethinking the Fur Trade: Cultures of Exchange in an Atlantic World*. Lincoln and London: University of Nebraska Press, 2009.

Smith, James G. E. "Chipewyan, Cree and Inuit Relations West of Hudson Bay, 1714–1955." *Ethnohistory* 28, no. 2 (Spring 1981): 133–56.

Smith, Vanessa. "Banks, Tupaia and Mai: Cross-Cultural Exchanges and Friendship in the Pacific." *Parergon* 26, no. 2 (2009): 139–60.

Spufford, Francis. *I May Be Some Time: Ice and the English Imagination*. London: Faber and Faber, 1996.

Stamp, Tom and Cordelia Stamp. *William Scoresby: Arctic Scientist*. Whitby: Caedmon of Whitby Press, 1976.

Steele, Peter. *The Man Who Mapped the Arctic: The Intrepid Life of George Back, Franklin's Lieutenant*. Vancouver: Raincoast Books, 2003.

Stern, Philip J. "Exploration and Enlightenment." In *Reinterpreting Exploration: The West in the World*, edited by Dane Kennedy, 54–79. Oxford and New York: Oxford University Press, 2014.

Stevens, Leonie. *Me Write Myself: The Free Aboriginal Inhabitants of Van Diemen's Land at Wybalenna*. Clayton: Monash University Publishing, 2017.

Stocking, George W., Jr. *Victorian Anthropology*. London: Collier MacMillan Publishers, 1987.

Stoler, Ann Laura. *Along the Archival Grain: Epistemic Anxieties and Colonial Common Sense*. Princeton: Princeton University Press, 2009.

Stoler, Ann Laura. "'In Cold Blood': Hierarchies of Credibility and the Politics of Colonial Narratives." *Representations* 37 (Winter 1992): 151–89.

Stoler, Ann Laura. "Tense and Tender Ties: The Politics of Comparison in North American History and (Post) Colonial Studies." *Journal of American History* 88, no. 3 (December 2001): 829–65.

Stone, Ian R. "'The Contents of the Kettles': Charles Dickens, John Rae, and Cannibalism on the 1845 Franklin Expedition." *Dickensian* 83, no. 1 (1987): 7–15.

St-Onge, Nicole. "'He was Neither a Solder Nor a Slave: He was Under the Control of No Man': Kahnawake Mohawks in the Northwest Fur Trade, 1790-1850." *Canadian Journal of History* 51, no. 1 (2016): 1–32.

Strzelecki, Paul Edmund. *Physical Description of New South Wales and Van Diemen's Land*. London: Longman, Brown, Green, and Longmans, 1845.

Tallie, T. J. "Indigeneity, Movement, and Disrupting the Global Nineteenth Century." In *World Histories from Below: Disruption and Dissent, 1750 to the Present*, edited by Antoinette Burton and Tony Ballantyne, 2nd ed., 188–225. London and New York: Bloomsbury Academic, 2022.

Taylor, Rebe. "The Polemics of Making Fire in Tasmania: The Historical Evidence Revisited." *Aboriginal History* 32 (2008): 1–26.

Teltscher, Kate. "The Sentimental Ambassador: The Letters of George Bogle from Bengal, Bhutan, and Tibet, 1770–1801." In *Epistolary Selves: Letters and Letter-Writers, 1600–1945*, edited by Rebecca Earle, 79–94. Aldershot: Ashgate, 1999.

Thompson, Carl. "Earthquakes and Petticoats: Maria Graham, Geology, and Early Nineteenth Century 'Polite' Science." *Journal of Victorian Culture* 17, no. 3 (September 2012): 329–46.

Thompson, Carl. "The Heroic Age of the Tin Can: Technology and Ideology in British Arctic Exploration, 1818–1835." In *Maritime Empires: British Imperial Maritime Trade in the Nineteenth Century*, edited by David Killingray, Margarette Lincoln, and Nigel Rigby, 84–99. Suffolk: Boydell Press, 2004.

Thorne, Susan. "'The Conversion of Englishmen and the Conversion of the World Inseparable': Missionary Imperialism and the Language of Class in Early Industrial Britain." In *Tensions of Empire: Colonial Cultures in a Bourgeois World*, edited by Frederick Cooper and Ann Laura Stoler, 238–62. Berkeley and Los Angeles: University of California Press, 1997.

Thrush, Coll. *Indigenous London: Native Travelers at the Heart of Empire*. New Haven and London: Yale University Press, 2017.

Thrush, Coll. "The Iceberg and the Cathedral: Encounter, Entanglement, and Isuma in Inuit London." *Journal of British Studies* 53 (January 2014): 59–79.

Tikoff, Valentina K. "Adolescence in the Atlantic: Charity Boys as Seamen in the Spanish Maritime World." *Journal of Early Modern History* 14 (2010): 45–73.

Torrens, H. S. and Janet Browne. "Fitton, William Henry (1780–1861)." In *Oxford Dictionary of National Biography*. Oxford University Press, 2004 (accessed May 1, 2013). doi:10.1093/ref:odnb/9525.

Tosh, John. *A Man's Place: Masculinity and the Middle-Class Home in Victorian England*. New Haven and London: Yale University Press, 1999.

Truelove: From War to Whaler, Hull City Council, 2008. http://www.hullcc.gov.uk/museum collections/collections/storydetail.php?irn=196&master=425 (accessed May 19, 2011).

Turnbull, David. "Boundary-Crossings, Cultural Encounters and Knowledge Spaces in Early Australia." In *The Brokered World: Go-Betweens and Global Intelligence*, edited by Simon Schaffer, Lissa Roberts, Kapil Raj, and James Delbourgo, 387–428. Canton: Science History Publications, 2009.

Turner, Mark W. "Periodical Time in the Nineteenth Century." *Media History* 8, no. 2 (2002): 183–96.

Van Kirk, Sylvia. *Many Tender Ties: Women in Fur-Trade Society, 1670–1870*. Winnipeg: Watson & Dwyer Publishing, Ltd., 1980.

Van Toorn, Penny. *Writing Never Arrives Naked: Early Aboriginal Cultures of Writing in Australia*. Canberra: Aboriginal Studies Press, 2006.

Vibert, Elizabeth. "Writing 'Home': Sibling Intimacy and Mobility in a Scottish Colonial Memoir." In *Moving Subjects: Gender, Mobility and Intimacy in an Age of Global Empire*, edited by Tony Ballantyne and Antoinette Burton, 67–98. Urbana and Chicago: University of Illinois Press, 2009.

Vickers, Daniel with Vince Walsh. *Young Men and the Sea: Yankee Seafarers in the Age of Sail*. New Haven and London: Yale University Press, 2007.

Vickery, Amanda, ed. *Women, Privilege and Power: British Politics, 1750-Present*. Stanford: Stanford University Press, 2001.

Vinkovetsky, Ilya. *Russian America: An Overseas Colony of a Continental Empires, 1804-1867*. Oxford and New York: Oxford University Press, 2011.

Wallace, Hugh N. *The Navy, the Company, and Richard King: British Exploration in the Canadian Arctic, 1829-1860*. Montreal: McGill-Queens University Press, 1980.

Warner, Kate, Tim McCormack, and Fauve Kurnadi. "Pathway to Truth-Telling and Treaty: Report to Premier Peter Gutwein." Hobart: Department of Premier and Cabinet, November 2021. https://www.dpac.tas.gov.au/__data/assets/pdf_file/0005/627242/Pathway_to_Truth-Telling_and_Treaty_251121.pdf (accessed August 27, 2021).

Wenzel, George. "Clyde Inuit Settlements and Community: From Before Boas to Centralization." *Arctic Anthropology* 45, no. 1 (2008): 1–21.

White, Paul. "Darwin Wept: Science and the Sentimental Subject." *Journal of Victorian Culture* 16, no. 2 (August 2011): 195–213.

Wiebe, Rudy. *A Discovery of Strangers*. Toronto: A. A. Knopf Canada, 1994.

Wilson, Kathleen, ed. *A New Imperial History: Culture, Identity and Modernity in Britain and Empire, 1660-1840*. Cambridge: Cambridge University Press, 2004.

Winter, Alison. "'Compasses All Awry': The Iron Ship and the Ambiguities of Cultural Authority in Victorian Britain." *Victorian Studies* 38, no. 1 (Autumn 1994): 69–98.

Winter, Alison. "The Construction of Orthodoxies and Heterodoxies in the Early Victorian Life Sciences." In *Victorian Science in Context*, edited by Bernard Lightman, 24–50. Chicago and London: University of Chicago Press, 1997.

Wisnicki, Adrian S. "Charting the Frontier: Indigenous Geography, Arab-Nyamwezi Caravans, and the East African Expedition of 1856-59." *Victorian Studies* 51, no. 1 (Autumn 2008): 103–37.

Withers, Charles W. J. "Mapping the Niger, 1798-1832: Trust, Testimony, and 'Ocular Demonstration' in the Late Enlightenment." *Imago Mundi* 56, no. 2 (2004): 170–93.

Wood, Rebecca. "Frontier Violence and the Bush Legend: The Sydney Herald's Response to the Myall Creek Massacre Trials and the Creation of Colonial Identity." *History Australia* 6, no. 3 (2009): 67.1–67.19.

Woodman, David C. *Strangers Among Us*. Montreal: McGill-Queen's University Press, 1995.

Woodman, David C. *Unravelling the Franklin Mystery: Inuit Testimony*. Montreal: McGill-Queen's University Press, 1991.

Woodward, David and G. Malcolm Lewis, eds. *The History of Cartography: Cartography in the Traditional African, American, Arctic, Australian, and Pacific Societies*. Vol. 2, book 3. Chicago: University of Chicago Press, 1998.

Woodward, Frances J. *Portrait of Jane: A Life of Lady Franklin*. London: Hodder and Stoughton, 1951.

Zastoupil, Lynn. "Intimacy and Colonial Knowledge." *Journal of Colonialism and Colonial History* 3, no. 2 (2002) (accessed April 4, 2013). doi: 10.1353/cch.2002.0053.

Unpublished Theses

Cave, Eleanor. "Flora Tasmaniae: Tasmanian Naturalists and Imperial Botany, 1829-1860." PhD thesis, University of Tasmania, 2012.

Chamberlain, Susan. "The Hobart Whaling Industry, 1830-1900." PhD thesis, La Trobe University, 1988.

Index

Aborigines' Protection Society (APS)   120, 175–6, 214
acculturation and assimilation   4, 10–11, 96, 103, 107, 114–16, 123, 176, 183, 223
Admiralty   1, 26, 35, 45, 46, 59, 72, 75–6, 78, 97, 105, 119, 142, 144–5, 148–9, 153, 155–6, 158–60, 171, 173, 175, 177–86, 188, 207, 209, 211, 213, 217, 219
   accusations of dereliction of duty   159, 177–9, 219
   Indigenous testimony   173, 183–6, 207
   Inuit maps   142, 152, 158–9, 179
   Jane Franklin   144–5, 153, 159–60, 188, 209
   petitioning   178–9, 188
   sailors' families   144, 159–60
   "Suggestions for the Relief of Sir John Franklin"   148–9, 159
Adolphus/Timemernidic   93–6, 98, 99, 102–3, 105–7, 116, 121, 122, 126
Advance and *Rescue* (USS)   161, 170–1, 174, 188
Africa   60, 74, 100, 103–4, 119, 175–6, 189, 194, *see also* Niger Expedition (1841)
Akaitcho (Yellowknives Dene leader)   25, 28–31, 33, 34, 40, 43, 46–7, 70, 71, 213, *see also* Indigenous geopolitics; Indigenous leadership; intermediaries and interpreters
   expedition documents   30, 34, 47
   Franklin's relationship   29, 34
   Inuit intermediaries   29–31
Alexander, Alison   104, 108, 119
American Arctic Expeditions (1848–60)   170–1, 181, 187–8, 191, 213

Anstey, Thomas   100, 101, 104, 107, 121, 122
Antarctica and Antarctic regions   93, 97–8, 104, 107–8, 111–13, 220
antislavery movement   9, 62–3, 100, 115, 119, 178, 189
Aotearoa New Zealand   96, 110–11, 115, 118–19, 141, 152, 190
APS, *see* Aborigines' Protection Society (APS)
archives and archival materials   2, 5–7, 11, 13, 57, 74, 126, 150, 170–87, 195, 205–7, 217, 219–23, *see also* relics; silences
   absences and silences   2, 5, 7, 13, 126, 138 n.262, 170, 180, 205–7, 222–3
   family archives   5, 6, 13, 74, 219–23
   relics and   170, 179–80, 205, 218–22
Arctic circles   2–4, 6, 11–13, 23, 27, 35, 57–82, 94–100, 102–5, 107–13, 120–3, 143, 148–51, 156, 162, 173, 180, 205, 221
   Australasia and   95–8, 100, 102, 104–5, 107–13, 120–3
   defined   3
   Franklin expedition and   143, 148–56, 180, 205, 221
   humanitarians and   62–4, 172–3, 175–80, 211, 219
   Indigenous information and   148–51, 156, 205
   institutions and   57, 97, 110–11, 143, 148–51, 180, 205
   Jane Franklin and   102, 107–8, 111, 113, 121, 126, 151, 162, 180, 205, 209, 219
   scientific sociability and   57–64
   vernacular Arctic circles   27, 70–3
Arctic Committee (1851)   180–6

"argument from negative evidence" 13, 171–2, 175, 177–82, 186, 188, 191–2, 194
  defined 171, 175, 177, 192
  humanitarians and 13, 175–8
  petitions and 172, 178–80, 186, 188
  Tasmanian settlers and 13, 191–4
armchair geographers 22, 74, 146
Arthur, George (Lt. Gov. of Tasmania, 1824–1836) 95, 96, 99–101
Arthur, Walter George (Indigenous Tasmanian man) 96, 98–101, 103, 106, 116, 122, 125, 126, 128 n.16, 189, see also Indigenous rights; Indigenous Tasmanians (*palawa/pakana*/Tasmanian Aborigines)
  political struggles of 106, 122, 125
  relationship with Adolphus/ Timemernedic 99, 103, 106, 122
assimilation, see acculturation and assimilation
Assistance (HMS) 161, 169, 171, 184, 186
Astronomical Society 73, 75, 97
Athenaeum 145, 147, 149–50, 176–8, 181, 209
Atwood, Margaret 221
Augustus, see Tattannoeuck/Augustus
Austin, Horatio 161, 169, 171, 179, 181–4, 186
authority 2, 4–9, 11–13, 22–31, 40, 43–4, 47, 60, 64, 68, 73–82, 93–4, 103–7, 110, 113–14, 121, 125, 139–44, 146–62, 171–2, 176, 180–8, 191, 193–5, 205, 209, 211–14, 219, 221–3, see also exploration and explorers; explorers' families; Indigenous leadership; intermediaries and interpreters; whalers and sealers; women
  Indigenous 9, 11, 13, 24, 25, 29–31, 68, 103, 106–7, 125, 139–40, 148, 150–2, 155, 162, 176, 185, 193–5, 205, 209, 212–14, 222
  vernacular 26, 43–4, 148–9, 153, 156–60, 162, 171, 179, 181–2, 186–7, 193–5, 205, 211

women and 6–9, 11–12, 22, 40, 60, 64, 69, 74–82, 93–4, 110, 113–14, 118–20, 124–6, 140–2, 152–4, 162, 172, 175–6, 188, 191, 194, 205, 212–12, 217, 219
Auty, Kate 120

BAAS, see British Association for the Advancement of Science (BAAS)
Back, George 26–7, 30–2, 34, 42, 45–7, 50–1 n.63, 58, 70, 72, 73, 76–7, 79–81, 96–100–100, 103, 121, 124, 148–9, 154, 160, 180–1, 215–16, see also Arctic Committee (1851); exploration and explorers; information and intelligence; Royal Geographical Society (RGS)
  Franklin rescue and 148–9, 154, 160, 180–1, 215, 216
  friendship with Willard Wentzel 42, 45–7
  Indigenous intelligence and 148–9
  Maconochies 98–102
  relationship with Franklin 31, 45, 50–1 n.63, 73, 96–7
  Relationship with Mary Anne Kay 45, 73, 96–7
  Ross rescue expedition (1832–4) 96–8
  rumors and 42, 45–7, 100
Back River (Back's Fish River, Great Fish River) 1, 78, 97–8, 129 n.30, 140, 205–7, 212–14, 217
Baffin Island 2, 11–12, 66, 126, 139, 141–2, 146–7, 153, 156, 208
Baffin's Bay 150, 158, 171, 174
Ballantyne, Tony 2, 4, 6, 106, 182
Banks, Joseph 26, 58
Barczewski, Stephanie 221
Barren Grounds 8, 11, 21–8, 31–5, 37, 39–42, 47, 71, 98–9, 102, 212–13, 215, see also caribou; Dene people; Indigenous geopolitics; Land Arctic Expeditions
Barrow, John Jr. 104, 140, 148–50, 152–3, 155–7, 173, 179, 181, 183, 187, 192–3

Barrow, John Sr.   26, 42, 45, 70, 103–5, 148, 157
Barrow, Peter   103–4
Bass Strait   95, 116, 121–2, 126, 222
Bayly, C. A.   142
Beagle (HMS)   61, 93, 110, 116, 121, 122, 191
Beatson, Donald   187, 192, 193
Beaufort, Francis   46, 59, 97, 98, 104–5, 110–11, 119, 121–4, 143, 148, 154, 159, 160, 180–1, 192, *see also* Arctic circles; scientific sociability
  Franklins' relationship with   104–5, 121–4, 154, 160, 180–1
Beaufort Sea   58, 141
Beck, Adam   94, 169–80, 183–7, 193–5, 200 n.140, 209, *see also* Arctic Committee (1851); authority; Indigenous intermediaries; literacy; petitions; relics
Beechey, William Frederick   45–6, 58, 75, 180
Beechey Island   170–1, 173, 175, 177, 179, 184, 187, 192–3, 205, 209, 213, 217, 219, *see also* "argument from negative evidence"; graves; relics
Beer, Gillian   75
Bering Strait   1, 8, 45, 58–9, 75, 141, 144–5, 156, 160–1, 173, 187–8, 190, 192–3, 202 n.181
biography and biographies   5–7, 13, 205, 211–13, 216–23
Bloody Falls, *see* Kugluktuk/Bloody Falls
Bock, Thomas   101, 107, 111, 118, 121, 123, 143, 220
books and reading   37, 41, 60, 71, 75, 77, 108–9, 122, 124, 142, 143, 174, 177, 192, 193, 217, *see also* expedition narratives; literacy; newspapers and periodicals
Boothia Peninsula   98, 146, 160, 206–7, *see also* Netsilingmiut Inuit
Bowdich, Sarah   67–8
Bowdich, Thomas   60, 74
Bravo, Michael   67–8
British Antarctic Expedition (1839–43)   93, 98, 104, 106, 108, 111–13, 119, *see also* Ross, James Clark; *Erebus* and *Terror* (HMS)

British Association for the Advancement of Science (BAAS)   97
British Empire   2–5, 7, 10, 12, 24, 221
Brown, Robert   26, 73
Buckland, Mary   59–60, 73
Buckland, William   59–61, 73, 110
Buettner, Elizabeth   6
Burton, Antoinette   6, 7
Buxton, Thomas Fowell   62, 63, 96, 119–20, 172–3, 176, 194, *see also* humanitarianism and humanitarians, imperial; Niger Expedition

Canada   7, 23, 43, 45, 72, 96, 141, 189, 215, 221
cannibalism   1, 11, 21–2, 34, 40, 47 n.4, 121, 140, 210–11, 217
  First Land Arctic Expedition (1819–22)   11, 21–2, 34, 40
  Franklin expedition (1845–8)   1, 140, 206–7, 210–11, 217
Cape York (Greenland), *see* Savissivik/ Cape York (Greenland)
Carey, Hilary M.   188
Carey, Jane   4
Caribou (reindeer)   5, 21, 23–4, 28, 32–4, 47, 57, 59, 97, 140, 206
Cartography, *see* maps
Cavell, Janice   142, 158, 171, 182, 217
children   7, 9, 11–13, 26, 31, 43, 60, 66, 77, 88 n.820, 93–6, 98–100, 102–3, 105–7, 113–26, 139, 169–70, 174–5, 187, 190, 194, 216, 222–3, *see also* fur trade and traders; intermediaries and interpreters; Métis people
  convicts and   63, 119–20
  education of   94, 96, 113–21, 123–6, 154
  Indigenous   7, 9, 11–13, 26, 31, 43, 77, 93–6, 98, 99, 102–3, 105–7, 113–21, 123–6, 159, 184, 187, 216, 222–3
  literature   60, 69
  removed from families   7, 11–12, 88 n.120, 93–6, 114–16, 118–20, 122, 125–6, 169–70, 173–4, 184, 222–3
  violence against   95, 99, 125

Chipewyan people 23, 141, 206, 215
civilization and civilizing missions 63, 93–6, 107–10, 113, 116, 119–20, 123–4, 208–11, 214
Clark, Robert 96, 120, 123, 138 n.262
climate change 24, 139–40, 205, *see also* Little Ice Age
collectors and collecting 4, 72–4, 100–2, 107–9, 113, 195, 217, 220, 223
  human remains 99, 103, 170, 184, 217
colonial governance 2, 4, 93–126, 211–12, 214–16, *see also* humanitarianism and humanitarians; settler colonialism and settlers
colonialism 2, 3, 7, 13, 223, *see also* British Empire; Hudson's Bay Company; humanitarianism and humanitarians; penal colonies; Russia and Russian Empire; settler colonialism and settlers
colonial knowledge, *see* knowledge
Colonial Office 25, 63, 75, 78, 95, 103, 104, 121–4
colonial science 12, 13, 101–2, 105, 108–13, 126, 190–1
convicts 4, 13, 63–4, 95–6, 99–101, 103, 106, 108, 109, 111, 115, 116, 118–20, 122, 152, 188–9, *see also* penal colonies
  anti-transportation campaign (Tasmania) 188–9, 192
  convict boys (Point Puer) 103, 116, 191
  convict discipline 99–101, 103–4, 119–20
  convict women 63, 119–20
Coppermine River 11, 21, 24–5, 27, 29, 39, 44–5, 80, 139, 143–4, 214
correspondence 1, 4, 6, 21–2, 32–3, 35–7, 39–41, 43–4, 47 n.3, 57, 71, 73–82, 104–5, 108–13, 153, 181–3, 191, 212
  credibility and 8, 73–82
  explorers and 73–82
  explorers' families and 1, 6, 8, 35–42, 73–82, 153, 182–3
  knowledge production and 73–82, 108–13

Craciun, Adriana 208, 217, 222
Cracroft, Isabella 46, 58, 71, 147
Cracroft, Sophia (Sophy) 1–2, 99, 104, 109, 145, 147, 149, 152–6, 159, 160, 172, 174–83, 186–7, 191, 211–14, 219–20
  "argument from negative evidence" and 172, 174–83, 186, 187, 191
  Indigenous people and information 1–2, 104, 147, 154, 156, 173, 175, 177–8, 186
credibility 1–4, 8–12, 21–3, 35, 57–64, 73–8, 81–2, 93, 98–103, 107, 143–4, 146, 149–52, 156, 174, 177–8, 183–7, 193–5, 205, 211–13, *see also* exploration and explorers; explorers' families; fur trade and traders; intermediaries and interpreters; whalers and sealers
  correspondence and 8, 74–82
  crises of 11, 98–103
  Indigenous 8–10, 22, 79–81, 103, 107, 150–1, 156, 174, 177, 183–4, 187, 193–5, 205, 211, 213–14
  interest and 12, 143–4, 148–51, 191, 211
  vernacular 143–4, 149, 156, 193–5, 205, 211
  women and 8–9, 12–13, 22, 40–2, 57–60, 66, 73–8, 82, 93, 98–103, 152, 205, 212
Cree people and language 23, 25, 28, 31, 66, 70, 173, 206, 207
Cresswell, Samuel Gurney 63, 64, 173, 186, 212
Crimean War 156, 208–9
Crooke, Robert 113–14, 118
Crozier, Francis Moira 58, 66, 93, 111, 121, 143, 170, 208, 217
Cumberland House 21, 27–9, 173, 176
Cumberland Sound 66, 142, 152, 179
curiosities 3, 57, 61, 73–82, 113, 123, 170, 190, 195, 220, *see also* collectors and collecting
  people treated as 3, 58, 113, 123, 220
Cuvier, Baron Georges 60, 175

Darwin, Charles   61, 75, 110, 124
Davis Strait   26, 66, 144, 153, 174, 179
Dease, Elizabeth   72–3
Dease, Peter Warren   70–3, 206
Dene people   21–5, 28, 29, 31–3, 41, 46, 66, 71, *see also* Indigenous geopolitics; separate peoples (e.g., Yellowknives Dene)
  Inuit and   24, 48 n.23
Denison, William   189–90, 192
Derwent Bank (Tasmania)   99, 100, 108, 122, 130 n.50, 133 n.124
diaries, *see* journals and written records
Dickens, Charles   194, 210–11
disease   23, 24, 28, 33, 37, 95, 139, 169–70, 208
Dog Ribs Dene   25, 31, 46, 70–1
  Edzo   70–1
domesticity   7, 9, 11, 37, 43, 58, 63, 77–8, 153, 210, 221
Driver, Felix   22, 146
Dumontier, Pierre Marie   107
D'Urville, Dumont   106

Eardley-Wilmot, John   124, 137 n.226, 189
Elce, Erica Behrisch   188
Eliza (vessel)   99, 116
Endersby, Jim   108
Enterprise (HMS)   61, 93, 116, 121, 122, 191
Erebus and *Terror* (HMS)   1–2, 8, 11–13, 93, 98, 110–11, 117, 124, 139–40, 154–5, 174–5, 191, 205–7, 220–2
  British Antarctic Expedition (1839–43)   93, 98, 111, 117, 119
  Franklin expedition (1845–8)   1, 8, 11, 124, 142–4, 205–6
Esquimaux, *see* Inuit
evangelicalism   33, 37, 40, 62–3, 95–6, 117–19
exhibitions   62, 175, 178, 184, 190, 208, 210, 223
  "Death in the Ice" (2017)   223
  Great Exhibition (1851)   175, 178, 184, 190
  "*taypani milaythina-tu*: Return to Country," (2022)   222

expedition narratives   4, 8–11, 13, 22–4, 34–47, 60, 62, 66–8, 70, 74, 77, 79, 81, 105, 112, 122–3, 142, 150, 158, 176–7, 193, 210, 213, 215, 217, *see also* correspondence; credibility; stories
  families and   11, 22, 35–47, 62, 77
  Indigenous people and   4, 22, 34, 41, 66–8, 79, 81, 150, 215
  women and   60, 62, 80, 105, 112, 122, 176–7, 193
  writing   4, 8–9, 22, 35–45
exploration and explorers   2–4, 8, 13, 22, 26, 30, 37, 40, 57–8, 60, 70–5, 77–9, 81, 96, 109, 110, 142, 152, 158, 171, 172, 177–8, 194, 210–11, 215, 220–3, *see also* authority; credibility; expedition narratives; explorers' families; information; intermediaries and interpreters; knowledge; maps; scientific sociability; trust and trustworthiness; truth and truthfulness
  domesticity and   7, 11, 37, 43, 58, 75, 77–8, 209–10, 221
  failure and   13, 41, 43, 47, 143, 144, 158, 173, 209, 220–1
  fur trade and   26, 30, 40, 69–73
  humanitarians and   62–4, 97–8, 119, 156, 172–80, 187
  Indigenous clothing and technology, use of   29, 59, 66, 72, 83 n.15, 166 n.109, 206
  Indigenous information and   29–31, 64–73, 146–9, 155–6, 169–71, 173, 211
  moral reform   62–4
  patronage   26, 29, 61, 69–73
  religious experiences   33, 35–42, 62, 143, 213
  women and   29–30, 35–42, 57–82, 143
explorers' families   1–13, 21–2, 34–42, 47, 57–8, 66, 69–71, 73–82, 96, 126, 139–62, 174–5, 178–9, 192, 205, 211–12, 221–3, *see also* correspondence; information; intermediaries and interpreters; intimacy; women

information and   35–42, 57, 73–82,
    139–62, 174–5, 178–9, 191–3
extinction   13, 108–10, 113–14, 118–20,
    125–6, 189–90, 216
  myth of Tasmanian   13, 110, 114,
    118–19, 125–6, 189–90, 216

Felix (vessel)   161, 169, 171
Fisch-Davis, Heather   5
Fitton, Sarah and William   60, 73
Fletcher, Eliza   59, 63
Flinders Island Aboriginal Establishment
    (Tasmania)   12, 95–6, 98–9,
    102–3, 106–7, 110, 113–18,
    120, 122–6, 128 n.16, 189,
    223, *see also* Indigenous
    rights; Indigenous Tasmanians
    (*palawa/pakana*/Tasmanian
    Aborigines); literacy,
    Indigenous; protection and
    protectorates; Wybalenna
  power struggles at   95–6, 106–7, 125–6
  removal of children from   96, 102–3,
    107, 113, 116
Forster, Matthew   99, 100, 103–4, 110
Forsyth, Charles   121, 159, 170, 172, 174
Fort Chipewyan   27, 34, 42, 45, 71, 73
Fort Churchill   11, 25, 44, 66, 79, 81, 98,
    195 n.6, 206–7
  interpreters from   11, 25, 79–82, 98,
    207
Fort Enterprise   29–34, 40–1, 43–5, 66,
    118, 143–4, 217
Fort Franklin   71, 78
Fort Resolution   28, 34–5, 70
Franklin, Eleanor, *see* Gell, Eleanor
    Franklin
Franklin, Eleanor Porden   22, 35, 37–42,
    45–7, 59, 61–2, 64–5, 69–71, 93,
    94, 98, 103–9, 111, 113–17, 119,
    121, 123, 126, 143
  Indigenous people and   37–9, 69, 71,
    143
  marriage to John Franklin   38–42,
    45–7
  poetry   37–9, 53 n.129, 64, 69, 143,
    163 n.23
  scientific sociability and   35, 61–2,
    64–5

Franklin, Jane Griffin   1–2, 6, 12–13,
    39, 57–60, 63–4, 69, 73–4, 82,
    93–4, 96, 99–126, 143–5, 147–50,
    152–60, 172–83, 185–8, 190–4,
    208–13, 215–17, 219–21, 223, *see
    also* authority; children; convicts;
    intermediaries and interpreters;
    Simpkinson, Mary; Tasmanian
    Society; rumors; women
  Arctic circles and   3, 11–12, 57–60,
    95, 102, 107–8, 111–13, 121,
    154, 171–7, 180, 209, 219
  authority   13, 93–4, 104, 113, 122,
    124–6, 144–5, 152–3, 188, 191,
    209, 217
  biographies and archives   13, 211–13,
    216–20
  expeditions financed by   169–72, 187,
    192–3, 216–19
  humanitarians and   9, 12–13, 63,
    118–20, 171–7, 219
  ideas of "improvement"   93–4, 102
  Indigenous children and education   7,
    102–7, 113–26
  Indigenous people and   1, 94, 102–7,
    113–26, 173–5, 185–6
  petitions and   120, 172, 178–80, 186,
    188
  rumors about   103–4, 107–8, 110–11,
    120–2
  scientific sociability and   57–60,
    102–13
  search for husband (1848–1860)
    139–220
  Tasmanian administration   93–4,
    98–126
Franklin, John   1–2, 5, 11, 23, 26–47,
    57–64, 66, 69–81, 93–4, 96–104,
    106–13, 115–18, 121–6, 139–40,
    145, 147, 150, 158–61, 170–1,
    177–80, 187–8, 191–2, 205, 208,
    210–12, *see also* Arctic circles;
    convicts; credibility; *Erebus* and
    Terror (HMS); exploration and
    explorers; explorers' families;
    intermediaries and interpreters;
    rumors; scientific sociability;
    trust and trustworthiness
  archives and   5–6, 11, 13, 23, 220–3

biographies and memory of 187, 191–2, 210–13
cannibalism 1, 11, 22, 34, 39, 121, 206–7, 210–11, 217
criticism 28–34, 95, 99–100, 102–4, 108, 110–11, 113, 120–1, 221
disappearance 2, 5, 8, 122
expeditions 5, 13
  (1819–22) 11, 21–3, 25–47, 58–9, 63, 70, 79
  (1825–7) 45–6, 57–8, 69–82
  (1845–8) 1–2, 13, 124–5, 141–3, 146, 147, 170–2, 184, 187, 205–7, 209, 211, 215
Indigenous people and 24–35, 69–73, 79–82, 116–17
relationships with other explorers 31, 76–8, 96
relationship with Richardson 11, 31–42, 45–7, 96–8, 139, 143, 213
religious faith 33, 35–42, 118, 143, 213
search for 8, 139–62, 169–95, 207–13, 216–18, 222
statues of 219–20
Tasmanian administration 12, 93–4, 96–126
Tasmanian search for 187–95
trustworthiness of 30, 35–42, 46–7, 70, 213
Franklin, Mary, *see* Price, Mary Franklin
Fry, Elizabeth 63–4, 69, 119–20
Fullagar, Kate 10
fur trade and traders 3, 8, 10, 24, 26, 27, 30, 40, 43, 47, 69–73, 76–7, 141, 215, *see also* authority; credibility; Hudson's Bay Company (HBC); Indigenous networks; North West Company (NWC);Russian American Company (RAC)
families 11, 24, 26, 69–73, 77
Fury (HMS) 45, 62, 64–8, 148

Gell, Eleanor Franklin 93–4, 96, 99, 103–9, 111, 113–17, 120–1, 123, 126, 145, 147, 152, 154–5, 160, 169, 180–1, 191, 195, 208, 219, 220, *see also* explorers' families; Mithina, Qalasirssuaq
  Arctic circles and 154–5

Indigenous people and 93–4, 99, 103–7, 113–17, 121, 123, 126, 154, 169, 195, 208, 220
Gell, John Phillip 108, 110, 115–16, 145, 155, 176, 181, 191, 195, 208
gold rushes and gold mining 192–3
Goodsir, Robert Anstruther 139, 140, 147, 150, 153
Gould, Elizabeth 102–3, 106
Gould, John 102–3, 106–7, 112
Graham, Maria 59–61, *see also* scientific sociability
graves 170, 212–13, 219–20, *see also* collectors and collecting; curiosities
  desecration of 170, 184, 190, 193
Great Exhibition (1851), *see* exhibitions
Great Fish River, *see* Back River
Great Slave Lake 21–2, 25, 28, 35, 37, 44, 46, 73, 78, 97–8, 176, 213
Greenland 143, 169, 172, 174, 187, 193–5, 209
  interpreters from 169, 172, 184, 187
Greenstockings (Yellowknife Dene girl) 29–31, 39–40, 50 n.54, 51 n.65, 69, 81, 143
  poetry about 39, 53 n.129, 69, 143, 163 n.23
Griffin, Jane, *see* Franklin, Jane Griffin
Grinnell, Henry 181, 188, 191
Gulf of Boothia 1, 98, 160, 207
Gunn, Ronald Campbell 98–9, 101, 105–6, 108–10, 112, 116, 119, 191
Gurney, Anna 13, 63, 64, 75, 96, 119–20, 172–9, 186, 187, 209, 219, *see also* "argument from negative evidence"; humanitarianism and humanitarians
Gwich'in Dene 80, 141

Hall, Catherine 7
Hall, Charles Francis 187, 207, 221
Hamilton, William (Secretary to the Admiralty 1845–55) 159, 173, 181
Harwood, Roger 157, 185–6
Hearne, Samuel 24–5, 77, 80
Hecla (HMS) 26, 45, 59, 63–8, 149

Index

Hepburn, John 26–7, 30, 32–4, 40, 42, 45, 70, 71, 83 n.15, 99, 103, 173–4, 191, 210, 212
 First Land Arctic Expedition (1819–22) 26–7, 30, 32–4, 40, 42, 70, 173, 210
 Prince Albert expedition (1851–2) 174, 191
 Second Land Arctic Expedition (1825–7) 71, 83 n.15
 Tasmania 99, 103, 191
Herschel, Caroline 59–60, 75
Herschel, John 59–60, 75, 102, 109–11
Hodgkin, Thomas 97, 98, 175–6
Hoeootoerock (Junius) 26, 32, 43, 79
homosexuality 62, 101, 189
Hood, Robert 26, 29, 30, 32–3, 35, 37, 40, 42, 44
Hooker, Joseph Dalton 111–12
Hooker, William Jackson 59, 76, 99, 108–12, 118
Hooper, William Harvey 66, 68
Hudson's Bay Company (HBC) 1, 21, 24, 28, 30, 34, 40, 44, 46, 70, 71, 77, 78, 97, 121, 141, 144, 160, 169, 172–4, 176, 178, 186, 206, 207, 211–16, *see also* fur trade and traders; Parliamentary Select Committee on the Hudson's Bay Company (1857)
 conflict with North West Company 24, 28, 30
 critiques of 97–8, 176, 211–16
 trading practices of 24, 97, 173, 176, 215–16
humanitarianism and humanitarians 3, 8, 11, 62–4, 94–7, 102, 104–5, 114, 119–20, 156, 172–80, 209–10, *see also* Africa; antislavery movement; authority; Indigenous rights; Niger Expedition; protection and protectorates; settler colonialism and settlers; women
 Arctic circles and 3, 11, 62–4, 96–8
 colonial governance and 4, 63, 95–6, 98, 119–20, 156, 158
 exploration and 11, 63–4, 97–8, 119, 156, 172–80, 187

 families 62–4, 75, 119, 173, 179
 imperial humanitarianism 4, 9, 172, 209, 210
 language and rhetoric 95, 114, 118, 156, 179–80, 188–9, 194, 219
 scientific networks and 57, 62–4, 173
 scientific sociability and 62–4
 women 9, 63–4, 69, 118–20, 172–3, 188
human remains 2, 99, 101, 103, 110, 118, 170, 184, 190, 193, 207, 212, 217, 221–3, *see also* collectors and collecting; graves; specimens
hunger 5, 8, 28, 78, 140, 151, 206–7, 216, *see also* provisions, starvation

ice and ice conditions 23–4, 38, 40, 58–9, 64–9, 93, 139, 141–3, 145–7, 160, 169–72, 205–7
Igloolik 63–9, 76, 145, 150
Iglulingmiut Inuit 57–8, 64–9, 166 n.109
Iligjaq/Iligliuk (Iglulingmiut woman) 65–9, 76, 148
imperial knowledge, *see* knowledge
improvement 7, 11–12, 62–4, 93–4, 102, 114
Indigenous geographical knowledge 25, 64–9, 139–40, 146–62, 185–6, *see also* authority; knowledge; maps
Indigenous geopolitics 10, 24–5, 44, 46, 48 n.23, 70, 140, 205–7, 215
Indigenous leadership 24, 25, 29–31, 43, 47, 98, 106, 125
Indigenous literacy, *see* literacy
Indigenous networks 10–12, 24–5, 29, 44–5, 58, 66, 70, 80, 107, 122, 126, 141–2, 145–6, 150, 156, 159–60, 205–7, 209, 213, 215
Indigenous Northwest Passage 1, 4, 6, 10, 12, 21, 24, 26, 29, 44, 45, 58, 66, 79, 97, 124, 139, 141–2, 186, 206, 211–13, 217, 221
Indigenous rights 10–13, 96, 107, 125, 171, 176, 178, 189, 193, 214–16, *see also* petitions
 petitions 13, 125, 176, 189, 214–15
 sovereignty 7, 9, 96, 105, 176, 189

Indigenous Tasmanians (*palawa/pakana*/Tasmanian Aborigines)   11–12, 93–6, 98–9, 101–3, 105–7, 110–11, 113–26, 127 n.4, 189–90, 220, 222, *see also* children; Flinders Island Aboriginal Establishment; Indigenous rights; Indigenous leadership; literacy; newspapers and periodicals; petitions; protection; *tyereelore*; Wybalenna; and individuals (e.g. Tunnerminnerwait)
   children   7, 11, 12, 93–4, 98–9, 105–6, 113–26, 174
   intermediaries   95, 100, 102, 128 n.16
   languages   95–6, 99, 110, 115–16, 126 n.1, 127 n.4
   literacy   106–7, 115–17, 126, 132 n.112, 172
   mortality and mortal remains   99, 101, 119
   myth of extinction   13, 99, 110–11, 114, 118–19, 125–6
   names and naming conventions   127 n.4
   networks of intelligence   107, 122
   political activity   13, 96, 178, 189, 193
   resistance   94–6, 120
   sealing and whaling   95–6
   sovereignty   96, 189
   violence against   94–6, 99, 101, 116, 125–6
Indigenous testimony   2, 8, 13, 125, 140–1, 146, 148, 162, 172–3, 175–7, 180, 183–6, 193, 205, 209, 214–17, 221–2, *see also* authority; credibility
   Inuit   140–1, 146, 148, 172–3, 175–7, 180, 185–6, 193, 205, 209, 222
information   1–13, 22, 24, 26–32, 34–5, 45, 57–8, 64–82, 94, 96–8, 100–3, 105, 109–11, 113, 118–21, 139–62, 169–95, 213, 221, *see also* correspondence; rumors; stories; women
   arrhythmic pulses of   2, 8, 11–12, 79, 140–2, 149, 156, 162, 172, 188, 209
   Indigenous   10, 24, 29–31, 64–73, 79, 122, 139–62, 169–71, 191, 205–17, 221
   intelligence   10, 27–30, 42–5, 47, 78–9, 122, 139–62, 191, 194, 206, 209, 213
   intimacy and   5, 11, 22, 28–31, 35–42, 64–9, 149, 152–4, 217–18
   panics   79, 142, 160
   trade in   1, 9–12, 28–30, 32, 34–5, 57, 66, 140–2
   women and   29–31, 39–42, 45–6, 57–82, 100–3, 109–11, 113, 118–21, 139–62, 169–95
intelligence and intelligence gathering, *see* information
intermediaries and interpreters   1–4, 7, 9–11, 21, 22, 25–30, 32, 34, 42–3, 47, 65, 71, 73–82, 93–6, 98–107, 121–3, 126, 128 n.16, 146, 151–2, 169–95, 222, *see also* authority; children; credibility; exploration and explorers; women
   credibility of   9, 13, 80, 169–87, 207–11, 214
   in explorers' correspondence   74–82
   explorers' families and   8, 9, 22, 65, 93–6, 98–107, 116, 121, 122, 126, 172–80, 185–6, 220
   intimidation of   184–7
   Inuit   3, 21, 25, 26, 29–33, 79–82, 139–40, 183–7, 207–11
   vernacular intermediaries   28, 42, 47, 146
intimacy   3, 6, 8, 11, 21, 23, 28, 30–42, 47, 64–9, 149, 152–4, 221, 223, *see also* explorers' families; fur trade; information; intermediaries and interpreters
   information and   5, 11, 22, 28–31, 35–42, 64–9, 149, 152–4, 217–18
Intrepid (HMS)   161, 169, 186
Inughuit Inuit   169–70, 178
Inuinnait Inuit   24–5
Inuit   1–3, 5, 8, 10–13, 21, 23–7, 29–33, 44, 45, 49, 51 n.66, 57–9, 63–71, 73–4, 76, 78–82, 97–8, 140–62, 169–74, 183–7, 191,

205–12, 214–15, 221–2, *see also* Indigenous geographical knowledge; Indigenous networks; Indigenous Northwest Passage; information; intermediaries and interpreters; knowledge; maps; and separate peoples, (e.g., Netsilingmiut)
conflict and avoidance   51 n.66, 68, 80, 184
Franklin relics and   1–2, 13, 205–9, 221–2
information and intelligence   10, 64–9, 76, 80, 148–9, 151–2, 157, 162, 191, 221
networks of trade and communication   10, 24, 32, 66, 98, 141, 145–6, 150, 156, 159–60, 162, 205–7, 209, 222
relationships with outsiders   24, 48 n.23, 64–9, 79–82, 205–7
shipwrecks and   2, 10, 98, 205–7, 221–2
stereotypes of   68–9, 80–1, 150–1, 183–7, 209–10, 214
territories   23, 64–9, 140, 205–7
testimony   1–2, 8, 13, 140, 155, 162, 171–2, 180, 183–6, 209, 221–2
travel to Britain   58, 141–2, 146, 151
women   64–9, 73, 76, 214
Inuluapik (Inuit youth)   142, 147, 152, 179, 184, *see also* intermediaries and interpreters; maps
Iñupiat (Alaska)   45, 80, 141, 145, 160, 190
Inuvialuit Inuit   70, 79–80
Investigator (HMS)   61, 93, 116, 121, 122, 186, 191, *see also* Cresswell, Samuel Gurney; Northwest Passage
Ipiirvik (Joe, Ebierbing)   184, 200 n.132, *see also* intermediaries and interpreters
Isabella (HMS)   26, 58
Isbister, Alexander Kennedy   13, 94, 172–3, 175–80, 189, 194, 206, 208–9, 211–16, 219
  Arctic Rewards and their Claimants   213–14

Jameson, Robert   26, 44, 59, 61, 76
Jeanneret, Henry   122, 125, 189
journals and written records   8, 26, 30, 32, 34–5, 43–4, 47, 52 n.104, 66, 102, 104–5, 170, 183–7, 205, 212–14, 217, 220, 222, *see also* archives and archival materials; books and reading; correspondence; *Erebus* and *Terror* (HMS)
  absence of   13, 150, 205, 220

Kalaalliit Inuit   169, 183–7, 194–5, 201 n.140
Kater, Henry and Mary   59–60
Kay, Joseph Henry (Henry)   1, 59, 111–12, 191–3, *see also* explorers' families
Kay, Mary Anne, *see* Kendall, Mary Anne Kay
Kay, Sarah Porden   40, 71, 75, 178, *see also* explorers' families
Kay, William Porden   1, 59, 191–2, *see also* explorers' families
Kendall, Edward   58, 73, 76, 78–80, 97, 143, 163 n.18, *see also* correspondence; explorers' families; Land Arctic Expeditions
Kendall, Mary Anne Kay   45, 59, 61–2, 73, 75, 77, 80–2, 83 n.18, 90 n.188, 97, 118, 143, 178, 180–2, 191, 219–20, *see also* "argument from negative evidence"; correspondence; explorers' families; scientific sociability
Kennedy, Dane   9, 74, 188
Kennedy, William   94, 172–6, 184, 189, 191, 193, 206, 208, 211, 213–16, 220, *see also* fur trade and traders; Indigenous rights
Kerr, David   145–7, 153–4, 156, 157, 159
Keskarrah, Yellowknives Dene man   29–30, 44
King, Richard   97–8, 214, 215
King William Island   5, 125, 140, 205–7, 217

knowledge 1, 3–6, 12, 21–2, 27, 40, 65–9, 73–82, 125–6, 140, 162, 209, 223, *see also* archives and archival materials; authority; colonial science; correspondence; expedition narratives; Indigenous geographical knowledge; information; journals and written records; maps; relics; rumors; stories
   colonial and imperial 2–3, 6, 22, 35, 74
   geographical 22, 24, 27, 65–9, 140, 146, 149, 162
   historiography 3–5
   Indigenous 10, 24, 29, 64–9, 146, 149, 173, 221
   intimacy and 3, 11–12, 22, 64–9, 73–82, 223
   production of 4–5, 21, 125–6
Kugluktuk/Bloody Falls 24, 31–2, 39, 48–9 n.23

Lady Franklin (HMS) 161, 169, 182, 193
LAE, *see* Land Arctic Expeditions (LAE)
Laidlaw, Zoe 11, 117, 174, 176, 214
Lamb, Jonathan 33
Lambert, Andrew 111, 187
Lancaster Sound 1, 8, 39, 66, 141, 143–4, 146, 155, 158, 160–1, 170, 174, 178, 193
Land Arctic Expeditions (LAE) 11, 21–35, 43–7, 57–9, 63, 69–82, 118, 121, 143–4, 206
   First Land Arctic Expedition (1819–1822) 11, 21–2, 25–35, 43–5, 47, 58–9, 63, 70, 79, 118, 121, 143–4, 206
   Second Land Arctic Expedition (1825–7) 45–6, 57–8, 69–82, 206
La Trobe, Charles 174, 189, 190
La Trobe, Peter 174, 185, 189
Lee, Sarah Bowdich 13, 60, 74, 172, 175–80, 187, 209, 219
letters and letter writing, *see* correspondence

literacy 10, 12, 80, 95, 105–7, 113–26, 132 n.112, 169, 173–80, 182, 189, 193–5
   "imperial literacy" 10, 178, 189, 193
   Indigenous 12, 80, 95, 105–7, 113–21, 123, 126, 132 n.112, 169, 173–80, 183–7, 193–5
   whalers and sealers 132 n.112, 182
Little Ice Age 10–11, 23, 58, 141, 216
Lydon, Jane 4
Lyell, Charles 59, 61, 73, 109
Lyon, George Francis 46, 58, 64, 66, 68–9, 72, 76

McClintock, Leopold 206, 216–20
McClure, Robert 186, 212–13
MacDonald, Charlotte 6
McDonnell, Michael 10
McKenzie, Roderick 43, 44, 77
Mackenzie River 24, 43–5, 70–1, 79–80, 141, 160
Maconochie, Alexander 8, 97–104, 149–50, 154, 191, *see also* convicts; mesmerism and clairvoyance
   Back and 97–100
   Franklin family and 97–104, 149–50, 154
Maconochie, Mary 98–103, *see also* women
   Back and 98, 100, 103–4
McVicar, Robert 28, 70–3, 78, 79
magnetic science 26, 59, 97–8, 110–12, 124, 150
Māori 115, 116, 190
maps 1, 8, 11, 12, 22, 25, 28–9, 44–5, 57, 64, 66–9, 74, 76–8, 139–62, 173–4, 184, 191, 209, 212–13
   blank spaces 7, 142, 211–12
   as domestic objects 57, 74, 77
   Indigenous 1, 8, 11, 12, 31, 45, 57, 66–9, 76, 78, 139–62, 174, 184, 191, 209
Mar, Tracey Banivanua 10, 105, 122, 178, 189, 193
maritime culture 7, 40, 74–5, 144–5, 152–3, 182
Mathinna, *see* Mithina

Meredith, Louisa Ann   108–9, 191
mesmerism and clairvoyance   8, 149–50, 153–6, 180, 191
Métis people   24, 32, 48 n.18, 73, 172–3, 176, 206, 215–16
missions and missionaries   4, 11, 79, 94, 95, 102, 115–17, 119, 152, 155, 169, 173, 178, 185, 188, 189, 195, 200 n.140, 216, 220
Mitchell, Thomas   104–5
Mitford, Mary Russell   61
Mithina (Indigenous Tasmanian child)   12, 93–6, 107, 113–21, 123–6, 127 n.4, 128 n.16, 135 n.173, 138 n.262, 195, 220, 223, *see also* children; Indigenous Tasmanians (*palawa/pakana*/Tasmanian Aborigines)
  discussion of extinction and   116, 118, 126
  education of   113–21, 123
  portraits of   121, 123–5
Mittimatalik/Pond Inlet   66, 139–41, 145–7, 151–2, 154, 156–60, 173, 191, 209
  Map drawn at (1849)   11, 147, 154–60, 173, 191
Montagu, John   96, 99, 100, 103–4, 120–4, 130 n.50, 143, 192, 219
Moriarty, William   104, 116, 135 n.85
Morning Chronicle (newspaper)   147, 157, 176, 177, 185
Murchison, Charlotte   59–60, 73
Murchison, Roderick   59–60, 73, 97, 174, 192
murder   11, 21, 22, 42, 121, 208–9
Murray, John (publishing house)   37, 65, 111, 122, 191, 227 n.81

narratives   11, 35–47, 65, *see also* expedition narratives; stories
national identity   6, 7, 11–12, 140, 145, 157–62, 171–2, 177–8, 187–8, 221
  and Arctic exploration   11–12, 140, 145, 157–62, 171–2, 177–8, 187–8, 221
natural history   36, 44, 46, 106–11, 113, 118

Netsilingmiut Inuit   1, 13, 98, 140, 205–7, 209–14, 217
newspapers and periodicals   11, 22, 34, 36, 47 n.4, 68, 75–6, 78, 99, 101–2, 104–6, 108, 110, 112–13, 120, 122, 126, 147–50, 157–8, 171–2, 176–81, 189, 191–3, 207–8, 212–13
  colonial   99, 101–2, 104–6, 112–13, 120, 122, 189, 191–3
  Indigenous   106, 194–5
New Zealand, *see* Aotearoa New Zealand
Niger Expedition (1841)   12, 119, 136 n.205, 173, 175–6, 194, 209, *see also* humanitarianism and humanitarians
Norfolk Island (Australia)   1, 104, 147, 149, 154, 191
North West Company (NWC)   21, 24, 26, 28, 30, 34, 40, 43, 44, 70, 71, *see also* fur trade and traders
  conflict with HBC   21, 28, 30
Northwest Passage   1, 11, 13, 21, 23, 26, 29, 45, 66, 68, 70, 76, 97, 124, 139, 141, 187, 207, 212–17, 221, *see also* ice and ice conditions; Indigenous Northwest Passage
  reward for completion   211–14
Nugent, Maria   183
NWC, *see* North West Company (NWC)

Ojibwe people   23, 206, 210, 214
Ommanney, Erasmus   161, 169, 170, 184, 195
open polar sea, theory of   8, 12–13, 26, 143, 169–95, 209, 215
  defined   171–2, 177
  humanitarians and   173–80
  philanthropic campaign   171, 177–81, 187–8
  Tasmania and   13, 187–95
Orkney Islands and Orkney Islanders (Orcadians)   24, 25, 27, 72, 88 n.120, 144–5, 147, 149, 173–4, 193, 206, 211, *see also* Rae, Dr. John; Kennedy, William; Isbister, Alexander Kennedy
  Arctic expeditions and   27, 72
  fur trade families and   11, 72, 88 n.120

Orphan School (Hobart, Tasmania) 96, 99, 103, 106, 116, 120–3, 138 n.262, *see also* children
Orr, Mary 60, 175
Osborn, Sherard 161, 170, 174, 219
Ouligbuck 79–81, 90 n.183, 139, 144, 206–7, 212, 214
Ouligbuck, William, Jr. 139, 140, 144, 206–7, 209–12, 214
Outram, Dorinda 35
Owen, Richard 109–10

Palle/Hannibal (Indigenous Tasmanian man) 115–17, 123, *see also* Mithina
Parker, John 139–40, 142, 146–9, 151–6, 158, 159
Parliamentary Select Committee on Aboriginal Tribes (1836) 12, 96, 98, 101, 119, 214, 216
    report 119, 173
Parliamentary Select Committee on the Hudson's Bay Company (1857) 214–16, *see also* Isbister, Alexander Kennedy
Parliamentary Select Committee on Transportation (1837–8) (Molesworth Committee) 101
Parry, Isabella 57, 59, 63–4
Parry, William Edward (Edward) 26, 45, 57–9, 61–70, 73, 75–9, 96, 104, 119, 120–4, 143, 148–58, 160–1, 173, 175–6, 180–1, 186, 220, *see also* Arctic circles; Arctic Committee (1851); exploration and explorers; explorers' families; humanitarianism and humanitarians
    Arctic circles and 57–77, 104, 121, 123–4, 148–9, 154, 160, 180
    Australia 96
    humanitarians and 62–4, 119–20, 173, 176
    Iglulingmiut and 64–9, 73, 76
    Indigenous knowledge and 65–70, 83 n.15, 148–52, 155, 173
    Inuit maps and 65–9, 148–52
    marriages 57, 59, 63–4, 68–9, 119
    Niger Expedition and 119, 136 n.202, 173, 176

penal colonies 1, 6, 8, 12, 93–8, 112, 149, 189–93, 215, *see also* convicts; Siberia; Tasmania
penal reform 98–102, 111, 149
Penny, Margaret 151, 153, 182–3
Penny, William 139, 140, 142, 145–7, 151, 153, 159–61, 169, 171, 174, 177–83, 186–8, 192–3, 208, 211, 220, *see also* "argument from negative evidence"; whalers and sealers
Perry, Adele 6, 30, 189, 214–16
petitions 1, 13, 63, 120, 125, 172, 176, 178–80, 186, 188–90, 214–15, *see also* "argument from negative evidence"; Indigenous rights
philanthropy 63, 116, 125, 126, 156–9, 171–3, 178, 179, 181, 187, 188, 190–2, 194, 209, 210, 214
    Arctic rescue as philanthropic cause 12, 171–2, 181, 187–8, 209, 221
phrenology 59, 101, 107, 118, 143, 150
Pioneer (HMS) 161, 169, 170, 186
Podruchny, Carolyn 27, 32
polite science, circles of, *see* scientific sociability
politics of truth 7, 22, 42, 47, 94, 124–6, 150, 172, 221–3, *see also* authority; credibility; rumors; stories; truth and truthfulness
    defined 7
Porden, Eleanor, *see* Franklin, Eleanor Porden
Port Phillip, Victoria (Melbourne), *see* protection and protectorates
Potter, Russell 221, 222
Price, Mary Franklin 1, 99, 147, 153, 191
Prince Albert (ship) 159, 161, 169–70, 172–4, 187, 191–2, 195 n.6, 216
Prince Regent Inlet 97, 140, 146–7, 155–6, 160
protection and protectorates 4, 10, 12, 96, 99, 102–5, 107, 119–20, 172, 173, *see also* Parliamentary Select Committee on Aboriginal Tribes
    Indigenous networks and 10, 116, 120, 122
    Port Phillip Protectorate 99, 102–5

provisions   5, 28–35, 40, 59, 66, 77, 97, 143, 159, 192, 207
  as curiosities   59, 97
  politics of   28–31

Qalasirssuaq, Kalli, Erasmus York   94, 169–71, 183–6, 195
Qallunaat (non-Inuit, non-Indigenous outsiders)   1, 25, 30, 64–8, 70, 141–2, 145–7, 169–71, 205–7

RAC, *see* Russian American Company (RAC)
Rae, John   1–2, 139–40, 144, 147, 155, 173, 177, 206–8, 210–17
reform   9, 12, 57, 62–4, 75, 96, 100, 104, 119, 121, 149, 157, 176, 209, 215, 220–1
Reid, Kirsty   189, 192
relics   1–2, 6, 13, 150, 170–5, 177, 179–80, 184, 186, 192, 195, 205, 208–9, 217, 221–3
  Inuit testimony and   150, 171, 173, 179, 205, 209
reputation   113, 121, 124, 188, 221, *see also* authority; credibility; trust and trustworthiness
Resolute (HMS)   161, 173, 186
Reynolds, Henry   118
RGS, *see* Royal Geographical Society (RGS)
Richardson, John   11, 21–2, 26, 29, 31–47, 57–9, 61–2, 69–81, 96–8, 100, 109, 111, 118, 122, 139, 140, 143–5, 154–5, 159–60, 180–1, 210, 212–13, 215–17, 220, *see also* correspondence; exploration and explorers; explorers' families; science and scientific networks; scientific sociability
  Arctic circles and   57–62, 70–3, 76–9, 96–8, 100–1, 109–11, 123–4, 159–60, 180–1
  cannibalism   21–2, 51 n.76
  First Land Arctic Expedition (1819–22)   11, 21–2, 26, 29, 31–47
  Franklin search (1848–60)   139, 140, 143–5, 154–5, 159–60, 180–1

  relationship with John Franklin   31–42, 45, 62, 70–81, 96–8, 123, 139, 143, 213
  religious faith and   35–42, 213
  Second Land Arctic Expedition (1825–7)   70–81
Richardson, Mary Booth   96–7, 100, 118, 124, 139, 143, 154, *see also* explorers' families
Richardson, Mary Fletcher   63, 139, 220, *see also* explorers' families
Richardson, Mary Stiven   11, 21–2, 32, 33, 35–7, 40, 45, 47, 70, 73, 76–8, 96, *see also* correspondence; explorers' families
Richardson, Peter   61, 73, *see also* scientific sociability
Robinson, George Augustus   95–6, 98–9, 102–7, 114–15, 120, 128 n.16
Robinson, Michael   172
Ross, Anne   124, 142, 155
Ross, James Clark   58, 66, 93, 97–8, 108, 111–13, 119, 122, 124, 139, 140, 142–3, 150, 151, 154–8, 160, 169–74, 178, 183, 184, 191, 217, *see also* magnetic science; Netsilingmiut Inuit
  Arctic circles and   58, 95–8, 124, 143, 154
  British Antarctic Expedition (1839–43)   98, 106, 108, 111–12, 119
  Franklin search   140–3, 150, 151, 154–8, 160, 169–74, 178, 183, 184, 191
  Inuit knowledge and   58, 66, 154–8
Ross, John   26, 58–9, 61, 97–8, 157, 161, 177, 183, 185
Routledge, Karen   68, 79, 184
Royal Geographical Society (RGS)   97–8, 100, 102, 110–11, 146, 206, 219
Royal Society   37, 61, 97, 111, 147
Royal Society of Tasmania   190, 192
rumors   2, 8, 11–12, 22–3, 30, 34, 42–3, 45–7, 68, 78, 103–5, 108, 110, 113, 120–2, 142, 152, 156, 189, 200 n.140, 205, 220, *see also* stories
  about expeditions and explorers   8, 11, 30–1, 42–3, 69–70, 72, 121

about Franklin family   12, 45, 95, 100–1, 103, 107–8, 121–2, 220
politics of truth and   30–1, 42–3, 47, 102–3, 113
silence and   2, 142, 156, 205
Rupert's Land   11, 45, 174, 189, 212, 214–15
Russell, Gillian   58
Russell, Lynette   116, 120
Russell, Penny   125, 145
Russia and Russian Empire   8, 10, 24, 45, 58, 70–2, 80, 141, 144–5, 160, 177, 187, 191–2, 208, 215–16, 221, 226 n.60
  Arctic exploration and   58, 70–2, 144–5, 160, 177, 187
  Indigenous trading networks and   8, 24, 45, 70–2
Russian American Company (RAC)   8, 10, 45, 70, 100, 102, 110, 111, 141, 160, 219

Sabine, Edward   62, 65–6, 69, 73, 97, 98, 102, 105, 111–12, 121, 124, 143, 154, 180, 191, *see also* magnetic science; scientific sociability
Sabine, Elizabeth Lieves   112, 124, 143, 177
  mother ("Mrs. Lieves")   177, 186
Savissivik/Cape York (Greenland)   169, 171, 183, 185
Schaeffer, Simon   3
science and scientific networks   4, 11, 44, 57–8, 62, 74, 97, 100, 102, 104, 108–10, 113, 122, 176, *see also* colonial science; correspondence; explorers' families; scientific sociability
scientific sociability   2–4, 9, 11, 38, 57–64, 69, 73–4, 82, 97, 104, 108–13, 119, 123, 175–6, 212, 220, *see also* Arctic circles; credibility; explorers' families; women
  humanitarians and   3–4, 9, 11, 26, 62–3, 98, 104, 119
  polite science, circles of   4, 57–64, 74, 81

Scoresby, William   26, 44, 61–2, 144, 148–9, 154, 156–9, 172, 175, 181, 212, 219
  Arctic rescue as philanthropic cause   156–9
  Indigenous information and   148–9, 157–9, 173
  whaling and   26, 44, 61, 153
Secord, James   58
settler colonialism and settlers   4, 13, 94–126, 172–3, 188–90, 194, 215–16, *see also* children; convicts; Franklin, John; Franklin, Jane; Indigenous Tasmanians (*palawa/pakana*/Tasmanian Aborigines); newspapers and periodicals; penal colonies
  claims of victimhood   189–90, 209
  philanthropy and   190
  self-government   188–9
  violence   12, 95–6, 98, 101, 118, 215
Siberia   24, 80, 112, 177, 187, 215–16
silences   2, 5–7, 11–14, 22, 35, 43, 47, 125–6, 140–2, 155, 160, 184, 194, 205–23, *see also* information
  archives and   5–7, 13–14, 125–6, 138 n.262
  Franklin expedition and   2, 12–13, 155, 222
  information and   2, 11, 35, 79, 140–2, 155, 194
  Inuit strategic use of   68, 184–5
Simpkinson, Francis (Frank)   104, 125, 181
Simpkinson, John   2, 57, 110
Simpkinson, Mary   1, 100, 103–5, 108, 109, 111, 113, 119–23, 154, 160, 176, *see also* scientific sociability
Simpson, Daniel   96
Simpson, George   34, 72, 206, 215, *see also* Hudson's Bay Company
Somerville, Mary   59–60
Sophia (HMS)   161, 169
specimens   73–82, 99, 100, 107, 110, 217, 222
  people treated as   99, 107, 110, 217

Stanley, Maria   64, 69
starvation   5, 11, 21–3, 26–8, 31–5, 40–1, 43, 58, 66, 98, 118, 140, 144, 159, 176, 205–7, 210, 216, *see also* hunger
Stephen, James   121
Stern, Philip J.   152
Stevens, Leonie   125
stories   7, 8, 11, 13–14, 22–3, 31–5, 43, 45, 47, 65, 68, 73, 78, 82, 94, 105, 125–6, 141–2, 162, 169, 173, 185, 190–1, 205–14, 216–23, *see also* rumors
   definition   22–3
   exchanges of   34, 45, 66, 78, 82, 141, 205, 207, 211
   politics of truth and   43, 47, 73, 125–6, 205–6, 216, 220–3
de Strzelecki, Count Paul Edmund   105, 123–5
suffering   21, 23, 31–5, 37, 40–2, 47, 64, 207–8, 210–11, 215–16
Sutherland, Peter   175, 182, 193
Swanston, Charles   100, 101, 104, 107, 121, 122

Tallie, T. J.   210
Tasmania (*lutruwita*)   1, 12, 43, 45, 70, 82, 93–126, 126 n.1, 141–3, 145, 149, 152, 154, 159, 172–4, 187–93, *see also* colonial science; convicts; Flinders Island Aboriginal Establishment; humanitarianism and humanitarians; Indigenous Tasmanians (*palawa/pakana*/Tasmanian Aborigines); settler colonialism and settlers
   anti-transportation movement   13, 188–9, 192
   Arctic circles and   98, 100, 102, 104–5, 108–13, 120–3
   Black War   12, 95–6, 98, 101, 118
   Franklin administration of   12, 93–126
Tasmanian Aborigines, *see* Indigenous Tasmanians (*palawa/pakana*/Tasmanian Aborigines)

Tasmanian Journal of Natural Science   108, 110–13, 116, 118, 120–1
Tasmanian Society   105, 108–13, 115, 121, 124, 190
Tattannoeuck/Augustus   25, 26, 30–4, 43, 66, 79–81, 90 n.188, 206, *see also* intermediaries and interpreters
tattoos and tattooing   64–5, 69, 73, 82
Teroahaute, Charles   46
Teroahaute, Michel   27, 32–3, 40, 42, 46, 70, 210
Thompson, Carl   60
Trent (HMS)   26–7, 58
Trugernanner/Truganini (Indigenous Tasmanian woman)   95, 103, 105, 120, *see also* intermediaries and interpreters
trust and trustworthiness   1, 3, 8–9, 11, 22–3, 30–1, 34–5, 39–42, 44, 47, 57, 60–4, 69, 70, 94, 146–51, 182–7, 209, 214, 221
   "trust at a distance"   9, 17 n.50
truth and truthfulness   1–2, 5–9, 11–13, 22, 42, 47, 94, 121, 124–6, 141, 146, 150, 152, 154, 171, 172, 180, 205, 207, 209, 211, 221–3, *see also* authority; credibility; rumors
   politics of   7, 22, 42, 47, 94, 124–6, 150, 172, 221–3
   truth-telling   7, 13, 221–3
Tunnerminnerwait/Pevay   99, 101, 103, 106, 116, 120, 128 n.16, *see also* Indigenous Tasmanians (*palawa/pakana*/Tasmanian Aborigines); intermediaries and interpreters
Turnbull, David   222
Turner, Mark W.   142
tyereelore   95–6, *see also* Indigenous Tasmanians (*palawa/pakana*/Tasmanian Aborigines)

Ugjulingmiut Inuit   205–7
Usky (Inuk man)   139, 140, 146–7, 153, 156–8, 160, 209
Utkuksalingmiut Inuit   205–6

Van Diemen's Land, *see* Tasmania (*lutruwita*)
Vansittart (vessel)   93, 99, 116, 121–2, 159
  Indigenous boys on   93, 116, 121–2, 136 n.185
Van Toorn, Penny   106
Vibert, Elizabeth   74
voyageurs   11, 21, 24, 27, 31–5, 40, 46, 73, 76–7, *see also* fur trade and traders

Walker, George Washington   100, 120, 122, 128 n.21
Walter, Maggie   7
Ward, Thomas   144, 145, 147, 149, 152, 158
Weld, Charles   177–8, 181, 219
Wellington Channel   143, 156, 160, 161, 170–1, 174–5, 177–8, 181–3, 186, 192–4, 216, 217, *see also* "argument from negative evidence"; Beechey Island
Wentzel, Willard   26–34, 41–7, 121
whalers and sealers   3, 8, 10–12, 44, 61, 66, 75, 78, 95, 98, 109, 120, 139–62, 169, 177, 179, 190–2, 202 n.181, 208, 212, *see also* authority; credibility; literacy
  Indigenous information and   146–9, 151, 153, 169–72, 174, 179
  Tasmanian Arctic whaling fleet   190–1, 202 n.181
Whewell, William   59, 110
Whitby   26, 157, 159
Winter, Alison   157
women, *see also* "argument from negative evidence"; convicts; correspondence; exploration and explorers; explorers' families; fur trade, families; humanitarianism and humanitarians; Indigenous Tasmanians (*palawa/pakana*/Tasmanian Aborigines); intermediaries and interpreters; Inuit; newspapers and periodicals; scientific sociability; *tyereelore*
  archives and   6–7, 11, 57, 74–82, 171–87, 195, 211
  authority of   9, 11, 40, 74–82, 93–4, 110, 113, 118–20, 124–6, 152–4, 188, 194, 209, 217
  authors   36–40, 57, 60, 62, 83 n.15, 108, 124, 191, 198 n.64
  colonial governance and   93–4, 103, 121–4, 126
  explorers and   11, 29–30, 35–42, 104, 139–62, 175
  information and   4, 8–9, 11, 29, 57, 74–82, 139–62, 172–87
  as intermediaries   73–82, 94, 104, 122–3
  intermediaries and   7, 39, 64–73, 93–4, 172–87, 195
  labor of   11, 24, 29, 31, 72, 77
  maritime culture and   7, 74–5, 144–5, 152–3, 182
  "petticoat influence" and government   71, 94, 100, 121–2, 124, 181, 213, 219
  public sphere and   4, 9, 11, 57, 63, 94, 171–88, 194, 209
  publishing and   4, 35, 38, 40, 46, 62, 108, 110–11, 113, 124, 172–3, 175–80, 191
  science and   8, 36–8, 59–64, 84 n.84, 99, 101, 104–5, 107–13, 172–3, 175–6, 188, 191
Wongerneep/Eveline (Indigenous Tasmanian woman)   114–15, *see also* Mithina
Woodman, David   221
Wrangel, Ferdinand Petrovich   112, 177
Wurundjeri people   102, 105
Wybalenna   96, 99, 103, 105–6, 114–18, 122, 125, 126, 138 n.262, 189, 222, *see also* Flinders Island Aboriginal Establishment; Indigenous rights; Indigenous Tasmanians (*palawa/pakana*/Tasmanian Aborigines); petitions

Yellowknives Dene   21, 24–5, 27–35, 40–1, 46, 70–1, 78, 97, 143, 216
York Factory   28, 45–6, 70, 72, 79

www.ingramcontent.com/pod-product-compliance
Lightning Source LLC
Chambersburg PA
CBHW071808300426
44116CB00009B/1243